The Cambridge Companion to Verdi

This *Companion* provides an accessible biographical, theatrical, and social-cultural background for Verdi's music, examines in detail important general aspects of its style and method of composition, and discusses stylistic themes in reviews of representative works. Aspects of Verdi's milieu, style, creative process, and critical reception are explored in essays by highly reputed specialists. Individual chapters address themes in Verdi's life, his role in transforming the theatre business, and his relationship to Italian Romanticism and the Risorgimento. Chapters on four operas representative of the different stages of Verdi's career, *Ernani*, *Rigoletto*, *Don Carlos*, and *Otello*, synthesize analytical themes introduced in the more general chapters and illustrate the richness of Verdi's creativity. The *Companion* also includes chapters on Verdi's non-operatic songs and other music, his creative process, and writing about Verdi from the nineteenth century to the present day.

The Cambridge Companion to

VERDI

....

EDITED BY
Scott L. Balthazar
Professor of Music History, West Chester University of Pennsylvania

CAMBRIDGE
UNIVERSITY PRESS

PUBLISHED BY THE PRESS SYNDICATE OF THE UNIVERSITY OF CAMBRIDGE
The Pitt Building, Trumpington Street, Cambridge CB2 1RP, United Kingdom

CAMBRIDGE UNIVERSITY PRESS
The Edinburgh Building, Cambridge, CB2 2RU, UK
40 West 20th Street, New York, NY 10011–4211, USA
477 Williamstown Road, Port Melbourne, VIC 3207, Australia
Ruiz de Alarcón 13, 28014 Madrid, Spain
Dock House, The Waterfront, Cape Town 8001, South Africa

http://www.cambridge.org

First published 2004

Printed in the United Kingdom at the University Press, Cambridge

Typeface Minion 10.75/14 pt.   *System* LaTeX 2$_\varepsilon$ [TB]

A catalogue record for this book is available from the British Library

ISBN 0 521 63228 5 hardback
ISBN 0 521 63535 7 paperback

Contents

Figures and table

Examples

Contributors

Scott L. Balthazar is Professor of Music History at West Chester University of Pennsylvania. His articles on nineteenth-century Italian opera and theories of instrumental form in the eighteenth and nineteenth centuries have appeared in the *Journal of the American Musicological Society, Journal of Musicological Research, Journal of Musicology, Opera Journal, Cambridge Opera Journal, Journal of the Royal Musical Association, Current Musicology, Opera Quarterly*, and *Music and Letters.*

Fabrizio Della Seta is Professor in the Faculty of Musicology at the University of Pavia in Cremona. He has edited Verdi's *La traviata* (1997), the autograph sketches and drafts for that opera (2000), and Rossini's *Adina* (2000). He is currently general co-editor of the *Edizione critica delle opere di Vincenzo Bellini.*

Andreas Giger is Assistant Professor of Musicology at Louisiana State University. His recent studies have focused on Korngold (*Journal of Musicology*), censorship (*Cambridge Opera Journal*), and prosody in Verdi's French operas (*Music and Letters*). He co-edited *Music in the Mirror: Reflections on the History of Music Theory and Literature for the Twenty-First Century* and is the founder of the Internet database *Saggi musicali italiani.*

Gregory W. Harwood is Professor and Director of Graduate Studies in Music at Georgia Southern University. His volume *Giuseppe Verdi: A Guide to Research* (1998) has become a standard reference tool in Verdi studies. Other research interests include topics related to Robert and Clara Schumann, Maurice Ravel, and Hector Berlioz.

Steven Huebner is the author of *The Operas of Charles Gounod* (1990) and *French Opera at the Fin de Siècle: Wagnerism, Nationalism, and Style* (1999), as well as numerous articles on Italian and French opera. He currently holds a James McGill Chair at McGill University in Montreal, where he has taught since 1985.

Luke Jensen is Director of the Office of Lesbian, Gay, Bisexual, and Transgender Equity at the University of Maryland, College Park, where he previously served as Associate Director of the Center for Studies in Nineteenth-Century Music and as Affiliate Faculty in the School of Music. His publications include *Giuseppe Verdi and Giovanni Ricordi with Notes on Francesco Lucca: From 'Oberto' to 'La traviata'* (1989) and a five-volume guide to the *Gazzetta musicale di Milano* for the series *Répertoire international de la presse musicale* (2000).

David Kimbell is Professor Emeritus of the University of Edinburgh, where he was Dean of the Faculty of Music from 1995 to 2001. His principal research interests are Italian opera and the music of Handel. His most recent publication was the completion, with Roger Savage, of *The Classics of Music*, Michael Tilmouth's edition of the previously uncollected writings of Donald Francis Tovey (2001).

Roberta Montemorra Marvin is Associate Professor at the University of Iowa. She is editor of Verdi's *I masnadieri* (2000) and his Secular Cantatas (forthcoming), co-editor of *Verdi 2001: Atti del Convegno internazionale* (2003), and editor of *Verdi Forum*. She has also published widely on Italian opera, including essays in *Cambridge Opera Journal*, *Music and Letters*, *Studi verdiani*, the *Bollettino del Centro rossiniano di studi*, the *Musical Quarterly*, and *Verdi's Middle Period* (Martin Chusid, ed., 1997).

Cormac Newark, having been Research Fellow in Music at Trinity Hall, Cambridge, is now engaged in a two-year program of research in Italy sponsored by the Leverhulme Trust. He has published in the *Cambridge Opera Journal*, the *Journal of the Royal Musical Association*, and the *Guardian*, and has contributed to various collections of essays, including *Reading Critics Reading* (Roger Parker and Mary Ann Smart, eds., 2001) and the *Cambridge Companion to Rossini* (Emanuele Senici, ed., forthcoming).

Mary Jane Phillips-Matz, a Co-Founder and Executive Board member of the American Institute for Verdi Studies at New York University, is the author of *Verdi: A Biography* (1993), which won the Royal Philharmonic Society Award in London and the ASCAP-Deems Taylor Award in New York, both in 1995, and has recently been published in French by Fayard and in Spanish by Paidós. Her book *Puccini: A Biography* appeared in 2002.

Harold Powers has taught at Harvard University, the University of Pennsylvania (jointly in Music and South Asian Studies), and Princeton University, and has been Visiting Professor at seven American and European universities. He is a member of the American Academy of Arts and Sciences, Corresponding Fellow of the British Academy, and honorary member of the American Musicological Society. He has published extensively on Indic musicology, Italian opera, and the history of music theory.

Alessandro Roccatagliati is Associate Professor of Musical Dramaturgy at the University of Ferrara. He is general co-editor of the *Edizione critica delle opere di Vincenzo Bellini* and is currently working on the critical edition of *La sonnambula*. His publications include *"Rigoletto" di Giuseppe Verdi* (1991) and *Felice Romani librettista* (1996).

Emanuele Senici is University Lecturer in Music at the University of Oxford and Fellow of St. Hugh's College, Oxford. Among his recent Verdian publications are "Verdi's *Falstaff* at Italy's Fin de Siècle" (*Musical Quarterly*, 2001) and "Per Guasco, Ivanoff e Moriani: le tre versioni della romanza di Foresto nell'*Attila*" in *Pensieri per un maestro: Studi in onore di Pierluigi Petrobelli* (Stefano La Via and Roger Parker, eds., 2002).

Mary Ann Smart is Associate Professor of Music at the University of California, Berkeley. She is author of the articles on Bellini and Donizetti in the *New Grove*, and editor of *Siren Songs: Representations of Gender and Sexuality in Opera* (2000) and (with Roger Parker) *Reading Critics Reading: Opera and Ballet Criticism in France from the Revolution to 1848* (2001). Her book *Mimomania: Music and Gesture in Nineteenth-Century Opera* was published by the University of California Press in 2004.

Rosa Solinas is currently Publications Editor for Wexford Festival Opera. She has worked in the opera industry in London and Bologna and lectured at Oxford University. Her research focuses on Italian late nineteenth- and early twentieth-century opera (especially Arrigo Boito) and theatre; her published work includes contributions to *Italian Studies* and *The Oxford Companion to Italian Literature* (2001).

Preface

One of the most beloved composers of the nineteenth century, Giuseppe Verdi has rightfully enjoyed a high standing among opera lovers that continues to grow as productions and recordings of his works – including those that are lesser known – multiply and as the sophisticated artistry of his mature style becomes increasingly apparent. This *Companion* examines Verdi's operas and other music in the context of his life, his social and cultural surroundings, and the tradition of nineteenth-century Italian opera. Since a number of exemplary life-and-works treatments of Verdi are already available, this volume proceeds differently. It centers on a series of essays, each investigating a different theme across Verdi's career, that reveal aspects of his style and lines of development that might be obscured if individual operas were discussed separately.

The *Companion to Verdi*, like other volumes in the series, is aimed primarily at students and opera lovers who already have a broad background in music history and theory but have not proceeded to a specialized level. Authors have provided the foundation for students and performers to begin reading more specialized literature and pursuing their own investigations or for other opera lovers to expand and enrich their experiences of Verdi's music. At the same time, many chapters offer the fruits of new research and explore a particular thesis, and consequently may interest scholars already working in the field. Although each chapter constitutes a free-standing article, the *Companion* has been designed to create a readably intensive, integrated overview of Verdi's oeuvre while avoiding unnecessary overlaps. So it might, for example, serve as a focus for all or parts of a course on Verdi, on nineteenth-century Italian opera, or on topics in nineteenth-century music.

The *Companion*'s opening chapters treat Verdi's personal and cultural environment. Mary Jane Phillips-Matz's biographical sketch introduces the reader to the composer's boyhood and education, his difficult entry into the operatic world, his relationships with librettists and performers, his involvement in Italian politics, and his activities in semi-retirement. Verdi's success as a composer depended to a great extent on understanding the conventions of the Italian theatre and surmounting its many obstacles. Alessandro Roccatagliati's chapter on the theatre business explains the basic circumstances of opera production when Verdi came onto the scene, then discusses the effect of Verdi's rising status on his dealings with management, performers, and censors, and on attitudes toward the integrity of the musical score. Mary Ann Smart reexamines Verdi's ambivalent engagement with Italian Romanticism and the Risorgimento, the "myth" of his artistic leadership of the revolutionary movement, and his handling of patriotic themes in political opera.

The next section explores aspects of musical and textual style in Verdi's compositions. The vast majority of Verdi's lyrical set pieces are based on conventional schemata that are the Italian equivalent of the Viennese Classical forms yet are much less familiar to students of opera. My own chapter explains the designs of arias, duets, concertato finales, *introduzioni*, and scenes that end operas, suggesting ways in which Verdi modified the practices of his predecessors to fit his increasingly plot-oriented approach, and also examines his principles for constructing choruses. Fabrizio Della Seta's introduction to Verdi's librettos provides a primer in the essentials of Italian versification and compares the ways in which Verdi and his librettists adapted literary sources, distributed singers' workloads, treated versification, and chose wording in four operas across his career. Verdi's music changed remarkably over the years as he personalized the style inherited from his predecessors and developed a remarkably flexible and acute language. Emanuele Senici looks at ways in which music amplifies text at an immediate expressive level, analyzing the interaction between melodic form and poetic syntax and meaning, dramatization of evocative words and visual gestures, and musical word painting. Verdi's introduction to French grand opera during his first sojourn in Paris (1847–49) left an indelible impression: from the 1850s on, virtually all of his operas synthesize French and Italian elements to varying degrees. Andreas Giger describes some of the broader textual and musical features of French grand opera and French influence on the forms of Verdi's arias and on his treatment of chorus and ballet, instrumentation, and melodic style. Verdi set himself apart from his predecessors and paved the way for such later composers as Puccini by viewing his mature operas as unified wholes rather than as sequences of independent scenes. Steven Huebner investigates scholarly theories of structural coherence involving sonority, musical motive, and tonality, and the problem of "historical" analysis, particularly in *Rigoletto*, *Il trovatore*, and *Un ballo in maschera*. Verdi was a leader among Italian composers in redefining the operatic role of the orchestra. David Kimbell introduces the various types of orchestral music in the operas – overtures and preludes for the opera and for individual acts, scenic music, dances and full-fledged ballets, mimetic music that captures localized gestures – and discusses Verdi's cultivation of *parlante*, vocal music in which the orchestra plays the lead role. In addition to operas, Verdi created a substantial body of other works for chorus, solo voices, and, to a much lesser extent, instruments. Roberta Montemorra Marvin surveys Verdi's non-operatic songs, chamber and keyboard music, and choral works, giving special attention to the Requiem.

The following chapters discuss in detail four operas that represent different stages of Verdi's career: *Ernani*, an early success from Verdi's "galley years"; *Rigoletto*, one of his most popular operas from his middle period; *Don Carlos*, perhaps the greatest of his French grand operas; and *Otello*, one of the two sublime masterpieces of Verdi's old age. Though the focus of each of these chapters was chosen by its author, three of them deal, in different ways, with the theme of "otherness," a coincidence indicative of recent scholarly directions. Rosa Solinas relates the evolution of the tenor role in the mid-nineteenth century to characterization of the hero in *Ernani* and his status as an outcast. Cormac Newark examines the alleged importance of the curse motive in the musical structure and genesis of *Rigoletto* and the detachment of the three leads – and even the most famous song in the opera, "La donna è mobile" – from their social, historical, and stylistic contexts. My chapter on *Otello* discusses ways in which Desdemona's defeat by Iago in their contest over control of her husband and her subsequent alienation are conveyed not only through words and actions but also through shifts in her musical style and through Verdi's organization of keys. In contrast to these three interpretive essays, Harold Powers introduces *Don Carlos* with a discussion of Verdi's adaptation of the source play, production history, and aspects of French style, and compares in close detail the several variants of this opera, guiding the reader through the extremely complicated textual problems created by the principal Italian revision (and others) of the French original. Powers also comments on recorded performances of various versions of this opera.

Two final chapters introduce the reader to some important tools of Verdi scholarship – the documentary sources used in studying the creative process and in editing scores – and to directions taken by Verdi scholars over the past century. Luke Jensen gives readers a behind-the-scenes look at Verdi's collaboration with librettists, theatre managers, performers, and publishers by tracing seven creative stages – from the scenario to revisions of the published score – and proposes subdividing Verdi's career into four periods based on shifts in his working methods. Gregory Harwood chronicles Verdi's rising fortunes in the critical literature, discussing the principal biographical and stylistic studies and identifying recent scholarly trends.

A word concerning citation of sources. Scenes from the play on which an opera was based are designated with the act and scene in upper- and lower-case roman numerals and the line(s) in arabic numerals (e.g. III, ii, 24); operatic scenes defined by locale are designated with upper- and lower-case roman numerals (e.g. III, ii); individual musical pieces follow

Martin Chusid's *A Catalog of Verdi's Operas* and are given with acts in roman numerals and pieces, numbered continuously across the opera, in arabic numerals (e.g. III, 12).

I wish to thank all the authors and my editors for their patience with the lengthy process of bringing the *Companion* to completion. Special thanks to my copyeditor Laura Davey for her superhuman attention to detail. Dean Timothy Blair of the West Chester University School of Music provided grants for translating two of the chapters. Roger Parker offered consistently helpful input concerning the selection of contributors. Judy Balthazar edited my own chapters and this preface. I am grateful to her and to our son David for their support during the minor trials involved in preparing this volume.

Scott L. Balthazar

Chronology

Year	Biography	Music and musicians
1813	Verdi born, October 9 or 10, in Roncole near Busseto, son of Carlo Verdi and Luigia (née Uttini)	Rossini, *Tancredi*, Venice, La Fenice, February 6 Wagner born, Leipzig, May 22 Grétry dies, Paris, September 24 Teresa Brambilla, soprano, born, Cassano d'Adda, October 23 Felice Varesi, baritone, born, Calais
1814		Napoleon exiled to Elba, April
1815		Napoleon defeated at Waterloo, June 18, and exiled to St. Helena, ending the "Hundred Days" Giuseppina Strepponi, soprano, born, Lodi, September 8 Léon Escudier born, Castelnaudary, September 15 Temistocle Solera, librettist, born, Ferrara, December 25
1816		Gaetano Fraschini, tenor, born, Pavia, February 16 Rossini, *Il barbiere di Siviglia*, Rome, Argentina, February 20 Paisiello dies, Naples, June 5 Rossini, *Otello*, Naples, Fondo, December 4
1817	Prior to age four, begins instruction in music and other subjects with local priests	Rossini, *La Cenerentola*, Rome, Valle, January 25 Madame de Staël dies, Paris, July 14 Méhul dies, Paris, October 18
1818		Marianna Barbieri-Nini, soprano, born, Florence, February 18 Erminia Frezzolini, soprano, born, Orvieto, March 27 Gounod born, Paris, June 17 Rossini, *La donna del lago*, Naples, San Carlo, October 24
1819		Offenbach born, Cologne, June 20

1820	Age seven, father buys him a spinet	Vittorio Emanuele II born, Turin, March 14
		Jenny Lind, soprano, born, Stockholm, October 6
		Carbonari-led Neapolitan revolution forces King Ferdinand I to promise a constitution
1821		Weber, *Der Freischütz*, Berlin, Schauspielhaus, June 18
1822	Age nine, becomes permanent organist at local church, San Michele	E. T. A. Hoffmann dies, Berlin, June 25
1823	Moves with family to Busseto	Rossini, *Semiramide*, Venice, La Fenice, February 3
1824	Age eleven, enters *ginnasio* in Busseto, is trained in Italian, Latin, humanities, and rhetoric	Bruckner born, Ansfelden, September 4
		Antonio Ghizlanzoni born, Lecco, November 25
		Cornelius born, Mainz, December 24
		Leone Giraldoni, baritone, born, Paris
1825	Begins lessons with Ferdinando Provesi, *maestro di cappella* at San Bartolomeo in Busseto, director of municipal music school and local Philharmonic Society	Winter dies, Munich, October 17
		Alessandro Manzoni, *I promessi sposi* (1825–27)
1826	Begins composing instrumental and vocal music	Sophie Cruvelli, soprano, born, Bielefeld, March 12
		Weber dies, London, June 5
1827		Beethoven dies, Vienna, March 26
		Bellini, *Il pirata*, Milan, La Scala, October 27
		Victor Hugo, preface to *Cromwell*
1828		Auber, *La muette de Portici*, Paris, Opéra, February 29
		Schubert dies, Vienna, November 19
1829	Applies unsuccessfully for position as organist in Soragna	Rossini, *Guillaume Tell*, Paris, Opéra, August 3
1830		Goldmark born, Keszthely, May 18
		Donizetti, *Anna Bolena*, Milan, Carcano, December 26
		Hugo, *Hernani*
1831	In May, moves into the house of Antonio Barezzi, his first patron	Bellini, *La sonnambula*, Milan, Carcano, March 6

Begins relationship with Barezzi's daughter Margherita
Is granted a scholarship by the local Monte di Pietà e d'Abbondanza for 1833; Barezzi supplies funds for 1832

Meyerbeer, *Robert le diable*, Paris, Opéra, November 21
Bellini, *Norma*, Milan, La Scala, December 26
Unsuccessful Carbonari-led revolutions occur in Bologna, Parma, and Modena
Mazzini founds nationalist society, Young Italy

1832 In May, Verdi moves to Milan, is rejected for admission to the Conservatory
Begins private study of counterpoint and free composition with Vincenzo Lavigna, previously *maestro concertatore* at La Scala

Camille Du Locle, librettist, born, Orange, July 16
Hugo, *Le roi s'amuse*

1833

Brahms born, Hamburg, May 7
Provesi dies, Busseto, July 26
Donizetti, *Lucrezia Borgia*, Milan, La Scala, December 26

1834 Assists at the keyboard in performances of Haydn's *Creation* by a Milanese Philharmonic Society directed by Pietro Massini

Ludovic Halévy, librettist, born, Paris, January 1
Teresa Stolz, soprano, born, Elbekosteletz (now Kostelec nad Labem), June 2 or 5
Ponchielli born, Paderno Fasolaro (now Paderno Ponchielli), August 31

1835 Completes studies with Lavigna
Co-directs Rossini's *La Cenerentola* with Massini

Bellini, *I puritani*, Paris, Italien, January 24
Bellini dies, Puteaux, September 23
Donizetti, *Lucia di Lammermoor*, Naples, San Carlo, September 26

1836 Appointed *maestro di musica* in Busseto
Marries Margherita Barezzi
Moves back to Busseto; directs and composes for the Philharmonic Society and gives private music lessons
Composes cantata for Massini's Philharmonic Society to honor Austrian Emperor Ferdinand I
Composes first opera, *Rocester*

Meyerbeer, *Les huguenots*, Paris, Opéra, February 29

Lavigna dies, Milan, September 14
Maria Malibran, mezzo-soprano, dies, Manchester, September 23
Giuseppe Mazzini, *Filosofia della musica*

1837	March 26, daughter Virginia is born	Mercadante, *Il giuramento*, Milan, La Scala, March 11
		Zingarelli dies, Torre del Greco, May 5
1838	July 11, son Icilio Romano is born	Bizet born, Paris, October 25
	August 12, Virginia dies	
	October, resigns position in Busseto	
	First publication, *Sei romanze*, appears in Milan	
1839	February, moves back to Milan	Paer dies, Paris, May 3
	October 22, Icilio Romano dies	
	November 17, *Oberto* (revision of *Rocester*) performed, Milan, La Scala	
1840	June, Margherita dies	Paganini dies, Nice, May 27
	September 5, *Un giorno di regno* fails, Milan, La Scala	Pacini, *Saffo*, Naples, San Carlo, November 29
	Verdi temporarily gives up composing	Giulio Ricordi born, Milan, December 19
1841		
1842	March 9, *Nabucco* succeeds famously, Milan, La Scala	Boito born, Padua, February 24
		Cherubini dies, Paris, March 15
		Massenet born, Montand, Saint-Étienne, May 12
		Wagner, *Rienzi*, Dresden, Kgl. Sächsisches Hoftheater, October 20
		Maria Waldmann, mezzo-soprano, born, Vienna
		Gazzetta musicale di Milano founded by Ricordi
1843	February 11, *I lombardi* performed, Milan, La Scala	Wagner, *Der fliegende Holländer*, Dresden, Kgl. Sächsisches Hoftheater, January 2
	Visits Vienna	Donizetti, *Don Pasquale*, Paris, Italien, January 3
		Adelina Patti, soprano, born, Madrid, February 19
		Pacini, *Medea*, Palermo, Carolino, November 28
1844	March 9, *Ernani* performed, Venice, La Fenice	
	November 3, *I due Foscari* performed, Rome, Argentina	

	Begins to buy property in and near Busseto	
1845	February 15, *Giovanna d'Arco* performed, Milan, La Scala	Wagner, *Tannhäuser*, Dresden, Kgl. Sächsisches Hoftheater, October 19
	August 12, *Alzira* performed, Naples, San Carlo	Mayr dies, Bergamo, December 2
1846	March 17, *Attila* performed, Venice, La Fenice	
1847	March 14, *Macbeth* performed, Florence, Pergola	Mendelssohn dies, Leipzig, November 4
	March until mid-1849, takes long trip beginning in London; lives in Paris with Strepponi for approximately two years	Romilda Pantaleoni, soprano, born, Udine
	July 22, *I masnadieri* performed, London, Her Majesty's	
	November 26, *Jérusalem* (revision of *I lombardi*) performed, Paris, Opéra	
1848	Visits Milan	Victor Maurel, baritone, born, Marseilles, June 17
	October 25, *Il corsaro* performed, Trieste, Grande	Donizetti dies, Bergamo, November 29
		First Italian War of Independence (1848–49)
1849	January 27, *La battaglia di Legnano* performed, Rome, Argentina	Meyerbeer, *Le prophète*, Paris, Opéra, April 16
	Returns to Bussetto with Strepponi	Nicolai dies, Berlin, May 11
	December 8, *Luisa Miller* performed, Naples, San Carlo	Chopin dies, Paris, October 17
1850	November 16, *Stiffelio* performed, Trieste, Grande	Wagner, *Lohengrin*, Weimar, Grossherzoglisches Hoftheater, August 28
		Francesco Tamagno, tenor, born, Turin, December 28
1851	March 11, *Rigoletto* performed, Venice, La Fenice	Spontini dies, Maiolati, January 24
	With Strepponi, moves to farm of Sant'Agata, near Busseto	
1852		Salvatore Cammarano, librettist, dies, Naples, July 17

1853	January 19, *Il trovatore* performed, Rome, Apollo	Giovanni Ricordi dies, Milan, March 15
	March 6, *La traviata* performed, Venice, La Fenice	Tito Ricordi becomes director of the Casa Ricordi (through 1888)
1854	Through 1855, spends two years in Paris, in which he completes and supervises production of *Les vêpres siciliennes*	Catalani born, Lucca, June 19
		Humperdinck born, Siegburg, September 1
		Wagner, *Das Rheingold* (first performed Munich, Kgl. Hof- und National, September 22, 1869)
1855	June 13, *Les vêpres siciliennes* performed, Paris, Opéra	
1856		Wagner, *Die Walküre* (first performed Munich, Kgl. Hof- und National, June 26, 1870)
		Schumann dies, Endenich, July 29
1857	March 12, *Simon Boccanegra* performed, Venice, La Fenice	Leoncavallo born, Naples, April 23
	Substantially expands his estate at Sant'Agata	
	August 16, *Aroldo* (revision of *Stiffelio*) performed, Rimini, Nuovo	
1858		Offenbach, *Orphée aux enfers*, Paris, Bouffes-Parisiens, October 21
		Puccini born, Lucca, December 22 or 23
1859	February 17, *Un ballo in maschera* performed, Rome, Apollo	Gounod, *Faust*, Paris, Lyrique, March 19
	Marries Strepponi	Wagner, *Tristan und Isolde* (first performed Munich, Kgl. Hof- und National, June 10, 1865)
	"Viva VERDI" appears as an acrostic message (standing for Viva *V*ittorio *E*manuele *R*e *D*'*I*talia) of Italian nationalism	Spohr dies, Kassel, October 22
		Second Italian War of Independence (1859–60)
1860	Renovates estate at Sant'Agata	Mahler born, Kaliste, July 7
		Garibaldi conquers Sicily and Naples
		1860–80, period of the *scapigliati* led by Boito
1861	Through 1865, serves as deputy for Borgo San Donnino (now Fidenza) in the first Italian parliament	Eugène Scribe, librettist, dies, Paris, February 20
		Cavour becomes first prime minister of Italy
		Cavour dies, Turin, June 6
		Marschner dies, Hanover, December 14

		Vittorio Emanuele II becomes King of united Italy
1862	Through 1863, travels twice to Russia for *La forza del destino*, and to Paris, London, and Madrid	Gustave Vaëz, librettist, dies, Paris, March 12
		Debussy born, Saint-Germain-en-Laye, August 22
	Collaborates with Arrigo Boito on the *Inno delle nazioni*, performed London, Her Majesty's, May 24	Alessandro Lanari, impresario, dies, Florence, October 3
	November 10, *La forza del destino* performed, St. Petersburg, Imperial	
1863		Mascagni born, Livorno, December 7
		Bizet, *Les pêcheurs de perles*, Paris, Lyrique, September 30
1864		Meyerbeer dies, Paris, May 2
		Richard Strauss born, Munich, June 11
		Antonio Somma, librettist, dies, Venice, August 8
1865	April 21, revised *Macbeth* performed, Paris, Lyrique	Meyerbeer, *L'africaine*, Paris, Opéra, April 28
		Felice Romani, librettist, dies, Moneglia, January 28
		Joseph Méry, librettist, dies, Paris, June 17
1866	Through 1867, travels to Paris for *Don Carlos*	Cilea born, Palmi, July 26
	With Strepponi, sets up winter retreat in Genoa	Sophie Loewe, soprano, dies, Budapest, November 29
		Annexation of Venetia
1867	March 11, *Don Carlos* performed, Paris, Opéra	Arturo Toscanini born, Parma, March 25
		Giordano born, Foggia, August 28
		Pacini dies, Pescia, December 6
		Rome won from France, becomes capital of Italy
1868	Takes first substantial trip to Milan in twenty years; meets Alessandro Manzoni	Boito, *Mefistofele*, Milan, La Scala, March 5
	Proposes the collaborative *Messa per Rossini*, to be created under the auspices of the Ricordi publishing house in Milan	Wagner, *Die Meistersinger von Nürnberg*, Munich, Kgl. Hof- und National, June 21
		Rossini dies, Passy, November 13

1869	Supervises production of revised *Forza del destino* in Milan, his first work with La Scala since 1845; performed February 27	Berlioz dies, Paris, March 8 Suez Canal completed
1870		Mercadante dies, Naples, December 17
1871	December 24, *Aida* performed, Cairo, Opera	Auber dies, Paris, May 12 or 13 Wagner, *Siegfried* (first performed Bayreuth, Festspielhaus, August 16, 1876)
1872	Enters semi-retirement at Sant'Agata	Mazzini dies, Pisa, March 10
1873		Manzoni dies, Milan, May 22
1874	May 22, *Messa da Requiem* in honor of Manzoni performed, Milan, San Marco	Cornelius dies, Copenhagen, October 26 Wagner, *Götterdämmerung* (first performed Bayreuth, Festspielhaus, August 17, 1876)
1875	Tours Europe directing the *Requiem*	Benjamin Lumley, impresario, dies, London, March 17 Alphonse Royer, theatre manager and librettist, dies, Paris, April 11 Montemezzi born, Vigasio, May 31 Bizet dies, Bougival, June 3 Bizet, *Carmen*, Paris, Comique, March 3
1876	Conflict with Strepponi over his relationship with Teresa Stolz reaches a crisis	Wolf-Ferrari born, Venice, January 12 Francesco Maria Piave, librettist, dies, Milan, March 5 Wagner, first complete performance of *Der Ring des Nibelungen*, Bayreuth, Festspielhaus, August 13, 14, 16, 17 Ponchielli, *La gioconda*, Milan, La Scala, April 8
1877		
1878		Vittorio Emanuele II dies, Rome, January 9 Solera dies, Milan, April 21
1879	Giulio Ricordi and Boito propose an operatic *Othello*	Merelli dies, Milan, April 10
1880		Pizzetti born, Parma, September 20 Offenbach dies, Paris, October 5

1881	March 24, revised *Simon Boccanegra* performed, Milan, La Scala	Vincenzo Jacovacci, impresario, dies, Rome, March 30
		Escudier dies, Paris, June 22
1882		Malipiero born, Venice, March 18
		Wagner, *Parsifal*, Bayreuth, Festspielhaus, July 26
		Garibaldi dies, Caprera, June 2
1883		Wagner dies, Venice, February 13
		Giovanni Mario, tenor, dies, Rome, December 11
1884	January 10, *Don Carlo* (revision of *Don Carlos*) performed, Milan, La Scala	Massenet, *Manon*, Paris, Comique, January 19
		Puccini, *Le villi*, Milan, Dal Verme, May 31
		Frezzolini dies, Paris, November 5
1885		Hugo dies, Paris, May 22
1886		Ponchielli dies, Milan, January 16
		Liszt dies, Bayreuth, July 31
1887	February 5, *Otello* performed, Milan, La Scala	Fraschini dies, Naples, May 23
		Lind dies, Wynds Point, Herefordshire, November 2
		Barbieri-Nini dies, Florence, November 27
1888	Verdi's hospital, Villanova sull'Arda, Piacenza, opens	Tito Ricordi dies, Milan, September 7
		Giulio Ricordi becomes director of the Casa Ricordi (through 1912)
1889	Boito proposes an opera based primarily on Shakespeare's *Merry Wives of Windsor*	Varesi dies, Milan, March 13
1890		Giorgio Ronconi, baritone, dies, Madrid, January 8
		Mascagni, *Cavalleria rusticana*, Rome, Costanzi, May 17
1891		
1892		Leoncavallo, *I pagliacci*, Milan, Dal Verme, May 21
		Massenet, *Werther*, Vienna, Hofoper, February 16
1893	February 9, *Falstaff* performed, Milan, La Scala	Puccini, *Manon Lescaut*, Turin, Regio, February 1
		Ghizlanzoni dies, Caprino Bergamasco, July 16
		Catalani dies, Milan, August 7

		Gounod dies, Saint-Cloud, October 18
1894		
1895		Brambilla dies, Milan, July 15
1896	Begins building the Casa di Riposo	Puccini, *La bohème*, Turin, Regio, February 1
		Bruckner dies, Vienna, October 11
1897	November 14, Strepponi dies, Sant'Agata	Brahms dies, Vienna, April 3 Giraldoni dies, Moscow, September 19 or October 1
1898		
1899	Casa di Riposo opens	
1900	December, arranges for his youthful compositions to be burned after his death	Puccini, *Tosca*, Rome, Costanzi, January 14
1901	January 21, suffers a stroke January 27, Verdi dies	

PART ONE

Personal, cultural, and political context

1 Verdi's life: a thematic biography

MARY JANE PHILLIPS-MATZ

Giuseppe Verdi, born in a country village in the Po Valley in 1813, rose to become the most popular opera composer of his century.[1] Across a career that spanned more than sixty years he won international fame, becoming the venerated and often decorated grand old man of Italy, "il gran vegliardo." Setting his stamp on two generations of performers, he transformed a show-case for *prime donne* and celebrated tenors into a serious theatre for singing actors. A patriot, Verdi was twice elected to political office and was honored as Senator for Life. He was also a farmer and philanthropist. At his death in 1901, he left behind a legacy of landmark works. Verdi's art has remained as accessible and popular as it was during his lifetime, his major operas constituting the backbone of today's standard repertory. Three of his homes and the home of Antonio Barezzi, his patron and father-in-law, are open to the public as museums. Now, as before, Verdi speaks to us all, even as he remains a beloved symbol of Italy and its culture, a man for his time and ours.

The child, the village, and the land

Verdi was born on October 10, 1813, in Roncole, a hamlet standing in open land about sixty-five miles southeast of Milan with the Apennines looming on the south and west and the River Po flowing to the north, where most income came from wheat, corn, and hogs. In this world of flat fields edged by rows of Lombardy poplars and irrigation canals, the only large buildings were the parish churches, among them Verdi's San Michele Arcangelo in Roncole. The people there spoke a sweet, liquid dialect that was heavily influenced by French and was the only spoken language of Verdi's early years. Peaceful today but chaotic during Verdi's infancy, the area was overrun with troops fighting the Napoleonic Wars.

Verdi's father came from a line of small farmers and tavern keepers whose roots reached back at least to the 1500s in the village of Sant'Agata. Although almost everyone in the area was illiterate, Carlo Verdi could sign his name, read, write letters, and keep accounts. Luigia Uttini, Verdi's mother, came from a family that had left its home in the Italian Alps in 1705 and settled in nearby Cortemaggiore, not far from Piacenza. Her people, also tavern keepers, operated inns and posthouses in tiny Chiavenna Landi and Saliceto di Cadeo. Modest innkeepers such as the Verdis and Uttinis led a life of drudgery and eighteen-hour days, because their establishments were the center of community life. In the Verdi house, the tavern and grocery occupied two rooms; the family lived in five other rooms on the first and second floors. They supplemented their income by leasing land and houses from the diocese, then subletting to tenant farmers. Verdi later used their system on a grand scale on the land he bought between 1844 and his death.

Education, music, and politics

Verdi's iron character was forged in this plain landscape. Seen by his boyhood companions as diffident and reticent, he disliked noisy games and stayed close to home. His closest friend in childhood was his sister Giuseppa, a seamstress who died in 1833. In Verdi's parish and hundreds like it, church music rang out for religious holidays, marriages, and funerals. Baptisms, saint's-day festivities, and fairs brought community dinners and secular music, most of it offered by itinerant musicians and bands of dedicated amateurs, many of whom belonged to local musical societies. Improvised programs were common, and lively concerts on summer evenings always ended with dancing.

Verdi was drawn early to music, and he was particularly fortunate because his intelligence and his musical gift were recognized when he was a child. Priests in Roncole began teaching him Italian grammar and arithmetic when he was about four. Soon he began to study with the organist in Roncole and the priest of the nearby pilgrimage church of La Madonna de' Prati. In 1821, when he was seven, his parents bought him a small spinet, probably using money from a bequest from his maternal grandfather. Verdi kept it until he died and provided for it to be saved afterward. That the son of rural tavern keepers should have had his own instrument at home was astonishing. Verdi proved worthy, learning so rapidly that when he was about ten the vestry of San Michele in Roncole hired him as church organist, a post he held for about nine years.

Many events reported from Verdi's childhood remain unverified anecdotes, but two that can be substantiated happened during religious services. As an altar boy in Roncole, he once failed to pay attention during Mass, irritating a priest who knocked him down the altar steps. The boy responded by cursing the priest, "May God strike you with lightning." As if in response to the boy's curse, the priest was killed in September 1828, when lightning struck the nearby church of La Madonna de' Prati during a holiday service.

Verdi, whose parents were catering a dinner for the clergy there, remembered the shattered altar and the charred bodies of four priests, two laymen, and two dogs who lay on the floor. He often told friends and relatives about the horrifying sight. In the countryside, where superstition ran abreast with the Catholic faith, Verdi's curse became a part of local lore. Still a teenager, he won new respect and was even a bit feared.

In 1823, Verdi's parents sent him to the *ginnasio* or upper school in Busseto, an ancient market town that was also a cultural center and seat of municipal government. Busseto offered the boy a classical education and a chance to work with the forty-odd amateur musicians of the local Società Filarmonica. A group that gave public concerts and served as the town band, they also invited singers to take part in concerts they presented in the grand town house of Antonio Barezzi, a distiller and grocer. In the summer, they rode around the countryside in lumbering, horse-drawn omnibus coaches, playing sacred and secular music in nearby towns. The teenaged Verdi served first as the Filarmonica's music copyist, then as its conductor and composer, writing hundreds of pieces for it and learning to compose for band, orchestra, and voice. In 1832, Barezzi became Verdi's patron, took him into his home, and treated him as if he were one of his own children.

In the 1830s, Verdi became ensnared in local politics, somewhat against his will. At that time Austria occupied much of northern Italy, including the major cities of Milan, Venice, Brescia, Padua, Verona, and Mantua. After Napoleon's defeat and exile, the duchy of Parma, where Verdi lived, was ruled by his wife, the Archduchess Marie Louise of Austria. Like other towns, Busseto was torn apart by factions: the Reds (including many members of the Filarmonica) were pro-French, anti-Austrian, anticlerical, and nationalist; the Blacks (including most of the clergy) supported Austria and the status quo. Verdi, still young, was regarded as the darling of the Reds because of his association with the Filarmonica. The bishop and local priests treated Verdi vindictively, calling him "the creature of Barezzi" and effectively preventing him from becoming parish organist. So much strife erupted over his candidacy that the Duchess sent soldiers to quell the riots. And Verdi had other issues with the clergy: in 1830 his parents' priest-landlords had evicted the family from the house they had rented for almost fifty years. Verdi's profound anticlericalism stayed with him all his life. He never forgot and never forgave.

Opera as an art and a trade

Needing further training, Verdi applied for admission to the Milan Conservatory in 1832 when he was eighteen, but was turned down. He then studied privately until 1835 with Vincenzo Lavigna, a composer of operas who had taught at the Conservatory and had played for many years at the Teatro alla Scala, northern Italy's most important opera house.

As the rehearsal pianist and conductor for the Milanese Società Filarmonica, an amateur group that gave concerts and operas in the Teatro dei Filodrammatici, Verdi gained valuable experience before circumstances forced him to leave the city. Forced back to Busseto, he fulfilled the duties of municipal music master for more than two years. In 1836 he married Margherita Barezzi, a spirited redhead who was his patron's daughter. A piano teacher whose father had once considered sending her to study singing at the Milan Conservatory, she fought fiercely for Verdi's cause both before and after their marriage. The couple soon had two children, named after heroic characters from the tragedy *Virginia* by Vittorio Alfieri, a revered poet and dramatist. Their daughter Virginia died in 1838. While teaching in Busseto he composed his first opera, which he tried in vain to get produced in Parma. Struggling to support his family and seeing that he could never advance his career from Busseto, he resigned his post in February 1839; and he and Margherita set up house in Milan, where their little son, Icilio Romano, died eight months later.

Verdi at first floundered in the rough world of impresarios, rival composers, singers, greedy publishers, librettists, agents, and publicity hacks. Only with the help of Lavigna and other friends was he able to persuade Bartolomeo Merelli, the impresario of La Scala and of the Kärntnerthor in Vienna, to stage *Oberto, conte di San Bonifacio*, which premiered successfully in 1839. With Merelli wanting more, and Verdi's career finally under way, misfortune struck again. Margherita died in June 1840, leaving him depressed and bitter, a childless widower at twenty-six.

Verdi closed the apartment in Milan, returned to Busseto, and tried unsuccessfully to get a release from his La Scala contract. Under pressure, he finished his second opera, *Un giorno di regno* (1840), a total fiasco that survived only one night. Afterward Verdi vowed to stop composing altogether; but Merelli turned a deaf ear and soon convinced him to try a new libretto, *Nabucco*, for which he finished the music in a remarkably short time. Despite Merelli's support, Verdi had trouble getting his new opera produced at La Scala until the *prima donna* Giuseppina Strepponi took up his cause. She and Giorgio Ronconi, a leading baritone, persuaded Merelli to put *Nabucco* on the calendar (March 1842), with Ronconi in the title role and Strepponi as the female lead. Its premiere, a triumph known by few composers, made Verdi a celebrity almost overnight and truly launched his career; its chorus "Va pensiero," sung by the Hebrews during their captivity in Babylon, remains Italy's favorite patriotic song and its unofficial national anthem.

As Verdi, the former music master from Busseto, began feeling his way through the labyrinth of the opera business, he was often helped by Strepponi, a gifted singing actress who knew the inside workings of the theatre. A graduate of the Milan Conservatory, she was the daughter of one composer and the niece of another. Her short but important career began in 1834 and ended in 1846. Traveling from one engagement to another, she adroitly manipulated agents and impresarios, among them Merelli and the powerful Alessandro Lanari of Florence, whose reach at various times extended from Tuscany and Milan to Verona and Venice and south to Rome and even Naples. Once Strepponi devoted herself to Verdi's career after *Nabucco* the pair soon became lovers.

Strepponi was an indispensable collaborator, fiercely loyal to Verdi, but their relationship created problems with his family and friends. She had tarnished her personal reputation with reckless love affairs, pregnancies, and the births – all in less than four years – of three (or perhaps four) illegitimate children. She abandoned all of them, leaving two with foster parents and one in a foundling home, although she did provide some money for her son. Unrecognized by her, all died as charity cases and were given third-class funerals. Her emotional scars never healed, and her tarnished reputation cost her dearly.

The composer and his librettists

Following *Nabucco*, Italian impresarios besieged Verdi with contracts and commissions; soon agents from European and American theatres were also courting him. His operas became so popular that they brought him a substantial income and filled the coffers of his Italian publisher, Giovanni Ricordi. His next opera for La Scala, *I lombardi alla prima crociata* (1843), was followed by the hugely successful *Ernani* (Venice, 1844), the first of five works Verdi composed for the Teatro La Fenice. *I due Foscari* (Rome, 1844) was followed by *Giovanna d'Arco* (Milan, 1845), *Alzira* (Naples, 1845), *Attila* (Venice, 1846), *Macbeth* (Florence, 1847), *I masnadieri* (London, 1847), *Jérusalem* (Paris, 1847), *Il corsaro* (Trieste, 1848), and *La battaglia di Legnano* (Rome, 1849). In all of these (apart from *Alzira*, which got a mixed reception and was written off as a failure), Verdi made steady progress and, above all, showed a growing ability to rule the box office.

Verdi remained constantly on the alert for promising librettos, the quality of which often determined the success or failure of a work. He closely managed the process of creating librettos, from scenario through finished poetry. After *Nabucco*, he might have looked back to Antonio Piazza, the journalist-poet who wrote the libretto of *Oberto*, or to the highly respected

Felice Romani, the author of *Un giorno di regno*. Instead, he collaborated again with Temistocle Solera, the headstrong poet and composer who had revised the libretto of *Oberto* for Merelli and had written *Nabucco* as well. Verdi engaged Solera as his librettist for *I lombardi, Giovanna d'Arco*, and *Attila*. But in 1845, when Solera fell behind on his work, the composer replaced him with the Venetian poet Francesco Maria Piave, who had written *Ernani*.

For more than twenty years, Piave remained Verdi's close collaborator and cherished friend. Their association lasted from 1843 until the late 1860s, when Piave was felled by a stroke. During Piave's protracted illness and after his death in 1876, Verdi provided financial assistance to him and his family. No other poet brought so much to the composer over such a long span of time: Piave not only wrote serviceable poetry but also provided expertise as a stage manager and tact as a negotiator with impresarios and censors, helping Verdi in Venice and elsewhere. Verdi wrote frankly to Piave about his joys and tribulations, sharing concerns that he rarely revealed to others. He called Piave "Dear Tom-Cat" and "Dear Lion-Cat," while Piave responded with salutations to "Adorable Bear" and "Dear Peppino," at a time when almost everyone else addressed Verdi as "Illustrious Maestro." The two men worked together in shared good faith, surviving private and professional crises even as they brought many successful operas to the stage. In addition to *Ernani*, Piave wrote *I due Foscari, Macbeth, Il corsaro, Stiffelio, Rigoletto, La traviata, Simon Boccanegra, Aroldo*, and *La forza del destino*.

Salvatore Cammarano, a Neapolitan librettist, sure-handed man of the theatre, and author of *Lucia di Lammermoor* and many other successful librettos, wrote *Alzira, La battaglia di Legnano*, and two operas of Verdi's maturity, *Luisa Miller* and *Il trovatore*. He also worked with Verdi on the libretto of *Re Lear*, based on Shakespeare, an opera that was never completed. Verdi trusted Cammarano's instincts because of his practical experience in poetry and stagecraft. Andrea Maffei, a distinguished translator and poet – and Verdi's close personal friend – was perhaps the most prominent literary figure among the composer's librettists. Maffei wrote *I masnadieri* and added sections of text to *Macbeth*. When Verdi got his first contract with the Paris Opéra, he collaborated with the French librettists Alphonse Royer and Gustave Vaëz. For his later French operas, he had several partners, including the venerable Eugène Scribe, Joseph Méry, Charles Duveyrier, and Camille Du Locle, who completed *Don Carlos* after Méry died and also translated several of Verdi's works into French. Among Verdi's later librettists in Italy was Antonio Somma, a former theatre manager, attorney, poet, and journalist, who helped with *Re Lear* after Cammarano died. Somma also wrote the libretto for *Un ballo in maschera* (Rome, 1859). The poet of *Aida*

(Cairo, 1871) was the eccentric former baritone and journalist Antonio Ghizlanzoni, the only Verdi librettist who had sung professionally.

Although Arrigo Boito eventually wrote the librettos for Verdi's sublime late operas, his association with the composer was not always cordial. After collaborating with Verdi on the *Inno delle nazioni* (1862), Boito insulted Verdi and the novelist Alessandro Manzoni when at a banquet he read aloud a nasty ode he had written about the decrepit "old men" who were ruining Italian art. Verdi, taking the insult personally and outraged over publication of the poem, kept Boito out of his inner circle for about fifteen years. However, when he read Boito's draft of a scenario of *Otello* their new collaboration began. It produced the revised *Simon Boccanegra* (La Scala, 1881), *Otello* (La Scala, 1887), and *Falstaff* (La Scala, 1893). A composer in his own right, Boito possessed a wide-ranging imagination, a sound understanding of the stage, and an impressive familiarity with Shakespeare, some of whose tragedies he translated into Italian; and he became indispensable to Verdi in the last years of his life.

Singers and impresarios

In the half-century that they lived together, Verdi and Strepponi worked as a team to advance his career. He valued her judgment about singers and leaned on her in battles with such agents and impresarios as Merelli in Milan, Benjamin Lumley in London, Lanari in Florence, and stingy Vincenzo Jacovacci in Rome; with the groups or individuals running the theatres in Paris, Naples, and Venice; and with the priests and local officials who wanted to censor his works. Through all this, Strepponi served as a tactful secretary, handling professional matters and negotiating disputes with colleagues and friends.

Verdi worked with many other celebrated performers, among them the dramatic baritone Ronconi and the sopranos Erminia Frezzolini and Sofia Loewe. In 1847, he wrote *I masnadieri* for Jenny Lind, who was then Europe's most famous singer. In that year and afterward he leaned heavily on the baritone Felice Varesi, who premiered the title roles in *Macbeth* and *Rigoletto*, sang the first Germont in *La traviata*, and appeared in dozens of other productions of Verdi's operas. Another respected baritone was Leone Giraldoni, who created the first Simon Boccanegra and the first Renato in *Un ballo in maschera*. The veteran tenor Gaetano Fraschini, one of the sturdiest artists of the century, sang Zamoro in *Alzira*, Corrado in *Il corsaro*, Arrigo in *La battaglia di Legnano*, and Riccardo in *Un ballo in maschera*. When Fraschini was almost sixty, Verdi even considered him for Radamès in *Aida*. Verdi admired the technique and versatility of Marianna Barbieri-Nini, the *prima donna* of his *Due Foscari*, *Macbeth*, and *Il corsaro*. For his first Gilda in *Rigoletto*, he chose Teresa Brambilla, who had gone to school with Strepponi. The German sopranos Sofie Cruvelli and Marie Sass sang in Verdi's operas in Paris; the Bohemian soprano Teresa Stolz and the Austrian mezzo Maria Waldmann were the stalwarts of his late works. At the end of his life, Verdi worked with the distinguished French baritone Victor Maurel, the first Jago in *Otello* and the first Falstaff, while the stentorian tenor Francesco Tamagno became the first Otello. Although he never named any singer as his favorite, Verdi particularly liked the intelligence, intensity, and beautiful voice of the celebrated soprano Adelina Patti, who sang his *Ernani*, *Giovanna d'Arco*, *Rigoletto*, *Il trovatore*, *La traviata*, and *Aida*. He regarded her far more highly than her predecessor, the diva Maria Malibran.

The view from the top

Although Verdi's career cannot be strictly divided along chronological lines, it is clear that he matured early and developed a deep understanding of his art in the late 1840s. His new command of opera, perhaps first foreshadowed in *Macbeth* (1847), gained momentum in the works that had their premieres between 1849 and the early 1860s.

Verdi had lived in Milan from 1832 until 1835 and from 1839 until the spring of 1847. Then Paris was his home base for nearly two years, as he began living with Strepponi, but he continued to travel to Italy. By then he was a cog in a huge machine, determined to promote his own interests above those of theatre managers and impresarios. As his reputation grew and as he aged, he became increasingly difficult, a tyrant who imposed his will on a whole industry. He also gradually changed the opera business, gaining control over his author's rights and productions of his works and choosing theatres, singers, and even set and costume designers. He amassed a fortune, his royalties coming from sales and rentals of scores and from direct fees paid for his services as composer and producer.

Like every frugal entrepreneur, Verdi sought safe investments; and for him, as for his parents, that meant land. Calling on his father for help, he began buying property in the mid-1840s, first a small farm near Roncole, then the Palazzo Cavalli, a fine town house in Busseto, and his Po Valley farm at Sant'Agata (1848). In 1849, when he decided to settle permanently in Italy, he moved to the Palazzo Cavalli and asked Strepponi to join him. It was a mistake, for the Bussetani, who remembered the scandals of her past, exploded when they saw her. People insulted her on the street and in church; at night, men hurled vile insults and even stones through the windows of Verdi's house. The ensuing scandal rocked the little community and led to conflicts involving Verdi and his parents, friends, father-in-law, brothers-in-law, and even common citizens of the town. Angry, Verdi forced his parents to accept legal separation from him, in a process he deemed "emancipation," and insisted that his relatives and friends give her the same respect they gave him. Afterward, he provided his parents with money, a house, and other amenities.

In May 1851, he and Strepponi left Busseto and moved into his farmhouse at Sant'Agata, a modest dwelling he later enlarged into the comfortable villa that we visit today. For the next fifty years, with fees and royalties covering his every need, Verdi composed in his study-bedroom in the country or in his winter quarters in Genoa. The works of his middle years included *Luisa Miller* (Naples, 1849), *Stiffelio* (Trieste, 1850), *Rigoletto* (Venice, 1851), *Il trovatore* (Rome, 1853), *La traviata* (Venice, 1853), *Les vêpres siciliennes* (Paris, 1855), *Simon Boccanegra* (Venice, 1857), *Aroldo* (Rimini, 1857), *Un ballo in maschera* (Rome, 1859), *Inno delle nazioni* (London, 1862), *La forza del destino* (St. Petersburg, 1862), and *Don Carlos* (Paris, 1867). In the 1860s Verdi often swore that he had retired, that his piano was locked, and that he could not remember a note of music. Why should he compose again? As he once said, people could hear *Il trovatore* everywhere, even in the Indies or the heart of Africa. He was right, as far as he went; but it is only one of his operas that captured the world's stages. And eventually he began to work again.

He revised *Forza* for La Scala (1869) and wrote *Aida* (Cairo, 1871), the opera that brought him a huge fee of 150,000 francs from the original commission and an uninterrupted stream of royalties that continued for more than thirty years. Immediately after its Cairo premiere, he supervised the important Italian premiere at La Scala (1872).

In this period he began to work with Teresa Stolz, the leading soprano in the La Scala *Forza* and *Aida*, and in his later *Messa da Requiem* (1874). Soon his marriage to Strepponi was seriously threatened, because of the attention he paid to Stolz. She had performed in many European cities, and had sung in Verdi's *Ernani, I due Foscari, Giovanna d'Arco, Macbeth, Luisa Miller, Trovatore, Traviata*, the Italian version of *Les vêpres siciliennes*, and the highly successful Italian premiere of *Don Carlos* at the Teatro Comunale in Bologna.

At first Strepponi was stunned at seeing how much Verdi cared for Stolz, and later she feared that he might abandon her altogether. Instead, he forced her to accept the soprano, so for years the three of them coped with oddly tangled emotions: Verdi was unyielding, Strepponi frightened and jealous, and Stolz confident and eager to cultivate an acquaintance with Verdi's wife (better a friend than an enemy). Beginning in 1869, Verdi kept a suite in the Grand Hotel in Milan and continued seeing Stolz, who lived nearby.

Shortly after Strepponi's death (1897), Verdi gave Stolz his autograph score of the *Messa da Requiem*. His letters to her, written when he was past eighty and she in her early sixties, express the immense joy he felt at being near her.

The gentleman farmer, the Deputy, the philanthropist

As Verdi's fortune grew, he added to his land holdings, creating a large estate in the backwater that was Sant'Agata. He found peace on the land he so loved, planting hundreds of trees from nurseries, digging wells, cultivating grapevines and his garden, and watching his crops grow. He bred horses, bought and traded livestock and produce in Cremona and other markets, and even sold hams and other cured meat products, sending out invoices for them on letterhead bearing his own name. He kept his accounts in tall ledgers, where he monitored his tenants, bales of hay and bushels of wheat, fodder, steers, and lengths of cut timber. Studying modern agriculture, he also worked on flood control and improved the situation of his employees and tenants, although he remained a strict and even intimidating *padrone*. In short, he was the very model of an enterprising, hard-nosed farmer, wearing his black, peasant-go-to-market suit and the broad-brimmed black hat that became his trademark. In a word, he loved his land. Although he appeared at public events in severe, elegant suits with top hat and silk scarf, he only reluctantly played a role in city society. Austere and guarded, he rarely spoke of his celebrity and sometimes made fun of it. He confided in few friends and remained wary, sometimes even of those closest to him. But when he entertained guests at Sant'Agata, he could relax.

Verdi might have remained the contented gentleman farmer forever, had he not been drawn into politics. Several revolutions were fought so Italy could win freedom from Austria, the Pope, and various petty rulers who held small areas of the peninsula. During that period, Verdi gave up his republican beliefs and accepted the idea that a king, Vittorio Emanuele II of the House of Savoy, might unify Italy and create it as a modern state. While the Italian people were taking the last steps toward unification, Verdi was elected to political office, first in September 1859 as a Deputy to the Assembly of the Parma Provinces. Only days before the election, he married Strepponi, legalizing their union after nearly sixteen years. Just afterward he headed the delegation from the Parma Assembly, carrying the results of the plebiscite to the King. In 1861 Verdi won higher office, as Deputy to the first parliament of Italy, where he served one term, often working effectively behind the scenes, although he claimed that he was an ineffective legislator. He chose not to run for a second term, but later was named Senator of the

Kingdom for Life. He also continued his career in theatre, though at a slow pace.

Verdi's charity was remarkable: he hid a vulnerable heart behind his diffident attitude. In the last forty years of his life, he gave money to hundreds of needy people, helping some directly, others through institutions and third parties. He established scholarships, founded and supported nursery schools and kindergartens, and gave money to hospitals and shelters for children, adults, the ill, the blind, and the poor. He paid for wet-nurses and shoes for school children, and sent poor arthritic peasants to local spas. He also fought illiteracy with cooperative adult education programs and circulating libraries, and in Busseto, Genoa, and Milan he donated to mutual aid societies to help those in desperate straits. Ongoing endowments or operating funds often followed his initial gifts.

The grand old man

Verdi sustained his artistic reputation and his personal image in the last years of his life. He never relinquished his anticlerical stance, and his religious belief verged on atheism. Strepponi described him as not much of a believer and complained that he mocked her religious faith. Yet he summoned the creative strength to write the *Messa da Requiem* (1874) to honor Manzoni, his "secular saint," and conduct its world premiere. In a singular tribute to Verdi's art, part of the *Messa da Requiem* was sung in Westminster Abbey in 1997 during the funeral service for Diana, Princess of Wales. Verdi gave life to the sublime phrases "Deliver me, O Lord, from eternal death on that dire day, when the heavens and the earth shall be moved, when Thou will come to judge the world by fire," "Let eternal light shine upon them," and finally "Remember me; do not forget me on that day of reckoning."

As Verdi worked on the artistic miracles of his old age, *Otello* and *Falstaff*, he embarked on new charitable projects. In 1888 he built, equipped, and helped manage a small hospital in Villanova sull'Arda at the edge of his fields. Still flourishing, it serves many patients, including disabled persons and accident victims. In the mid-1890s, he built a large retirement home in Milan to shelter old, poor folk from the theatrical trade. This is the Casa di Riposo per Musicisti, which every Milanese taxi driver knows as the "Casa Verdi." It remains a landmark and is full today, recently restored thanks partly to a bequest from the late Wanda Toscanini Horowitz.

In 1901, Verdi suffered a stroke at his suite in the Grand Hotel in Milan and died there on January 27. He was eighty-seven. He had ordered that he have no funeral ceremony, only a brief rite with no music, and his wishes were carried out. He was buried beside Strepponi in Milan's Monumental Cemetery with the understanding that as soon as the Casa di Riposo opened their bodies would be moved to the little chapel in its courtyard. For that occasion, Italy staged a full state funeral, for which about 300,000 people crowded the streets. The young Arturo Toscanini conducted the music for the event, directing a huge chorus in "Va pensiero" from *Nabucco*.

2 The Italian theatre of Verdi's day

ALESSANDRO ROCCATAGLIATI

Within Verdi's long life and career, Italy witnessed two Wars of Independence (1848–49, 1859–60) and a social and political revolution: in 1861, the previous collection of small absolutist states became a single constitutional monarchy which subsequently enjoyed decades of rapid economic and civic development (particularly in the north) resulting from bourgeois liberalism. The theatrical world, with Verdi in a leading role, experienced corresponding changes: by the time of *Falstaff*, almost none of the system in which Verdi began his career – one that belonged essentially to the previous century – remained intact. To understand better Verdi's influential relationship to the opera industry and its gradual restructuring within a more modern environment before and after Italian unification, we first must examine the operatic world of 1825–40.

Although the peninsula was united by little more than an elite language written and spoken by educated citizens (and then only on formal occasions), the economic and cultural phenomenon of the "opera in musica" had become a central element of Italian identity and increasingly homogeneous since the mid-seventeenth century. Operatic style was based on widely known literary, musical, and theatrical conventions; while they differed from genre to genre and changed gradually over time, they nonetheless satisfied audience expectations and accelerated the composer's output. Operatic performances were widespread, and a growing number of theatres were open at various times of the year in both cities and smaller towns: eighty-two could boast working theatres in 1785–86 compared with forty at the end of the seventeenth century; one hundred and seventy-five different opera seasons were offered in 1830, around fifty more by 1840. Theatrical production was handled virtually the same way everywhere, providing a single cohesive marketplace for itinerant artists and impresarios. At the height of their careers, composers such as Rossini, Pacini, and Donizetti traveled throughout Italy to stage as many as three to four new operas per year.

Accustomed as we are to today's wealth of accessible theatre, we cannot easily understand the significance of attending an opera at the beginning of the nineteenth century. In this regard, the papal governor's justification for ordering the Teatro Comunale in Ferrara to be open for the carnival season of 1833–34, despite a financial crisis, is revealing:

Most people love to go to the theatre, where there are great crowds, to be diverted not only by the entertainment on stage but by the many conversations in the boxes and stalls. Without this gathering everyone is more or less isolated, consumed by boredom and idleness... The people of Ferrara love the theatre, but it is at its most pleasing to them during carnival, when everyone is in the city, and the nights are long and tiresome. Many, perhaps, reckon on financial savings by going to the theatre rather than staying at home to hold court and spending money on oil, fire, light, and sometimes even a small entertainment. In the theatre, society comes together more easily, and people are content.[1]

Today this description might be applied more easily to a club than to a theatre, a club for cultivating social relations, discussing business and politics, and flaunting wealth and fashion. At the height of the season, one might attend as many as three or four performances each week but concentrate on the stage only at the most salient moments, particularly when viewing the same production numerous times.

The audience for the lavish theatres built by sovereigns, rich patrons, or the municipality consisted of the social upper crust: nobles, bankers, professionals, and merchants, who used their owned or rented boxes as surrogate drawing rooms. Complete with a partitioned-off area at the back, boxes provided both a setting for entertaining guests and a vantage point for viewing the stage. They were also status symbols, their distinction and price determined by their distance from the central box of the second balcony, which was usually reserved for the most important local luminary.

Social standing was thus demarcated in the crowded auditorium: boxes of different rank looked out over the stalls, where soldiers, domestic workers, and occasional opera-goers stood or purchased seats, while artisans and clerical workers climbed a separate staircase to the so-called "loggione" (literally "big box"), the unpartitioned gallery at the very top of the house. In this way the opera house mirrored the authoritarian *ancien régime* and its hierarchies – appropriately, since the system of operatic production revolved around and was sustained by the ruling classes. Aristocrats and other socialites were not only the most devoted opera-goers, paying for entrance every night in addition to holding seasonal subscriptions. They were also the governors who promoted and subsidized the opera with public money, the "theatre directors" who administered the daily workings of the season, the police authorities who maintained decorum, morality, and good order through censorship and not infrequent arrests of offending impresarios and singers, and the box owners who sometimes – as at La Fenice in Venice – planned the operatic season.

But the key player in operatic productions in pre-unified Italy, the impresario, had more humble roots. He was contracted by the governing

authorities, through open bidding or private negotiation, to manage a theatre for one or more seasons according to precise stipulations. Three main
seasons ranged in prestige and lavishness: first in importance was the carnival
season (from December 26 through the end of February or the beginning of
March), then spring (from the end of April through the beginning of June),
and finally autumn (September through October). However, each normally
required three or four operas and a pair of ballets ("balli"), an opera and
a ballet being coupled to comprise an evening's entertainment ("spettacolo
completo"). Any worthwhile season would boast at least one newly composed opera – from the 1820s increasingly a tragic *melodramma serio* rather
than an *opera buffa* – and often another opera new to that theatre. The "ballo
principale" was also normally new or at least "di cartello" (a local premiere
that had already succeeded elsewhere). Titles already familiar to the local
audience completed the bill.

The impresario faced this heavy workload without respite. As one season
concluded he would secure his next contract, often for a different theatre,
and estimate a budget. Fixed expenditures could be planned accurately:
the singers, orchestra, composer, and staging took up around 50, 12–15, 8,
and 20–30 percent of the total budget respectively. And government subsidies that provided as much as half the total revenue were commonplace:
from the 1830s theatres depended on them to offset income lost through
the suspension of gambling in theatre foyers ("giochi d'azzardo"), which
had balanced the books under Napoleon (and at Naples as late as 1820).
Revenue from theatre attendance was less predictable, however. Although
subscription fees for theatre boxes could be depended on (at least in theory),
the actual proceeds from nightly ticket sales to box holders were not reli-
able, since owners could decide not to use their boxes and the impresario
sometimes failed to rent them. Ultimately, profits hinged on such factors as
the effectiveness of the singers, or the reception of the music and staging,
as well as on side-stepping external impediments such as wars, fires, and
deaths of sovereigns.[2]

His own contract in place, the impresario engaged a company of singers
through written negotiations supervised by the theatre directors and facilitated by theatrical agents who earned 5–6 percent of the singers' fees.
He also hired on the national market the composer, choreographer, and
dancers; orchestral musicians, chorus members, stage and costume designers, theatre staff (stagehands, box office attendants, etc.), and to a lesser
extent the librettist were usually local. As the librettist and the composer
started to create a new opera the cast was a central consideration. For example, the choice of subject had to suit the voice types available: if a good
soprano, tenor, and bass had been hired, a pair of lovers opposed by the
woman's father would suit; a conflict between two rival women over the

same man was possible only with two "prime donne assolute" and a passable tenor.

The chosen subject was then shaped into an outline consisting of discrete musico-dramatic "situations" – the "orditura," "ossatura," or "selva," as Verdi called it – which satisfied not only the logic of the drama, but also the singers' expectations for showpieces. Taking this outline as a starting point, librettist and composer worked in alternation, often in different cities. Little by little the libretto was versified and delivered, frequently piece by piece, to the composer, who set it to music that accentuated the individual strengths of the singers. Meanwhile the poet would also supply the set and costume designers with descriptions of locales and characters.

With the vocal score completed but not yet orchestrated, the composer began rehearsing the principal singers. If the opera was not the first of the season, the singers prepared the new opera during the day, performing the current opera at night while the composer orchestrated his score. The last few days before the premiere were even more hectic: singers rehearsed on stage in costume with the composer conducting the orchestra from the keyboard and the librettist giving stage directions. By the opening curtain everyone was exhausted, particularly the singers, and fatigue sometimes affected the performance. Obstacles aside, the best operas ran throughout the season at the demanding pace of three to four shows per week. The composer, by standard contract, left the city after the first three performances.

The elite theatre-goer measured the success of a season by the number of stimulating evenings it provided. Similarly, the impresario's profit rose or fell with the number of well-attended performances, which themselves depended on a harmonious marriage of cast, music, words, and staging. Within the fiercely competitive market of the hundred or so Italian theatres, only good results could ensure the impresario, singers, and composer future contracts at more prestigious venues. Music was a means to the "artistic fact" of the performance, not an end in itself: the composer was only one of many essential contributors, like the poet or scenographer, and much less significant than the solo singers (a state of affairs reflected in their respective fees). The material product of his engagement, the score, was sold just once to the impresario or theatre management, who used it as they wished: the concept of authorial property and copyright protection had yet to filter into Italian opera. Popular composers were sought not only for new operas but also to flesh out seasons with titles that had already succeeded elsewhere, being hired to adapt existing scores to new singers by altering vocal contours or even composing new pieces. Since composers' creations changed when they were restaged, the score – both words and music – was not considered to be a self-contained and inviolable "work of art." How was it, then, that the works of the greatest Italian composer of the century soon came to be recognized as precisely that?

In the twenty years preceding unification in 1861, Italian theatres maintained these traditions of commissioning and producing opera. It was within this system that Verdi began his career in 1839, won acclaim in 1842, and soon became the patriarch of Italian opera. As a provincial composer, he initially faced daunting obstacles: he had received his only professional training from a private teacher (albeit a knowledgeable *maestro concertatore* at La Scala) and consequently lacked references from a conservatory or prestigious mentor that could convince an impresario to produce his operas. Musicians and other acquaintances in Milan who as amateurs had been conducted by Verdi were pressed into service; but additional interventions were necessary before he could make his debut in the autumn of 1839 with *Oberto, conte di San Bonifacio*. Recommendations by two well-known singers seem to have been decisive: after rehearsing the opera at La Scala in the spring for an aborted charity performance, Giuseppina Strepponi (his future wife) and Giorgio Ronconi spoke well of it to the Milanese impresario Bartolomeo Merelli.

Following a successful debut (that of *Oberto* was fairly good), a composer's willingness to adapt to the demands of the theatres was crucial, and the first years of Verdi's career can be seen from this point of view. Since Merelli managed the best houses in Milan and Vienna, Verdi was happy to agree to write three operas over the next two years, ensuring his entry into the Milanese theatrical world, then unsurpassed in Italy. This agreement carried obligations: for the autumn of 1840 Merelli wanted an *opera buffa*, so Verdi laid aside the tragic libretto on which he was working and wrote the disastrous *Un giorno di regno*. Verdi also set ready-made librettos. Commissioned by the impresario, they could be exchanged between composers as in the case of *Nabucco*: having refused it, Otto Nicolai set *Il proscritto*, which Verdi had rejected, and the latter accepted Nicolai's unwanted goods. Librettos could also be rescued from previously used stock and modified if necessary: *Il finto Stanislao*, which became Verdi's *Un giorno di regno*, had been written by Felice Romani in 1818 for Adalbert Gyrowetz. As for the standard practice of adapting the score to the soloists, Verdi made adjustments for the revival of *Oberto* he directed in Genoa (February 1841), and a solo *scena finale* was omitted from *Nabucco* after two performances, probably because the soprano, Giuseppina Strepponi, was not in good form. Finally, *Nabucco* exemplified the hasty preparations that especially afflicted operas that did not top the season's bill: two short weeks of rehearsal, thrifty staging (Merelli was persuaded to engage Verdi on condition that they recycle warehoused backdrops and costumes from the ballet of the same name staged in 1838), and hurried stage rehearsals (at the premiere, the band practically improvised their entrance). And yet it was an epoch-making success.

Not unexpectedly, every Italian city wanted to see operas by the most fashionable composer. Verdi seized the opportunity and signed up with several theatres, writing for three seasons per year while also overseeing revivals in major houses. In the years that followed, which Verdi later referred to as his "anni di galera" (1858), the pace was frenetic, as an account of the period 1845–46 indicates. In February 1845 Verdi rehearsed both the revival of *I lombardi* and his new opera *Giovanna d'Arco* at La Scala. A few days later he began planning for the following carnival; then, with a mid-March Milan performance of *Ernani* barely begun, he traveled to Venice to oversee *I due Foscari* at the San Benedetto. On returning to Milan he fell ill, but an obligation to the San Carlo in Naples for June was imminent, and between April and May he negotiated a postponement, eventually leaving for Naples on June 20, where *Alzira* premiered on August 12. Having spent September at home in Busseto, he worked in Milan during October and November on *Attila*, to be staged in Venice. He arrived in Venice at the beginning of December for a revival of *Giovanna d'Arco*, and stayed through the premiere of *Attila* on March 17, 1846. Suffering from fatigue during the production period, in February he had a relapse of week-long gastric fevers likely related to his work rhythms, forcing him to delay another opera contracted for London.

Knowing that the singers were central to the success of an opera, Verdi always paid close attention to their suitability to and readiness for their dramatic and vocal roles, as shown by his concern over casting in negotiations with various theatres.[3] He took pains to avoid having the impetuous hero of *Ernani* played by a contralto *en travesti* in 1844; for *Il corsaro* in 1848 he demanded a specific *prima*; for *La traviata* in 1853 he flatly vetoed hiring a contralto for the title role; for *Simon Boccanegra* in 1857 he recommended "for Paolo's part... and this is very important... a baritone who is a good actor," only to refuse the one chosen by the theatre after seeing him in rehearsal.[4] Each case was different, because Verdi's growing fame allowed him to impose his views more and more forcefully. This expanded authority promoted greater respect for the original score by singers when they revived it. But if the young Verdi had few qualms about providing new pieces on request – for the soprano Sophie Loewe (a revival of *Giovanna d'Arco*, Venice, La Fenice, December 1845) or the tenor Giovanni Mario (a revival of *I due Foscari*, Paris, Théâtre Italien, December 1846) – neither was the mature and famous Verdi unwilling to adapt his scores, as for the revival of *La traviata* in 1854, which needed "some shifts of keys, and some adjustments that I myself have made in order to suit it better to these singers."[5]

Such events attest that within the world of Italian opera the "artistic fact" was still the performance – a changing event by nature – rather than the operatic text, the authoritative score which embodied the work of the authors. Although a "repertory" of best-loved operas was developing, it was still the specific production that won attention and appreciation. Critical reviews of revivals reflect this orientation: plot and music are given short shrift compared with the attention to singers, chorus, and scenographers. Verdi considered himself not only an "author" but even more a "man of the theatre." So naturally, for the success of his own revivals, which benefited both his finances and his reputation, Verdi tolerated revisions of his operas necessitated by circumstances. Especially striking were revisions of Verdi's operas in the 1850s, following the suppression of the 1848–49 uprisings, which reflected the reinforced authoritarianism of some Italian governments. Stripped of any moral, religious, or political liberalism, especially in the Papal States and the Kingdom of Naples, "bold" operas such as *Rigoletto*, *La traviata*, *Stiffelio*, and *Les vêpres siciliennes* were restaged with Verdi's music more or less intact but with new texts which radically altered the plot, characters, and settings while retaining the original poetic forms.[6] Having shed their original conceptions, the shows nonetheless – and with the composer's consent – went on and the producers cashed in.

While Verdi adhered completely to these traditions of Italian opera, he also found ways of using conventions to gain a towering artistic individuality, a number of personal and historical factors influencing this process.[7] For example, he was much more interested in literature and the spoken theatre than most of his fellow Italian opera composers. By the mid-1840s he was manifesting considerable dramatic intuition and frequented the Milanese salons, interacting with the lively minds of Italian literary Romanticism – Tommaso Grossi, Carlo Tenca, Giulio Carcano, and Andrea Maffei. In the spring and summer of 1846 Verdi spent several weeks with Maffei, a translator of Schiller and an ardent admirer of Shakespeare. His choice of librettos during this period is scarcely surprising: *Macbeth* (Florence, March 1847), for which Maffei made the final adjustments to Piave's libretto, and *I masnadieri* by Schiller (London, July 1847), which Maffei versified. On his return from London Verdi remained mostly in Paris for two years, its lively artistic environment providing crucial stimuli. There, as in London, the spoken theatre had a deep-rooted tradition and international scope unknown in Italy. Little is known of Verdi's contact with it. But from then on he was increasingly exacting, bold, and original in choosing subjects for his operas. His partiality for the generic contrasts of the sublime and trivial, tragic and comic, that still scandalized Italy now came to the fore.[8] Within a few years, in projects merely sketched (*Re Lear* after Shakespeare) or fully realized (*Rigoletto* after Hugo's *Le roi s'amuse*, *Il trovatore* after Gutiérrez's *El*

trovador, *La traviata* after Dumas *fils*'s *La dame aux camélias*), Verdi fertil-
ized the conventions of Italian opera with the more up-to-date sensibilities
of Romantic theatre.

The system of operatic production in Paris also substantially reshaped
Verdi's attitudes toward the status of the composer. Centered primarily on
the Opéra and the Opéra-Comique, it diverged fundamentally from Italian
practices. Director-impresarios, companies of singers, librettists, orchestras
and scenographers held long-term positions instead of seasonal contracts,
and the process of staging an opera was much more laborious than in
Italy. Productions were carefully scrutinized by many individuals, since a
successful opera could enter the fixed repertory of a theatre, as had been
customary at the Opéra since its inception during the reign of Louis XIV
(1672). Owing to the potential longevity of the score, the composer enjoyed
the status of primary "author," and his creation constituted an independent
"artwork" that might be printed and distributed for decades under copyright
protection.

Having worked in a musical environment that observed such traditions –
he had prepared *Jérusalem* for Paris in 1847 and *Les vêpres siciliennes* in
1854–55 – Verdi became increasingly aware that he had to control all facets
of operatic production, musical, textual, and visual. He not only insisted that
librettists adhere closely to their models (Hugo's *Le roi s'amuse* for Piave's
Rigoletto), but also wrote one *selva* on his own (for *Il trovatore*, by the
already expert Cammarano) and suggested poetic meters and styles (for *Un
ballo in maschera*, by the relatively inexperienced Somma). Verdi personally
attended to the smallest details of the special effects for *Macbeth* at Florence
(Banquo's ghost, the apparitions, etc.), supported in this case by Alessandro
Lanari, the impresario most scrupulous about staging at this time. And
he abandoned La Scala for many years because of Merelli's indifference
toward the stage sets for revivals of *I lombardi* and *Attila* in 1845–46. For
Giovanna di Guzman he adopted from the Paris Opéra the custom of printing
"disposizioni sceniche," which, in conjunction with directions in the score,
preserved for revivals his original staging, including the costume designs,
scenery, and stage movements.[9]

In his business relationships Verdi's growing stature and rural pragmatism often led to impatience and intransigence, particularly with impresarios. He broke with Merelli, who had been helpful at the beginning of
his career; he mistreated Flaùto and Lumley, who had questioned his ill-
nesses; he excoriated Jacovacci's stinginess, challenging him to stage relics
by Paisiello, Gluck, or Lully if *Un ballo in maschera* were too expensive.[10]
Whenever possible he dealt directly with the theatrical management, who
could browbeat impresarios when necessary. At La Fenice, for example, the

Marzi brothers were compelled to take on *Simon Boccanegra* after being warned by the proprietors of the "threat to the smooth proceeding of the season" if public expectations of the great maestro's engagement were disappointed.[11]

Following the revolutions of 1848–49 and consequent financial difficulties for theatres, the old system of seasons and new works as well as management by impresarios became less feasible. Meanwhile, music publishers exerted increasing power. In particular, Giovanni Ricordi in Milan had foreseen – as early as the Rossini vogue between 1813 and 1817 – that repertory operas would become the norm and recognized that a cadre of enthusiasts would welcome printed arrangements of the best-known pieces to perform at home. From 1816 he began systematically acquiring exclusive rights to new operas staged in Milan, buying them from theatres even before their premieres, and in 1825 he purchased the entire collection of manuscript scores from La Scala. Ricordi dealt increasingly with the composers themselves, in order to control distribution of printed editions and manuscript copies. The agreement enacted in 1840 among the states of northern and central Italy for the protection of music copyright was advantageous to this process.

Verdi, who had a good head for business, quickly realized the benefits of such changes for the composer. As early as *Nabucco* he involved himself in the negotiations between Merelli and the publishers Ricordi and Francesco Lucca concerning ownership of the score and libretto. Encouraged by the composer, their competition to acquire his operas from theatres all over Italy lasted for years. Lucca even drew up contracts with Verdi that sold him future scores (which turned out to be *I masnadieri* and *Il corsaro*) and obliged him to produce them in important theatres. From mid-1847 on, however, Ricordi was Verdi's chief associate. Beginning with *Jérusalem* and *La battaglia di Legnano* the composer sold him scores directly prior to performance but not all at once: payments were stipulated for the initial production, for the sale of printing and distribution rights abroad, and for each revival for ten years, the last of these shifting after 1850 from fixed fees to percentages (at first 30 and later 40 percent of the rental). So even when Verdi contracted directly with a theatre as in the case of *Rigoletto*, he maintained the rights for himself, to exploit through sales to publishers. The financial benefit to a composer whose work circulated widely was clear: in 1854 Verdi boasted to Nestor Roqueplan, the director of the Opéra (perhaps exaggerating slightly), that "an opera *chez nous* makes five or six times what it used to make in a dozen years."[12] In this context, the task of arranging revivals with theatres increasingly fell to the publisher, with Verdi himself ready to intervene to relaunch scores that had failed at their premieres (*La traviata* in Venice, May

1854; *Simon Boccanegra* in Reggio Emilia, June 1857). The impresario was losing his preeminent status in the theatrical world, a clear sign that the whole system, like Italian society, was about to change.

After 1861, if the new state of Italy were to succeed alongside more advanced European nations, it needed to establish a suitable political administration and foster industrial development. Both of these concerns greatly influenced the world of opera, as did the opening of the national market to French and German music.

The new Italian government had different priorities – raising literacy, building infrastructure, eliminating banditry in the southern regions – than the theatrical entertainments for affluent urbanites that had always been a primary concern for the authorities of the *ancien régime*. In 1867, the burden of subsidizing opera was transferred from the state to municipalities, a responsibility they were not obligated to fulfill; moreover, from 1869 the state government taxed performances. Townspeople and representatives soon debated municipal subsidies that supported with common resources lavish operatic seasons that many could not enjoy, and these local grants were abolished in many cities at the turn of the century following referendums engineered by radicals and socialists. The unreliability of subsidies resulted in fewer seasons each year for the theatres that were co-financed by box owners, and even in closures, for example at the Carlo Felice in Genoa (1879–83) and at La Fenice (twelve carnival seasons eliminated between 1872 and 1897). Entrepreneurs, sometimes non-Italians, compensated in part by opening new theatres. Their greater capacity and more democratic design – two to three thousand seats, extended single balconies in place of individual boxes – allowed opera to be offered at a lower price to a broader audience.

Under these circumstances it was less risky to stage tested, popular operas than to commission new ones. So between 1860 and 1880 the traditional impresario system based on seasonal novelties was replaced by one revolving around successful "repertory operas." This repertory gradually expanded, but new works were created at a less frenetic pace than before and were meant to last. To compensate, many foreign scores were now imported onto the Italian stage.

The rise of such a repertory was made possible by modern international regulation of artistic copyright. It was not accidental that Verdi – who was called to the first parliament by Prime Minister Cavour (1861–65) and later became a senator (from 1874) – advocated legislation on composers' rights (passed in 1865, improved in 1875), establishment of a national Società degli Autori charged with the collection of copyright fees (1882), and adherence by Italy to international copyright conventions such as the 1888 Berna Agreement. His early partnership with the Casa Ricordi, in which he ceded scores but received percentage royalties, had blazed the trail along which the whole production system of Italian theatres now proceeded.

Now the key player was the publisher, who usurped the prior role of the impresario, whose responsibilities were now confined to arranging daily rehearsals, managing the ticket office, and supervising theatre employees. Active nationwide and abroad, heading companies of increasingly industrial dimensions, and commanding sufficient capital for long-term investments, Ricordi and Lucca exerted maximum control over any aspect of opera that would enhance future earnings from hired scores. Especially for the decisive premiere, but also for each revival, the publisher had to secure a suitable company of singers, a competent musical director, appropriate costumes, and effective scenery, even helping by publishing *disposizioni sceniche* to arrange the stage movements of soloists and chorus. This level of involvement was matched in Italian premieres of foreign operas to ensure the profitability of the investment in performing rights. To compete with Ricordi's stars (Rossini, Donizetti, Bellini, and Verdi), Lucca specialized in imports: the grand operas of Meyerbeer, Auber, and Halévy in the 1860s, and the operas of the young Wagner, staged at Bologna from 1871 beginning with *Lohengrin*.

Within this new system, the integrity and inviolability of the score became the premise of the publisher's commercial rights and the author's artistic ownership. So the idea took hold that opera composers should be considered true "authors" of veritable "artworks." The most successful of them could not only earn sums that would have been unimaginable only decades earlier but also, through the publisher, demand respect for the printed score, obtain the best singers, and exercise nearly unquestioned authority over the theatres, including power of veto over impresarios, singers, librettists, directors, and scenographers.

And Verdi, beyond a doubt, was at the pinnacle of Italian opera. From the time of his election to parliament Verdi was a living monument, a symbol of the new country for Italians only recently united within it. A wealthy man, he owned and worked a large farm at Sant'Agata near Busseto where he lived quietly with his wife Giuseppina, wintered at his apartments in the seaside town of Genoa, traveled in Europe whenever career or interest drew him, and skillfully managed his fortune. A true celebrity, he saw his activities chronicled in the national newspapers, as in 1868 when he provocatively returned the Cross of the Crown of Italy after the Minister of Education insulted his music. Composing new operas was no longer urgent: he could work at his leisure in the most stimulating circumstances while royalties from works written since 1847 poured in.

In his eminent position, Verdi was always a leading actor in the general developments described above. As Italy joined the European operatic market (with its offshoots in the Near East and the Americas), Verdi became a standard-bearer, the only Italian composer richly compensated for writing new works for foreign capitals: *La forza del destino* for St. Petersburg (1861–62), *Don Carlos* for the Paris Opéra (1866–67), and *Aida* for Cairo after the opening of the Suez Canal (1869–71), his only operas of the decade. In view of his astronomical fees, Italian theatres preferred to revive his operas rather than launch them. Ricordi earned royalties from these revivals, so naturally he tried to make each of them a real event, persuading the composer to attend or widely publicizing performances that featured new music. An example is *La forza del destino*, presented at La Scala in 1869 with long passages rewritten (Verdi had been dissatisfied with the first version), an event that signaled the composer's triumphant return to the Milanese stage after more than twenty years.

Verdi's international fame, cultivated by Ricordi and the publisher Léon Escudier (who owned the French rights of many of his operas until 1882, when they were auctioned to various Parisian publishers), deepened his pride and consciousness of his status as his nation's most influential artist at a time when French and German elements were permeating Italian musical life as never before. As early as the 1860s the "scapigliati," a group of young composers and writers in Milan that included Arrigo Boito, Franco Faccio, critic Filippo Filippi, and (in the early days) Ricordi's heir Giulio, had loudly proclaimed that Italian music must abandon the conventions of *melodramma* and follow French models such as Gounod's influential *Faust* (La Scala, 1862). Disappointing performances of two operas – Faccio's *Amleto* in 1865 and Boito's *Mefistofele* in 1868 – quelled years of debate in the *Gazzetta musicale di Milano*, Ricordi's fortnightly house organ. This turn of events pleased Verdi – who had viewed the polemics with vexation and suspicion – particularly when the progressives bowed to his music a few years later. Faccio, at La Scala from the early 1870s, became his most faithful director, Boito his patient and respectful librettist for *Otello* and *Falstaff*, and Giulio Ricordi his dynamic entrepreneurial partner for the last twenty years of his career.

Verdi also kept a respectful distance from the later diffusion of German music in Italy. Although the Bologna stagings of Wagner's operas in the 1870s provoked an outcry, encouraged by the publisher Lucca through his journal *L'Italia musicale*, subsequent polemics between musical xenophiles and nationalists (who wrote primarily in the Ricordi *Gazzetta*) clearly had commercial implications, so they ceased promptly in 1888 when Ricordi acquired Lucca's catalog. Although the Austro-German instrumental tradition was initially praised only by connoisseurs who established the first quartet societies in Florence (1861) and Milan (led by Boito from 1864), it was soon widely absorbed through the addition of Classical and Romantic music to the curricula of the new conservatories which, unlike the theatres, were restructured and financed directly by the state government. Verdi did not appreciate these cultural and political decisions, and attempted in various ways to oppose or correct them (even though he himself was assimilating useful elements of foreign styles).[13] In spite of his efforts, these trends quickly reshaped the musical scene: when at the end of the century the young composers of *verismo* educated in conservatories – Puccini, published by Ricordi, and Mascagni and Leoncavallo, published by the new competitor Sonzogno – established themselves in theatres with innovative vocal and instrumental writing, opera might still take pride of place, but orchestral and chamber concerts were gaining a good following.[14]

Although Verdi benefited from the new theatrical organization more than most, he too still contended at times with its conditions. In November 1868, after Rossini's death, he tried to coordinate a collaborative anniversary Mass to be performed in Bologna where Rossini had studied. Each piece was to be written by a different Italian composer, resulting in a work of truly "national" consequence. Appealing at first, the project stalled within a few months, above all for business reasons. Ricordi balked, since commercial exploitation was prohibited: the music would be "sealed and deposited in the archives of the Liceo musicale," the "object neither of curiosity, nor of speculation."[15] The impresario of the current season at the Teatro Comunale resisted, because singers already engaged for operas would need to be reassigned. Nor was the municipality of Bologna, inclined toward progressiveness and already in touch with Lucca about *Lohengrin*, enthusiastic about the project.

In the absence of state support, aspects of municipal involvement in theatres were also still a fact of life for Verdi and others. For example, in 1874 it was necessary to ask the mayors of Milan and Florence to persuade a Florentine impresario to release the mezzo-soprano Maria Waldmann for another anniversary homage, Verdi's *Messa da Requiem* for the writer Alessandro Manzoni (performed in Milan and marketed by Ricordi). The mayor of Turin requested performances of Verdi's operas so that the carnival season of 1883 would be successful enough to persuade the town council to renew its subsidy. Similarly, according to Ricordi, the mayor of Milan declared in 1886 that "if Verdi completes and stages *Otello*, La Scala is saved . . . we shall win over the three or four determined opponents, and fix the subsidy for the next ten years!!!"[16] Verdi continually urged the state government to take greater responsibility for Italian theatre. In 1869, after taxes were levied on performances, he wrote to his influential friend Senator Piroli, "it is a shame that the government should abandon this art so pitilessly . . . will it be able to hold out without the government's help? No: impossible." Two years later he turned to the Ministry of Education, asking "that the Minister revive the theatres . . . For example, establish three of them . . . one in the capital, the other in Naples, the third in Milan. Orchestra and chorus paid for by the government."[17] Unsuccessful in these efforts, Verdi settled for helping several cities in the difficult years 1872–73 by personally overseeing revivals such as those of *Aida* and *La forza del destino*.[18]

Verdi's zealous protectiveness of his own works also contributed to his involvement in even minor revivals. After *Aida*, Verdi sought contracts that allowed only for complete performances and was furious when singers – even famous ones appearing in the best salons – performed pieces out of context (as *prima donna* Adelina Patti did in Paris in 1880). Whether at his farm, his winter home in Genoa, or abroad, he fastidiously supervised revivals from a distance, sending detailed instructions to the publisher, who then acted as his intermediary with impresarios, singers, directors, scenographers, and costumers, heading off proposals that might displease him. So their correspondence of the 1870s–80s shows Verdi's dictatorial attention to the merits of various theatres, the qualifications of singers for specific roles, the direction and disposition of orchestras, and the quality of costumes and scenery.

Giulio Ricordi handled all these concerns meticulously, particularly when dealing with La Scala, where he dominated the administrations of the latter part of the century. His greatest achievement was the premiere of *Otello* in 1887, having suggested the idea to Verdi as early as 1878 and nurtured the project throughout the next decade. A host of supporters catered to the elderly composer: Boito, who was committed to the project from the start; famous singers such as Francesco Tamagno and Victor Maurel, who coveted the parts of Otello and Jago respectively (the latter even offering to lower his customary fee); the costume designer Alfredo Edel, whose work Verdi demanded be redone; and even manufacturers of a special bass drum (at Milan) and trumpets (as far away as Belgium).

Ensconced in his drawing room with the entire theatrical world revolving around him, Verdi had left behind the age of domineering singers and impresarios. This did not mean that Verdi lost, even at the height of his world fame, his old flexibility as a true "man of the theatre." For example, he lodged the soprano Romilda Pantaleoni, the first Desdemona, at Sant'Agata while he composed *Otello* so that he could tailor her part to her and discuss "what would be best for the two refrains" of her last aria.[19] But on that morning in February 1901 when the people of Milan walked behind his coffin to the strains of "Va pensiero" from *Nabucco*, the theatrical world for which that chorus had been conceived had completely disappeared, nobody remembering it. Yet its legacy lived on, in music still capable of moving men in a new century.

Translated by Laura Basini

3 Verdi, Italian Romanticism, and the Risorgimento

MARY ANN SMART

> Among its other meanings romanticism has assumed that of a special
> relationship or bond between intellectuals and the people, the nation. In
> other words, it is a particular reflection of "democracy" (in the broad
> sense) in literature ... And in this specific sense romanticism has never
> existed in Italy.[1]

The writings of Antonio Gramsci might seem a strange place from which
to launch a consideration of the vexed topic of Verdi's ties to the Risorgimento, particularly since Gramsci disapproved of opera and never had
anything kind to say about Verdi. He did, however, possess a visionary
understanding of the role of culture in nineteenth-century Italy, one all
the more revealing for its unfriendliness to Verdi. Gramsci saw the popularity of opera in Italy as both a substitute for and an impediment to the
development of his preferred vehicle for Romantic sentiment, a popular
literature that demanded a solitary and reflective mode of consumption
diametrically opposed to the experience of the opera house. His suspicion
of opera was aroused partly by ties he perceived between operatic song and
an oratorical style that reminded him of fascist speechifying: elsewhere in
the *Prison Notebooks* he lamented the "operatic" taste of the "man of the
people," who seeks in poetry only the singsong rhymes and "hammering of
metrical accents" that he enjoys in popular oratory.[2] It was this willingness
to be swept away by the "operatic," Gramsci argued, that militated against
the formation of what he called a "national-popular" style of literature in
Italy and against a truly popular Romanticism.

Gramsci's diagnosis – especially his insistence on entwining the Romantic and the national – might help to clarify the complex issue of Verdi's
position as a Romantic composer as it intersects with the Risorgimento.
While an influential strand of scholarship has celebrated Verdi as an exponent of both a populist style and northern European high-art trends, recent
research has revealed the first of these views to be largely unfounded. In the
two main sections of this article, I shall examine contrasting facets of Verdi's
so-called "Risorgimental" style: his mythical image as creator of patriotic
choruses and the more intimate brand of patriotic sentiment he adopted
in his only opera composed specifically for a Risorgimento occasion, *La
battaglia di Legnano*. To set the scene, however, I should consider briefly
what the word "Romantic" meant to Italian artists, and particularly to Verdi.

In search of Romanticism

Italy may never have experienced a full-blown Romantic movement, but it certainly had heated Romantic debates. The most feverish arguments took place in 1816–18 in response to Madame de Staël's call for Italian writers to broaden their horizons by translating works by German and French writers. These polemics touched on many of the same topics as the nearly contemporaneous debates in France and Germany: the role of literature as an imitation of the world, the use of mythological subject matter, and the importance of the dramatic unities. But the Italian debates distinguished themselves in two ways.[3] First, the Italian pamphleteers were explicitly concerned with questions of national self-definition, an orientation evinced in their choice of exemplars. Along with the expected references to the northern European Romantic pantheon of Goethe, August Wilhelm Schlegel, *et al.*, they cite as models Dante, Petrarch, and Ariosto, elevating these authors to the status of honorary Romantics. Perhaps more relevant to *operatic* Romanticism, the polemicists also show a surprising sympathy toward certain aspects of Classicism, a willingness to tread a middle path between styles of past and present. Thus while Alessandro Manzoni advocated sweeping away mythological plots and embracing instead subjects drawn from everyday experience, he remained cool to the Romantic doctrine of originality, allowing that imitation of Classical models could be desirable. Writing in 1823, Manzoni distanced himself from Romantic orthodoxy when he noted that Romanticism "was talked much about a while ago, but today is talked about no more; the word itself is forgotten."[4]

Measured against Verdi's output, the idea that Romanticism was passé by 1823 seems bizarre, but a similar periodization is suggested in a text often regarded as the blueprint for creating a Romantic style in Italian opera, Giuseppe Mazzini's *Filosofia della musica* (1836). For Mazzini, Romanticism was largely a pejorative term, associated with individualism and the artist's private struggle to escape from convention. When he accorded Rossini the dubious honor of having "accomplished in music what romanticism accomplished in literature," he was promoting an operatic reform that would move *beyond* Romanticism, and especially beyond Italian opera's enthralment with melodic beauty and vocal ornament – both traits that Mazzini saw as manifestations of excessive individualism and lack of social consciousness.[5] Mazzini counseled composers to replace or enrich these "individualistic" tendencies with a new musical style based on such techniques as an expanded role for the chorus, vivid local color, and more precise characterization achieved by associating principal characters with recurring themes or motives.[6]

Musical evidence suggests that Mazzini's call to transcend Romanticism may have been premature, at least in the sense that the label is usually applied to composers such as Berlioz or Weber. Certainly the Italian opera of the first half of the century contains little that approaches the formal or harmonic experiments of contemporary French or German music. For Italian composers, Romanticism was less a full-fledged doctrine than a manner to be applied selectively in individual works. Rossini tried on the Ossianic mode in *La donna del lago* (1816), Bellini experimented with the Gothic in *Il pirata* (1827), and Donizetti shocked the Milanese censors by adapting Victor Hugo in *Lucrezia Borgia* (1833).[7] But for all three composers these remained isolated experiments within a predominantly conservative style based in predictable aria structures and vocal display.

Verdi, too, indulged in some Romantic impulses during the first decade of his career, setting texts by the heroes of French Romanticism, Victor Hugo (*Ernani*, 1844) and Shakespeare (*Macbeth*, 1847).[8] There was also an encounter with Byron in *I due Foscari* (1844), in which, unknowingly following Mazzini's advice, Verdi experimented with a system of identifying themes for the principal characters. But these are the exceptions. Perhaps because most of Verdi's early works take as their subject matter clashes between opposing national groups, musical techniques emphasizing an almost "Classical" balance and contrast prevail over any "Romantic" blurring of form. These scenarios of stark confrontation call for clear, forceful musical treatment and almost beg for allegorical decoding in terms of the domination of Italy by its Austrian invader. *Nabucco* (1842) and *I lombardi* (1843) both feature religious conflicts; the equally martial *Giovanna d'Arco* (1845) and *Attila* (1846) showcase potent warrior women, waving swords and driving out invaders in a manner reminiscent of the French emblem of nation, Marianne.[9] In *La battaglia di Legnano* (1849), Verdi's only work composed specifically to celebrate Risorgimento victories, he veered away from overt historical commentary, focusing instead on the private agonies of its principal characters, locked in a traditional love triangle.

The political views Verdi expressed privately are almost as various as the messages of his operas, shifting with the vicissitudes of his career and those of the struggle toward Italian unification. At the earliest stages of his career, Verdi could cater to the Austrians governing Milan when it was professionally efficacious. In 1836 he composed a cantata in honor of Ferdinand I, the new Emperor of Austria, and he dedicated two early scores to Austrian duchesses resident in Milan. Verdi's clearest endorsements of the Risorgimento date from the spring of 1848, when the Austrians had been driven from Milan and Venice and the Pope had fled Rome, leaving the city to be governed, briefly, by a triumvirate of rebels that included Mazzini. Having braved considerable physical inconvenience to return to Milan when news of the fighting there (the so-called "Cinque Giornate") reached him in Paris, Verdi expressed his excitement in phrases that would fit quite comfortably into one of Piave's librettos:

> Honor to these heroes! Honor to all Italy, which is now truly great!
>   The hour of her liberation is here; be sure of that. The people want it: and when the people want it, there is no absolute power that can resist...
>   You talk to me about music! What has got into you? Do you think that I want to bother myself now with notes, with sounds? There cannot be any music welcome to Italian ears in 1848 except the music of the cannon! I would not write a note for all the money in the world: I would feel immense remorse at using up music-paper, which is so good for making shells.[10]

Rather than stuffing scores down the throats of cannons, Verdi instead took action by composing an *Inno popolare* ("Suona la tromba") to a patriotic text provided by Mazzini. When Verdi sent Mazzini the completed piece, he noted that he had "tried to be as popular and easy as possible," and hoped that the piece would "be sung on the Lombard plains, to the music of the cannon."[11] This was not to be: by the time the music arrived, France had come to the aid of the Austrians and the Italian rebels were in retreat, no longer in need of a new anthem.

   After this reversal, Risorgimento leaders became more pragmatic, eventually forging an alliance with King Vittorio Emanuele II of Sardinia, a move that undercut the popular revolution. This shift to a strategy of compromise and consensus brought disillusionment to the most committed revolutionaries, but it was probably coincidence that Verdi turned away from political subject matter around this time, favoring instead domestic subjects often drawn from recent Parisian plays. While Verdi clearly felt some political disappointment, personal circumstances – his increasing financial and professional security and his extended periods of residence in Paris – were probably more influential. In the 1850s, only *Les vêpres siciliennes* (1855) portrays an oppressed nation straining against a foreign tyrant, and the opera takes no sides in the colonial conflict, simply killing off everyone in a massacre in the brief final scene.[12] A decade later in *Don Carlos* (1867), Verdi reexamined his own youthful (if intermittent) revolutionary fervor, by way of the opera's jaded but sympathetic presentation of the Marquis de Posa's idealistic attempts to change the world.[13] But there is much more to the political world of *Don Carlos* than Posa. The opera could be heard as a summation of Verdi's relationship to politics, as multi-voiced as Verdi's own statements. Every principal character expresses political beliefs at some point, and all are musically envoiced vividly enough that listeners can sympathize with each in turn.

The myth of "Va pensiero"

How, amid all these conflicting attitudes, did Verdi come to be mythologized as the bard of the Risorgimento? The story usually goes that the people ordained him through spontaneous demonstrations and appropriations of his music. However, recent research has revealed that Verdi's patriotic reputation originated much later, that it was in fact constructed retrospectively.[14] The origins and perpetuation of this myth form a fascinating episode of historiography, worthy of detailed consideration here.[15]

First, the myth. Details vary, but stories of the political uses of Verdi during the Risorgimento tend to concern choruses, and they usually center around spontaneous outpourings of emotion, moments when Verdi's music enabled the populace to express patriotic sentiments forbidden in any guise except the relatively "safe," "meaningless" medium of song.[16] The best known of the Risorgimento anecdotes concerns Verdi's first great success, *Nabucco*. As the story goes, the audience at the Milanese premiere (1842) demanded a repetition of the famous chorus of chained Hebrew slaves, "Va pensiero," in contravention of the Austrians' prohibition of encores. Afterward, enthusiasm for "Va pensiero" spread across Italy, sparking not only more encores, but also spontaneous choral outbursts, with Verdi's catchy tune moving entire audiences to burst into song.[17]

Contrasting this fervid reception is the incongruous calm and repose of both words and music in the chorus itself:

Va pensiero sull'ali dorate	Fly, thought, on wings of gold,
Va ti posa sui clivi, sui colli	go, settle on the slopes and the hills,
Ove olezzano libere e molli	where the sweet airs of our native land,
L'aure dolci del suolo natal!	free and gentle, waft fragrantly.
Del Giordano le rive saluta,	Greet the banks of the Jordan
Di Sïonne le torri atterrate...	and Zion's toppled towers...
Oh mia patria sì bella e perduta!	Oh, my country, so lovely and distant!
Oh membranza sì cara e fatal!	Oh, fond and painful memory!
Arpa d'or dei fatidici vati	Golden harp of the prophetic bards,
Perchè muta dal salice pendi?	why hang mute on the willow?
Le memorie nel petto raccendi,	Rekindle the memories in our breast,
Ci favella del tempo che fu!...	tell us of times past!...

Example 3.1 Verdi, *Nabucco*, III, 11, "Va pensiero" (chorus)

Even if one were to substitute the Tiber and "*Rome*'s toppled towers" for the geographical markers of the Promised Land, the words would still lack urgency, evoking only a dulled, remote pain. In a sense, the words of "Va pensiero" enact the exile's imagined *recovery* of the homeland, by means of peripatetic thoughts, breezes, and bardic song. In keeping with this peaceful, familiar poetic landscape, Verdi's music sets up a static musical paradise, through its rocking rhythm and a melodic outline that hardly alters throughout the piece. Patterns of melodic repetition create musical symmetry and closure, but never attempt to illustrate individual words or ideas from the text. As a nostalgic invocation of nation "Va pensiero" is exemplary, but it carries no impulse toward action, change, or movement that might inspire supposed patriotic outbursts.

In preparing the critical edition of *Nabucco*, Roger Parker attempted to trace the story of the spontaneous, unruly "Va pensiero" encore back to reviews of the opera's premiere, only to discover that the encore had actually been demanded for a completely different chorus in *Nabucco*, the Hebrew prayer "Immenso Jeovha." The routine biblical sentiments of "Immenso Jeovha" lack the political potential of the pastoral nostalgia of "Va pensiero," and one only needs to listen to the first few phrases of each chorus to understand why Verdi biographers have preferred to sustain the fantasy of the "Va pensiero" encore.[18] This single instance of misapprehension turns out to be emblematic of a far-reaching exaggeration of associations between Verdi's music and the emerging Italian sense of nation of the 1840s.[19] Reports in the *Gazzetta musicale di Milano*, the house organ of Verdi's publisher,

Ricordi, show that following the Cinque Giornate, when La Scala closed for several months, opera was replaced by concerts of newly composed patriotic hymns and military music. But strangely, when the "papa dei cori" should have been a leading figure, Verdi's name is nowhere to be found on concert programs. Ricordi's *libroni*, the logbooks that record publications, tell the same story. During this period the presses were dedicated almost entirely to engraving patriotic anthems, but Verdi's name is missing from these lists too. Even more surprising, the *libroni* lack entries for any reprints of "Va pensiero" as an independent piece, inexplicable if it had really been receiving such frequent popular performances.[20]

One chorus that Ricordi *did* print in 1848, Pietro Cornali's *Canto degli italiani*, can perhaps provide some clue to Milanese tastes in moments of revolutionary fervor. Published in the last issue of the *Gazzetta musicale* to appear before the Austrians returned to Milan (July 26, 1848), Cornali's chorus can stand in for the reams of such popular pieces published during the year. Its text, credited only to "un toscano," consists of eight four-line stanzas, and calls for guerrilla action, urging citizens to defend Italy against the invader with stones and bits of roofing tile. Internal stanzas celebrate nation-defining moments of the distant past – "Viva il Vespro di Palermo!" "Viva il patto di Pontida!" ("Long live the Sicilian Vespers! Long live the Oath of Pontida!") – and the chorus concludes with a ringing affirmation of the power of the Pope and the Holy Cross to support the campaign waged by the sword:

Finchè Italia non sia nostra	Until Italy belongs to us
Non si dorma, non si taccia;	we will not sleep, we will not be silenced.
Segua il fatto alla minaccia,	Suit the action to the word:
Italiani alla tenzon.	Italians into the fray!
Chi lo schioppo non ha pronto	He who does not have his rifle at the ready,
Piglia un tegolo d'argilla;	take up a piece of tile;
Viva il sasso di Balilla	long live the stone of Balilla,
Che potè più d'un cannon.	which achieved much more than a cannon.
[five stanzas omitted]	
Chi di voi non può la spada	Those of you who do not have a sword,
Osi almen alzar la voce	dare at least to raise your voices;
Viva il Pio che la Croce	long live Pius, whose Cross
Fè segnal di libertà.	has been the signal for our freedom.

Parker has written that "it is hard... to be much interested in Cornali's music, hard even to take it seriously."[21] But in the context of Verdi's peculiar absence in 1848, it would seem hard *not* to take Cornali seriously, if only for the access this music promises to popular and revolutionary musical taste. Indeed, "Finchè Italia" could hardly be more different from "Va pensiero."

Example 3.2 Pietro Cornali, *Canto degli italiani*

Although Cornali sets up a similar lilting dotted rhythm, the rhythmic figure here is underpinned by a series of repeated chords forceful enough to impel brigades forward in a slow march (see example 3.2). Where "Va pensiero" sustains a single mood throughout, the *Canto degli italiani* is full of passing dissonances and fleeting melodic responses to individual words in the poetic text, effects that jar the listener from private contemplation and aggressively call attention back to the meaning of the words. In the second stanza, voices and piano accompaniment suddenly join in a unison tattoo figure to paint the lines "Chi lo schioppo non ha pronto / Piglia un tegolo d'argilla," and the stanza ends with an even more overstated onomatopoeic effect for "più d'un cannon." Judged according to any high-art aesthetic, these points of literal text–music correspondence verge on the absurd. But it may well have been partly these devices – Cornali's willingness to take the text "at its word" – that made the chorus suitable for revolutionary occasions. Together with the sensual layering of a melody line embellished by frequent chromatic

Example 3.2 (continued)

dissonances over a comfortingly monotonous bass line, Cornali's music skillfully combines soothing, memorable melody with surges of heightened sensation and surprise.

If in the 1840s Verdi's operas neither alarmed the Austrians much nor focused popular patriotic feeling as usually thought, his reputation as the "vate del risorgimento" nonetheless gained strength as the nineteenth century progressed. The senatorial post granted Verdi in the first Italian parliament and his identification with Vittorio Emanuele II through the slogan "Viva VERDI" (for "Viva Vittorio Emanuele, re d'Italia") may have represented the beginnings of this trend, which culminated in the singing of "Va pensiero" by mourners at Verdi's funeral in 1901. This last "spontaneous" outburst, which happens to have been led by Arturo Toscanini and supported by the chorus and orchestra of La Scala, seems the perfect symbol for a process of retrospective mythologization, in which the significance

Example 3.2 (continued)

of Verdi's music for the Risorgimento is pushed further and further back in time, the nostalgic-pastoral hymn "Va pensiero" playing an ever more central role.[22]

Confronted by this evidence, we could discard the formulation "Verdi and the Risorgimento" altogether, erecting in its place the rigorously empirical view that art and politics are basically unconnected, or are connected only in incidental ways unworthy of serious scrutiny. But this would be to ignore evidence that Verdi himself at times cared deeply about his role in articulating a national sensibility. Perhaps more important, it would overlook evidence in the operas themselves. Even the arch-skeptic Parker has allowed that in later compositions Verdi deliberately imitated the musical features that make "Va pensiero" inherently suitable as a patriotic hymn.[23] The unison melody and decasyllabic meter that characterize "Va pensiero" reappeared the following year in "O Signore dal tetto natio" (*I lombardi alla prima crociata*), with poetry by the same librettist as *Nabucco*, Temistocle Solera. Verdi returned to the topos in both *Ernani* ("Si ridesti il Leon di Castiglia") and *Macbeth* ("O patria oppressa"), as if making a concerted effort to establish the patriotic chorus as a new operatic genre.

"Digli ch'è sangue italico"

While Verdi's attempt to create a patriotic-popular idiom is clearest when he musters familiar rhythms and melodic types, he also directed his attention toward the broad fabric of images and archetypes that constituted the culture of the Risorgimento. Commissioned to write an opera for Rome's Teatro Apollo specifically commemorating the events of 1848, Verdi turned to this inventory, choosing a sequence of events that had already received a good deal of attention from Risorgimento writers and historians.[24] Like *Nabucco*, *La battaglia di Legnano* glorifies the struggle for independence through historical analogy, but here Italy finally plays herself, with the role of the foreign aggressor assigned to Frederick Barbarossa. As Adrian Lyttelton has shown, the twelfth-century formation of the Lombard League and its successful resistance to Barbarossa at Legnano was a foundational tale for Risorgimento artists and historians, treated as a climactic moment in Sismondi's *History of the Italian Republics*, in a historical novel by Cesare Balbo (1816), and in Giuseppe Diotti's painting *The Oath of Pontida* (1837).[25] Surprisingly, handed this chance to fashion an opera from Italian sources, Verdi and his librettist, Salvatore Cammarano, instead grafted the story of the Lombard League onto a French play about conflict between France and England, Joseph Méry's *La Bataille de Toulouse* (1828).[26]

Equally intriguing is the absence in *Battaglia* of a patriotic chorus along the lines of "Va pensiero." This omission points to a larger innovation in *Battaglia*, the shift of attention from the clash of national (or religious) groups to a focus on familial relationships, and especially on the mother's role in raising a brave and virtuous son of Italy. As the curtain rises, Lida (soprano) loves Arrigo (tenor) but, believing that he has died in battle, has married Rolando (baritone). Her guilt and torment over her continuing love for Arrigo provide the opera's central emotional conflict. It is an indication of the new importance of family ties that the opera's lyrical high point comes not during the ceremony in which the "Squadron of Death" swears to die for Italy, nor in a love duet for the adulterous couple, but in an exchange between Lida and her husband. Just before he goes into battle, Rolando charges his wife with the moral education of their son, saying in the introductory recitative, "Tu resti insegnatrice di lui" ("You shall be his teacher"). The slow movement that follows proposes a new Risorgimento archetype, an alternative to the collective melancholy of "Va pensiero." Rolando's words concern heritage, and – crucially – position Lida as vessel or intermediary. Ideally blank and passive herself, she conveys father's heroic message to son, and thus perpetuates the Nation:

Digli ch'è sangue italico,	Tell him he is of Italian blood,
Digli ch'è sangue mio,	tell him he is of my blood,
Che de' mortali è giudice	that the judge of men
La terra no, ma Dio!	is not on earth, but God!
E dopo Dio la patria	And after God, teach him
Gli apprendi a rispettar.	to respect the homeland.

The music Verdi wrote for the two characters seems designed to reinforce a traditional gender opposition, a contrast most apparent in the choice of accompanying instrument: Rolando's solo statement is underpinned by French horns playing insistent repeated notes, while Lida's reply (expressing guilt and sorrow) is supported by more introspective oboe and clarinet, playing sobbing figures she herself takes up toward the end of the passage (see example 3.3). As if to emphasize the sacramental nature of this exchange, the duet ends without a *cabaletta*, closed instead by a slow prayer-like coda. Harp, tremolo strings, and woodwind accompany as Rolando blesses his kneeling and silent son.

The depiction of Lida as virtuous mother plays on a discourse linking Woman and Nation that extends far beyond the world of this opera, and even beyond the borders of Italy. It also brings to mind a specific precedent, a passage in Mazzini's *Filosofia della musica* in which music is personified as a pure woman having the power to redeem both culture and country:

Music, like a woman, is so holy with anticipation and purification, that even when men sully it with prostitution, they cannot totally obliterate the aura of promise that crowns it. Even in the midst of that music which we today condemn, there is still a ferment of life that foretells new destinies, a new development, a new and more solemn mission... You might say that an angel, out of the abyss into which he has been thrown, still manages to address us as if from paradise. Perhaps in the future it will fall to woman and to music to carry a broader responsibility for resurrection than has so far been anticipated.[27]

This characterization of music as redemptive woman and angel (with its strange anticipations of Wagnerian rhetoric) prefigures the Victorian archetype that feminist literary critics have called the "angel in the house," a phrase that also seems apt for the images of domestic women so popular in contemporaneous Italian painting. While *French* revolutionary art (whether of 1789, 1830, or 1848) tended to feature flag-waving Amazon figures, the images of women in *Ottocento* painting are almost exclusively

Example 3.3 Verdi, *La battaglia di Legnano*, III, 7, "Digli ch'è sangue italico" (Rolando, Lida)

Example 3.3 (continued)

domestic, placed mostly in genre scenes of husbands leaving for the front, or groups of girls reading letters or sewing red shirts.[28]

Stronger evidence of *Battaglia*'s status as a "Mazzinian" opera is provided by Verdi's treatment of the opera's principal chorus, "Viva Italia! sacro un patto." By far the best-known passage from Mazzini's *Filosofia* is an oracular paragraph that calls out for the "new" Italian opera to elevate the chorus, that "born interpreter of the voice of the people," to the status of a "collective individuality . . . [having] an independent and spontaneous life of its own."[29] Mazzini's wish-list has often been seen as foreshadowing Verdi's achievements, even though Mazzini himself later singled out Meyerbeer as the realization of his hopes for operatic reform. In his approach to the patriotic chorus in *Battaglia* Verdi seems not only to partake of a Mazzinian aesthetic, but also to have learned from Pietro Cornali and other successful composers of popular revolutionary music. The musical substance of "Viva Italia! sacro un patto" is actually far less interesting than that of "Va pensiero" or any of Verdi's subsequent attempts to recapture that nostalgic style. But it *is*

Example 3.4a Verdi, *La battaglia di Legnano*, I, 2, "Viva Italia! sacro un patto" (chorus)

eminently singable, and *march*-able. Sung by male voices in unison with the sparse accompaniment of an on-stage brass band, this curtain-raising number convincingly creates the impression of performance by a gaggle of unschooled singers eagerly striding into battle (see example 3.4a).

The lesson of 1848 is felt most strongly when this chorus returns at the opera's melodramatic climax. At the end of the third act, Rolando surprises Lida in a tête-à-tête with Arrigo. Suspecting marital betrayal, Rolando locks them in a tower and leaves for battle. As Arrigo desperately searches for a means of escape, the chorus "Viva Italia!" is heard offstage, announcing the departure of the "Squadron of Death" to which both Rolando and Arrigo belong. Taunted by the strains of the patriotic march, Arrigo rushes to the window and hurls himself from the balcony to follow his fellow soldiers (see example 3.4b). Here the chorus "Viva Italia!" works as a dramatic agent, its sounds irresistibly spurring Arrigo into action. In *Battaglia* Verdi dared to eschew musical beauty, and aimed instead to create a kind of music that could be integrated directly into action and that could inspire wild heroic deeds. This stance seems an explicit rejection not only of the leisurely aestheticization of "patria" spun out in "Va pensiero," but also of Romanticism's traditional glorification of music as transcendent, surpassing

Example 3.4b Verdi, *La battaglia di Legnano*, III, 9, *scena, terzetto*, finale

both word and action. The chorus in *Battaglia* celebrates a music that is based in movement and acts forcefully on the body, compelling physical action.

These two examples from Verdi's "1848 opera" demonstrate a kind of pragmatism that is usually demonized in the aesthetic realm, and one that is viewed as particularly antithetical to Romanticism. The brand of "political opera" embodied by *La battaglia di Legnano* may initially seem less compelling than that transmitted in familiar anecdotes, based not in flouting the censors or sparking popular outbursts but in tailoring an occasional work for a particular audience and in manipulating the cultural archetypes understood by that audience. But another way of hearing *La battaglia di Legnano* is as a grasp at a different kind of popular idiom: not the broad sweep of the unison choruses that appealed to *fin-de-siècle* reconstructions of Risorgimento sensibility, but an aesthetic truer to Italian taste at mid-century. In this sense, the style of *Battaglia* verges on Gramsci's Utopian category of the "national-popular"; certainly it has much in common with the French serial novels he cites as examples of the popular idiom he desired for Italy.

To hear *La battaglia di Legnano* this way is to locate the opera at a crucial stylistic intersection, between the rhythmic energy of Verdi's "Risorgimento" operas and the renewed wave of Romanticism that permeated his domestic dramas of the 1850s. For it is above all in middle-period works such as *Rigoletto* and *La traviata* that Verdi, perhaps freed by the focus on individual passions in his (mostly) French literary sources, truly began to manipulate forms and break with conventions of vocal writing in a way that music historians have conventionally recognized as typical of Romanticism. It is tempting to suggest that Gramsci, deafened by the demagogic "hammering of metrical accents" he heard in Verdi and by the music's jingoistic fascist-era reception, failed to recognize that Verdi's operas proposed not one, but many Romanticisms, all of them at once popular, cosmopolitan, *and* Italian.

The style of Verdi's operas and non-operatic works

4 The forms of set pieces

SCOTT L. BALTHAZAR

Like his predecessors, Verdi relied on an elaborate system of conventions – termed the "customary forms" ("solite forme") of set pieces (or "lyric numbers") by Abramo Basevi in 1859 – for organizing introductions, arias, duets, and finales.[1] Gradually narrowing the diversity of approaches found at the end of the previous century, composers such as Gioachino Rossini, Vincenzo Bellini, and Gaetano Donizetti had "standardized" designs sufficiently that even a provincial critic such as Carlo Ritorni, writing in 1841 about Bellini, could formulate accurate templates for the most extended version of each form.[2] However, while adhering to shared outlines composers also revised internal details for new dramatic effects, a process that Verdi embraced in his own operas.[3] Whereas Rossini's lyric numbers had summarized relationships presented in the *scena* or reacted to its events, Verdi's take an increasingly expository role in the foreground action, weakening the traditional polarized relationship between an active *scena* and static lyric number. Dramatic continuity is paralleled by continuity of musical style: the more frequent appearance of lyrical melody in the *scena* and declamatory singing in lyric numbers allows more flexible expression and stronger characterization in both sections. Innovative treatment of individual movements within the lyric numbers also enhances dramatic momentum, undercutting traditional dichotomies between active and reflective passages and weakening musical disjunctions. Verdi made the presence of these forms less obvious and adapted them to more diverse dramatic circumstances by varying the internal designs of movements, omitting movements, interpolating additional sections (particularly in extended ensemble scenes), and changing the complement of characters within scenes.

Arias

The grand aria described by Ritorni and Basevi includes three movements: the slow movement (often termed "cantabile" or "adagio"), the *tempo di mezzo*, and the *cabaletta* (see figures 4.1a and b). It developed from the two-movement slow–fast *rondò* of the late eighteenth century, the *tempo di mezzo* of the three-movement aria apparently an outgrowth of the declamatory section that had sometimes begun the fast movement of the *rondò*.[4]

[49]

Figure 4.1a Nineteenth-century Italian aria form, Rossini

Section:	Scena	Aria		
		Movement 1 *Primo tempo/cantabile*	Movement 2 *Tempo di mezzo*	Movement 3 *Cabaletta*
Style and internal form:	Recitative; may be preceded by a chorus or orchestral introduction	Open melody — Closed melody	Dialogue; may include chorus and/or secondary characters	Theme — Transition — Theme' — Coda
Key:	Modulation V/I	I — I or V/I (modulation) $V/?$	(I) modulation V/I	I
Action:	Interaction	Reflection/reaction	Interaction/reappraisal	Reflection/reaction
Poetry:	Recitative verse	Lyric verse		

Figure 4.1b Nineteenth-century Italian aria form, mid-nineteenth century

Section:	Scena	Aria		
		Movement 1 *Primo tempo/cantabile*	Movement 2 *Tempo di mezzo*	Movement 3 *Cabaletta*
Style and internal form:	Recitative; may be preceded by a chorus or orchestral introduction	Melody following the lyric prototype	Dialogue; may include chorus and/or secondary characters	Theme — Transition — Theme' — Coda
Key:	Modulation $V/?$	I	Modulation $V/?$	New key
Action:	Interaction	Reflection/reaction	Interaction	Reflection/reaction
Poetry:	Recitative verse	Lyric verse		

Rossini had often omitted the *tempo di mezzo*, relying on the two-movement form (slow movement–*cabaletta*) most associated with him. While Bellini, Donizetti, and even Verdi sometimes reverted to this arrangement (see Eleonora's *cavatina*, *Oberto*, I, 3: slow movement, "Sotto il paterno tetto," and *cabaletta*, "Oh potessi nel mio core"), the three-movement design is heard much more often, most famously in Violetta's Act I aria in *La traviata* (slow movement, "Ah, forse è lui che l'anima," *tempo di mezzo*, "Folie! delirio vano è questo," and *cabaletta*, "Sempre libera degg'io"). Whether two or three movements appear, the designation "cavatina" is normally given to an extended aria for a lead singer at his or her first appearance on stage; otherwise "aria" is used.

The number of three-movement arias declined in Verdi's middle operas as single-movement solos increased.[5] Typically they are stage songs, prayers, or narratives, realistic performative events incorporated within large ensemble scenes. Moreover, Verdi's increasingly pliable treatment of the aria's form, influenced by the flexibility of French melody, resulted sometimes in pieces that adhere only loosely to the conventional design, if at all.[6] Leonora's *romanza* "Me pellegrina ed orfana" (*La forza del destino*, I, 2) glides seamlessly through short, expressively diverse passages without resorting to formulas. Melitone's "Che? Siete all'Osteria?" (*La forza del destino*, IV, 14) unfolds as continuous comic dialogue with beggars and Guardiano, disguising its identity as an aria and anticipating the fluid style of Verdi's late masterworks.

Even within traditional grand arias, Verdi's overriding concern with realism and expressiveness shaped his adaptations of individual movements. Rossini's slow first movements had typically begun with a passage of flexibly paced, short-phrased "open melody" followed by more periodic "closed melody" in longer phrases, both passages heavily ornamented. Normally they would modulate from tonic to dominant, creating a tonal upbeat resolved by return to the tonic at the beginning of either the *tempo di mezzo* or the *cabaletta*. Like Bellini and Donizetti, Verdi eliminated this anacrustic quality by avoiding long-range modulation, cadencing in the original key, and relying on the stable lyric prototype for its internal form.[7] By confining *fioriture* (ornamentation) to the ends of phrases and including declamatory passages he made the slow movement even more expressive while tying it back to the preceding *scena*, as in Luisa's *preghiera* "Tu puniscimi, o Signore" (*Luisa Miller*, II, 8).[8] Verdi's two-part melodies, normally progressing from minor to major, reinforce musical momentum and changes of mood in the text. In her "D'amor sull'ali rosee" (*Il trovatore*, IV, 12) Leonora shifts optimistically at "Com'aura di speranza" from F minor to A flat major and from more constricted to more mobile melody. Strophic forms derived perhaps from the *couplets* of French comic opera allude realistically to popular song in performative circumstances. Examples include Oscar's *ballata* "Volta la terrea," a one-movement *sortita* within the *introduzione* of *Un ballo in maschera*, and Leonora's *racconto* "Tacea la notte placida," which opens her three-movement *cavatina* (*Il trovatore*, I, 2). In their texts, Verdi's slow movements (and to a lesser extent his *cabalette*) not only react to prior events but also take a more active role, often contributing revelations, establishing new relationships, and in some cases prefiguring future activities.

The second movement – the *tempo di mezzo* – is normally a dialogue that revives action suspended in the slow movement, often by bringing soloists or chorus on stage with news. Thus it connects the aria proper to the preceding *scena*, motivates the ensuing *cabaletta*, and expands the range of mood and visual effect within the aria. Verdi's *tempi di mezzo* range considerably in length and complexity depending on dramatic circumstances, from modest recitative-like sections (Germont's vain attempt to dissuade Alfredo from following Violetta to Paris, "Nè rispondi d'un padre all'affetto," *La traviata*, II, 6) to elaborate sequences in all styles of text setting. The *tempo di mezzo* of Carlo's grand aria (*Ernani*, II, 8) involves three soloists and chorus, touching keys as distant as F sharp minor and F major/minor across seventy-one measures of score, and incorporates a set piece for Carlo's knights and lyrical moments for Elvira and Silva alternating with declamatory exchanges.

The familiar form of the third movement, the *cabaletta*, involves a showy theme, a transition dominated by orchestra and chorus and incorporating a groundswell or "Rossinian crescendo," recapitulation of the entire theme, and a coda borrowing music from the transition. It became so standardized by the 1830s that composers indicated the reprise with signs instead of writing it out. Although the *cabaletta* provides a stable ending through its thematic and tonal stasis and predictable pattern, as well as an effective display piece for singers, it creates a disruptive articulation antithetical to sustained action, and Verdi took steps to minimize its effect. In various cases he eliminated the reprise (as early as Nabucco's "Cadran, cadranno i perfidi," III, 12); introduced both presentations of an abbreviated, moderately paced theme with dialogue (Rodrigue's "Carlos, écoute," *Don Carlos*, IV, 19); camouflaged the principal melody by beginning it in the orchestra as an accompaniment to dialogue (Aroldo's "Ebben, parlatemi," *Aroldo*, I, 1); merely alluded to the *cabaletta* through melodiousness, patterned accompaniment, and reprise when ending a slow aria (Philippe's "Elle ne m'aime pas," *Don Carlos*, IV, 15); or eliminated the *cabaletta* entirely (Leonora's "Pace mio Dio," *La forza del destino*, IV, 17, which ends with an Allegro, "Ma chi giunge," suggesting a *tempo di mezzo*). Such *cabalette* that take slow or moderate tempos, allude to the conventional form without adhering to it completely, or avoid it entirely provide a more individualized, responsive ending and undercut the monolithic nature of the three-part form.

Duets

The grand duet as conceived by Ritorni and Basevi included four movements: the *tempo d'attacco* (literally the movement that "attaches" the duet
to the preceding *scena*), the slow movement (often termed "cantabile" or
"adagio"), the *tempo di mezzo* (middle movement), and the *cabaletta* (see
figures 4.2a and b). In Rossini's duets this design divided into two phases
(*tempo d'attacco* – slow movement and *tempo di mezzo–cabaletta*), each
comprising an interactive, musically unstable section followed by a more
introspective, musically stable one. This polarization began to disintegrate
across the careers of Bellini and Donizetti, however, encouraging variability
of form and continuity of music and action. Verdi embraced these developments, omitting movements as dramatic events dictated and sustaining
interaction and dramatic progression across the duet.[9]

Rossini's *tempi d'attacco* had normally consisted of two long, closely
matched solos, followed by a passage of dialogue (see figure 4.2a). A modulation leading to a half cadence left tension to be resolved in the following,
more stable slow movement. Although Verdi relied on this traditional design
in some cases, after 1850 he emulated Donizetti's contrasting solos, sometimes unevenly balanced and imbedded in dialogue, avoiding the formality
of Rossini's treatment and reducing the break with the *scena* (see figure 4.2b).
For example, in Carlo and Alvaro's confrontation duet (*La forza del destino*,
IV, 16), Alvaro's lyric *risposta* ("Vissi nel mondo intendo") ends after two
phrases and the characters resume their dialogue that had begun the movement. Verdi further enhanced continuity with the preceding *scena* through
freely structured *tempi d'attacco* that set continuous, modulating dialogue in
a mixture of *parlante*, *arioso*, and recitative-like styles (Amelia and Riccardo's
"Teco io sto. Gran Dio," *Un ballo in maschera*, II, 4, for example). In contrast
to Rossini's *tempi d'attacco*, which had normally restated conflicts already
broached in the *scena*, Verdi's tend to introduce new events and information, continuing dramatic exposition, as in Germont and Violetta's "Pura
siccome un angelo" (*La traviata*, II, 5), in which he gradually manipulates
her into leaving Alfredo.

Like his *tempi d'attacco*, Verdi's slow movements show increased energy:
no longer always ruminative asides, they sustain foreground action, reinforcing prior entanglements or initiating new relationships. Whereas Rossini
had favored simultaneous singing in parallel thirds or sixths for his *cantabile*
movements (see figure 4.2a), Verdi (like Bellini and Donizetti) began most of
his with successive solos and confined singing *a due* to the end of the movement, finishing with a codetta (see figure 4.2b). This approach provides an
interactive transition from the dialogue ending the *tempo d'attacco* to the
vocalization that ends the *cantabile*. Furthermore, as in his *tempi d'attacco*

Figure 4.2a Nineteenth-century Italian duet form, early Rossini

Section:	Scena	Duet Movement 1 *Tempo d'attacco*	Movement 2 *Slow movement/adagio*	Movement 3 *Tempo di mezzo*	Movement 4 *Cabaletta*
Style and internal form:	Recitative dialogue	Dialogue Solo 1 Solo 1'	Simultaneous singing in 3rds or 6ths	Dialogue	Simultaneous singing in 3rds or 6ths Theme Transition Theme' Coda
Key:	Modulation V/I	I I or V modulation V/?	New key, typically natural or flat mediant or submediant of I	(I) V/I	I
Action:	Interaction	Interaction	Reflection/reaction	Interaction	Reflection/reaction
Poetry:	Recitative verse	Lyric verse			

Figure 4.2b Nineteenth-century Italian duet form, mid-nineteenth century

Section:	Scena	Duet Movement 1 *Tempo d'attacco*	Movement 2 *Slow movement/adagio*	Movement 3 *Tempo di mezzo*	Movement 4 *Cabaletta*
Style and internal form:	Recitative dialogue	Dialogue	Solo 1 Solo 2 Simultaneous singing in counterpoint and 3rds and 6ths	Dialogue	Theme Transition Theme' Coda Solo 1 Simultaneous singing in Solo 1' counterpoint and 3rds and 6ths
Key:	Modulation V/?	Modulation V/?	New key	Modulation V/?	New key
Action:	Interaction	Interaction	Interaction	Interaction	Reflection/reaction
Poetry:	Recitative verse	Lyric verse			

Verdi preferred contrasting solos, which maintain musical progression, facilitate individualized characterization, and reduce the formality of the design. In his middle and late duets, Verdi sometimes reinforced these tendencies by making the solos asymmetrical, setting one of them primarily as declamation, changing key from one to the next, or abbreviating the section of simultaneous singing. "Se voi scacciate" in Leonora's duet with Guardiano (*La forza del destino*, II, 6) incorporates all of these techniques. Her solo is much longer and more expressive than his, fluctuating between lyricism and declamation. Each uses a different key (A minor and F major), and the reprise includes only her closing phrase followed by an economical codetta.

Development of the *cabaletta* from the 1820s to the 1840s paralleled the slow movement by promoting interaction and asymmetry. The Rossinian form had typically comprised a lively melody sung in thirds or sixths, a transition dominated by the orchestra, a recapitulation of the main theme, and a coda (see figure 4.2a). In his late operas Rossini often replaced simultaneous singing with successive solo performances of the main theme at both its first presentation and its recapitulation. Bellini, Donizetti, and Verdi in many cases kept the opening solos but shortened the second half by reviving Rossini's previous simultaneous reprise (see figure 4.2b). Verdi's treatment of the *cabaletta* also seems conservative in another respect: unlike Donizetti, he rarely used contrasting solos, apparently valuing the stability inherent in static repetition of a single melody for closing the scene. As in the *tempo d'attacco* and slow movement, however, Verdi sometimes telescoped the opening solos by alternating phrases of a single melody between singers (see both the *tempo d'attacco* "L'alto retaggio non ho bramato" and *cabaletta* "O meco incolume" of Walter and Wurm's duet, *Luisa Miller*, II, 9), or he abridged or eliminated entirely the reprise and coda. In addition, Verdi's duet *cabalette* normally seem better motivated and less redundant than Rossini's, because his *tempi di mezzo* redefine relationships between characters rather than merely reviving a conflict established previously in the *tempo d'attacco*.

The first father–daughter duet in *Rigoletto* exemplifies Verdi's mature duets and his handling of form in general. It includes all four movements of the grand duet as Verdi treated them. The reunion begins with the duet proper, the interactive *parlante* dialogue of the *tempo d'attacco* "Figlia! Mio padre!" making a preliminary *scena* superfluous. Lacking a traditional coda, the slow movement "Deh, non parlare al misero" consists of imbalanced contrasting solos of different moods, Gilda's sounding especially brief because most of it doubles as the concluding section of simultaneous singing, Rigoletto providing counterpoint. The *tempo di mezzo* "Il nome vostro ditemi" is equal in weight to the other movements, its centerpiece a closed, lyrical *a due*, "Culto famiglia," which is followed by additional dialogue. Although Verdi started the *cabaletta* "Ah veglia o donna" with traditional matching solos, he chose a moderate tempo that avoids inappropriate levity, shifted key for the second solo to reduce stasis, and postponed the reprise. Hearing noises outside, Rigoletto scouts intruders and exhorts Gilda's guardian before resuming their melody, the interruption bringing the *cabaletta* into the unfolding action. Verdi maintained musical cohesion among all movements by eliding the slow movement with the *tempo di mezzo* and giving the latter a non-traditional role in thematic exposition by including the *a due* mentioned above. As in many of Verdi's set pieces, even traditionally introspective movements contribute to the plot: Rigoletto's slow movement *racconto* introduces family history, the *cabaletta* initiates the threat by Gilda's abductors. Tonal progression from C major through A flat to E flat across the duet emphasizes dramatic progress.

Central finales and mid-act trios and quartets

Ritorni and Basevi described finales that occur mid-opera in much the same terms as duets, although the second and fourth movements have other names (see figure 4.3). For example, after an opening chorus ("Lo vedeste? Fulminando"), the Act I finale of *Nabucco* includes a *tempo d'attacco* ("Viva Nabucco") beginning with *parlante* dialogue, an extended *largo concertato* ("Trema gl'insani"), a declamatory *tempo di mezzo* ("O vinti, il capo a terra"), and *stretta* ("Mio furor, non più costretto"). Like their predecessors, Verdi and his librettists gave the *tempo d'attacco* and *tempo di mezzo* expository roles while the *largo* and *stretta* react to and summarize preceding events, a progression through two phases of action and reflection that further resembles traditional duets.[10] Mid-act trios and quartets rely on the same formal template, although they occur less frequently, appearing occasionally from *Oberto* through *I due Foscari*, then not again until *Luisa Miller*. Verdi included them in his middle operas only when an ensemble finale is not present in that act (the quartet in Act II of *Luisa Miller*, which precedes Rodolfo's aria finale) or as prefatory episodes to finales (the trio in Act II of *Un ballo in maschera*). Independent trios and quartets were likely omitted to avoid upstaging the finale, to minimize overcrowding within acts as individual pieces lengthened, and to eliminate redundant confrontations.

Owing partly to its roots in comic opera, the finale had traditionally been a forum for on-stage action, a tendency that Verdi emphasized, particularly in the *tempo d'attacco*.[11] Even more frequently than in duets, Verdi and his librettists avoided the parallel solos that had dominated Rossini's

Section:	Scena	Finale			
		Movement 1 *Tempo d'attacco*	Movement 2 *Largo concertato*	Movement 3 *Tempo di mezzo*	Movement 4 *Stretta*
Style and internal form:	Recitative dialogue	Series of dialogues and lyric set pieces	Series of themes: single, paired, or grouped soloists / Simultaneous singing by full ensemble	Dialogue	Theme: series of solos or simultaneous singing / Transition / Theme' / Coda
Key:	Modulation V/?	I Modulation V/?	New key	Modulation V/?	New key
Action:	Interaction	Interaction	Interaction/reflection/reaction	Interaction	Reflection/reaction
Poetry:	Recitative verse	Lyric verse			

Figure 4.3 Nineteenth-century Italian central finale form, mid-nineteenth century

and Bellini's opening movements, instead relying primarily on dialogue. In addition, the events of this opening section are often expanded with small arias, ensembles, choruses, and mimetic movements such as marches and dances. In his early works, Verdi typically put these pieces ahead of the *tempo d'attacco* and gave them separate designations, such as Zaccaria's *preghiera* (II, 6) and the chorus of Levites (II, 7) in Act II of *Nabucco*. As early as *Ernani* (1844), however, the Act I finale incorporated Silva's solo "Infelice!...e tu credevi." And beginning with the Act II banquet scene in *Macbeth*, in which Lady Macbeth's *brindisi* occurs during the *tempo d'attacco*, he increasingly drew subsidiary set pieces into the finale proper. This approach resulted in imposing designs such as the fortune-telling scene in *Un ballo in maschera* (I, 2), which includes solos for the sorceress Ulrica (in effect a full aria including a slow movement, "Re dell'abisso affrettati," and *cabaletta*, "È lui, è lui, ne' palpiti") and for her first client (the sailor Silvano, "Su, fatemi largo"), a slow trio movement for Ulrica and the lovers Amelia and Riccardo ("Della città all'occaso"), and a strophic song for Riccardo ("Di' tu se fedele") interspersed with dialogue, all prior to the *largo concertato* "È scherzo od è follia."

As in his duets, Verdi sustained momentum even through the two reflective movements, made more dynamic than those of his predecessors by their progression through different melodies, individualized characterization, and interaction. Slow movements of finales incorporate the broad range of textures found in duets: simultaneous singing ("Io tremo, sol io, per te," *Ernani*, I, 5), similar solos ("S'appressan gl'istanti," *Nabucco*, II, 8), contrasting solos ("Di sprezzo degno," *La traviata*, II, 7), and melodies divided between characters ("Qual voluttà trascorrere," *I lombardi*, III, 13). However, Verdi tended more and more to open with dissimilar solos and divided melodies, which sustain musical momentum, distinguish allies from adversaries, and give the effect of dialogue. Because of the greater number of soloists, pairs or groups are often contrasted rather than single soloists, as in the Act II finale of *Il trovatore*, in which Manrico and di Luna pass off phrases of a broader melody following Leonora's breathless opening ("E deggio e posso crederlo"). Typically the leads are joined by secondary characters and chorus in an additional idea, and massed recapitulation of at least one melody and a coda normally end the piece.

The *stretta* tends to follow the same theme–transition–theme'–coda form as the duet *cabaletta* and relies on a similar repertory of textures to the *largo concertato*, typically beginning with solos, the entire ensemble joining in as the opening section proceeds. Yet, as in his duets, Verdi often undercut this formulaic ending, substituting an aria-like piece for Nabucco that vacillates between slow and fast tempos ("Oh mia figlia, e tu pur anco," II, 8), using Rodolfo's *più mosso* "Tutto tentai...non restami" (*Luisa Miller*, I, 7) to suggest the excitement of the missing *stretta* within the concluding dialogue, or writing a reprise of earlier choral melodies ("Gloria all'Egitto," *Aida*, Act II) to take its place.

The multiplication of events in the *tempo d'attacco* together with Verdi's increasing orientation toward linear, non-repetitive drama made the second phase of action and reflection (*tempo di mezzo–stretta*) potentially redundant. Consequently Verdi was more inclined than his predecessors to truncate the finale, the form *tempo d'attacco–largo concertato* seen as early as Act III of *I lombardi* (1843). In some cases he retained the *tempo di mezzo*, the arrangement *tempo d'attacco–largo concertato–tempo di mezzo* appearing for the first time in Act II of *La battaglia di Legnano* (1849). The informal texture and tonal instability of the *tempo di mezzo*, bereft of the summarizing, stabilizing *stretta*, creates unresolved tension and leaves the act dark and open-ended.

Beginnings

Verdi's *introduzioni* are lyric numbers that begin acts and spotlight the chorus, providing, in Ritorni's terms, "an introductory ceremony," sound and activity to grab the audience's attention.[12] The majority of Verdi's soloists in these openings are male, often tenors. The chorus voices solidarity with and characterizes the lead by describing his situation or reputation or by establishing his ethnic, political, and occupational identity through membership in their cohort. Arias or ensembles reveal his alliances and conflicts, state of mind, and plans. The demands of theatrical conventions, in particular the insistence of the *prima donna* on a dazzling entrance later in the act, may in part account for the rarity of female leads in these scenes. When women are featured – Odabella in *Attila*, Luisa in *Luisa Miller*, Hélène in *Les vêpres siciliennes*, and Violetta in *La traviata* – they tend to dominate dynamic situations, compensating for their premature appearances.

Verdi used the term "introduzione" most consistently in his first acts, to designate two types of pieces that have roots in Rossini.[13] Up to *Attila* (1846) the term refers almost exclusively to a substantial opening chorus, its participants remaining on stage for an ensuing three-movement aria (generally designated "cavatina"), after which everyone exits. This chorus-plus-aria opening erodes after *Attila*: the chorus is sung offstage in *I masnadieri* (1847, where it is also severely curtailed), *Il corsaro* (1848), *Aroldo* (1857), and the original *Don Carlos* (1867); it is confined to dialogue with the soloist in *Il trovatore* (1853); the aria is reduced to a single movement in *Aroldo* (1857) and *Don Carlos* (1867); and the aria *cabaletta* is replaced by an ensemble *stretta* in *Luisa Miller* (1849) and *Les vêpres siciliennes* (1855).

Verdi's expanding preoccupation with action-oriented scenes fostered a second type of *introduzione*, an extended ensemble involving chorus, which appeared first for Verdi in *I lombardi* (1843) and then in eight operas from *Macbeth* (1847) through *Aida* (1871). Although these longer *introduzioni* vary considerably in form, they all share features with the chorus-plus-aria type and with other ensembles, often beginning with a chorus and almost always including sections that mimic movements of central finales or duets (see figure 4.4). Their action starts in an extended dialogue that mixes declamation and *parlante*, resembling Verdi's *tempi d'attacco*. One or more single-movement solos typically break up the dialogue and fulfill the traditional aria function of the *introduzione*. The remaining movements vary in number, but normally correspond to the *largo concertato*, *tempo di mezzo*, and/or *stretta*.

The *introduzione* of *Un ballo in maschera* (1859) exemplifies this second type. After a chorus pitting Riccardo's supporters against his detractors, we learn about Riccardo's magnanimity, the threat he faces, and Ulrica's invitation in an extended dialogue with solos for Riccardo ("La rivedrà nell'estasi"), Renato ("Alla vita che t'arride"), and Oscar ("Volta la terrea"). Plans to visit the sorceress are finalized in the *stretta* "Ogni cura si doni al diletto." The flexibility of these extended *introduzioni* is evident in *La traviata*, where, preceding the ensemble *stretta* "Si ridesta in ciel l'aurora," the two set pieces are duets: Violetta and Alfredo's shared stage song "Libiamo ne' lieti calici" with chorus; and their tête-à-tête in the anteroom, which comprises a *tempo d'attacco*, "Oh qual pallor," slow movement, "Un dì felice," *tempo di mezzo*, "Ebben? che diavol fate," and *cabaletta* beginning approximately at "Oh ciel! domani!" elided with the previous movement. The revelers part in an ensemble *stretta* "Si ridesta in ciel l'aurora." For the party scene from *Rigoletto* (1851), Verdi diverged from the finale template by substituting a fast *concertato* (its beginning fused with the previous fast dialogue around "Ah sempre tu spingi") for the more traditional *largo*, the resulting continuity through the first half of the scene making Monterone's entrance in the *tempo di mezzo* ("Ch'io gli parli") more shocking and avoiding the problem of upstaging the courtesans' horrified reaction in the *stretta* ("Oh tu che la festa").

Introduzioni in the second through final acts are exclusively choruses, sometimes leading to arias in which the chorus participates. Instead of the designation "introduzione," some are called "coro," while others bear more descriptive titles: "festa da ballo" (dance party, *Ernani*, Act IV), "marcia" (march, *Giovanna d'Arco*, Act III), "giuramento" (oath, *La battaglia di Legnano*, Act III), or "preghiera" (prayer, *La battaglia di Legnano*, Act IV). From *Luisa Miller* (1849) on, Verdi more often used arias to open later acts.

Section:	(Scena)	Introduzione	Tempo d'attacco	Largo concertato, tempo di mezzo, and/or stretta
Style and internal form:	Recitative dialogue	Chorus	Series of dialogues and lyric set pieces	
Action:	Events/interaction	Events/interaction or reflection	Events/interaction	Interaction/events/reflection
Poetry:	Recitative verse	Lyric verse		

Figure 4.4 Nineteenth-century Italian ensemble *introduzione* form, Rossini and Verdi

Endings

The death of one or more principal characters in the final scenes of Verdi's
serious operas – usually the baritone or bass up to *Macbeth* (1847), later
the soprano – is essential for the experience of catharsis and completion.
These death scenes normally include three sections: the preparation, slow
movement, and conclusion (see figure 4.5).[14] The last two and at least part
of the first occur within the concluding piece in the opera, designated by
Verdi as the "finale" or "finale ultimo."

In the preparation section a mortal wound is inflicted, an announcement
made that the victim is already dying, or a conflict reestablished that leads
inevitably to death. Like the opening passages of a central finale, this preparation consists primarily of dialogue set in a mixture of declamation, *parlante*, and *arioso*, within which at least one set piece is normally embedded:
a one-movement aria (Fenena's *preghiera* "Oh dischiuso è il firmamento" in
Nabucco), a duet (Luisa and Rodolfo's slow movement, *tempo di mezzo*, and
cabaletta, beginning "Piangi, piangi il tuo dolore" in *Luisa Miller*), a chorus
(the funeral march "Un suon funereo" in *Giovanna d'Arco*), or a more complicated ensemble. Often lengthy, this phase of action may span pieces prior
to the finale proper, which are designated separately in the score but take
place in the same locale. For example, the entire third act of *Rigoletto* up to
the *scena e duetto finale* (III, 14), including the Duke's *scena e canzone* "La
donna è mobile" (III, 11), the *quartetto* best known for its *largo concertato*
"Bella figlia dell'amore" (III, 12), and the trio and *tempesta* in which Gilda
is stabbed, may be regarded as the preparation phase of one long final scene.

The slow movement of the *finale ultimo* proper is an extended trio or
larger ensemble resembling the *largo concertato* of a central finale (rarely
a solo with chorus, as in *Nabucco*, or a duet movement as in *Rigoletto*)
during which the protagonist dies slowly without losing vocal proficiency,
consoled by friends, relatives, and former enemies seeking reconciliation.
Less often, reconciliation is avoided, conflicts inflamed, and the death blow
struck afterward. In *Attila*, for example, Odabella waits to kill Attila until
she and Foresto have confronted him in the *concertato* movement "Scelerati
su voi sanguinosa." Normally this ensemble is longer than the preceding set
piece and its complement of characters greater, *Rigoletto*'s final scene being
a noteworthy exception.

The conclusion is most often a brief dialogue, sometimes involving no
more than a cadential progression, in which the protagonist dies and onlookers react. Rigoletto's outburst "Ah! la maledizione!" over a cadence in D flat
minor after Gilda expires is the best-known example. In some cases dialogue
is replaced by action mimed to the concluding music (*Giovanna d'Arco*, IV,
16). More elaborate treatments of this section incorporate a second death

Section:	Scena	Final scene (may include pieces prior to *finale ultimo*)		
		Preparation	Slow movement	Conclusion
Style and internal form:	Recitative dialogue	Series of dialogues and lyric set pieces	Series of themes: single, paired, or grouped soloists — Simultaneous singing by full ensemble	Dialogue
Action:	Events/interaction	Events/interaction	Reaction/reflection	Event (death)/reaction
Poetry:	Recitative verse	Lyric verse		

Figure 4.5 Nineteenth-century Italian final scene form, Verdi

(Corrado jumps into the sea following Medora's death in *Il corsaro*), a revelation (Azucena tells di Luna he has killed his own brother in *Il trovatore*), or transfer of political power (Gabriele is named Doge in *Simon Boccanegra*).

An elaborate version of this form concludes *Un ballo in maschera*. Its preparatory section begins with a *scena* and one-movement solo for Riccardo ("Ma se m'è forza perderti," designated "romanza e finale ultimo," III, 10), connected scenically to the finale proper (III, 11), which also begins in Riccardo's chambers before moving to the ballroom. *Parlante* dialogue, in which Riccardo is warned and the conspirators prepare to murder him, alternates with a chorus of revelers heard three times ("Fervano amori e danze") and Oscar's strophic *ballata* ("Saper vorreste"), leading to a duet movement for Riccardo and Amelia ("T'amo, sì, t'amo, e in lagrime") after which Renato stabs Riccardo and the chorus reacts. The slow movement ("Ella è pura") brings reconciliation with the conspirators once Riccardo attests to Amelia's innocence and pardons Renato. In the concluding section Riccardo dies in a brief cadential *arioso*, to which others grieve.

This design appeared early in Verdi's career, its basic elements already present in the *finale ultimo* of *Nabucco* (as written): a preparation including Fenena's set piece (the *preghiera* "Oh dischiuso è il firmamento") and a dialogue in which Nabucco frees the Jews and announces that Abigaille has poisoned herself; a slow ensemble hymn "Immenso Jeovha," celebrating Nabucco's reconciliation with the Jews; and a conclusion bringing Abigaille's reconciliation with her enemies, her death, and reaction by onlookers. The flexibility of this design – particularly that of the preparation section – allowed its adaptation for diverse situations throughout Verdi's career. Moreover, its resemblance to the sequence *tempo d'attacco–largo concertato–tempo di mezzo* – the form of the central finale minus the *stretta* – might have eventually suggested truncating the central finale, a signature feature of Verdi's middle period.

Choruses

As evidenced above, choruses figure prominently throughout Verdi's operas, occurring in a wide range of situations as self-contained numbers and as parts of larger set pieces, especially *introduzioni*, arias, and finales. They evoke many different textual, visual, and musical topoi: patriotic anthems (most famously "Va pensiero," *Nabucco*, III, 11) and military marches ("È l'Assiria una regina" earlier in the same opera); prayers (the dirge "Charles Quint, l'auguste Empereur," *Don Carlos*, II, 4), and sacred scenic effects (the chorus of damned and elect that opens the Act I finale of

Giovanna d'Arco); rustic dances (the *tarantella* "Nella guerra è la follia," *La forza del destino*, III, 11) and pastoral hunts (the antiphonal chorus "Sciogliete i levrieri," beginning the Act I finale of *Luisa Miller*); and choruses that are ethnic (the gypsies' "Vedi! le fosche notturne spoglie," *Il trovatore*, II, 4), festive (the *baccanale* "Largo al quadrupede," *La traviata*, III, 9), exotic (the chorus of Egyptian priests and priestesses that opens the Act I finale of *Aida*), or diabolical (the witches' choruses in *Macbeth*).[15]

Throughout his career Verdi used choruses not only for traditional spectacular decoration but also in significant dramatic roles. They provide specific social, geographical, and ethnic contexts – textual, visual, and musical – against which the leads function, and characterize directly through their commentary. Their history lessons and revelations, both in formal *racconti* and in dialogue with the leads, motivate other set pieces. Choruses contribute subtext when they carry covert political messages.[16] And in extraordinary cases they participate in the plot, as do the partisans in *Simon Boccanegra* or the priests in *Aida*.

In their music, Verdi's choruses play equally diverse and essential roles. They enhance volume, textural density, and activity in *tempi di mezzo* and in the transitions and codas of *cabalette* and *strette*, providing a sonic foil for the soloists. They also frame scenes through timbral or melodic reprise, as in the muleteers' chorus "Holà! Holà!" that opens and closes the tavern scene in *La forza del destino*, II, 4. Verdi used the chorus offstage for sound effects (the wind in *Rigoletto*, III, 13) and, like Meyerbeer, as a continuing background against which foreground action unfolds (the Act II finale of *Il trovatore*, in which nuns pray offstage, "Ah! se l'error t'ingombra," while di Luna and company prepare to abduct Leonora).

Unlike other types of set pieces, choruses seem to have had no "customary form," and their variability in Verdi's operas makes them difficult to categorize. Internally, shifts among different complements of characters and among the full range of text-setting styles, textures, modes, tempos, and musical and poetic meters articulate sections. The music often proceeds toward more lyrical styles of text setting, fuller textures, faster tempos, and major mode (in pieces that begin in minor). And their arrangement of parts tends to draw upon and combine the following organizing principles:

(1) The lyric form prototype (*a a′ b a″/c*) and its adaptations. In some cases a single lyric form melody constitutes an entire chorus (for example, "Quale un sorriso," *Luisa Miller*, I, 5, in which an additional repeated closing phrase expands the lyric form prototype), while in many others it serves a section or movement within a longer piece.

(2) Repetition. Strophic forms in two stanzas appear as early as the nuns' prayer "A te nell'ora infausta" (*I lombardi*, I, 2) and in all three free-standing choruses in

Il corsaro (1848). Coming at a time when other elements of grand opera were entering Verdi's style, they perhaps show the influence of French *couplets*, although they contain no textual refrains. The matadors' chorus "È Piquillo un bel gagliardo" in the Act II finale of *La traviata* has a loose strophic form in three stanzas, which includes several melodies in each stanza, introduces a new melody for the middle stanza, and shifts performers as the piece proceeds. Several of Verdi's early choruses adapt a repetitive form similar to the *stretta* (theme–transition–theme'–coda) for their concluding sections. For example, the second section, "O duce, noi sempre mirasti sui campi," of the soldiers' chorus in *Giovanna d'Arco*, II, 7, repeats words and music following a brief solo transition by Talbot.

(3) Musical reprise, normally lacking concurrent textual reprise. A B A′ forms occur occasionally throughout Verdi's career, appearing as early as "Gerusalem… Gerusalem…la grande" (*I lombardi*, III, 10), in which the da capo follows a section of declamatory exclamations and does include textual reprise, and later in *Les vêpres siciliennes* alongside da capo arias. In the middle sections of some pieces (for example, the gypsy chorus "Noi siamo zingarelle" in the Act II finale of *La traviata*, in which fortunes are told in the middle section) dialogue involving soloists replaces lyrical melody. French-influenced rondo forms also appear in *Les vêpres siciliennes* and occasionally elsewhere (*La traviata*, III, 9, *baccanale*). Probably inspired by Meyerbeer, Verdi deployed elaborately nested, multiple melodic returns, an approach appearing on the grandest scale in the Act II finale of *Aida*.

(4) Serial form. Some choruses consist of a sequence of two or more different lyric melodies or passages of *parlante* or declamation (for example, A B or A B C…), some of which may return (for example, A B C A). As illustrated in figure 4.6, the *introduzione* of *Ernani* (I, 1) combines a series of four different melodies (A–D)

A   "Evviva! beviam!"

B   "Giuochiamo, chè l'oro"

C   "Allegri! beviam!"

D   "Beviam! beviam! nel vino cerchiam"

codetta

E   "Ernani pensoso"

B′   "Qual freccia scagliato"

C   "Allegri! beviam!"

D   "Beviam! beviam! nel vino cerchiam"

codetta′

Figure 4.6 Verdi, *Ernani*, I, 1, *introduzione*

and a passage of *parlante* (E) with reprise of melodies B–D. This example bears a relationship to strophic *couplets* because B and B' have different words, whereas C and D function as refrains, repeating both music and text.

(5) Through-composed form. Across Verdi's career choral set pieces increasingly take on the flexible character of choral dialogues heard in *tempi di mezzo*, promoting closer interaction with other characters. These dialogues involve members of one or more groups, or most often chorus and soloists, likely reflecting influence by French opera. An early example occurs in the choral funeral march prior to Joan's resurrection that begins the *finale ultimo* of *Giovanna d'Arco* (IV, 16). In Verdi's middle period, choruses having extensive dialogue sections become increasingly common; in the chorus that opens Act II of *Luisa Miller*, interactive passages surround the *racconto* concerning the imprisonment of Luisa's father; Melitone's exchange with the beggars in *La forza del destino* (IV, 14) is a continuous dialogue. This tendency toward integration and continuity is paralleled by the expanded presence of chorus within complex ensemble scenes and the less frequent appearance of free-standing choral *introduzioni*. Thus, beginning in the 1850s choruses are less evenly distributed across all scenes but contribute more effectively to the action whenever they participate.

Though deservedly venerated for its flexible and sensitive marriage of music and action, and despite the absence of designated musical numbers in its printed score, *Otello* (1887) nonetheless represents an outgrowth of formal developments observed in Verdi's earlier works rather than a unique miracle of his old age. Set pieces remain embedded in the dramatic flow, and although less prominently detached from surrounding dialogues than in earlier operas they typically receive musical articulation, follow traditionally rooted internal forms, and sound more uniform than their matrices in texture and scoring.[17] Moreover, their inconspicuous presentation draws on adaptations tested across Verdi's career: emotionally responsive fluctuation of text setting and musical motive, continuity of action, omission or truncation of movements, emphasis of dialogue within set pieces, substitution of transitions for cadences and codas, and distribution of movements within traditional forms among different groups of performers. Four-movement designs based on conventional ensembles underlie the storm scene and love duet in Act I, Otello and Jago's duet in Act II, and the trio (*tempo d'attacco* and *stretta* only) and finale (lacking the *stretta*) of Act III. As one example, the opening chorus has four sections that resemble the principal movements of ensemble *introduzioni*, the first and third more eventful, the second and fourth more static: "Una vela" (like a *tempo d'attacco*), an opening dialogue in which chorus and soloists watch Otello's ship founder; the prayer "Dio, fulgor della bufera" (like a *largo concertato*); "È infranto l'artimon" (like a *tempo di mezzo*), a second dialogue presenting Otello's rescue and entrance; and the celebratory hymn in the style of a *stretta* ("Vittoria! Sterminio!"). Although the piece closes with a tonally static orchestral postlude, its correspondence with traditional forms is obscured by the lack of caesuras between sections, the constant tempo up to the *stretta*, the brevity of the prayer, and the exclusion of soloists from the reflective sections. Verdi's use of popular forms as a naturalistic element in stage songs – strophic form with refrain for the ensemble *brindisi* in Act I ("Inaffia l'ugola") and elements of strophic form and song form (*a a' b a''*) for Desdemona's Willow Song in Act IV ("Piangea cantando") – also has numerous precedents, as noted previously. Here again, refinements tested in earlier works, such as interaction within potentially soloistic pieces, replacement of the lyric prototype with self-contained (and now interchangeable) phrases, and disintegration of melodies in response to stage action, mold these forms better to dramatic circumstances. Even numbers that are essentially through-composed and replace traditional forms with sequences of alternating and developing motives in the French style – Otello and Desdemona's duets in Acts III and IV, Jago's Credo in Act II – have roots in earlier pieces that emphasize free declamation. In short, *Otello* represents a summation of Verdi's transformation of form in operatic *melodramma*, through which conventional forms – and the traditionally discontinuous modes of action and reflection that they had helped to delineate – were reshaped and dissolved to create a more cohesive linear dramaturgy.

5 New currents in the libretto

FABRIZIO DELLA SETA

From the beginning, the libretto ("little book" because of its small printed format) played a fundamental role in operatic structure and style.[1] Until the mid-eighteenth century, a *dramma per musica* was considered a literary text, judged according to the canons of spoken theatre. It led an autonomous life, and its music constituted an aspect of staging, one that could change over time. By the nineteenth century, however, this relationship was inverted: the music became more important, and composers intervened in writing the libretto, assuming the role of "musical dramatists." This trend culminated in Germany with Wagner and in Italy with Verdi, who did not write his own librettos but influenced their genesis profoundly. Through this reversal, nineteenth-century librettos lost importance as a literary genre. They were compared unfavorably to their literary sources (especially when these were the greatest examples of dramatic literature by Shakespeare, Schiller, and others) and criticized for unrealistic plots and purportedly bombastic, antiquated language. In the last thirty years, however, literary critics as well as musicologists and those in theatre studies have recognized the non-literary values of the libretto and have reappraised its function in musical dramaturgy.[2]

In considering Verdi's librettos, it is useful to distinguish between dramatic, poetic, and literary design. The fact that Verdi intervened in the first category most and the third least implies that they should be considered as being of decreasing importance.

Dramatic structure

Almost all opera librettos, including Verdi's, draw on preexisting models: spoken dramas, other librettos, or – less often – novels. Usually the libretto is much shorter than its source, allowing for musical expansion. Its creation involved selection and alteration: the number of characters might be reduced, the number of acts changed, scenes omitted, added, or shuffled, and the most important verbal exchanges from the original text reworded. Acts and scenes were reconfigured as a series of musical numbers in an outline of the main scene divisions, stage actions, and dialogue called the "programma" or "selva." Verdi participated in drafting these "selve," sketching them in person or discussing them with the librettist. He apparently devoted more time and attention to this operation than to composing the music, realizing that dramatic effect hinges on the organization of action, as he suggested at the time of *Ernani*: "I have seen myself that many compositions would not have failed had the distribution of pieces been better, the effects better calculated, and the musical forms clearer."[3] Since the character of a drama depends on the way in which conflicts between the principals are presented, it is the dramatic structure of the libretto that determines its status as a new artwork distinct from its model.

Poetic structure

Italian librettos were written in verse, following rules and conventions that dated back to the Renaissance. The choice and organization of poetic forms contributed to both dramatic and musical organization.[4] Throughout the nineteenth century, seven meters were used: *quadrisillabo* (four syllables per line, extremely rare), *quinario* (five), *senario* (six), *settenario* (seven), *ottonario* (eight), *decasillabo* (ten), and *endecasillabo* (eleven), each possessing its own distinct characteristics. The meter is determined by the number of syllables and the position of accents in the line; to identify line length we count through to the syllable following the last accent.

Consider this famous example from *Rigoletto*:

La donna è mobile
Qual piuma al vento,
Muta d'accento
E di pensier.

All four lines are *quinari*. The first, however, has *six* syllables, termed *quinario sdrucciolo* since the final accent falls on the antepenultimate syllable. The second and third lines have five syllables, the accent falling on the penultimate, and are termed *quinario piano*, the standard type. The fourth has *four* syllables, the accent falling on the last syllable: *quinario tronco*. Note that in singing the words "donna è" and "piuma al," the adjacent vowels fuse into a single syllable in an effect of elision (*sinalefe*).

These principles hold for other meters. In all cases, save the two longest lines (*decasillabo* and *endecasillabo*), "double" forms (*doppio*) also exist, for example *quinario doppio* (not to be confused with *decasillabo*, which has a different pattern of accents). In general, accents in lines that have an even number of syllables (*senario, ottonario,* and *decasillabo*) recur in fixed positions, giving those meters regularity and predictability; longer lines with an odd number of syllables (*settenario* and *endecasillabo*) have greater flexibility.

Example 5.1a Verdi, *Il trovatore*, IV, 13, "Mira, di acerbe lagrime" (Leonora)

Example 5.1b Verdi, *La traviata*, II, 4, "De' miei bollenti spiriti" (Alfredo)

A fundamental distinction is made between recitatives and set pieces (arias, duets, and the like). For the former, *versi sciolti* are used, freely alternating *settenari* and *endecasillabi* and avoiding patterned rhymes and stanzaic organization. In set pieces, lines of the same type arranged in regular rhyme schemes – aabb…(*rime baciate*, "kissing rhymes"), abab…(*rime alternate*, "alternating rhymes") – or more complex patterns form stanzas of four to twelve lines or more. These *strofe liriche* (lyric stanzas) mark the different sections that constitute each musical number (*tempo d'attacco, cantabile, cabaletta*, etc.).

The choice of poetic meters not only contributes to the formal structure of the work but also shapes musical phrases and entire melodies. Since a musical phrase generally sets one or two lines of poetry, length of line affects breadth of melody. The choice of poetic meter also influences the underlying musical rhythm, as in the examples of *settenari sdruccioli* in examples 5.1a and b. Furthermore, certain meters have traditionally been associated with particular moods or situations. For example, the regular accents of *ottonario* and *decasillabo* convey a popular character suited to narrative, as in "Da Gusman, su fragil barca" (*Alzira*, II, 5, *ottonario*) and "Un ignoto, tre lune or saranno" (*I masnadieri*, III, 11, *decasillabo*). Since populism can be heroic, Verdi chose *decasillabi* and *ottonari* for the "patriotic" choruses in his early operas: "Si ridesti il Leon di Castiglia" (*Ernani*, III, 11, *decasillabo*); "Viva Italia! sacro un patto" (*La battaglia di Legnano*, I, 2, *ottonario*). *Endecasillabo*, the most noble meter in Italian poetry, is used – sparingly – for

sublime situations, particularly for religious choruses such as "Gerusalem...
Gerusalem...la grande" (*I lombardi alla prima crociata*, III, 10) and
"Miserere d'un'alma già vicina" (*Il trovatore*, IV, 12). *Sdrucciolo* lines, when
intoned repeatedly, are associated with the supernatural and the demonic; in
this capacity they occur frequently in *Macbeth*: "Tre volte miagola / La gatta
in fregola" (III, 10). These associations were not invariable, of course; all
meters cited above, in particular the very common *settenario* and *ottonario*,
might be employed in any context.

Literary structure

"It seems to me that, as far as effect goes, the best subject I have set to music
so far (and I do not mean to speak at all about literary or poetic merit) is
Rigoletto."[5] Verdi's words suggest that he considered the literary aspect of the
libretto second to theatrical effect, his main concern being clear and concise
expression. Since he collaborated with many poets of different personalities
and generations, however, his librettos are not homogeneous, but reflect
changes of literary taste across almost sixty years.

Verdi's librettists were educated in one of the oldest, most conservative poetic traditions in the world. For an Italian writer, it was practically
impossible to resist the influence of Petrarch, Ariosto, Tasso, the Roman
Virgil, or more recent Arcadians such as Metastasio. Not even the greatest poets of nineteenth-century Italy, Ugo Foscolo and Giacomo Leopardi,
could detach themselves from this heritage, so that a "classicizing" tendency
persisted well into the 1800s. Italian Romanticism was born late, around
1810, and interested primarily a small group of intellectuals. Decades earlier,
however, Romantic taste had infiltrated popular culture, primarily through
distribution of late eighteenth-century English and German novels and
poetry: Melchiorre Cesarotti's translations of James Macpherson's poems,
attributed to the mythic Ossian (1763), were particularly important. Later,
French theatre was influential, from the innumerable *mélodrames* imported
by itinerant theatre companies to the plays of the young Victor Hugo. The
language, images, and poetics of these models guided early nineteenth-
century Italian librettists from Gaetano Rossi to Felice Romani, and are
found in the works of Verdi's most frequent collaborators – Temistocle
Solera, Salvadore Cammarano, Andrea Maffei and Francesco Maria Piave –
and in other Romantic poetry. Even Verdi's last librettist, Arrigo Boito,
avowedly distanced himself from these models only to present them in
revamped form.[6] In short, the Italian nineteenth-century libretto documents a diffusion of a literary taste that permeated social custom and general parlance. Only a few decades ago, familiar phrases from librettos could
still be heard in the everyday language of the Italian middle class.

Produced over more than fifty years, Verdi's librettos gradually adopt a freer, more personal style, yet also manifest traits that withstood time and his collaboration with fourteen different librettists. These variables and constants are illustrated by four important operas, each from a different period, by a different librettist, and related to its source in a different way.

Luisa Miller (1849)

Between 1848 and 1849 Verdi engaged in a lively correspondence with Salvadore Cammarano, official poet at the Teatro San Carlo in Naples, whose theatrical experience he valued highly.[7] After many difficulties, they settled on a subject that Verdi had proposed to Cammarano as early as 1846: *Kabale und Liebe* (1784) by Friedrich Schiller, a vehement polemic against social conventions, class prejudice, and tyranny in eighteenth-century Germany. Verdi was familiar with an Italian translation and French adaptations, including one by Alexandre Dumas *père*.[8] Cammarano, who had read both Dumas's adaptation and Schiller's original, judged the play "rich in lively situations, and in warm affections," having a "catastrophe...exceptionally terrifying and pitiful." But he noted three obstacles: "first, I should be obliged to remove whatever might prove unacceptable to the censorship; secondly, I should have to raise the Drama, or at least certain of its characters, to a nobler plane; thirdly, I should have to reduce the number of those characters."[9]

Cammarano addressed these issues in his "Progetto d'un melodramma tragico," titled *Eloisa Miller*, a scenario sent to Verdi on May 3, 1849, from which we can infer his reasons for altering Schiller's drama.[10] For example, he shifted the setting from a small city in the German Rhineland to the Tyrolean mountains, from a bourgeois environment to a rustic one; Walter, father of Rodolfo, is not a prince's minister, but himself a count. These and other changes justified spectacular staging and allowed the chorus of villagers a greater role. Lady Milford, the Prince's lover and Walter's choice for his son, was omitted altogether, Verdi yielding to Cammarano's arguments that the censorship would not permit the Prince a lover, and that Lady Milford would have been a second *prima donna* competing with the heroine, a risk no singer would accept.

Cammarano's version has been criticized as suppressing Schiller's revolutionary message. Such criticism, however, unfairly expects opera merely to translate or reproduce its source, when it should rather be evaluated as an independent work that projects themes resonant with the ideology of librettist and composer. Verdi was most interested in highlighting the theme of oppression, the central motive of Alessandro Manzoni's great nineteenth-century novel *I promessi sposi* and a universal conflict easily set in different times and places. Furthermore, for Italians, particularly southern

Italians like Cammarano, the relationship between a feudal lord and his peasants provided a more tangible image of power than that between a minister and the urban bourgeoisie. The alpine setting also links *Luisa Miller* to the tradition of *opera semiseria*, to Bellini's *La sonnambula* and Donizetti's *Linda di Chamounix*, whose heroines share a slandered innocence that evokes oppression and misspent power. Finally, Verdi recognized in Schiller's tragedy a recurrent theme in his own dramaturgy: paternal authoritarianism. Although the two fathers in *Luisa Miller* view the happiness of their children differently, both conceive the paternal role as Miller frames it: "In terra un padre somiglia Iddio" ("On earth a father resembles God"). Cammarano embraced these themes while remaining faithful to the basic events of his source, which Verdi then made into the most effective moments of the opera.

The division of *Luisa Miller* into musical numbers was discussed thoroughly by Verdi and Cammarano. On May 15, 1849, Cammarano sent Verdi an outline that may be compared with the final structure of the opera:[11]

Cammarano's proposal	*Structure of the completed opera*	
	1	Sinfonia
ACT I		
Chorus	2	*Introduzione*
Eloisa's *cavatina*		
Trio closing the *introduzione*		
Miller's aria	3	Miller's *scena* and *aria*
	4	Walter's *scena* and *aria*
Chorus	5	Recitative and chorus
Duet – Rodolfo and Federica	6	Recitative and duet
Grand finale	7	Finale
ACT II		
Chorus	8	Chorus
Eloisa's aria		Luisa's *scena* and *aria*
	9	Recitative, *scena* and duet – Walter and Wurm
Concertato	10	*Scena* and quartet
Rodolfo's aria	11	Rodolfo's *scena* and aria
ACT III		
Chorus	12	*Scena* and chorus
Duet – Eloisa and Miller	13	*Scena* and duet
Eloisa's *romanza*		
Duet – Eloisa and Rodolfo	14	*Scena*, duet and *trio finale*

Verdi requested an added aria for Walter and a duet for him and Wurm to emphasize the second father figure, also wanting the *romanza* in Act III omitted and the duet expanded into a *trio finale* to unite the three victims before the violent conclusion. He also advocated a duet between Luisa and Wurm in place of Luisa's aria (II, 8), a more dramatic solution that would have displaced the heroine's mandatory aria. The aria was ultimately kept, but the action in its *scena* and *tempo di mezzo* was radically expanded. Lastly, Verdi feared that finishing Act II with Rodolfo's aria ("Quando le sere al placido") would not be sufficiently exciting, but Cammarano convinced him that its ending would be intensified by a despairing *cabaletta* and chorus ("L'ara o l'avello apprestami").

The poetic structures of most pieces reflect Cammarano's roots in the 1830s and 1840s. Out of thirteen numbers, six were conceived in the basic *cantabile-cabaletta* formula (nos. 2, 3, 4, 6, 11, 13). Verdi apparently did not even ask for more innovative forms, insisting only that the Act I finale should not end with the conventional *stretta* but with a fast-paced dialogue that he sketched himself. Cammarano's conservatism is also seen in his choices of meter:

Verse type	Number of lines	Percentage
versi sciolti	243	32
versi lirici	516	68
settenari	220	29
quinari doppi	118	15.55
ottonari	110	14.50
senari doppi	42	5.55
decasillabi	24	3.15
quinari	2	0.25
Total	759	100

The total number of lines and the relationship between *versi sciolti* and *versi lirici* is customary for librettos before 1850. Traditionally prevalent meters – *settenari* and *ottonari* – abound. *Quinario* is used only in doubled lines (*quinari doppi*), which compensate for its brevity and uneven number of syllables, encouraging rhythmic symmetry in the melody. More distinctive meters such as *decasillabo* make Walter seem more noble (I, 4), or serve narrative sections, as in the choral *racconto* that begins I, 8.

Although Cammarano was considered an exponent of Romantic taste, his Romanticism (aside from choice of subject, which he controlled only in part) was limited almost entirely to using early nineteenth-century forms. Verdi's Romantic taste, on the other hand, derived from his familiarity with French theatre (primarily Hugo) and with Shakespeare. In vain Verdi asked Cammarano to give Wurm "that certain comical something" to contrast with the tragic plot.[12] Cammarano, as noted, was more disposed to "raise the Drama, or at least certain of its characters, to a nobler plane," eliminating all vulgarity from Schiller's text. The (classicist) nobilizing impulse in fact extended to all characters. Consider the village girl Laura's invitation to Luisa (Act III), its convoluted phrase structure and the obscure adjective "affralite" (enfeebled) derived from "frale" ("frail"), a word only used in poetry: "O dolce amica, e ristorar non vuoi / Di qualche cibo le affralite membra?" ("Sweet friend, would you not like to refresh your enfeebled limbs with some food?"). The peasant chorus's description of Luisa's situation (III, 12) is even more extraordinary: "Sembra mietuto giglio / Da vomere crudel" ("She seems a lily cut down by a cruel ploughshare"). This simile paraphrases two famous lines of Virgil, "Purpureus veluti cum flos succisus aratro / Languescit moriens" ("As a purple flower, severed by the plow, falls slack in death"), *Aeneid,* IX, 435, an image that had already been adopted in the Italian tradition by Ariosto: "Come purpureo fior languendo muore, / Che 'l vomere al passar tagliato lassa" ("As languishing a purple flower lies, its tender stalk cut by the passing plough"), *Orlando furioso,* XVIII, 153.[13] Cammarano transformed Virgil's and Ariosto's "purple" flower (the poppy) into a white lily, a cogent symbol of Luisa's purity.

La traviata (1853)

Verdi's interest in Alexandre Dumas *fils*'s *La dame aux camélias* dates to September 18, 1852, when he wrote to Léon Escudier requesting a copy of the play. According to the librettist Francesco Maria Piave, the "plot set Verdi on fire and I... had five days to do the outline."[14] The libretto was written for the most part between October and November 1852, then revised in February 1853. Since correspondence concerning its genesis is virtually non-existent, and neither the *selva* nor a manuscript draft seems to survive, direct comparison of the two texts is the only means of reconstructing the conversion of play into libretto. The number of characters was reduced to accommodate the cast engaged by the Teatro La Fenice in Venice: nineteen *personaggi* shrank to twelve, most of these stripped of any individuality. There are only three real characters, the three leads: Violetta, Alfredo, and Germont. Piave and Verdi omitted Dumas's second act, which contained important psychological details but dispensable events. Four scenes remained, articulating the visual rhythm of the opera: the first (I, party and Violetta's aria) and third (II, ii, party) are grand and vibrant, hosting many characters and chorus, while the second (II, i, at Violetta's country house) and fourth (III, in Violetta's apartment) are private, concentrating almost exclusively on the three principals. This alternation defined the fluctuation of musical color from scene to scene, brilliant and riotous or intimate and chamber-like.

An important difference between play and opera is the disappearance of Violetta's friends from the "private" scenes (II, i, and III), an omission highlighting the progressive marginalization of the heroine from society. Contrasts between treatments of the father are equally significant. In Dumas, the father participates in only one conversation with the heroine, convincing her to leave Alfredo. Piave and Verdi, on the other hand, had him appear three more times: at the end of II, i, to exhort Alfredo, at the end of II, ii, to reproach him, and at the end of III to witness Violetta's final moments. Amplification of his role was necessary because the third principal could scarcely disappear halfway through the opera, having sung for less than twenty minutes; he had to have an aria and participate in the most important ensembles. Moreover, the change was consistent with Verdi's dramaturgy: Dumas's *comédie de moeurs*, centered on the problematic relationship between heroine and society, became a struggle of individuals, a clash between Violetta and Germont over different concepts of life and love. The embodiment of social order in a father-figure who must accept responsibility for the tragedy is entirely Verdian.

Parallel to the organization of dramatic events was the choice and distribution of musical numbers. Two arias for soprano, one each for tenor and baritone, and at least two duets were necessary. The decisive confrontation between Marguerite (Violetta) and Duval (Germont) and the lovers' last meeting were easily chosen for the duets; it was more difficult to place the arias, since there were no long monologues in Dumas's play. However, Violetta's initial grand aria ("È strano ... Ah, forse è lui," I, 3) had been envisioned in the earliest musical sketches, source material having been spotted by Verdi in brief sections of the play's first and second acts. The *romanza* ("Addio del passato," III, 8) mirrored her first aria in its placement at the beginning of the third act, but was preceded by an expansive *scena* into which Piave condensed scenes ii–vi of the play. Alfredo's aria ("De' miei bollenti spiriti," II, 4) was extracted from a brief dialogue between Armand and Prudence at the beginning of Dumas's Act III. Positioned at the start of Cammarano's Act II, it has the double function of recapitulating events since Act I and introducing the theme of money. The biggest problem was the aria for Germont ("Di Provenza il mar, il suol," II, 6), which necessarily delayed the end of the scene. However, while this aria has always been considered the weakest dramatic point of the opera, it has the important function of characterizing Alfredo's relationship with his father. And its placement is significant: after Violetta's passionate "Amami Alfredo," Alfredo falls out of his lover's arms into those of his father, illustrating the forces impelling the drama.

Two other long numbers account for almost half the entire opera: the *introduzione* (I, 2), which summarizes Act I of Dumas's play, and the central finale (II, 7), which corresponds to Act III in Dumas (except for the choruses of gypsies and matadors, which construct a social atmosphere and create contrasts of musical color with the surrounding darker sections). In these two numbers Verdi advanced a tendency already clear in earlier operas – above all *Rigoletto* – to encapsulate different pieces in one continuous scene. The Act I *introduzione* consists of private conversation between Violetta and Alfredo, framed by the worldly exchanges of other guests. The central finale is traditional, particularly in its introductory choruses and grand *concertato* ("Di sprezzo degno"); but the dramatic kernel is in the two middle passages (the gambling scene and the dialogue between Violetta and Alfredo), in which the lovers' difficult relationship again comes to the fore. In short, with the exception of Germont's aria, Piave and Verdi succeeded in achieving a hard-won balance between the demands of coherent action and respect for the laws of Italian musical theatre.

Discussion of the versification of *La traviata* is rare in the Verdi–Piave correspondence. In the structure of arias there are no particular novelties, aside from an unusual preponderance of strophic forms in slow tempos (three out of the four arias: "Ah, forse è lui," "Di Provenza," and "Addio del passato"), *couplets* that embody the French tone of the drama. Neither do the two duets present any real novelty, except for the expansion and differentiation of sections in the *tempo d'attacco* of the Violetta–Germont duet. But Piave's choice of meters is interesting:

Verse type	Number of lines	Percentage
versi sciolti	286	36.50
versi lirici	499	63.50
settenari	178	22.65
ottonari	100	12.75
quinari doppi	79	10.05
decasillabi	56	7.15
settenari doppi	28	3.55
quinari	26	3.30
senari	12	1.525
senari doppi	12	1.525
ottonari doppi	8	1
Total	785	100

Notice the increase of *versi sciolti* compared to *Luisa Miller*, which reflects both unusually long sections of recitative and increased reliance on *parlante*, in which relatively free vocal declamation is supported by independent orchestral discourse. *Parlante* is used in *La traviata* for conversational scenes that characterize the social setting. A particularly good example is the dialogue in *versi sciolti* between Violetta and Alfredo ("Oh qual pallor," I, 1) that unfolds against a waltz. Piave used other types of verse for the same function: *decasillabi* for the opera's opening conversation ("Dell'invito trascorsa è già l'ora"), and *ottonari* for agitated dialogue between Violetta and Alfredo in the Act II finale ("Mi chiamaste?...Che bramate?"). These meters lose their traditional connotations, becoming vehicles of a new, flexible musical discourse in which lines are broken down or combined into units varying from a half measure to four measures. *Settenario doppio*, an uncommon meter that would later be important in Boito's librettos, is employed to the same end. In the gambling scene this verse is fragmented into smaller units determined by the sense of the text more than the poetic meter, as illustrated in the following example:

FLORA	Solo?		
ALFREDO	No, no, con tale, che vi fu meco ancor:		
	Poi mi sfuggia...		
VIOLETTA		(Mio Dio!)	
GASTONE			(Pietà di lei.)
BARONE			Signor!...

FLORA	Alone?		
ALFREDO	No, no, with the one who was with me,		
	then left me...		
VIOLETTA		(My God!)	
GASTONE			(Pity on her.)
THE BARON			Sir!...

Although *La traviata* is a *melodramma*, its setting and character types resemble comedy. Verdi had already achieved a rapprochement between "high" and "low" styles in *Rigoletto*, following the examples of Hugo and Shakespeare, a rapprochement that primarily involved musical genres, while the verbal language remained elevated because of the court setting in the distant past.[15] But Piave could not ignore the problem in *La traviata*, where language is essential in characterizing the bourgeois setting. Coming from a generation that struggled to comprehend the first stirrings of Naturalism, he was not inherently suited to achieve this synthesis and produced a hybrid (and in some respects clumsy) libretto in which expressions used frequently in Romantic librettos lie uneasily in their new contexts. For example, in the lines "L'amistà qui s'intreccia al diletto" and "Solo amistade io v'offro" ("Here friendship mingles with pleasure" and "I offer you only friendship"), "amistà" and "amistade" are literary forms of "amicizia" (friendship), "diletto" a more formal term for "piacere" (pleasure). On the other hand, *La traviata* is the only Verdi opera before *Falstaff* in which money is discussed without reticence: Alfredo: "e v'abbisognan!" Annina: "Mille luigi" (Alfredo: "and how much is needed?" Annina: "A thousand *louis*"); and elsewhere, Violetta: "Quale somma / V'ha in quello stipo?" Annina: "Venti luigi"

(Violetta: "How much is there in that cabinet?" Annina: "Twenty *louis*").
The *louis* (in Italian, "luigi") was one currency of the time; "venti luigi" was
more concrete than the "venti scudi" with which Rigoletto pays Sparafucile.
Annina goes to Paris to "alienar cavalli e cocchi" ("sell the horses and car-
riages"), using the legal term "alienare" ("to alienate," transfer property),
and Violetta waits for "un uomo d'affari" ("a businessman"). *La traviata* is
also the first opera in which the heroine dies of so prosaic an illness as tuberculosis, named specifically in the text: "La tisi non le accorda che poch'ore"
("The tuberculosis will not allow her more than a few hours"). These examples betray a tendency that would lead in forty-five years to the realism of
La bohème.

Aida (1871)

Aida is unprecedented among Verdi's works in being his first subject not
derived from a play, preexisting libretto, or other literary source. It was
conceived in 1869 by the French archaeologist Auguste Mariette, supposedly
after an ancient Egyptian story, and was suggested to Verdi by Camille Du
Locle. Three poets and Verdi himself created the libretto; since Mariette
did not work in the theatre, and Du Locle was French, it was necessary to
recruit a professional, Antonio Ghislanzoni, to versify the text in Italian. The
genesis of the libretto can be reconstructed in detail thanks to the following
surviving documents:[16]

(1) Mariette's scenario in French, published by the author in a twenty-three-page
    pamphlet containing the complete plot of *Aida* (divided into acts and scenes that
    correspond to those of the opera), rich descriptions of scenery, and most of the
    content of the dialogue.
(2) An outline in French prose drafted by Du Locle in 1870, under Verdi's supervision.
    Significant changes were made to the dramatic content of the scenes in Mariette's
    scenario, and the dialogues were reworked in direct speech.
(3) Verdi's revision of this outline in Italian prose with indications for music.
(4) The manuscript libretto by Antonio Ghislanzoni, a versification of Verdi's out-
    line. Verdi made many alterations in the manuscript itself and on pages of notes.
    This phase is also documented in detailed correspondence between the com-
    poser and poet dating from the summer and fall of 1870, and the summer of
    1871.
(5) The librettos printed for the world premiere in Cairo (December 24, 1871) and
    the European premiere in Milan (February 8, 1872).

The dramatic structure of the opera was defined in phases 1–3 and its poetic
and literary form in phases 4 and 5, throughout which further adjustments
continued to be made.

The plot of *Aida* presents a classic love triangle, in which the passions of Aida, her lover Radamès, and rival Amneris clash with their feelings of duty, patriotism, and loyalty toward two peoples, the Egyptians and the Ethiopians. The tension between public and private is typical of Parisian grand opera, a genre in decline in France by 1870 but at the height of its international success. Mariette envisaged a grand opera in its most spectacular form, enhanced by an exotic setting. For Verdi, choosing *Aida* meant revisiting themes dominant in his operas: the unhappy fates of individuals overwhelmed by history and society, the destructiveness of jealousy (Amneris is related to Eboli and di Luna), and the oppressive weight of paternal authority (compare Amonasro to Walter and Germont).

In adjusting Mariette's scenario, Verdi and his collaborators emphasized the personal events of the plot, clarifying with the spectacular setting the historical-political backdrop:

Act I: Mariette's scenario opens with the march and chorus of King's ministers, followed by dialogue between Amneris, Radamès, and Aida. Du Locle and Verdi eliminated this spectacular (and conventional) introduction and began the opera with Ramfis and Radamès in mid-conversation, informing us of the imminent Ethiopian attack and emphasizing the High Priest's importance. Verdi and Ghislanzoni added Radamès's *romanza* "Celeste Aida," highlighting his love for Aida and her nostalgia for Ethiopia.

Act II: Mariette envisioned a single scene; consequently, the Amneris–Aida exchange takes place in public. However, the King's pardon occurs only after the crowd has dispersed. Thus the march and ballet were conceived according to the classic model of *divertissement* in grand opera, as insertions which can be omitted. Du Locle and Verdi divided the act into two scenes, the first of which takes place in Amneris's rooms, where the dialogue between Amneris and Aida develops into a full duet. In the second scene, Amonasro's plea is an integral part of a series of choruses, dances, and ensembles.

Act III: Mariette's setting is a garden of the royal palace at sunset. The first scene spotlights Aida alone, her monologue centered on her love for Radamès. Du Locle and Verdi shifted this scene to a remote locale in the dead of night, added the chorus of priests offstage and the short scene between Ramfis and Amneris, and focused Aida's monologue on her longing for Ethiopia, reinforcing that sentiment by inserting the *romanza* "O cieli azzurri." Aida's nostalgia is crucial to her subsequent duet with Amonasro, who exploits it for his own purposes.

Act IV: Dividing the stage into two parts for the second scene (inside and outside the tomb) was Verdi's wish. The arrangement is visually effective, but its real aim dramatic: it brings all three victims together by having Amneris enter to pray for her lover, ironically unaware that her rival is with him.

In its musical structure, *Aida* typifies Italian opera after 1860. The aria with *cabaletta* has disappeared; tenor and soprano alone have only one-movement *romanze*; the central finale retains its importance and indeed is made even more imposing. But the dramatic heart of the opera is its five duets, work on which Verdi painstakingly guided.[17] No other libretto shows such a decisive contribution by the composer in defining musical forms, specific wording, and poetic meter.

Verdi's preoccupation with concise and effective expression at the expense of "poetic" language is distilled in the term "parola scenica," defined by him as "the word that clarifies and presents the situation neatly and plainly."[18] Its meaning is further elucidated by his requests that Ghislanzoni rework lines precisely because they were not "theatrical" enough. For example, at the end of Act III Ghislanzoni's original lines for Radamès, who gives himself up to Ramfis, "Sacerdote, io qui resto: / In me sfoga il tuo furor" ("Priest, here I yield: release your fury on me") were initially changed to "Io qui resto, su me scenda / Il tuo vindice furor" ("Here I yield, may your avenging fury come down on me"). Verdi approved the latter version, but maintained that "it would not be more beautiful, but it would be more dramatic, to say simply 'Io qui resto o sacerdote'."[19] In the final version this line was made even more emblematic through abbreviation, and because Radamès addresses his adversary directly: "Sacerdote, io resto a te" ("Priest, I yield to you").

Finally, compare the following statistics regarding poetic meter in *Aida* with those from *Luisa Miller* and *La traviata*:

Verse type	Number of lines	Percentage
versi sciolti	235	30.55
versi lirici	505	69.45
settenari	264	34.30
ottonari	78	10.15
quinari doppi	62	8.05
endecasillabi	57	7.5
decasillabi	55	7.15
senari	16	2.05
quinari	2	0.2
Total	769	100

Notice that there are now more *settenari lirici* than the sum total of *versi sciolti*. Verdi's mature style blurs recitative and *cantabile*: increasingly the former admits passages of *arioso* and the latter approaches *parlante*, for which *settenario* provides a neutral base unconstrained by regular accents. The final scene, for example, shifts almost imperceptibly from recitative ("La fatal pietra sopra me si chiuse... E qui lontana da ogni umano sguardo / Tra le tue braccia desiai morire") to *cantabile*, in which *settenari* are mixed with *quinari* and *endecasillabi*:

> Morir! sì pura e bella!
> Morir per me d'amore...
> Degli anni tuoi nel fiore
> Fuggir la vita!
> T'aveva il cielo per l'amor creata,
> Ed io t'uccido per averti amata!
> No, non morrai!
> Troppo io t'amai!...
> Troppo sei bella!

This mixture of meters was expressly demanded by Verdi to obtain "uncommon forms," following the example of "the French [who], even in their poetry set to music, sometimes use longer or shorter lines."[20]

The use of *endecasillabo* for lyric verse is also interesting. Its traditional role in "sacred" passages is seen in the priests' intonation "Spirto del nume, sovra noi discendi," at the beginning of the trial scene. Ghislanzoni had chosen *senari*, but Verdi observed "that [the] six-syllable line seems short to me for this situation. Here I would have liked a full line, Dante's line, and also in tercets."[21] *Endecasillabo* also provides flexible support for melodic lines of unusual breadth, enabling such melodies as "O terra addio, addio valle di pianti." Much of the third act, from the *romanza* "O cieli azzurri... o dolci aure native" to the opening movement of the duet "Rivedrai le foreste imbalsamate," is written in *endecasillabi*, which blend into the surrounding recitative to create unity and continuity.

Falstaff (1893)

Verdi turned to Shakespeare four times in his career, considering him a model for creating drama through profound characterization. After *Macbeth*, he worked fruitlessly on *King Lear* throughout the 1850s; *Otello*, on a libretto by Arrigo Boito, began to take form in 1878. This last collaboration represented a new direction not only in Verdi's own work but also in the tradition of the Italian libretto. Himself a composer, Boito was an author of classical cultivation and a refined versifier. Steeped in recent currents of European literature, from Parnassianism to Baudelaire, he was suited to interpreting Shakespeare through *fin de-siècle* Decadentism rather than through Verdi's Romanticism.[22] In 1889 Boito proposed a new Shakespearean project based on *The Merry Wives of Windsor*. The libretto was written quickly, and Verdi requested only a few alterations while composing the music.

Boito described the difficulties involved in adapting the play for *Falstaff* as follows: "I wanted to write colorfully and clearly and concisely to outline the musical plan of the scene so that an organic unit results that is a *piece of music* and at the same time is not; I wanted to make the merry comedy come to life from beginning to end, to make it live in a natural and communicative merriment."[23] He reduced the number of characters, demoted Mistress Page (Meg) to a secondary character, while Anne Page (Nannetta) became the daughter of Ford and Alice Ford (who encourages her love for Fenton and organizes the masked wedding). These characters nevertheless retained their personalities, as did Falstaff, Bardolph, Pistol, Dr. Caius, Mistress Quickly (apart from her inclination to obscene puns), and Fenton. Shakespeare's intricate plot was rearranged, some episodes cut, combined, and their order reversed:

The Merry Wives of Windsor	Falstaff
I, i; I, iii	I, i
II, i	I, ii
II, ii; III, v	II, i
III, iii; IV, ii	II, ii
III, v; IV, iv; V, i	III, i
V, v	III, ii

By comparison with the play, the libretto develops in a more linear manner, with each of the six scenes organized around a pivotal event: (1) Falstaff begins to woo the two ladies; (2) a double conspiracy is devised; (3) Quickly and Ford, each on her own account, lure Falstaff into their traps; (4) the two conspiracies converge in a single punishment for Falstaff; (5) a new trick, devised by both men and women, is prepared; (6) Falstaff's second punishment is unleashed. Verdi feared that interest would lag in Act III, but Boito, while admitting that a slackening toward the end was almost inevitable in comedy, resolved the problem by revealing Nannetta's trick marriage in the final scene, fusing it with the main action.

Faithful adaptation of *The Merry Wives of Windsor* would not itself have sufficed to make *Falstaff* a masterpiece. Many feel that it is one of Shakespeare's weakest plays, devised to exploit the popular character Falstaff, while the source of his theatrical greatness lies elsewhere, in the two parts of *Henry IV*. Boito's decision to extract from the "chronicle play" the passages that best delineate the hero was crucial:

King Henry IV		Falstaff	
Part 2, III, iii:	"Thou hast saved me a thousand marks in links"	I, i:	"So che se andiam la notte"
Part 2, IV, iii:	"I have a whole school of tongues in this belly"	I, i:	"In quest'addome / C'è un migliaio di lingue"
Part 1, V, i:	"Can honour set to a leg?"	I, i:	"Può l'onore riempirvi la pancia?"
Part 1, II, iv:	"When I was about thy years, Hal"	II, ii:	"Quand'ero paggio / Del Duca di Norfolk!"
Part 2, IV, ii:	"A good sherry-sack hath a two-fold operation"	III, i:	"Il buon vino sperde le tetre fole"
Part 1, II, iv:	"Go thy ways, old Jack, die when thou wilt"	III, i:	"Va', vecchio John, va', va', per la tua via"
Part 1, I, iv:	"This sanguine coward, this bed presser"	III, ii:	"Pancia ritronfia"
Part 2, I, ii:	"Men of all sorts take a pride to gird at me"	III, ii:	"Ogni sorta di gente dozzinale / Mi beffa"

Here is the real "Old Jack," an arrogant, lying scoundrel who elicits sympathy by pitting down-to-earth humanity against the heroic world of the King and dynastic wars. Transplanted into the bourgeois world of *The Merry Wives*, the character who asserts his right to delight in a world that no longer wants him transforms the play of intrigue into a bitter moral fable on old age.

Against this theme Boito set the young love of Nannetta and Fenton, unessential to the plot but conceived as a contrasting "color": "I like that love of theirs, it serves to make the whole comedy more fresh and more solid ... I would like to sprinkle the whole comedy with that lightened love, like powdered sugar on a cake, without collecting it in one point."[24] Initially, Verdi was not sure about keeping the love interest and would have ended the opera without the wedding had Boito not held his ground. The poet had his own doubts about Fenton's sonnet (III, ii), which seemed "pasted in there to give the tenor a solo"; but Verdi was so convinced about this solo that he began setting it before finishing Act II, "not because the piece is very important to me ... but because this passage adds a new color to the musical composition, and rounds off Fenton's character."[25] Boito had seen in the lovers "a color, which seems good to me,"[26] and Verdi took up the idea in the same spirit, demonstrating the shared motivation of poet and composer.

Comparison of metric structure with earlier operas has limited use here. The only passage conceived in a traditional form is Nannetta's Fairy Song (III, ii), a *romanza* in two *couplets* meant as a stage song. The other solo is not an aria, but Fenton's sonnet, a poetic form completely outside the operatic tradition which alludes to Shakespeare's sonnets.[27] Exclusive use of *endecasillabi* allowed Verdi to unwind a broad-breathed melody like many in *Aida* and *Otello*. The distinction between *versi sciolti* and *versi lirici*, between recitative and *cantabile*, is essentially erased. Sequences of *endecasillabi* and *settenari* alternating with *quinari* occur but are organized by rhyme in a manner reminiscent of traditional arias. An example is Ford's Jealousy Monologue (II, i):

> È sogno? o realtà?... Due rami enormi
> Crescon sulla mia testa.
> È un sogno? Mastro Ford! Mastro Ford! Dormi?
> Svegliati! Su! ti desta!

Falstaff's Honor Monologue (I, i) is constructed according to the same principle, based on *settenario doppio*, that "long line" found sporadically in *La traviata*. Boito used this meter virtuosically, as in Act I, scene i, in which one line of *settenario doppio* – "Collo di cigno! e il labbro?! / un fior. Un fior che ride" – may be read as three *quinari* – "Collo di cigno! / e il labbro?! un fior. / Un fior che ride." This technique is suited to Verdi's late style, in which melodies divide into phrases of variable lengths determined primarily by sense and syntax.

Different types of verse delineate groups of characters. While *settenari doppi* predominate in the scenes led by Falstaff, *senario* is the Mistresses' meter, *ottonario* the men's, and *quinario* the lovers'. This differentiation serves another virtuosic technique involving different meters superimposed in poetic counterpoint, as in the *concertato* toward the end of Act II, scene ii:

Men around the screen: *ottonari*

FORD	Se t'agguanto!	
DR. CAJUS		Se ti piglio!
FORD	Se t'acciuffo!	
DR. CAJUS		Se t'acceffo!

Women around the basket: *senari*

| QUICKLY | Facciamo le viste |
| | D'attendere ai panni. |

Lovers behind the screen: *quinari*

| NANNETTA | Mentre quei vecchi |
| | Corron la giostra. |

These metric gymnastics are accompanied by a linguistic artifice verging on mannerism. Boito's taste for formal, archaic literary vocabulary is akin to that of the most famous Italian poet of the late nineteenth and early twentieth centuries, Gabriele d'Annunzio, whose first collection of poetry had been published in 1879. There are words in Nannetta's Fairy

Song that even scholars have difficulty decoding: "etesio" (the name of a wind), "cesio" (used as an adjective, meaning "of a white-silver color"), "alluminate" (illuminated). Boito did not limit himself to deploying obsolete words, but also invented new ones. In the torrent of insults flung at Falstaff in Act II, scene ii, "falsardo" is a mutation of "falsario" (counterfeiter), by analogy with "codardo" (coward); other contortions are "sugliardo" ("sudicio," dirty, low-down), "scanfardo" ("scanfarda," prostitute), "scagnardo" ("malvagio," wicked), and "pappalardo" (glutton, from "pappare," to wolf down) and "lardo" (bacon fat), all being extremely rare. In Falstaff's torment by the fairies (III, ii), words such as "scarandole," "scorribandole," and "rintuzzola" are modeled by rhythmic analogy on other words present in the same context, such as "farandole" and "ruzzola."

Boito has often been reproached for this linguistic preciosity, seen as corrupting Verdi's simplicity and populism. The composer, however, apparently understood the dramatic function of invented language. The humor of the preceding examples relies on the play of onomatopoeia and rhythm more than the sense of the text. In the vocabulary of pieces such as Nannetta's Fairy Song, Boito recreated the atmosphere of *A Midsummer Night's Dream*, enhanced by Verdi's magical music. Similarly, in the love scenes he recreated Shakespeare's courtly wit, as in the clever conceits concerning love as tournament in the lovers' second duet (I, ii). Verdi's last opera is a supreme homage to the spirit of the English playwright, realized equally in music and language.

Translated by Laura Basini

6 Words and music

EMANUELE SENICI

In Verdi's operas words are set to music in order to produce drama, to establish communication between the stage and the audience. Words and music are never entirely separate or completely independent domains, and therefore can never be fully understood in isolation. This aesthetic principle and its interpretive corollary have not always been obvious to Verdians, but now seem to be accepted by most. However, as soon as attention turns to the ways in which the aesthetic principle has been translated into practice, which involves applying the hermeneutic corollary to concrete examples, matters become more complex. There is no simple answer to the question of how drama is produced in Verdi's operas. Communication between the stage and the audience can be established at any given moment in many different ways. Moreover, both the concept and the practice of drama evolve through time. This means not only that Verdi's ideas on how communication might be established changed during his very long compositional career, but also that our ideas of drama might be significantly different from Verdi's and from those of his original audiences.

The paths to drama in Verdi's operas are not infinite, however, since interaction of words and music is always filtered through a set of conventions. Far from being a constricting presence – and notwithstanding what Verdi might have said about the matter in his letters – conventions make theatrical communication possible, and dialectic engagement with them seems to have been the composer's attitude through most of his career. Much of this chapter will therefore be devoted to operatic conventions that impinge on the relationship between words and music. I have decided to concentrate on three areas that best demonstrate Verdian conventions and their evolution: the interaction between text and music within the movements that constitute an operatic number; the so-called "parola scenica" and other moments of especially important communicative significance; and word painting.[1]

A preliminary warning is in order. The assumption governing most discussions of words and music in Verdi – my own included – is that the text came first, and that only when the composer had it before him did he set it to music. As recent investigations have shown, however, this is not always the case. In discussing an instance of music preceding the words, Roger Parker has gone so far as to suggest that the customary state of coexistence between words and music in nineteenth-century Italian opera is one of "uneasy disjunction."[2] We could do worse than keep in mind that, despite Verdi's and his librettists' efforts to make words and music work together toward drama, and despite our own efforts to interpret them as somehow fused, words and music stubbornly remain two very different systems of communication.

"To make music one needs stanzas"

One convention that Verdi never completely abandoned was a requirement for stanzas, constituted mainly by lines of equal length, as a necessity for composing melodies. As the composer wrote to the librettist Antonio Somma in 1853, "to make music, one needs stanzas for cantabile sections, stanzas for ensembles, stanzas for largos, for allegros, etc., and all these in alternation so that nothing seems cold and monotonous."[3] The number of stanzas for any given set piece depends largely on its type and the number of characters involved. The text for the *cabaletta* of an aria, for example, will be much shorter than for the *largo concertato* of an internal finale. The number of lines per stanza is in most cases four (in Italian, "quartina"; in English, "quatrain").[4] six is the next most likely possibility. Regardless of the number of lines in a stanza, the basic syntactic and semantic unit with which librettists operated seems to have been two lines of poetry, the couplet (in Italian, "distico").

A good example of the standard textual organization for a lyric movement is Luisa's *cabaletta* in Act II of *Luisa Miller*, given below as printed in the standard libretto that Ricordi circulated immediately after the premiere (1849):

A brani, a brani, o perfido,	O perfidious man, you have ripped
Il cor tu m'hai squarciato!...	my heart to shreds!...
Almen t'affretta a rendermi	Hasten at least to give me back
Il padre sventurato...	my hapless father...
Di morte il fero brivido	The cruel shudder of death
Tutta m'invade omai...	now invades me completely...
Mi chiuda almeno i rai	May my eyes at least be closed
La man del genitor![5]	by my father's hand!

This text is presented as a single eight-line unit not only by virtue of its layout, but also because the only *verso tronco* – a line in which the final accent falls on the last syllable, the usual marker of the end of a stanza – comes at the end. However, the rhyme scheme changes from lines 1–4 ($a^s bc^s b$) to lines 5–8 ($d^s eef^t$), suggesting an internal articulation.[6] The first four lines alternate between *versi sdruccioli* (lines having an accented antepenultimate syllable, and usually not expected to rhyme) and rhymed *versi piani*

Example 6.1 Verdi, *Luisa Miller*, II, 8, "A brani, a brani, o perfido" (Luisa)

(in which the accent falls on the penultimate syllable, by far the most common case). Lines 5–8 open with another *verso sdrucciolo*, continue with a pair of rhyming *versi piani*, and close with the obligatory *verso tronco*.

Syntax and meaning separate the text into four couplets, each an independent sentence having a different tense or mode of the verb. Moreover,

Example 6.1 (continued)

each couplet centers on a single image: the heart torn to pieces, Luisa's father, the shiver of death, and the father's hand closing Luisa's eyes. The second and fourth couplets have in common not only the image of the father ("padre" first, "genitor" later), but also the word "almeno" ("at least"). From a phonetic point of view, the first six lines are characterized by consonant groups containing the letter "r": "*brani*," "*perfido*," "*cor tu*," "*squarciato*," "*affretta*," "*rendermi*," "*padre*," "*morte*," "*brivido*." The last unit, on the other hand, although featuring "*rai*" and "*genitor*," lacks the peculiarly aggressive sound produced by "r" coupled with a non-sonorant consonant such as "b," "f," or "t."

Verdi's setting exemplifies the ways in which music articulates different levels of poetic structure, depicts significant images, and establishes connections among them (see example 6.1). Although the two-line units are maintained, the first quatrain displays a melodic consistency created through varied repetition of the opening phrase. This varied repetition acknowledges that Luisa addresses Wurm in both couplets, while also separating the different images of the heart torn to pieces and the hapless father. The modulation to the relative major (mm. 8–9) might indeed be inspired by Luisa's tenderness towards Miller, particularly since emphasis is placed on "padre," the only word repeated in this quatrain, rather than on his misfortune.

The death shiver in the text of the third unit is accompanied by a return to the tonic minor (mm. 10–14), while the downward scale on "brivido" ("shudder") (m. 11) can be heard as word painting. Word painting is more obvious in the scale up to high B♭ on "tutta" (m. 12), a musical shiver that invades Luisa's entire body and most of the body of her vocal range. The rhythm of the vocal line at m. 10 also connects this unit with the setting of "il cor tu m'hai squarciato" (mm. 4–5). The fourth unit returns to the father, and to the major mode, although this time the tonic major. The shift is emphasized by the silence of the orchestra in mm. 13–14, and by the appearance of a new rhythmic pattern in the accompaniment at m. 15, related, however, to that at mm. 8–9, the prior appearance of the father. As befits the markedly different affect of this last couplet, the melody is also new (although its shape could be related to mm. 2–3); and equally unheard thus far is the near-identical repetition of two measures (mm. 15–16 and 17–18).

At m. 18 the text has been exhausted, but the double repetition of the last two lines that follows can hardly be called a coda. Measure 18 lacks a structural cadence, since the voice ends on scale degree 3, not 1, and on the third beat, not the first. Moreover, mm. 19–20 and 23–24 bring back the accompanimental figure of the beginning of the aria, as well as a shadow of minor color. The awaited cadence occurs finally in mm. 24–28. There the sense of closure is heightened by the scale in m. 24, which reawakens and resolves the musical tensions created by the one at m. 12, through its different metrical placement of the high B♭ and resolution through contrary stepwise motion.

Verdi's setting does not simply articulate the text, then, but actively interprets it, selecting among the structural, semantic, and rhetorical elements that the text presents, and highlighting some of these elements at the expense of others. However, this interpretation takes place within a set of conventions that permit, or at least promote, certain interpretive choices, while impeding others.

Scholars have long identified a conventional framework that Verdi inherited from his predecessors, within which he seems to operate for a substantial part of his career, and of which Luisa's *cabaletta* constitutes a good example. This "lyric form" or "lyric prototype" is most often summarized as *a a′ b a″*, or *a a′ b c*, where each letter indicates a four-bar musical unit that sets two lines of text, with the *b* section often divided into two members of two measures each.[7] There is significant evidence of theoretical awareness of this framework in the writings of nineteenth-century Italian commentators.[8] James Hepokoski has recently suggested a nomenclature that addresses the function of the different sections of the lyric form: the initial zone, or initial phrase-pair (*a a′*); the medial zone (*b*); the final zone (*a″* or *c*); and the coda space.[9] In the case of Luisa's *cabaletta* the initial phrase-pair comprises mm. 2–5 (obviously including the pick-up in m. 1) and mm. 6–9; the medial zone mm. 10–14; and the final zone mm. 15–28, internally divided at m. 19 by the exhaustion of the text. The coda space is constituted by the cadential measures that appear only after the repetition of the *cabaletta* (and therefore are not included in example 6.1).

Such a framework leaves large room for manoeuvre. There are many instances, even in early- and middle-period operas, of texts that do not fit the quadripartite structure, and of melodies that manipulate the lyric pro-totype considerably. Strict sixteen-measure *aaba/c* forms are rarely found in arias, even in the early operas: Luisa's *cabaletta*, which follows the form but extends *c*, is the rule rather than the exception. As a consequence, its standard description does not provide us with adequate tools to deal with the sec-tion following the completion of the text presentation. And although duets and other ensembles offer examples of the sixteen-measure lyric prototype in the form of statements by a single character, most often in slow move-ments and especially *cabalette* (for example, the *cabaletta* of the Radamès-Aida duet in *Aida*, "Sì, fuggiam da queste mura"), the form frequently undergoes modification, usually through expansion of either *b* or *a″/c*, or both.

The slow movement of Luisa's aria presents an extreme example of such modifications. Its text is as follows:

Tu puniscimi, o Signore,	Punish me, O Lord,
Se t'offesi, e paga io sono,	if I offended you, and I will be content,
Ma de' barbari al furore	but do not abandon me
Non lasciarmi in abbandono.	to the fury of the cruel ones.
A scampar da fato estremo	To save an innocent father
Innocente genitor	from a mortal fate
Chieggon essi . . . – a dirlo io fremo! –	they ask for . . . – I shudder to say it! –
Della figlia il disonor!	his daughter's dishonor!

As in the previous example, there are elements of versification that both support and undermine the division into two stanzas. The rhyme pattern, ababcd^tcd^t, changes at the fifth line, but the *tronco* ending at line 6 and the offset placement of line 7 in the original libretto suggest a six-plus-two division. Note, moreover, that if the regular, non-truncated forms of the rhyme words at lines 6 and 8 were used, they would rhyme with lines 1 and 3: "Sign*ore*," "fur*ore*," "genit*ore*," "dison*ore*" (more on this feature later).

In its syntax this text is much more complex than that of the *cabaletta*. The first two lines contain a conditional sentence ("punish me... if I offended you") and an independent clause ("I will be content"), while the second couplet consists of a single independent clause that indicates an opposition to the concept expressed in the first one. The second quatrain is occupied by a single unit, constituted by a subordinate phrase in lines 5–6 and the controlling main clause in lines 7–8; but the latter is interrupted by another independent clause that functions as an aside ("I shudder to say it!"). A rhetorical reading of this text reveals a potentially problematic tension. The image that causes Luisa's lyric outburst, her dishonor – that is, the unwilling sacrifice of her virginity to Wurm (a central theme, perhaps *the* central theme of the opera) – is placed in the final line, a conventional feature of aria texts in nineteenth-century Italian opera. Syntactically, however, this image is weak, since Luisa refers to it in the third person as "his daughter's dishonor" (no doubt to emphasize the connection with the father), and as the object of somebody else's request ("they ask for"), without the emphasis produced by the first- and second-person verbs of the first quatrain. The prayer, stated in the imperative form, has already been heard more forcefully in lines 3–4 ("do not abandon me"), and in a much weightier syntactical and rhetorical context.

Verdi set this text as an Andante agitato in A major (see example 6.2). This movement contains the components of a traditional lyric form, but they are separated by interpolated sections and expanded so radically as to render the form barely recognizable. The conventional sections are phrase *a* (mm. 3–6); *a′*, an almost entirely new melody which acts harmonically, however, as a consequent to the preceding antecedent (m. 7 through the beginning of m. 9, which connects to the end of m. 15 and m. 16); *b* (mm. 17–20); *c* (mm. 21–24, substituting the music for the repetition of "della figlia il disonor" with that for "non lasciarmi in abbandon" at mm. 30–31). If the movement were constituted only by these sections, text repetition would be limited to "non lasciarmi" in mm. 9/15 and, from the last couplet, "chieggon essi" and "della figlia il disonor." We could consider such a setting a sensible, logical response to Cammarano's text.

Verdi found a much more creative solution, however, that addresses the syntactical and rhetorical tensions of the text head-on. The obsessive repetition of "non lasciarmi in abbandono" in mm. 9–16 – as far as I know the most extended internal text repetition in Verdi's arias – promotes this line to the rhetorical high point of the movement. At the same time, the melody fixates on the semitone C♯ – D, supported harmonically by a

Example 6.2 Verdi, *Luisa Miller*, II, 8, "Tu puniscimi, o Signore" (Luisa)

directionless alternation between V/vi and iv/vi (mm. 10–11) that threatens to move to vi (and therefore alludes to the vi harmony in m. 5) but eventually evades it. The rhetorical opposition contained in the first quatrain is compressed and heightened at mm. 13–15 by rearranging the text: "se t'offesi mi punisci, ma non lasciarmi." The deceptive cadence on the downbeat of

Example 6.2 (continued)

m. 24, again involving V/vi, recalls m. 10 and introduces a further repetition of line 4 similarly harmonized. The ascent to B and the subsequent coloratura passage resolve the tension created by the isolated high A at m. 21, partly filling the tenth left open previously. Only in m. 31 does the music reach a structural cadence, the coda beginning no sooner than this point.

Example 6.2 (continued)

Here Verdi exploits the possibility of truncating "abbandono" and "Signore" and ends the movement with two *tronco* lines, "abbandon" and "Signor," thus reinforcing closure and retroactively making the first four lines into a separate stanza, while undercutting Cammarano's *tronco* endings in lines 6 and 8. Normally the last two lines would be repeated, but Verdi must have regarded them as rhetorically and syntactically unfit to provide the climax of the piece, and therefore decided to alter the standard form.[10] As a consequence, Verdi's setting changes the perception of Luisa's state of mind. While in the text she expresses terror and desperation but remains in control of her discourse, the music portrays her as almost beside herself. The shadows of obsession and perhaps even hysteria loom large over Verdi's Luisa.

Unquestionably the principal model for text setting until the 1850s, the lyric prototype became one possibility among others as Verdi's career unfolded. The increasing presence of formal types imported from French opera is especially noticeable, in particular strophic and *couplet* structures and large ternary forms (ABA′). Different forms are not only juxtaposed, but also mixed and overlapped, as when one stanza of a strophic form is shaped according to the lyric prototype principle.[11] One of the most complex examples of formal mixture, and of Verdi's text setting in general, is Renato's entrance aria "Alla vita che t'arride" in the *introduzione* of *Un ballo in maschera*. The text of the first printed libretto, by Antonio Somma, and the one actually set by Verdi differ substantially, but the words in the score are Somma's except for line 2; they constitute the first draft of a text that went through at least five versions, mainly in an effort to cope with censors' requests:[12]

Alla vita che t'arride	To the life that smiles at you,
Di speranze e gaudio piena,	full of hopes and joy,
D'altre mille e mille vite	the fate of thousands and thousands
Il destino s'incatena!	of other lives is linked!
Te perduto, ov'è la patria	If you are lost, where is the fatherland
Col suo splendido avvenir?	with its splendid future?
E sarà dovunque, sempre	And will the way to wounds
Chiuso il varco alle ferite,	be always, everywhere, blocked,
Perché scudo del tuo petto	because the love of the people
È del popolo l'affetto?	is a shield for your bosom?
Dell'amor più desto è l'odio	Hatred is quicker than love
Le sue vittime a colpir!	to strike its victims!

Somma's text is divided into two six-line stanzas, signaled by the offset placement of lines 1 and 7 in the original libretto and by the same *tronco* rhyme in lines 6 and 12. The rhyme scheme, ababc^{s}d^t eaffg^{s}d^t, links the two stanzas by way of the return of the "-ite" and "-ir" rhyme in the second, but differentiates the succession of rhymes in the first four lines of each.[13] Prosody, syntax, and, above all, meaning separate the first four lines of each stanza from the last two, which function as a more concise, forceful restatement of the concept expressed in the preceding quatrain. The final couplet sounds almost like a proverb, as if Renato were reminding Riccardo of the wisdom contained in a popular saying.

The first twelve measures of Verdi's setting (see example 6.3) have been analyzed as a manipulation of the lyric prototype, in which the developmental function of the *b* section and the closure provided by *a″/c* are fused in a single four-measure segment that features both sequential expansion (mm. 11–12) and cadential progression (mm. 12–14).[14] But mm. 15–23 could also be interpreted as the expanded *b* section of a lyric prototype, of which they present many characteristic features: new thematic material, a shift to the relative minor, a two-measure repetition at mm. 16–17 and 18–19, and a cadential progression leading to V of the relative minor in m. 23. In this light, the function of the next section (mm. 24–31) could be understood in terms of the *a″/c* section of the standard prototype – that is, to provide closure, in this case both thematic and tonal. This enormously expanded lyric prototype can be understood equally well, however, as a modified version of French ternary form: A (mm. 1–14), B (mm. 15–23), A′ (mm. 24–31), coda. The tonal open-endedness of the B section would constitute a modification of the usual form, which normally features a tonally closed middle section. In conclusion, we might regard Renato's aria as an example of the mixture of formal types increasingly common in Verdi's operas of the 1850s.[15]

In the context of a discussion of the relationship between words and music, however, the striking feature of "Alla vita che t'arride" is its lack of coordination between textual and musical logic. To put it bluntly, Somma's text is either too short or too long: too short for the lyric prototype hypothesis, so that lines 5 and 6 must be repeated in order to bring the form to conclusion; too long for the French ABA′ hypothesis, so that the return of A does not correspond with a return of the initial text. In light of other ternary-form arias from the 1850s, such as Amelia's Act II aria in *Ballo*, or a different Amelia's entrance aria, "Come in quest'ora bruna" in Act I of *Simon Boccanegra* (1857), in which the A′ section sets an entirely new text, Renato's text is, again, too short: there are not enough lines to bring this A′ section to conclusion, and lines 5 and 6 must come back. From a semantic point of view, the setting of the last two lines of the second stanza seems especially problematic. If indeed they condense into a proverb

Example 6.3 Verdi, *Un ballo in maschera*, I, 1, "Alla vita che t'arride" (Renato)

the concept expressed in the first four lines of the second stanza, why are they separated from the preceding material by such an emphatic tonal non-sequitur (mm. 23–24)? And why are they set to the music associated with the first four lines of the first stanza, which express a different concept altogether?

Example 6.3 (continued)

Roger Parker and Matthew Brown have deemed Renato's musical discourse in this aria conventional by comparison with other parts of the
introduzione, pointing to the uniform stress pattern of his *ottonari* and
Verdi's strict adherence to it, to the restriction of Renato's modulations
to the relative minor, and to the contrast between his opening dominant

Example 6.3 (continued)

pedal and the more piquant tonic pedals supporting dominant harmonies in the other set pieces.[16] One could add that the motivic elaboration of Riccardo's immediately preceding "La rivedrà nell'estasi" sets in relief the substantial amount of near-literal repetition in Renato's piece, and that the latter's vocal cadenza is a rather conventional gesture, concluding that the most conservative character in the opera, a traditional jealous baritone, is appropriately introduced through a conservative, even old-fashioned aria.

But the problematic relationship between words and music in this piece merits further consideration. The plot presents Riccardo as a complex, divided personality, while Renato seems much simpler, lurching from absolute devotion to absolute hatred. Yet the contrast between the straightforward lyric prototype of Riccardo's "La rivedrà nell'estasi" and Renato's formally complex "Alla vita che t'arride" suggests a less distinct contrast between characters. And what of Renato's near-obsessive repetition of "te perduto, te perduto ov'è la patria, te perduto ov'è la patria…"? At what point does repetition begin to make a rhetorical question sound real? And why does the quasi-proverbial last couplet, arguably the semantic climax of the text, receive a relatively non-emphatic setting, at least before the coda? Is Renato such a conventional character after all? Such questions suggest the crucial interpretive issues that a critical engagement with the relationship between words and music brings to the fore.

"Words that carve out a situation or a character"

"Parola scenica" is one of those expressions – another being "tinta" – that have become "buzzwords" among Verdians. Verdi used it for the first time, however, no earlier than 1870:

> I would not want *theatrical words* [*parole sceniche*] to be forgotten. By theatrical words I mean those words that carve out a situation or a character, words whose effect on the public is always most powerful. I know well that sometimes it is difficult to give them a properly literary and poetic form. But... (pardon the blasphemy) both poet and musician must sometimes have the talent and the courage to make neither poetry nor music... Horror! Horror![17]

Commentators differ on the meaning of this expression. On the one hand, Harold Powers has suggested that it refers to words that function as "launching pads for a set-piece that will follow forthwith."[18] On the other, Fabrizio Della Seta has connected it with the concepts of "theatrical" and "dramatic," suggesting that examples of *parola scenica* can be found in other formal contexts, including within set pieces.[19] Whatever Verdi actually meant – and he probably meant different things at different times – one can trace through his career a constant interest in expressions that "carve out a situation or a character," that "powerfully sum up the situation and make it immediately clear and evident."[20] Verdi and his librettists seem to have aimed at encapsulating a situation or emotion in a concise and incisive expression and then setting it to music whose main function is to make the words as audible as possible and to enhance their impact on the audience.

Parole sceniche are indeed often found immediately before set pieces. Powers mentions several instances, from Nabucco's "Non son più re, son Dio!" ("I am no longer King, I am God!") before the *stretta* of the Act II finale, to the "sonorous kiss" between Fenton and Nannetta that launches the *largo concertato* of the Act II finale of *Falstaff*.[21] "Tutto è finito," the words with which Macbeth announces to his wife that he has murdered Duncan (Shakespeare's "the deed is done"), and which immediately precede the *tempo d'attacco* of their duet (*Macbeth*, I, 5), constitute a particularly eloquent example. This duet stages the different reactions of the two characters to their crime and the progressive realization of its possible consequences; from the point of view of the music, both the melody (C and Db) and the rhythm of Macbeth's unaccompanied declamation become structural elements not only of the *tempo d'attacco* but of the entire duet.[22] Other instances could be mentioned: for example, Rigoletto's "No, vecchio, t'inganni. Un vindice avrai" ("No, old man, you are wrong. You will have an avenger"), which introduces the idea of revenge before it is developed in the *cabaletta* of his duet with Gilda, "Sì, vendetta, tremenda vendetta" (II, 10).[23] It seems relevant that many of these instances of *parole sceniche* immediately precede *cabalette* or *strette*, the types of set pieces whose text is usually the hardest to hear, and whose content therefore needs to be summarized and conveyed to the audience with particular clarity immediately before they begin.

There are many other phrases, however, that fulfill the function of *parole sceniche* but do not introduce set pieces. Violetta's reaction to Germont's letter in Act III of *La traviata* is an extreme example. After reading the letter, she exclaims "È tardi!" ("It's late!") still in her spoken voice over a diminished-seventh chord in the orchestra. Verdi accompanied the intonation that makes the words easiest to hear with his standard harmonic means of expressing maximum emotional intensity: the effect is shattering. Several such moments come at the end of operas and function as "punch lines": Stiffelio's "Sì, perdonata... Iddio lo pronunciò" ("Yes, pardoned... God has pronounced it"), (III, 10); Rigoletto's "Ah! la maledizione!" ("Ah! The curse!"), (III, 14); Azucena's "Egli era tuo fratello!... Sei vendicata, o madre!" ("He was your brother!... You are avenged, o mother!") (*Il trovatore*, IV, 14); Alvaro's "Morta!" ("Dead!") and Padre Guardiano's rejoinder "Salita a Dio!" ("Ascended to God!") (revised version of *La forza del destino*, IV, 18).[24] This seems to be a Verdian innovation, since earlier in the century operas usually terminated with an aria, almost always for the *prima donna*.[25] Verdi's successors would often imitate his final *parole sceniche*, from a nameless peasant woman's shriek, "Hanno ammazzato compare Turiddu!" ("They have killed Turiddu!"), at the end of Mascagni's *Cavalleria rusticana* to Tosca's "O Scarpia, avanti a Dio!" ("O Scarpia, before God!").

In all the instances of *parola scenica* mentioned thus far, notwithstanding their placement within the opera, the words carry the burden of expressing a dramatic situation, while the music enhances their impact, often in very powerful ways. There are other moments, however, in which the action on stage is also essential to meaning, in which the text is indeed incomprehensible without images. *Luisa Miller* presents two exemplary cases. Miller's "Prostrata!... No" ("Prostrate!... No") before the *largo concertato* of the Act I finale makes sense only after Luisa falls on her knees in front of Walter and exclaims "Al tuo piè" ("At your feet"). Similarly, Rodolfo's final words to his father "La pena tua... mira..." ("Look at your punishment") are inseparable from his subsequent action of falling dead to the ground. Here the words have a double function: they explicitly call attention to the action ("look!") with a performative act comparable to the customary verbal gesture preceding narratives in nineteenth-century opera ("listen!"); at the same time they direct the audience's attention to a specific interpretation of that action ("this is your punishment").

Verdi similarly strove to enhance the role of the visual component in reworking a scene for the revised version of *Simon Boccanegra* (1881). In the first version (1857), the *cabaletta* of the Amelia-Simone duet in Act I concludes with an *a due* and is followed by a brief recitative in which Simone suggests that their newly discovered relationship as father and daughter be kept secret for the moment. In 1881 the recitative is discarded and the *a due* is followed by an orchestral statement of the melody with which Simone opened the *cabaletta*, leading into a repetition of the key words of the duet, Simone's "Figlia!" and Amelia's "Padre!" The subsequent orchestral coda, memorably scored for harp and bassoon, ends with one last "Figlia!" by Simone. The *disposizione scenica*, published in 1883 and compiled according to Verdi's staging of the opera at La Scala in 1881, describes this moment as follows:

> At the end of the *a due*, the Doge kisses his daughter on the forehead, and accompanies her towards the palace. Amelia says farewell to the Doge, but, after a few steps, she turns to him again and, overcome by filial love, runs to him and exclaims, "Father!..." ... The Doge remains motionless, ecstatic, as though gazing at his daughter, who has entered the palace; in this position and in the tenderest tone he whispers one last time the word "Daughter!..."[26]

The recitative section of the 1857 version, a purely text-driven moment whose purpose is to convey information relevant for the following action, is replaced by a rare instance of *parole sceniche* summing up the affective content of a preceding, rather than following, set piece. At first its placement might be considered the only trait that separates this example from the ones previously mentioned. In the light of the *disposizione scenica*, however, one could argue that here the words have lost much of their essential role in conveying meaning, and function merely as an enhancement of the visual action. This moment differs from Rodolfo's words at the end of *Luisa Miller*, since in the revised *Boccanegra* the text does not perform any interpretive activity, does not tell the audience how to decipher what happens on stage. The emphasis has shifted from *parola* to *scenica*.

Carl Dahlhaus has rightly noted that while the *parola scenica* immediately clarifies the situation, the situation enhances the impact of the verbal discourse, this relationship transforming words into *parole sceniche*.[27] The examples discussed above allow us to qualify this interpretation chronologically. Across Verdi's career the visual component – which includes not only the action immediately relevant to the plot, but also the enactment of affects and emotions – progressively gains privileged status. Words and music become more and more a function of what is seen on stage, and are less comprehensible in their own right.[28] The shattering effect of one of the most striking moments in late Verdi, Desdemona's desperate cry "Emilia, addio" ("Farewell, Emilia") at the end of the Willow Song in Act IV of *Otello*, owes much to its visual implications. The *disposizione scenica* is again revealing:

> Seeing Emilia leave, Desdemona, with a passionate cry, "Ah! Emilia!", calls her back and takes two or three steps towards her. Emilia stops and turns, then runs towards Desdemona, who takes her affectionately in her arms, then dismisses her with a kiss on the forehead. These various movements should be planned in such a way that the embrace take place exactly on the second "Emilia, addio."[29]

The final injunction, with its request for the precise timing of words and music to a specific movement on stage – a recurring preoccupation throughout the *disposizione scenica* for *Otello* – is especially telling. The enormous impact of this moment owes much to the fact that its music and words are expressions of Desdemona's movements, which break the passivity and near immobility that have physically characterized Desdemona thus far in the act, and eventually reveal the crushing weight of her desperation.

"Singing a madrigal"

Despite substantial scholarly attention to the relationship between text and music in Verdi's operas, little has been written about word painting. This lacuna betrays an underlying discomfort with an aspect of text setting considered suspect by critics since at least the late Renaissance and discredited by the German Romantic idealism that shaped twentieth-century aesthetic discourse on music. Yet investigating Verdi's operas with an eye for mimetic text setting – usually called, perhaps with a tinge of superciliousness, "madrigalisms" – reveals more than is normally thought.[30]

A few examples show the different ways in which word painting works. Mimesis is most easily detected when it is literal. The rising vocal line to which the last couplet of the slow movement of Lady Macbeth's Act I aria is set, "Che tardi? accetta il dono, / Ascendivi a regnar" ("Why wait? Accept the gift, ascend the throne and rule") can be interpreted as a response to the verb "ascendervi" (to ascend). The musical gesture is inspired by a single word but spans several measures that cover an entire couplet of poetry. In other cases mimetic music sets single words, as in Ernani's slow movement and *cabaletta* in Act I of *Ernani*, where "fiore" (in the slow movement) and "infiorare" (in the *cabaletta*) elicit short ornamental turns.[31] Since flowers were often used as ornaments for a person or an object, the term "infiorare," initially meaning "to adorn with flowers," became synonymous with ornaments in general and musical adornment or ornamentation in particular (in Italian, "fioriture"; compare the English "florid melody"). In this case, therefore, mimesis does not work literally, as in the example from Lady Macbeth's *cabaletta*, but through etymology and metaphor.

The accompaniment to Macbeth's words "Banco! l'eternità t'apre il suo regno" ("Banquo! Eternity opens its kingdom to you") (*Macbeth*, II, 7) offers an example of word painting affecting instrumentation rather than vocal line. The choice of trumpets and trombones for the loud chords that punctuate and sustain the voice can be understood against the image of the final judgment that the kingdom of eternity evokes: brass chords anticipate the trumpets that will sound on Judgment Day. Again, mimesis can be invoked only through a linguistic and cultural contextualization.

A different type of contextualization helps identify another kind of word painting. The staccato articulation of Luisa's "Lo vidi, e il primo palpito" ("I saw him, and my first heartbeat") in Act I of *Luisa Miller* and the alternation between notes and pauses of Gilda's "Caro nome" in Act I of *Rigoletto* evoke the palpitations that both heroines experience as they fall in love for the first time. This textual image and musical response had become a topos by the 1840s, thanks mostly to Amina's *cabaletta* "Sovra il sen la man mi posa" in Bellini's *La sonnambula* (1831) and Linda's *cavatina* "O luce di quest'anima" in Donizetti's *Linda di Chamounix* (1842). In these cases Verdi's practice can be evaluated only in light of an ongoing convention of text setting.[32]

Much has been made of the sonority of B in Azucena's music in *Il trovatore*, which recurs especially when she describes her mother's death at the stake. Few have noticed, however, that the rhythmically distinctive ornamentation of B at the beginning of her *canzone* "Stride la vampa" ("The flame crackles") depicts the oscillating flames described in the text.[33] Azucena's first textual and musical image in the opera immediately presents the gipsy's visual memory and imagination. Azucena thinks through images from her very first appearance to the final scene, in which she emphasizes her mode of expression with terms such as "mira" ("look") – significantly "la terribil vampa" ("the terrible flames") – "osserva" ("watch"), and "spettacolo" ("spectacle").

The orchestral writing of the first scene of *Aida* is characterized by pervasive imitation in three-voice counterpoint. This texture responds to Ramfis's opening words, "Sì, corre voce" (literally, "voices are running around," i.e. rumors are circulating): circulating rumors are depicted in the circulating voices of the orchestra. The dialogue between Ramfis and Radamès is punctuated by references to voices reporting: for example, "un messo recherà il ver" ("a messenger will report the truth"), "ella ha nomato" ("she has

named"), and "reco i decreti al Re" ("I report the decrees to the King").
Here word painting depends on musical terminology: the convention of
calling contrapuntal lines "voices" allows a pictorial hearing of the orchestral accompaniment. Although comparable to the ornamental turns on
"fiore" and "infiora" in Ernani's *cavatina*, here word painting relying on the
names of musical procedures works on a much larger scale, as word painting
of any kind often does in Verdi's late operas.

It will come as no surprise, then, that the opera in which word painting
takes center stage is *Falstaff*. Boito's text might have led to the pervasive
occurrence of "madrigalisms" in the score: the libretto is rich not only in
images and objects but also in words referring to music, giving Verdi ample
opportunity for moments in which the music becomes self-referential – yet
another form of parody in this opera.[34] The oft-proposed relationship of the
opera's opening scene to sonata form is verbally articulated by expressions
such as "Ecco la mia risposta" ("Here is my answer") at the beginning of the
presumed second subject and "Non è finita" ("It's not over") at the beginning of the development. Its conclusion is signaled by Bardolfo and Pistola's
chant of "Amen," to which Falstaff responds "Cessi l'antifona, la urlate in
contrattempo" ("Stop the antiphon, you are shouting it off the beat"), a
reaction to their lack of synchronization. The even more famous final fugue
is announced by Falstaff's exhortation "Un coro e terminiam la scena" ("A
chorus, and then we'll end the scene"). Boito's extravagant verbal *divertissement* on the word "trillo" at the beginning of Act III receives from Verdi an
appropriately excessive setting, a massive crescendo of trilling instruments
that ends up in what the text describes as "una demenza trillante" ("a trilling
dementia").

One of the most interesting instances of self-referential musical word
painting occurs when "Fontana" (Ford in disguise) complains that Alice's
virtue left him empty-handed ("a bocca asciutta," or "dry-mouthed"), "cantando un madrigale" ("singing a madrigal"). Verdi set the word "madrigale"
to a long *fioritura* that evokes not only the act of singing, but also the type
of "mechanical," "literal-minded" word painting for which madrigals –
and, more generally, Italian vocal music of the preceding centuries – were
scorned by nineteenth-century music critics and historians.[35] Given the
deep current of self-parody that runs throughout *Falstaff*, this mockery
of "madrigalisms" should alert us to its likely presence in Verdi's previous
operas.

Discourse on music in the text becomes especially prominent in Act III,
where it is paralleled by musical meta-discourse. Besides the trill episode
and the final "chorus" mentioned above, one finds, among other examples,
the "blando suon" ("soft sound") of Nannetta's song (first violins and harp
playing harmonics), and the "crepitacoli, scarandole, nacchere" ("rattles,

clappers, castanets") of the torture scene, in which the orchestra plays exactly these instruments. But the most striking instance of musical references in the libretto is Fenton's sonnet "Dal labbro il canto estasiato vola" ("From my lips the song flies in ecstasy"), an extended description of the act of singing involving terms such as "nota" ("note") "accordo" ("chord") and "suon" ("sound"). An analysis of the sonnet's setting in terms of the correspondence between the textual description of singing and its musical realization would require more space than is available here, but would reveal the extent to which the former shaped the latter.

In fact, the entire last scene of *Falstaff* could be interpreted as music about music, a walk through a portrait gallery of musical and especially operatic moments of the preceding one hundred years. Many of these portraits are of course primarily self-portraits: the threefold ritual scene (compare Act II of *La forza del destino*, or Act IV of *Aida*), the church-music topos of the "Domine/Addomine" passage (many instances in operas from all periods), Nannetta's strophic song (the Veil Song in *Don Carlos* and Jago's drinking song in *Otello* among others). But other composers make their appearances too. The orchestral writing of Nannetta's song is pure "fairy music" in the tradition of the overture to Mendelssohn's *A Midsummer Night's Dream* and the Queen Mab scherzo in Berlioz's *Roméo et Juliette*. The final fugue and its subversively moralizing text may ironically allude to the fugato texture and ethical platitudes of the ending of Mozart's *Don Giovanni*. Verdi even found room for a sort of irony by absence. In a letter to the composer Boito insisted on a wedding scene before the ending: "The nuptials are necessary; without weddings there is no happiness . . . and Fenton and Nannetta must marry. I like that love of theirs; it serves to make the whole comedy more fresh and more solid."[36] These words are perhaps reminiscent of Figaro's suggestion in the Act II finale of *Le nozze di Figaro*: "Per finirla lietamente / E all'usanza teatrale, / Un'azion matrimoniale / Le faremo ora seguir" ("In order to close it [the scene] happily and according to theatrical custom, a wedding scene should now follow"). And indeed Mozart's opera features an extended wedding scene at the end of Act III, introduced by a wedding march. Boito's final text includes a sentence comparable to Da Ponte's: "Coronerem la mascherata bella / Cogli sponsali della / Regina delle Fate" ("Let's crown this merry masquerade with the wedding of the Queen of the Fairies"). But Dr. Cajus's and Bardolfo's subsequent entry, announced by Ford's words "Già s'avanza la coppia degli sposi" ("Here comes the wedding couple"), is accompanied by a minuet, not a march (as on- and offstage practice would require). Verdi's non-wedding-march seems appropriate when an old pedantic doctor marries a drunkard. But it might also be viewed as an ironic comment on the topos of the wedding march, perhaps even as a more specific reference to *Le nozze di Figaro*.

In *Falstaff*, then, and especially in the last scene, the practice of finding musical equivalents for textual images, common throughout Verdi's career, turns in on itself when it responds literally to musical images present in the text. In this case mimesis looses its externally referential quality, since words do not evoke external images or objects, but music. The subject of music has become music. Or, better, the subject of words and music in opera has become opera itself.

7 French influences

ANDREAS GIGER

After the French Revolution, Paris emerged as Europe's foremost political center and indisputable cultural capital, and the city began to attract composers both for occasional visits and for extended residencies. The Académie Royale de Musique (the Opéra), the most prestigious of the three major opera houses, held a particular allure. Combining splendor, technical innovation, and quality of performance, it became the institution in which any ambitious composer hoped to score lasting success. A number of Italian composers in particular made Paris their temporary or permanent home: Luigi Cherubini, Gaspare Spontini, and Gioachino Rossini wrote some of their most important works for the Opéra. Gaetano Donizetti and Giuseppe Verdi continued this tradition, the former with *La favorite* (1840) and *Dom Sébastien* (1843), the latter with *Jérusalem* (1847, an extensive reworking of *I lombardi*, 1843), *Les vêpres siciliennes* (1855), and *Don Carlos* (1867). By the time of *Don Carlos*, Verdi had mastered French grand opera to such a degree that Rossini declared him the genre's leading representative. Referring to the possibility that Verdi might again compose for the Opéra, Rossini asked the publisher Tito Ricordi to "tell [Verdi] from me that if he returns to Paris he must get himself very well paid for it, since – may my other colleagues forgive me for saying so – he is the only composer capable of writing grand opera."[1]

Verdi realized early in his career that inspiration for exciting and original new works – and especially new dramatic concepts – had to come from outside Italy.[2] His love for Shakespeare is well known. And although one of the most effective features of Shakespearean drama – the inclusion of comic and grotesque elements for dramatic contrast and thus greater effect – was frowned upon in Italy, in France it played a major role not only in plays performed at the Parisian boulevard theatres but also in French grand operas.[3] French plays provided the source for some of Verdi's earliest operas, including *Nabucco* (based on *Nabuchodonosor* by Anicet-Bourgeois and Francis Cornu, 1836) and *Ernani* (based on Hugo's *Hernani*, 1830). However, the fusion of dramatic styles did not begin to take hold until *Macbeth* (1847). There for the first time Verdi interpolated grotesque elements, giving the witches an idiosyncratic vocabulary, abrupt rhythms, awkward leaps, appoggiaturas and slides, and misaccentuations of poetry, and instructing them in the score to sing in a "hacked and cackly voice."[4]

Verdi introduced more profound dramaturgical changes only after spending nearly two years in Paris.[5] In 1849 at the Théâtre Historique (one of the boulevard theatres), Verdi saw *Intrigue et amour*, Alexandre Dumas *père*'s adaptation of Friedrich Schiller's *Kabale und Liebe*. Unlike Verdi's operas up to this point, *Intrigue et amour* focused on everyday characters, not on the nobility or life at court. Furthermore, it drew on the mixture of styles, adapting it to the modern subject of social injustice. In adapting this source for his opera *Luisa Miller* later the same year, Verdi specifically asked his librettist, Salvadore Cammarano, to draw on the polarity between the serious and comic for dramatic effect:

> In the second act take special care over the duet between Wurm and Eloisa [later to become Luisa]. The terror and despair felt by Eloisa will make a fine contrast with the infernal indifference of Wurm. In fact it seems to me that if you were to impart a certain comical something to Wurm's character, the situation would become even more terrible.[6]

While Cammarano still toned down the innovative aspects of *Intrigue et amour*, Francesco Maria Piave fully developed them in *Rigoletto* (1851, based on Victor Hugo's *Le roi s'amuse*), thus gaining for opera a title character Verdi considered to be "a creation worthy of Shakespeare."[7]

In addition to this Shakespearean dramaturgical concept, audiences of French grand opera came to expect productions of great sophistication. Stage effects, comparable to special effects in present-day action films, became as essential an ingredient as highly realistic sets and elaborate costumes. The latter replaced the conventional stock costumes, which had commonly been reused with only minor adjustments. A composer, too, had to consider an extensive set of conventions when writing for the Opéra, including a four- or five-act structure with standard aria forms and an elaborate part for the chorus and the ballet. On the level of musical style, adaptation to French taste was more difficult to determine and accomplish. Nineteenth-century critics occasionally even questioned whether, for example, the melodic style at the Opéra could truly pass as French. In reaction to a review in a Berlin paper that detected French influences in Verdi's *Rigoletto*, the *Gazzetta musicale di Milano* responded:

> Of what French opera does the Berlin paper speak here? We cannot recognize the true physiognomy of French melody except in comic operas. In serious opera, of which the major temple is the grand Opéra, as someone else has observed, French music is cosmopolitan; and in fact, quite rarely are we given the chance to perceive in the grand works performed in that theatre the vices inherent in the melody and the music of the French in general.[8]

Even those critics of the time who insisted on fundamental differences between French and Italian styles described them in vague terms. The critic of the *Gazzetta musicale di Milano* implies that "French influences" may first have appeared in one of Verdi's Italian works rather than in one specifically written for the Opéra. A particular characteristic may have come to Paris in the first place through an Italian composer, or migrated from France into an opera by one of Verdi's predecessors and thence into his own work, or both national styles may have been influenced by a common source. Nevertheless, if a stylistic feature first appears in one of Verdi's French operas, in one of his Italian operas shortly after he heard a French work, or while he was living in Paris, we can speak with reasonable certainty of an immediate French influence.

Aria forms

With the gradual integration of French dramatic principles within Italian opera came an increasing employment of French musical forms, particularly the ternary aria and strophic aria with refrain. While the former had characterized French opera since Gluck, the latter found its way from *opéra comique* into grand opera only after 1830.[9] In Verdi's work, both made their first appearance not in a French opera but in Italian operas written immediately after *Jérusalem*, while the composer was still living in Paris.

The first example of a strophic *romanza* (albeit without refrain) appears in *Il corsaro* (1848, "Non so le tetre immagini," I, 4). Strophic forms *with* refrain become prominent in *La traviata* (1853), appropriately enough since the story is set in Paris.[10] These refrains differ from the culminating phrases (a''_4 or c_4)[11] of typical mid-nineteenth-century Italian melodies (a_4 a'_4 b_2 b'_2 a''_4/c_4) in constituting self-contained musical periods with their own symmetry and in introducing a contrasting mode, rhythm, accompaniment, and sometimes even tempo.[12]

"Ah, forse è lui" (I, 5) illustrates these departures from the mid-century lyric form (see example 7.1). Following customary parallel opening phrases *a1 a1′* (eight measures each in short meter), and a sequential medial section consisting of four (instead of the usual two) rhythmically parallel designs (*b1 b1′ b1″ b1″ b1‴*), the climactic *c* phrase then introduces a rhythmically and tonally distinct refrain with a new accompaniment and its own lyric form (*a2 a2′ b2 b2′ c2*).

True *couplets* – that is, those strophic songs that borrow from *opéra comique* not only the refrain form but also the light character – first appear in *Les vêpres siciliennes*.[13] The popular flavor of Hélène's "Merci, jeunes

Example 7.1 Verdi, *La traviata*, I, 5, "Ah, forse è lui" (Violetta)
(a) opening

(b) refrain

amies" (V, 2), for example, derives from the bolero rhythm in the accompaniment and often conflicting melodic accents (see example 7.2). The strongest accents of the melody's first phrase fall on "Mer*ci*," "*jeu*nes," and "a*mies*" (all with prosodic accent and musical lengthening), and "am*ies*" (musical lengthening only), whereas those in the accompaniment fall mainly on beats 1 and 3 of the measure and thus partly on unaccented syllables. Grace

Example 7.2 Verdi, *Les vêpres siciliennes*, V, 2, "Merci, jeunes amies" (Hélène)
(a) opening

(b) refrain

notes add to the lightness of the style.[14] The refrain introduces a new mode
(A major, as opposed to the preceding A minor), rhythm, and accompaniment and is self-contained on account of its independent parallel phrases
and their development.

With regard to tripartite arias, "Ah! m'abbraccia… d'esultanza" from
La battaglia di Legnano (I, 2) remains the only example until *Les vêpres
siciliennes*, where the form appears on a much larger scale. In Montfort's

Example 7.3 Verdi, *Les vêpres siciliennes*, III, 3, "Au sein de la puissance" (Montfort)

Example 7.3 (continued)

"Au sein de la puissance" (III, 3), for example, it extends across 101 measures (as opposed to the thirty-seven measures of "Ah! m'abbraccia"): A ("Au sein de la puissance," mm. 1–30), B ("La haine égara sa jeunesse," mm. 30–44), A′ (mm. 45–73), coda (mm. 74–101) (see example 7.3).[15] The length of "Au sein" allows for elaborate modulations that are usually absent from Italian arias. In the A section, for example, the music modulates to the dominant minor (m. 8), sidesteps to the Neapolitan (mm. 9–10), loses its sense of key (mm. 11–16), and finally establishes the parallel major with an independent melody (mm. 21–30).

Chorus and ballet

Traditionally more prominent in French operas than in Italian ones, choruses played particularly important musical and dramatic roles in grand opera, which required elaborate crowd scenes. Directed at providing a social and political context for the unfolding action, the chorus establishes the interests of competing social forces, clarifies the relationships between individuals and groups, contributes plot lines, and enhances the *tinta* (the overall color and atmosphere) of the work. Composers frequently employed a double chorus to juxtapose different segments of the populace, setting each part in a distinct musical style.[16]

Markus Engelhardt has singled out *Luisa Miller* as a turning point in Verdi's handling of the chorus.[17] While the chorus does indeed contribute to the drama on both psychological and musical levels, it was in his previous opera, *La battaglia di Legnano*, that Verdi first drew significantly on all the important choral achievements of French grand opera: polychoral passages, musical and dramatic continuity (as opposed to set pieces), and grandeur.[18] Verdi's instructions to his librettist Cammarano for the opera's final act reveal a decidedly French aesthetic:

> At the beginning, in front of the basilica of Sant'Ambrogio, I would like to combine two or three different melodies: I would like, for example, the *priests* inside [and] the people outside to have a separate [poetic] meter and Lida a *cantabile* with a distinct meter: leave it up to me to combine them. One could also (if you agree) assign the priests lines in Latin ... do whatever you believe to be best, but be sure the passage makes an effect.[19]

At this point in the opera, the Milanese are awaiting the return of the men who fought against the invading army of Frederick Barbarossa. Lida prays for the return of Arrigo, whom she loves, and Rolando, whom she married at a time when she believed Arrigo dead. The priests inside the basilica intone a Latin psalm verse ("Deus meus, pone illos"). Over the chant, both Lida and a second chorus pray, the chorus in lines of seven syllables (*settenari*, "O tu che desti il fulmine"), Lida in double lines of five (*quinari doppi*, "Ah se d'Arrigo, se di Rolando").[20] Even though the individual melodies are not particularly distinctive (they are both prayers, after all), Verdi succeeded in combining three ideas (two choral, one solo) of distinct melodic contours and rhythms (see example 7.4). For the conclusion of the opera, Verdi built up the forces in a typically French manner. After a short trio for Lida, Rolando, and the dying Arrigo, he introduced a chorus of townspeople and then brought back the priests, singing a *Te Deum laudamus* in four-part harmony. Gradually assimilating the initially distinct themes of the two choruses, he finally added the soloists to create a magnificent apotheosis.

Example 7.4 Verdi, *La battaglia di Legnano*, IV, 1, "Deus meus" (priests) / "O tu che desti" (people) / "Ah se d'Arrigo" (Lida)

It was this sort of double chorus that delighted the Parisian audiences during the first run of *Les vêpres siciliennes* in 1855. The situation unfolds outside Palermo, Sicily: soldiers of the French occupying force have just abducted Sicilian women dancing with their fiancés. Stunned, the Sicilian men launch a rhythmically conceived chorus ("Interdits – accablés") but

Example 7.5 Verdi, *Les vêpres siciliennes*, II, 8–9, "C'en est trop" / "Jour d'ivresse" (chorus)

are soon distracted by a boat carrying French officers and their Sicilian mistresses to the ball of the ruling French governor Montfort. The lyrical *barcarolle* of the guests ("Jour d'ivresse") contrasts diametrically with the fragmented melody of the Sicilian men. When the two ideas converge (the Sicilian men now singing the words "C'en est trop"), they remain perfectly distinct (see example 7.5). P. A. Fiorentino, the critic for the daily newspaper *Le constitutionnel*, described the scene as follows: "The piece that literally made *furore* (never has the term been better applied) is the double chorus sung by the conspirators on stage and by the ladies and gentlemen who pass by in a boat. This beautiful song, first emerging in the distance, coming

Example 7.5 (continued)

gradually closer, and then fading away *pianissimo*, produces a magical effect."[21]

In grand opera, ballet played an equally essential role. Composers were expected to include a short ballet in Act II and a longer one in Act III, allowing the members of the influential Jockey Club to arrive at the Opéra after supper in time to admire their protégées among the *corps de ballet*.[22] When Verdi wrote a new work for Paris or adapted an old one, he always added a substantial ballet, in part to comply with tradition but also because he believed in its dramatic effectiveness.[23]

In *Macbeth*, Verdi for the first time succeeded in fully integrating the ballet. In the original version (1847), he had already insisted on a short ballet, in spite of the objections of Alessandro Lanari (the impresario of the Teatro

Example 7.6a Meyerbeer, *Robert le diable*, III, 7, ballet of the debauched nuns

Example 7.6b Verdi, *Macbeth* (1847), III, 4, "Ondine e Silfidi," mm. 89–94

della Pergola in Florence, where *Macbeth* received its first performance). The ballet with chorus (*ballabile*, "Ondine e Silfidi") features water spirits and aerial spirits trying to revive Macbeth, who has fainted after hearing the witches predict that Banquo's descendants will live. The musical allusions to Meyerbeer's ballet of the debauched nuns from Act III of *Robert le diable* did not escape early reviewers, who noted similarities not only in melodic contour but also in Verdi's scoring of string staccatos over a harp accompaniment (see example 7.6a and b).[24]

In the 1865 revision, a new ballet was inserted immediately after the witches' chorus that opens Act III. Inspired by a passage from Carlo Rusconi's 1838 translation of *Macbeth*, Verdi depicted the appearance of the goddess Hecate among the witches, chastising them for casting Macbeth's fate without consulting her. The style of the new *Macbeth* ballet departs considerably from Verdi's earlier scores. The melodies repeatedly sound in the low register of the cellos and brass, accompaniments frequently abandon formulaic patterns, and the instrumentation displays the originality demanded by French audiences. Instead of writing a string of independent melodies, Verdi developed them, which in turn allowed him to integrate contrasting ideas effectively. For example, the opening "rondo" theme, played by cornets and trombones, is soon accompanied by previously heard running sixteenth notes in the low strings. Verdi then drew on this accompanimental figure for an effective transition to the subsequent contrasting section (see example 7.7).

Verdi insisted that portions of his ballets be mimed and not danced, as in the ballet's entire middle movement. This lengthy section – accounting for half of the ballet's ten-minute duration! – largely abandons the square phrases associated with the regular step patterns of traditional ballet music.

Example 7.7 Verdi, *Macbeth* (1865), III, 2, ballet of witches, mm. 69–80

Verdi depicted Hecate's apparition with an unpredictable sequence of harmonies grouped into two five-measure phrases, following it with a simple melody in the cellos and bassoons consisting of a four-measure antecedent and a five-measure consequent (see example 7.8).

Critics immediately recognized the new style of the *Macbeth* ballet; an 1874 review in the Milanese paper *Il secolo*, summed it up perfectly: "The third act includes another ballet that has all the zest of modern music: these are three pieces that correspond to three masterworks of symphonic music."[25]

Instrumentation and accompaniment

The French prided themselves on the originality both of their accompaniments and of their instrumentation, limiting the use of "oom-pah-pah" and related patterns and creating dramatic effects with distinctive scoring.[26] French composers frequently relied on string tremolos, which allowed for greater rhythmic freedom in the vocal parts, though sometimes at the cost of rhythmic and metric clarity.

In *Les vêpres siciliennes* Verdi adapted Meyerbeer's use of tremolos in very high registers to convey Hélène's feelings when French soldiers force her to entertain them with a song.[27] She responds with the *cavatine* "Viens à

Example 7.8 Verdi, *Macbeth* (1865), III, 2, ballet of witches, mm. 120–41

nous, Dieu tutélaire" (I, 2), a prayer invoking God's salvation, to which the strings add a sustained tremolo supported by running triplets in the flutes and clarinets in a relatively low register (see example 7.9). This accompaniment avoids melodic and rhythmic patterns, a sense of meter being conveyed solely through harmonic rhythm and the natural accents of the text.

Verdi sometimes employs instrumentation with such skill that sound combines with the dramatic situation to create a climactic moment, as for example in the Act II love duet between Elisabeth and Carlos in *Don Carlos.* King Philip II of Spain has married the French princess Elisabeth

Example 7.9 Verdi, *Les vêpres siciliennes*, I, 2, "Viens à nous, Dieu tutélaire" (Hélène)

of Valois for purely political reasons; she, however, is in love with Philip's son, Carlos. Returning her feelings, Carlos cannot bear to see Elisabeth at his father's side, and in a passionate duet he begs her to obtain his passage to Flanders. Carlos responds to her farewell with a stereotypical *cabaletta* text:

Ô prodige! mon coeur déchiré se console!	O wonder! My torn heart finds consolation!
Ma douleur poignante s'envole!	My poignant pain is dissipating!
Le ciel a pitié de mes pleurs...	Heaven has pity on my tears...
À vos pieds, éperdu de tendresse, je meurs!	At your feet, overcome with tenderness, I die!

Instead of launching a *cabaletta*-like movement, however, Verdi wrote a declamatory vocal line over an orchestral canvas that relies primarily on instrumentation for its atmosphere (see example 7.10). The blend of high-pitched violins and violas, the melodic doubling in the woodwinds (the first bassoon in an unusually high register), and the soft background colors of the low brass and the harp (the latter a favorite instrument of the French) combine with the initial harmonic shift from B flat major to D flat major

Example 7.10 Verdi, *Don Carlos*, II, 9, "Ô prodige!" (Carlos)

Example 7.10 (continued)

and the deliberate lack of rhythmic distinction to evoke an otherworldly feeling of suspended reality and sheer ecstasy.[28]

Melodic style

Some stylistic aspects of French opera can be better explained by the distinct rhythmic qualities of French verse than by the expectations of French audiences. Like their Italian counterparts, French librettos consist entirely of verse, sometimes but not always grouped in stanzas. But while Italian verse relies heavily on regular accents, French verse allows for a wide variety of accentual positions. With the gradual disappearance of the melismatic melodic style, Italian composers came to rely on prosodic regularity in order to comply with the Italian preference for symmetry, regular rhythms, and their natural development.[29] For example, lines of six syllables (*senari* in Italian terminology) always have an accent on the second and fifth syllable; lines of eight syllables (*ottonari*) always on the third and seventh. Even if the prosodic accents are less regularly spaced – as in some types of lines of five syllables (*quinari*) and seven syllables (*settenari*) – Verdi could nevertheless draw on regular musical rhythms because Italian theory allowed violation of some prosodic accents.[30] The following quatrain of *settenari* from Act I of *La traviata* provides a good example (accented syllables are italicized; see also example 7.1 above):

	Prosodic accents (syllables)	*Musical accents (syllables)*
Ah, for*se* è *lui* che *l'* a*nima*	1 (or possibly 2), 4, 6	1, 4, 6
So*linga* ne' tu*multi*	2, 6	1, (4), 6
Go*dea* so*vente pingere*	2, 4, 6	1, 4, 6
De' suoi co*lori* oc*culti!* ...	4, 6	1, (4), 6

Although some French theories allow for scanning against the inherent accentual structure of the line, French composers tended to restrict such freedom to lighter numbers associated with *opéra comique*.[31] In serious numbers, they usually observed at least the most important syntactic and semantic accents of a line, even if these are spaced irregularly. To accommodate this irregularity, the prestigious French critic Castil-Blaze suggested creating a melody that is "*vague, without determined character*, that does not create too much sense of rhythm and does not shock the prosody too much," an appropriate suggestion for a language having generally weak word accents.[32] Nineteenth-century French composers increasingly drew on this solution, but it is not always clear whether the "vagueness" was the result of irregular accentuation, the composer's expressive ideal regardless of accentual structure, or both.

In writing such melodies, a composer might continuously vary the rhythm or use equal note values to distribute the weight of syllables evenly; he might introduce broad meters and accompanimental patterns or avoid formulaic accompaniments altogether; or he could reflect prosodic accents by duration (i.e. long notes) rather than stress (i.e. by placing notes on metrically strong beats), thus neutralizing the underlying metric structure with its implied accentual positions. The latter solution was particularly intriguing because French theorists of the nineteenth century could not agree as to whether their prosodic accent was primarily an accent of duration or one of stress.[33]

Several types of French line challenged Verdi's compositional instincts. The most prominent of these is the *octosyllabe*, the line of eight syllables according to the French system of counting and nine syllables (*novenario*) according to the Italian.[34] Whereas *novenari* are virtually absent from nineteenth-century Italian opera librettos, precisely because their accentual structure lacks regularity, *octosyllabes* occur commonly in French librettos.[35] Two examples from *Les vêpres siciliennes* may illustrate Verdi's treatment both of unusual syllable counts and of irregular patterns of accents. The first opens the duet proper between Henri and Hélène (II, 3):

Com*ment*, dans ma reconnais*sance*	(2, 8)
Pa*yer* un pa*reil* dévoue*ment*?	(2, 5, 8)
À *vous*, ma *seule* provi*dence*,	(2, 4, 8)
À *vous* et ma *vie* et mon *sang*!	(2, 5, 8)

Verdi could have set this quatrain in triple meter with accents on [2,5,8], violating only the accent on "seule" and overemphasizing only one additional syllable ("re[connaissance]"). Nevertheless, the dance-like quality of regular triple meter would not have conformed to the passionate dialogue between Hélène and Henri, and aligning the accents with the strongest metrical beats would have caused difficulty in the fast tempo of this movement. Verdi responded to the unusual rhythmic qualities of the text with predominantly even note values in the context of a vague musical meter. Only the end of each line provides some distinction between longer and shorter syllables and thus a greater sense of metric clarity (see example 7.11). The unusually long upbeat of three quarter notes, the chromatic harmony at the beginning of the first two distichs, the lack of symmetry within the four-measure phrases, and the metrically vague accompaniment all contribute to the sense of instability, indicating the discharge of passion in this passage. The accompaniment plays a particularly crucial role in this process: the pattern, shortened to the duration of a single quarter note, does not lend any

Example 7.11 Verdi, *Les vêpres siciliennes*, II, 3, "Comment dans ma reconnaissance" (Hélène, Henri)

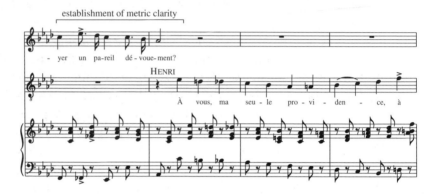

metrical support to the melody because it stresses every note to the same degree.

The opening melody of the quartet "Adieu, mon pays" (*Les vêpres siciliennes*, IV, 5) is also based on *octosyllabes*:

A*dieu*, mon pa*ys*, je suc*com*be
Sans bri*ser* ta captivi*té*!
Je *meurs* sans ven*geance*! et ma *tom*be
Est *cel*le de ta liber*té*!

The irregularity of their rhythmic groups calls for either textual or musical adjustments if parallel phrasing and reasonably regular rhythms are to be maintained. Verdi decided on a small lyric form, setting the first two lines

Example 7.12 Verdi, *Les vêpres siciliennes*, IV, 5, "Adieu, mon pays, je succombe" (Procida)

to parallel *a* and *a′* phrases, part of the third line to shorter *b* and *b′* phrases, and the remaining text to the concluding cadential *c* phrase (see example 7.12). The accommodation of the lyric form required word repetition in two instances ("Sans briser" and "Je meurs sans vengeance"); parallel musical phrases, the solemn pace suggested by the sense of the text, and avoiding misaccentuations required interpretation of prosodic accents as accents of duration. In accommodating this rhythm, Verdi consistently set prosodic accents to longer notes or groups of notes, with exceptions only in the cadential flourish at the end.

These textual irregularities and Verdi's decisions regarding form and prosody had consequences for the melodic rhythm. Measuring the rate at which syllables are delivered against the predominant harmonic half note rhythm, we find a wide range from one to six syllables (see example 7.12). As a consequence, most melodic subphrases feature distinct rhythms.

While the Italians tended to understand "development" as building an extended formal section from a memorable rhythmic idea, the French emphasized the meaning of "developing the passions" through a series of contrasting though not diametrically opposed melodic ideas.[36] To Italian audiences, therefore, French arias or duets seemed to lack unity, appearing incoherent, fragmented ("spezzate"), and constantly contrasting. The frequent change of poetic meter in French librettos and the importance of expressing the sentiment of the text at any given moment led to a musical style that differed fundamentally from the Italian one. In stanzas with irregular accentuation and poetic meter, composers often repeated words early in a stanza for reasons of proportion and balance, or they introduced a new idea sooner than the Italians would have done. The latter distinction did not escape Italian critics. Alberto Mazzucato censured the broken phrases of *Le prophète*, arguing, "And if [the phrase] does not break off, it is transformed into a new design, sets out on a new and unexpected path, so that its second part no longer seems to have any regular connection with the first."[37] Both French and Italian reviews noted this characteristic in *Les vêpres siciliennes* – either as praise or criticism, depending on the point of view.[38] For example, Pietro Torrigiani recognized the new melodic quality of *Les vêpres siciliennes* but blamed Verdi for poor craftsmanship:

> Chief among the defects observed in this score is the lack of a nexus and a connection between the melodic ideas; so that rather than fused they appear stitched together, to the detriment of the musical language, which, though composed of parts that are very regular in themselves, seems to proceed without any aim.[39]

Verdi again used this approach in *Don Carlos*, as may be seen in the second duet for Carlos and Elisabeth (II, 9). Inspired in part by the change of poetic meters from *octosyllabes* in the stanza for Carlos to polymeters for Elisabeth and back to *octosyllabes* and then alexandrines for Carlos and by the constant emotional shifts (even in mid-verse), he wrote a succession of melodies that progresses freely, in a chain of rhythmically and melodically independent ideas that express the changing moods of the poetry (see example 7.13).

In the following text, asterisks denote the beginning of a new melody or a rhythmically independent phrase.[40]

CARLOS

*Quoi! pas un mot, pas une plainte,
Une larme pour l'exilé!
*Ah! que du moins la pitié sainte
Dans votre regard m'ait parlé!
*Hélas! mon âme se déchire...
Je me sens mourir... *Insensé!
J'ai supplié dans mon délire
Un marbre insensible et glacé!

CARLOS

Ah, not a word; you would send me
into exile with no farewell!
Calmly you turn aside and leave me,
no glances of tender regret!
Alas! My soul is in torment...
Alas! In despair I'll die. Cruel heart!
So I have cried to a statue of marble,
yes, marble, quite unfeeling and cold!

ÉLISABETH

*Carlos n'accusez pas mon coeur
    d'indifférence.
Comprenez mieux sa fierté... son
    silence.
*Le devoir, saint flambeau, devant mes
    yeux a lui,
Je marche conduite par lui,
Mettant au ciel mon espérance!

ÉLISABETH

Oh, Carlos, how can you call my heart
    unfeeling and cruel?
Can you not tell why I'm stern, why
    I'm silent?
Like a flame, clear and bright, duty
    shines to light my path,
and her light must be my guide.
For God alone can help and save me!

CARLOS

*Ô bien perdu... Trésor sans prix!
Ma part de bonheur dans la vie!
Parlez Élisabeth: enivrée et ravie,

Mon âme, à votre voix, rêve du paradis!

CARLOS

O love, once mine, O love I lost!
My one hope of joy, all I live for!
Speak on, fill my soul with
    enchantment,
for, when I hear your tender voice,
    paradise then is mine!

French stylistic traits continue to play an essential role in Verdi's last two operas, *Otello* and *Falstaff*, where they become integral elements of his personal style. Melodic rhythm and mood vary continuously, and instrumentation and accompaniment maintain a high level of sophistication. In the love duet at the end of Act I of *Otello*, for example, the passage "Ingentilìa di lacrime... e gli astri a benedir" constitutes a short but distinct limb in the chain of melodies, devoid of symmetry, and shows the rhythmic variety characteristic of French opera (see example 7.14). As in examples from French operas discussed earlier, the orchestral accompaniment lacks any pattern, allowing for a free unfolding of the melodic rhythm with long upbeats and a tendency to mark accents by duration rather than stress. In addition, the beauty of the instrumentation with its initial combination of high violins, expressive bassoon line, and blend of lower strings and winds,

Example 7.13 Verdi, *Don Carlos*, II, 9, "Quoi! pas un mot" (Carlos, Élisabeth)

Example 7.13 (continued)

Example 7.13 (continued)

the reinforcement of the sighing half step at "di sospir" by horn, bass clarinet, and English horn, and the expansion of the sound at "paradiso" add distinction to this passage while supporting the sense of the text. Even the phrasing, though apparently regular, consists of irregular subphrases of 3 + 1 and 1 + 2 + 1 measures respectively (marked by brackets above the staff).

Passages from *Les vêpres siciliennes*, *Don Carlos*, and *Otello* discussed here indicate that French influences on Verdi's operas went far beyond the use of characteristic forms, choruses, and ballets. Thanks to Verdi's strong musical personality, these influences never constricted his musical development. Following his first newly composed opera for Paris, *Les vêpres siciliennes*, Verdi created some of his most original and successful compositions, and his talent for successfully assimilating the best of existing musical traditions into original creations marks him as one of the most significant composers of nineteenth-century opera.

Example 7.14 Verdi, *Otello*, 1, 2, "Già nella notte densa" (Otello, Desdemona)

Example 7.14 (continued)

8 Structural coherence

STEVEN HUEBNER

A burgeoning interest in music theory beginning in the 1960s led scholars to settle new empires, among them nineteenth-century Italian opera.
Increasing sophistication of operatic analysis has been indebted to what
Thomas Christensen has called "presentist" music theory, for which the
craft of the critic/theorist provides a key to principles of order and value,
and, by extension, an analogue to technological progress.[1] In the early days
of the academic bull market for Verdi's stock, even Pierluigi Petrobelli, a
commentator not aligned to the Anglo-American theoretical establishment,
observed:

> Of course, we are still a long way from identifying, confidently and with
> absolute precision, the formal principles according to which Verdi's scores
> were composed and the structural laws they obey. Surely their amazing
> richness – testified to by our continuous rediscovery of values and
> meanings in these works, which have been with us for quite some time –
> cannot be explained in any other way than through the presence of formal
> principles whose determining power is directly related to, and measured
> by, the manifold and complex relations it establishes.[2]

By suggesting that the "determining power" of "formal principles" is nested
in a web of "complex relations," Petrobelli posits a fertile line of investigation that seems partly to attribute the "amazing richness" of Verdi's scores
to immutable laws – by implication, deeply buried and ingenious ones –
waiting to be discovered by perspicacious scholars with the right tools. Is
there a secret method similar to that "discovered" by Alfred Lorenz in the
works of Wagner, one which will reveal the craft behind the magic?

Theoretical tools designed to show unity have long been used implic-
itly to substantiate the integrity of composers (and theorists) faced with
the commodification of culture, functioning as tropes for creative authority
and autonomy and a ready criterion for value judgment. In the wake of
Romantic aesthetics that cast aspersions on conventional harmonic syntax
and stereotypical melodic figures as a basis for coherence, such tools became
particularly urgent. "Everyone knows," wrote Roger Parker over a decade
ago in a study of motivic development in *Aida*, "[that] in good music a search
for 'motivic coherence' will almost always be rewarded in overabundance."[3]
These kinds of remarks have most often been tested with reference to the

German repertory extending from Bach to Wagner and beyond. But for quite some time now the wall erected by critics such as Arnold Schoenberg and Carl Dahlhaus between works that putatively follow their own internal designs and those beholden to social practice and institutions (such as nineteenth-century Italian opera) has crumbled, not only because the former have been seen as grounded in ideology and society but also because the latter have been subjected to a new and wide variety of theoretical tests of what constitutes "good music."

Yet while the new apparatus of music theory has modernized Verdi research – just as productions of the works themselves have been modernized – it has come under fire over a range of concerns. The house lights have dimmed somewhat on the type of musical "logic" in which similarity relationships particular to individual pieces assume primordial importance. Some scholars have objected to a tendency to "terrorize" historical Others and crush figures of the past with the heavy armor of modern analytical techniques, others to a plethora of graphs and charts and tedious prose.[4] These complaints have been effective in encouraging greater nuance in critical and analytical discussions, but often do not seem to foster methodological pluralism any more than their targets. We would do well to remember that methodologies are the product not only of ideologies, authority structures and/or consensus-seeking communities, but of personal temperaments as well.

One prominent suggestion that opera criticism should forgo analyses that seek coherence in unity came from James Webster in the late 1980s.[5] He admonished readers "to conduct our searches for tonal coherence as skeptically as we know how, and to accept from the beginning and without bias the possibility that we may not find it."[6] Ostensibly sound advice, but it is grounded in the assumption that coherence is located *entirely* in the text itself. We might legitimately ask to what degree structural relationships exist apart from the purposes and interpretive strategies of the critic, as well as in implicit contracts among composers, listeners, performers, and institutions of the past as styles and genres evolved. In other words, is the longevity of interpretations contingent on community values, pragmatics, rhetoric, and persuasion or the "facts" of the text as critics repeatedly test hypotheses against these "facts" over time? While the first set of criteria would seem to be the most compelling, the second cannot be discounted entirely.

Whatever the answer, no quest for transcendent criteria for validating similarity relationships will be easily rewarded. Although avoiding errors in describing tonal syntax seems one hardy value in the natural selection of ideas, the critic's purpose may not necessarily require such knowledge and, where it does, one may well imagine many instances where understanding basic syntax amounts to interpretation (especially in late nineteenth-century chromatic music).[7] To distinguish purposefulness (of either creator or critic) from statistical randomness can be slippery, and interpretation of coherence depends on the breadth and focus of our field of vision. For a "neutral level" description of even a single aria in a Verdi opera would reveal dozens of similarity relationships in rhythm, motif, voice-leading, and harmony.[8] Application of paradigms to privilege any of these is complicated by the likelihood that these paradigms will operate on many different levels and in an unhierarchical manner. It is hard to deny, for example, that any Verdi opera has a degree of coherence resulting from his personal style (which includes structure). Because a work represents a particular set of relationships forged out of a style, it will not always be evident where the particular emerges from the general. On the other hand, documents may reveal that a composer might have conceived of certain syntactical commonplaces as structurally significant. Obvious points of emphasis in the text or ways of parsing syntactical units would seem to be another important guidepost to unity. What analysts do with this information will vary, and the "obvious" can change with the critic.

Transplantations to Italian opera of methodologies customarily applied to symphonies and sonatas have been vulnerable to charges of what may be called "analytical inauthenticity."[9] Over twenty years ago Julian Budden opined that the polarity of tonic and dominant projected dramatically in symphonic writing finds few echoes in nineteenth-century Italian opera:

> It is useless to look in the operas of Verdi and his contemporaries for
> any large-scale key-scheme such as can be found in Wagner's scenes or
> Mozart's finales . . . There is no structural reason why the Act II duet in
> *Rigoletto* should begin in E minor and end with a cabaletta in A flat major;
> it was merely that what Schoenberg called the "tonal regions" were no part
> of Verdi's way of thinking.[10]

Aside from Budden's debatable assumption about Wagner and Mozart, such assertions are problematical at an epistemological level. Although premised on period vocabulary and paradigms, "authentic" studies use such evidence to recompose the score vicariously (as do composers in commenting on their own finished works). Vicarious recomposition brings to mind what literary critic Stanley Fish calls "the strenuous act of imagination that strives to match the act performed by the poet."[11] Fish refers here not to a particular methodology but to creative energy, an umbrella that covers a wide array of different purposes, from Verdi's to ours. The "strenuous act of imagination" is historically situated in both cases: "Verdi's way of thinking" cannot be invoked to distinguish between a historicist and an anti-historicist approach. "Given that all actions are historically embedded . . . Being historical is not an option," notes Fish in another context, "but an inevitability, and therefore historicity cannot be the basis of distinguishing between interpretive styles."[12] It is not enough to recognize that authentic paradigms interact with modern perspectives. The rub in any such dialogic model comes because the historically situated critic actually organizes the whole conversation, manipulating the thoughts, concepts, and rhetoric of an interlocutor and subjecting them to routines sanctioned by current professional practice. Furthermore, complete understanding of the interaction of past practice, no matter how thickly described, with present day culture, academic or otherwise, requires a dislocation impossible for any of us to achieve. That said, there is a good deal to recommend Fabrizio Della Seta's argument that to avoid at least some of the questions we ask of German music for the sake of cultural sensitivity would be to create an artificial insularity that undermines the participation of Italian opera in the wider European scene.[13]

Reconstruction of "Verdi's way of thinking," then, is a limited strategy, though obviously not without importance in understanding coherence. Writers such as Harold Powers and Scott Balthazar have expanded clues dropped by Verdi and acolytes such as Abramo Basevi into an elaborate theory, contending that form constituted both a common basis of understanding between Verdi and his audiences and a field of compositional options.[14] The "structural coherence" of standardized forms may be characterized as one of *functional* relationships in which musical units interlock (in syntax and affect) to produce a composite musico-dramatic whole on the level of the number, and function as generic and stylistic norms governing the succession of movements and numbers.

Studies of *associational* relationships – the attachment of dramatic meaning to thematic, motivic, harmonic, and tonal recurrence – are supported by Verdi's allusions to contemporaneous pan-European musical developments. In an oft-quoted letter to Salvatore Cammarano concerning their initial plan for *Il trovatore*, Verdi observed that "if in opera there were neither cavatinas, duets, trios, choruses, finales, et cetera, and the whole work consisted, let's say, of a single number I should find that all the more right and proper."[15] Budden remarks, "These are the words of a Wagner or a Berlioz."[16] To an interviewer in 1875 Verdi spoke of Wagner's great contribution in weakening the foundation of aria opera and acknowledged that he had taken a tentative step in this direction himself in *Macbeth*.[17] An operatic ideal (however fleetingly expressed) that gives short shrift to set pieces surely leaves open to question whether "large-scale key-schemes" or a web of motivic relationships were completely foreign to "Verdi's way of thinking." One might say the same of Verdi's diatribes against the mosaic construction of Meyerbeer's operas, their lack of an organic creative vision.[18] During the Ottocento the

Italian opera libretto became much more cohesive, with careful attention to event preparation, significant details, and smooth transitions from scene to scene within well-motivated plot lines.[19] Verdi's references to the *tinta* of individual works, an allusive coloristic category, also invites contemplation of musical unity. In short, just as with conventional forms, period writings furnish plausible triggers (for those modern analysts who seek them) to develop more systematic theories about similarity relationships and tonal groundplans.

Although conventional narratives of Verdi's life celebrate a composer who imposed his will on centrifugal institutional practices, to the end of his career Verdi embraced compromises in which organic unity could be negotiated. A good example, because it originated when Verdi's authority was at its height, is the transposition of the Act II quartet in *Otello* from B major to B flat major at the end of October 1886, during final retouchings of the orchestration. Having heard his singers, Verdi reported to Ricordi, "It is very likely that I will lower the quartet by a semitone. As it is, it shrieks too much, and all those Bs for the soprano and tenor are too daring."[20] For some, this would seem to weaken the case for B major and a network of keys around it as a generator of unity in *Otello*. But James Hepokoski has argued that such decisions do not necessarily invalidate analytical inquiries into tonal coherence.[21] Not only can a B major or a B flat major quartet be contextualized in different but equally plausible ways in *Otello*, but the analyst need not assume that tonal-dramatic associations *must* be deployed with absolute consistency at all structural levels throughout a work (even though the symmetries and multivalence of the tonal system often encourage such investigations). Nor, of course, must Verdi's own attitude necessarily be privileged by an analyst temperamentally inclined to take a different tack.

Because Budden referred to the Act II Gilda-Rigoletto duet in criticizing methodologies that violate "Verdi's way of thinking," that piece will be our starting point for a more grounded discussion of structural coherence in Verdi's operas. How to account for the E minor beginning of the duet? Harold Powers has focused on the original sequence of keys in Verdi's continuity draft, as well as the composer's preoccupation with baritone high c^1 as composition progressed. Figure 8.1a reproduces Powers's outline of the key schemes in both the draft and the definitive score and figure 8.1b his outline of keys in Rigoletto's preceding aria "Cortigiani, vil razza dannata." Powers observes that because of the transposition in the duet, duplication of the progression F minor to D flat major heard in Rigoletto's aria shifted from Gilda's solo in the duet draft to Rigoletto's transition from *tempo d'attacco* to *adagio*.[22] Furthermore, Powers attributes modulations from

[end of the SCENA: *versi sciolti*]

		draft	published score
(Rigoletto, Gilda)			
"Parla, siam soli. Oh ciel! dammi coraggio!"		C → V/f	C → V/e

[beginning of the duet: *versi lirici*]

[*TEMPO D'ATTACCO*]			
(Gilda)			
"Tutte le feste al tempio"	Andantino	f → Db	e → C
"Furtivo fra le tenebre"		f → Db	e → C
"Partì, il mio cor aprivasi"		Db	C
(Rigoletto)			
"Solo per me l'infamia"	Più mosso	f♯	f
[*ADAGIO*]			
(Rigoletto, Gilda, *a 2*)			
"Piangi, fanciulla, e scorrere"	Più lento	D	Db
"Padre, in voi parla un angelo"			
[*TEMPO DI MEZZO*]			
(Rigoletto)			
"Compiuto pur quanto"	Recitativo	(modulates)	(modulates)
(Usciere, Monterone, Rigoletto)			
"Schiudete, ire al carcere"	Moderato	c =	c
"Poichè fosti invano"			
"No, vecchio, t'inganni"			
[*CABALETTA*]			
"Sì, vendetta, tremenda vendetta"	Allegro vivo	Ab =	Ab

Figure 8.1a *Rigoletto*, II, 10 (following the *scena*), duet Gilda-Rigoletto (after Powers, "One Halfstep at a Time," 154)

"Cortigiani, vil razza dannata"	Andante mosso agitato	c
"Quella porta, assassini, m'aprite"		(c)
"Ah! voi tutti a me contro venite"		V/f
"Ebben, piango... Marullo, signore"	Meno mosso	f
"Miei signori, perdono, pietate"		Db

Figure 8.1b *Rigoletto*, II, 9 (following the *scena*), aria Rigoletto (after Powers, "One Halfstep at a Time," 156)

C major to F minor, and then from F minor to D flat major, to Rigoletto's prominent delivery of baritone c^1 at both sectional junctions (a possibility unavailable in the previous version). Since other revisions allowed baritone c^1 elsewhere (most famously at the music of the curse), "resonances to be obtained from a halfstep downward transposition of the *tempo d'attacco* and slow movement of the duet *must have forced themselves irresistibly on Verdi's attention*" (my emphasis).[23] As irresistibly, one is led to suppose, as upon the modern-day critic. The transposition of the *tempo d'attacco* to E minor/C major had the ancillary result of supplying Gilda with her own tonal space following "Cortigiani, vil razza dannata."

Powers credits Petrobelli with first demonstrating that pitches control key sequences in *Il trovatore* – where b^1 in Azucena's mezzo-soprano range assumes real importance. In addition to "vague notions and historical memories of tonal affect" that might play a role in key choice, Powers holds that Verdi usually integrated tonalities with reference to a specific sonority:

A "sonority" can be fifth, third or root in a number of triads, any of which in turn can be tonic in one or another key. The analytic hierarchy, therefore, is first the pitch, then the triad and finally the tonality – not the other way around as it may or may not be in the German instrumental music on which most of us cut our analytical teeth.[24]

To buttress Powers's hierarchy with documentary evidence, one might begin with Verdi's request to the composer Prince Józef Poniatowski concerning Emilia Goggi, the mezzo intended for Azucena at the premiere:

> I hope you will not mind writing a second [report], sending me a musical scale through the range of her voice, annotating each note, good bad, weak strong, etc.... If that disturbs you, Signora Goggi can do it herself without any fear of confessing her sins: it will be under the seal of the confessional, and will be of great assistance both to her and to me.[25]

One imagines, then, that Felice Varesi, the first Rigoletto, had a stellar c^1, an assumption supported by his music in *Macbeth*, his other big Verdi creation. Powers's cogent approach has obvious ideological and methodological uses. His premise that voice and melody (instead of harmony) generate structure lends it an "authentic" flavor, supporting critical positions that emphasize the indigenous characteristics of Italian musical culture.

David Lawton made many of the same observations about the Gilda-Rigoletto duet in 1982, including recognition of the importance of baritone c^1.[26] Nevertheless, differences between Powers's and Lawton's interpretations of the sonic "facts" are revealing. Lawton calls the replication of key sequences such as F minor–D flat major in the duet and Rigoletto's preceding aria a "double cycle," defined as "a distinctive tonal plan which is repeated in another number in order to unify musically a larger scene-complex, or else to underline a parallel between two different dramatic situations."[27] For Lawton, double cycles are deployed in *Rigoletto* to prolong (in a loosely Schenkerian sense) D flat as a tonic, a key attached to the "impact of the seduction and later events upon the father-daughter relationship."[28] Pitch class C (and, more specifically, baritone c^1 in Act II) is vital as a leading note to D flat, as the mediant of A flat (the dominant to D flat, powerfully projected in the curse theme itself), and as the dominant of F (the third degree of D flat, important in arpeggiations of the "tonic" triad). Like Powers, Lawton attributes his theoretical methodology to "Verdi's way of thinking" by grounding such compositional choices in the composer's early training: "We know that Verdi was thoroughly acquainted with the Mozart operas from his early studies with Lavigna. It is therefore not surprising to find him treating tonal structure in an analogous way."[29] Those wishing to de-emphasize national segregation of operatic culture have a good starting point here.

Though silent on the late transposition of "Tutte le feste" from F minor to E minor, Lawton suggests another critical/compositional purpose for the revision. He notes that each double cycle is initiated with prominent articulation of E minor (to make an overall sequence of E minor/C major–F minor/A flat major–D flat major). The *scena* for Rigoletto and the courtiers ("Povero Rigoletto! La rà, la rà, la rà") preceding his aria is not only in E minor (unacknowledged by Powers) but also exhibits similar texture and tempo as "Tutte le feste." The two parallel passages are each cast in a different relationship to C. After his suspicious, nervous *scena* in E minor, Rigoletto explodes at "Cortigiani, vil razza dannata" (C minor). For her part, Gilda begins a *racconto* in E minor by adopting her father's perspective on the events. But each of her strophes ends in luminescent C *major*, a tonal analogue both for her attraction to the Duke and her separation (by virtue of the modal shift) from her father.[30]

One might also speculate whether Verdi's transposition of Gilda's Act I "Caro nome" from F major (in the draft) to E major led him to do the same for "Tutte le feste" in order to retain a common tonic.[31] Or one might further observe that the beginning of Rigoletto's "Solo per me l'infamia" (the second part of the *tempo d'attacco* in the Act II duet) may be heard in A flat major, before the passage fragments over the dominant of F minor (that gives way to D flat major), thereby producing an explicit tonal relationship with the *cabaletta*. That is, Rigoletto tentatively touches A flat in self-pity before that key and emotion are absorbed into his call for vengeance at the end of the duet.

Thus Powers's "analytic hierarchy" must share space with other musico-dramatic strategies, some of which privilege keys over pitch. Baritone c^1 may be fashioned into a sign of the curse itself, D flat major into one signifying its unfolding. This is not to deny that for most listeners the musico-dramatic pervasiveness of the curse does indeed stop at the repeated iterations of "Quel vecchio maledivami!" as *Rigoletto* unfolds in performance. But ultimately we have little basis, epistemic and even moral, to cut off the act of criticism and analysis at this limited experiential level.[32]

In an analysis of *Rigoletto* Martin Chusid has noted that "D flat … is of such importance to the overall key design and the dramatic course of events that it might well be understood as a kind of tonic for the entire opera," raising the question: can an act of a Verdi opera, or even an entire opera, be "in" a key?[33] The answer depends on what it *means* to say that any piece is "in" a key, a concept never isolated from the act of interpretation (except as a matter of naming pieces in the instrumental repertory). Symphonic analyses frequently speak of movements closely or distantly related to the home key in narratives premised on stability, departure, and return within a context of large-scale tonal closure that does not usually apply in Verdian opera. Yet analytical purposes may take many forms. Analysts of opera may *also* prioritize some keys – according to such factors as ubiquity, placement within acts, or decisiveness of associated dramatic action – and structure their narratives accordingly.

In a short article on *Un ballo in maschera*, Siegmund Levarie has identified B flat as the tonic of the opera.[34] That tonic (in major or minor mode) sounds at the last three (of five) curtains and elsewhere, reminding the listener "where he is heading," and reflecting the increasing weight given to the conspirators as the plot unfolds.[35] Its dominant F (and keys said to substitute for the dominant) occurs at catalytic events, an analogue to its cadential function. And the tonalities ending Acts I to III spell an ascending chromatic progression A flat–A–B flat. In response, Joseph Kerman has counseled scholars to stay away from abstract key schemes and overly systematic tonal dramatic associations, and to concentrate on how keys are approached on the local level, how they are perceived as the work unfolds. Kerman broadens intent to incorporate effects that "fall safely within the range of Verdi's musical technique and dramatic psychology in the late 1850s."[36] Studies of key relations and drama should be conducted with "tact, common sense, an awareness of history, and respect for the integrity of each individual composer."[37]

Notwithstanding some unconvincing references to authorial intent in Levarie's piece, his conclusions should not be dismissed too hastily. The "integrity" of the composer does not always march in lockstep with the "integrity" of the text itself. Current methods of analytical discourse steer around the black hole of chance by demonstrating the *utility* of analytical propositions. We may apply this test to Levarie's reductionist statements, particularly his more robust example from *Il trovatore* which begins in E major and ends in E flat major, an "enharmonically reinterpreted Neapolitan cadence."[38] He *might* have supported his case by pointing out that these two tonics belong to separate spheres in the drama, E minor (and related keys) to Azucena and her world, and E flat major (especially as understood in the orbit of A flat) to Leonora.[39] Positioning of these keys at the beginning and end of the work, then, has an iconic significance: the whole story begins with the calamity that befell Azucena's mother and, arguably, ends as a tragedy of lovers. Such an analytical strategy, one deployed by Balthazar, traces the extent to which tonality mirrors the course of the plot: relative stagnation in the unfolding of events finds resonance in a limited range of modulations, forward momentum in a wider palette.[40]

Another approach might seek to relate local detail to the wider tonal groundplan. Chords on E and E flat are juxtaposed (and perceptible in relation to one another) at two important junctures in *Il trovatore*. In the

Act II finale, just before the *concertato a tutta ribalta*, an E major harmony (spelled as F flat) is the culmination of a chromatic bass ascent coinciding with Manrico's appearance to rescue Leonora. The F flat chord gives way to an E flat harmony, dominant of the A flat *concertato* as he moves from the gypsy world back to courtly love. In the next act, during the *tempo di mezzo* before the *cabaletta* "Di quella pira," an explosion on E major *follows* an E flat dominant, precisely the moment where Manrico returns to the gypsy world by deciding to rescue Azucena.

The significance of E–E flat poles is further underscored by their allusions to Phrygian cadential motion conventionally associated with death. A morbid aura extends from the Act I duel and the subsequent battle between rebels and the Count (where Manrico is left for dead) to Azucena at the stake and the conclusion of the opera. Of course, such wide-spanning "cadences" detected by Levarie (and by analysts of opera from Mozart to Wagner) are unlike true cadences that involve adjacent chords. Nevertheless, like literary figures these cadences share at least one characteristic with the normative concept, here a succession of sonorities (however separated) reminiscent of real cadences.

That the Phrygian motion involves E flat confirms its macabre topos, at least according to Martin Chusid's identification of E flat with Manrico's cruel destiny and death in one of several studies in which he proposes associating tonality with dramatic elements and characters in various Verdi operas.[41] At his first appearance Manrico sings in E flat minor of his "rio destino." He is later executed in that key. En route, the bell in the "Miserere" scene tolls in E flat accompanied by anapestic rhythmic figures conventionally associated with death. Some analysts will also grant purpose to Manrico's metrically stressed E♭s at "pagina / De' miei destini" ("the page of my destiny") in the aria "Ah sì, ben mio," a movement that begins in F minor, tonicizes A flat (at "pagina / De' miei destini"), and finishes in D flat. Although Chusid's core of tonal-dramatic associations always seems well motivated, the question that it raises is the *extent* to which a set of relationships might be spun out. His willingness to embrace single chords and pitches combined with wide latitude in interpreting the libretto makes for a large field indeed. Accepting the general premise that Leonora and her world revolve tonally around A flat, statistical probability suggests that E flat will almost certainly be prominent and will coincide with references to fate and death. In the second act, where the offstage chorus of nuns is in E flat, the dominant of the ensuing *concertato* in A flat, few critics will want to explain that key with reference to poetic lines such as "Che un'ombra, un sogno fu, / Anzi del sogno un'ombra / La speme di quaggiù" ("That was but a shadow, a dream; rather, the hopes of this world are a shadow of a dream"), which suggest, in Chusid's words, "the convent is a place to prepare for the initiate's second existence, the heavenly one, after *death*" (my emphasis).[42] In short, one might roll dice within these parameters and come up with the same type of coherence. In the absence of a document showing that Verdi himself thought of his choice of key here in this way, the mastery of the critic/composer seems to evaporate into the thin air of chance.

Returning to Levarie's "Neapolitan cadence," we have observed how his structural frame can be put to a number of critical and analytical uses, an important affirmation of validity. The effectiveness of the A flat–A–B flat curtain sequence which Levarie identifies in *Ballo* is not as clear. To be sure, dyads from this chromatic set seem significant. For example, the martial ensemble "Dunque l'onta di tutti sol una" in A flat is followed almost immediately by Oscar's frothy "Di che fulgor" in B flat at the end of Act III, scene i; likewise, the dance music of the ball is first heard in A flat before it breaks out *tutta forza* in B flat. And, as Roger Parker and Matthew Brown show so well, A major plays an important role at several dramatically significant junctures during prolongations of the dominant of B flat.[43] In such juxtapositions one senses the effect of tonal *Steigerung* implied by Levarie's wide-spanning model. But the *complete* chromatic succession A flat–A–B flat is not articulated on local levels, nor resonant in successions of curtains in other Verdi operas. Perhaps the best case for Levarie's observation lies in the intellectual appeal of the concept of rising tonal levels at curtains (however unrelated to the rest of the opera) culminating in the "tonic." The statement cannot be completely invalidated, but it is difficult to make further claims or delineate other purposes.

Today radically reductionist statements such as Levarie's face an uphill battle. Parker and Brown warn that

> the musical structure of the opera [*Ballo*], whether geared to motivic or harmonic matters, or to both, lies essentially in an accumulation of detail rather than in any abstract pattern . . . It may at times be tempting to cut through this web, to shape an empyrean path along which all details can be neatly arranged: but the unity of purpose thus achieved can only be chimerical, and will be attained only by ignoring or distorting contradictory evidence . . . What all this proves is that any *one* explanation of the tonal or motivic structure of a piece as complex as *Un ballo in maschera* is bound to be unsatisfactory. That those irremediably wedded to organicism are doomed to distort this repertory.[44]

As with Kerman, one senses a well-meaning desire to shield Verdi, an impulse to preserve the integrity of Italian operatic culture and protect it from distortions. The Parker and Brown article masterfully resists the chimera they draw. It begins with a discussion of the "coherent, symmetrical structure" exhibited by the first scene of *Ballo*, although the authors also point out musical features that run counter to the five-part form they propose. They describe the important role of B flat in the scene and although they repudiate B flat as the "tonic" of the entire opera, their analysis traces analogous uses of that key in various parts of the work, attending to strategies for preparing and prolonging its dominant. Coherence is described in tandem with *process*, tonal relationships appearing at different structural levels. The reader is alerted that these relationships do not inform every part of the work, and that networks around other keys in *Ballo* might also yield rich analytical discourse.

Given their concentration on B flat, it is striking that Parker and Brown do not mention the sounding of that key at the three final curtains. In what sense might it be construed as the tonic of the opera? One might credibly argue that the play of light and shade at the core of *Ballo* occurs most often in the context of B flat with effects of modal mixture that include shifts to D flat major and ominous utterances of flat VI (G flat).[45] That is, B flat might be conceived as fundamental to the *tinta* of the work. For example, Amelia's aria at the beginning of Act II is in F minor/major, with D minor as an important subsidiary key. As Parker and Brown point out, the slow section and *tempo di mezzo* of the subsequent Amelia-Riccardo love duet play out some of the very same keys (F major, D flat major, A major) that hovered around B flat in Act I (and will do so again in Act III). These keys are redeployed as a chain of modulations through thirds appropriate for the ecstatic context (starting from Amelia's "Ah, deh soccorri tu"). When part of the *tempo di mezzo* ("Ebben, sì, t'amo!") is recalled during the C major *cabaletta*, the fresh key of E major is introduced. F, D flat, and A are untouched in the *cabaletta*, but immediately afterward the tonal course winds back to F, with local references to D flat (as in the earlier slow section of the duet). A trio in D minor follows (recall the importance of that key in Amelia's aria) and later F appears as a tonic (for the entrance of the conspirators), giving way to yet another sequence of major thirds (D flat to A). B flat major follows at the final movement of the act (with appropriate tonic minor inflections). In short, keys are tightly integrated, and the network spawned by B flat in the first act is never gone for very long. In light of the emphasis on F (dominant of B flat) and the arrival on B flat to culminate the accumulation of characters on stage, one might even consider B flat as the goal of this act. At any event, the biggest turn sharpward in Act II – for the *cabaletta* in C and "Ebben, sì, t'amo!" in A and E, an interlude of sharpward motion that defines the love music – may surely be "heard" against the foil of the B flat conclusion to the act, the assorted flat keys on the way (including the shift from F to D flat for Amelia's earlier prayerful expression of distress in the duet), and even the gloomy stage set. Similarly, the beginning of *Ballo* in B major and F sharp major stands radiant against the B flat minor with which the opera ends (as in *Il trovatore*, a semitone relationship), as well as against the first appearance of the murderer Renato, for which B flat minor/major is the tonic. And on one might go, just as in analytical discourse about the rotation of keys against a tonic key in a German symphony.

Rather than see "unity of purpose" as chimerical, one might examine "purpose" and ruminate on the entwinement of musicological style and perceptions of validity. To hear (or see) details against a constant or repeating element is one approach; to fill an entire essay with these findings is a legitimate way to recompose the score vicariously; and to posit abstract patterns (at whatever level) is not necessarily incongruent with accumulating detail. Nor is the critical strategy of providing a *single* explanation for a passage, aria, or opera, or of using a *single* musico-dramatic element – such as a single tonic – as a focal point "unsatisfactory" *per se*. Since no analysis or interpretation will reflect the complete musical and dramatic texture of a discrete musical section – in other words, since all analyses *select* or even *reduce* in light of a purpose – it would seem that the best lesson to draw from Parker and Brown is the truism that interpretation is open-ended. Like all high art forms opera is dense, complex, and polysemous. How, and *to what extent*, method and discourse in studies with finite numbers of words should reflect this awareness is another matter, one of critical style.

The critic of Verdi's operas has many further techniques for studying constraints on tonality (and structural coherence more generally) than those touched upon here. She might follow an intertextual route, considering analogous coordination of tonality with dramatic action in scenes from other works (by Verdi or someone else) as decisive to her analytical purposes. For instance, the anvil chorus from Azucena's world in *Il trovatore* seems to lurk behind the major mode reprise of Ulrica's aria in the first act of *Ballo*: both C major passages for ethnic outsiders emerge from extended preparations on E pedals and begin with melodic emphasis of the mediant, tonic, and dominant. Or, to take another example, in three passages I have discussed (the Gilda-Rigoletto duet, Manrico's Act III aria, numerous examples in *Ballo*) the key moves from F to D flat. The modulatory context is different in each case and dramatic parallels are difficult to see, except that a "bright" color does not seem appropriate for these situations. Here intertextuality merges with stylistic reflex, which, as we have observed, is a compelling criterion for restricting analytical options.

We thus return to that hazy border between the particular and the general, between purposes confined to the work and those that reach beyond. Parker and Brown refer to the shifts from F (as the dominant of B flat) to D flat in the first act of *Ballo* as "unusual" and "anomalous," their point apparently being that the exceptional nature of the progression strengthens the opera's individuality and, hence, coherence. Yet both shifts occur after articulation of B flat *minor* and, thus, belong to the nineteenth-century toolkit of modal mixture. The same network of keys is played out, somewhat differently, before another well-known regicide in Verdi's oeuvre, during Macbeth's long recitative "Sappia la sposa mia" in the first act of *Macbeth*. That a modulation from F to D flat is sometimes extended to A major in *Ballo* reflects a more general tendency of Verdi's harmonic language to explore major third relations.[46] This procedure might be contextualized against symmetrical division of the octave in the work of non-Italian composers. That is, aspects of this modulatory sequence are *not* particular to this opera. Or, to cite another modulation sequence, one might note that the E major "bacio" theme in the Act I *Otello* duet emerges out of C major, like the reprise of "Ebben, sì, t'amo!" in the *Ballo* duet. To be sure, syntactical differences between the two passages leap out irresistibly: an ecstatic sequential ascent to E major in *Ballo*, melting, side-slipping diminished-seventh harmonies in *Otello*. But E major plays a role elsewhere in both works, and a succession of the *same* two major keys related by major third forms the culminating point of expressions of love. Do these intertextual connections mean that *Ballo* and *Otello* are tonally less coherent than some analysts have made out? That would not be the consensus today, if only because musical ideas relate to purposes that operate within a work as well as outside it.

One could follow the same path further and arrive at even more contentious territory. Amelia prays in E major to resist Riccardo in the first act of *Ballo*, protests her innocence in that key at the beginning of the third ("Un istante, è ver, l'amai / Ma il tuo nome non macchiai"), and is compelled by Renato to choose Riccardo's murderer over an E major harmony a short time later. Should we argue that the last passage helps weld together the entire opera by functioning as an ironic manipulation of the key of "Ebben, sì, t'amo"? For one might also note that E results from local motion out of E flat, a chilling juxtaposition, rather than through broader correspondences, particularly since E is uncommon elsewhere. Verdi had used this effect at least once before in the second act of *Macbeth*, after Macbeth sees Banquo's ghost a second time ("Ma fuggi! fantasma tremendo").[47] Local expression or structural coherence? Once again, although many will argue that more than one purpose might be reflected in Renato's extended E major harmony, many will also feel that these purposes do not carry the same weight.

That analysts such as Parker and Brown choose *not* to take up questions about style and intertextuality – an entirely defensible option – limits the premises of their "complex web of interlocking relationships." While their path is hardly "empyrean," it does avoid certain neighborhoods. One might envisage a continuum of constraints and purposes spanning structural coherence considered as "an accumulation of detail" within a work (following Parker and Brown), abstract patterns as they apply to individual works, abstract statements about Verdi's style (which in themselves deal in a certain kind of coherence as manifest in individual works), and broad observations about pan-European musical developments after 1850. The more widely focused end of the continuum might in some instances lead to inflection, or even disconfirmation, of certain interpretations about the coherence of individual works. But there is also a circular element: interest in motivic and tonal coherence also informs perceptions of style (as a comparison between the Wagnerian and the Verdian analytical traditions will reveal). My point is this: rather than dismiss reductionist statements and the subordination of details to paradigms, we would do well to recognize that paradigms reflect analytical purposes, and that reduction and subordination occur at one level or another in all analysis. Different ways of arguing for and molding coherence, even different fields for the play of chance, will yield different perspectives on the panorama between detail and whole.

9 Instrumental music in Verdi's operas

DAVID KIMBELL

My essay is concerned with the overtures (*sinfonie*) and preludes; the storms and battle scenes; the stage music accompanying marching armies, religious ceremonies, dances, and balls; ballets, and shorter episodes of pantomime; and certain other episodes where the burden of the musical argument is carried by the orchestra.[1] This is the music by means of which Verdi places his operas in their social frame; since so much of it functions as sounding décor and sounding spectacle, it provides some of the most thought-provoking insights into how he wished his operas to be staged; it also forms the locus for some of his boldest experiments in exploring the balance between "realism" and stylization in the operatic medium.

Verdi's overtures enjoy a life of their own – that is, independent of the operas to which they belong – less securely than those of the German tradition, less securely indeed than Rossini's overtures. One reason is certainly that they are less firmly rooted in a Classical, sonata-based symphonic ideal.[2] Verdi knew those German overtures, and occasional traces of their influence are discernible; but in general his *sinfonie* occupy a space fascinatingly poised between the symphonic ideal and the idea of a potpourri, a medley or parade of themes from the body of the opera. What gives them their distinctive Verdian character is the manner in which the themes are set out: the formal framework plays on our sense of movement, alternating kinetic or transient episodes with episodes that seem suspended in time, in a manner that is surely evocative of an operatic *scena*. And though they may fall into several movements, they typically highlight a slow *cantabile* and a rousing Allegro.

In *Nabucco* the *cantabile* takes the form of a 3/8 variation on the chorus "Va pensiero," the theme being given first to solo oboe and solo clarinet playing in octaves, and then at its reprise to solo oboe and solo trumpet in unison, with ornamental patterns woven around it by flutes and clarinet. The procedures are typical of the orchestral style of Verdi's early years, when distinctiveness of instrumental timbre mattered less to him than that the instruments should give the melody a specific density and weight. The *cantabile* is preceded by an extensive introduction, in which a chorale-like melody for the brass (see example 9.1) – though it is not taken from the opera, it anticipates the priestly tone of some of its most important episodes – is interrupted by more and more extensive counterforces: bleakly powerful

Example 9.1 Verdi, *Nabucco, sinfonia*, opening

(m. 9), sinister (m. 16), militaristic (at the first Allegro). This last passage is based on the chorus "Il maledetto non ha fratelli" from Part 2 of the opera; a further working of the same theme, now set over a dominant pedal, performs the function of a transition between the Andantino and the principal Allegro in D major.

Despite some superficial resemblances (a "second subject" in the dominant key at rehearsal letter F, a "recapitulation" at G), this Allegro has no real kinship with sonata form. Its two most important themes – one Babylonian, one Hebrew – are both in the tonic; starkly and directly set against one another, they have rather the effect of that type of duet *cabaletta* that employs dissimilar solos.[3] The theme in the dominant is a mere episode, providing a temporary shift of perspective before the restatement of the same juxtaposition of themes (the *cabaletta* repeat, so to speak) at G. The "maledetto" theme that had galvanized the introduction and supplied the energy for the transition between *cantabile* and "*cabaletta*" recurs a last time to form the coda.

The most sonata-like of the overtures, and surely Verdi's finest essay in the symphonic style, is the *sinfonia* to *Luisa Miller*. In striking contrast to the potpourri overtures, this is a monothematic movement, based on a theme which recurs in various guises throughout the opera – but especially in Act III – as a symbol of the malign fate that destroys the lovers' happiness (see example 9.2). Originally Verdi conceived it in a relatively conventional sonata form. In the event, he foreshortened the recapitulation, canceling the reprise of the first subject and launching directly into the second, which is rescored, with flute and oboe added at the upper octave and a new sparkle in the accompaniment figuration. A coda brings further transformations of the theme. The result of these modifications of the sonata scheme is

Example 9.2 Verdi, *Luisa Miller, sinfonia*
(a) opening

to transform the overture into another manifestation of the characteristic Italian alternation of drama and lyricism, action and stillness. The first subject area is full of strong contrasts: music and silence, concertino and tutti scoring, rapidly shifting modulation, all of which are intensified in the development. The second subject is a lyrical distillation of the same theme, sustained for more than thirty measures. Then, at the point where in a Rossini overture one would expect the *crescendo*, a celebratory, clinching cadence theme rounds off the exposition.

The *sinfonia* of *Les vêpres siciliennes* is sonata-like too. But here the thematic obsessiveness of *Luisa Miller* is replaced by an extravagant profusion of lyrical material. Of all Verdi's overtures it comes closest to Weber, in the sense of being a fully coherent sonata movement in which all the material has dramatic or poetic connotations.[4] Evidently the selection of themes was made with some care, giving the piece a coherence which is poetic as well as musical and suggesting, indeed, a latent program. For everything in the introductory Largo proves to be expressive of the condition of Sicily and its people at the time in which the opera is set: its national and political hostilities, its oppressions, its religious faith. The Allegro agitato, on the other hand, is built from themes that might be said to contain the yeast that sets the drama fermenting: themes associated with conspiracy and with family bonds (of anguished complexity).

The orchestra had commonly been used in Italian opera as an adjunct to the art of the scenographer. By the time of Verdi's immediate

Example 9.2 (continued)
(b) mm. 82–113

predecessors, each change of scene was accompanied by a brief, usually untitled orchestral movement that helped create the ambience for the next stage of the drama. In Bellini, for example, three favorite types of prelude can be distinguished: (1) scene-setting pieces, directly linked with the fol- lowing (usually) choral movements; (2) preludes which, while still setting the scene, provide elements of thematic cross-referencing and/or architectural grandiosity besides, by taking up themes heard elsewhere in the opera; (3) evocations of the mood of the character who sings the following scene, a song-without-words type of movement sometimes featuring an obbligato solo instrument. The music of these commonly spills over into the following *scena*, providing background or punctuation for its recitative musings.

Verdi's own early mastery of all these preludial functions is clear in the 1847 *Macbeth*, an opera with an unusually large number of scene changes:[5]

(1) II, 5: *Magnificent hall, etc.* This prelude falls into two contrasting parts. The first eight measures set a gestural tutti against a lighter-footed woodwind response; deep bows and gracious acknowledgments are all but visible in the music, and in due course the two phrases prove to represent the exchange of courtesies between, respectively, Macbeth and nobles and Lady Macbeth and nobles. From m. 9 a more regular wind-band-dominated theme evokes the festive occasion; this functions later (both at rehearsal figure 14 and at figure 20) as the orchestral theme for the *parlante* in which the Macbeths try to animate their increasingly heavy-spirited guests.

(2) II, 1: *A room in the castle.* Essentially this prelude is an instrumental quotation of the "tutto è finito" motif from the Act II duet, and that stretch of the *tempo d'attacco* that depicts Macbeth's inner perturbation, "Fatal mia donna." The music breaks free from its vocal model only to reach a half cadence, in which, however, the sighing Db–C semitone echoes on.

(3) IV, 3: *A hall in Macbeth's castle, etc.* The longest and most remarkable of the preludes, a substantial part of which also serves as *preludio* to the opera as a whole. In the broadest terms it comprises a tragic *cantilena* for first violin, clarinet, and English horn framed by atmospheric and graphic figurations of a more discontinuous kind. Both in key and in the highlighting of the Db–C semitone, the soft string motif at the start takes us back to the murder duet of Act I; a high tiptoeing motif later recurs at both the entrance and the exit of the sleepwalking Lady Macbeth.

If the *Macbeth* preludes combine traditional scene-setting functions with a keener than usual sense of psychology, that is no doubt partly due to the effect of Shakespeare's play on Verdi's imagination. The tendency might also have been stimulated by a remarkable experiment Verdi had made a few years before in his adaptation of Byron's *Two Foscari*. In *I due Foscari*, prompted perhaps by the peculiarly obsessive characterization of the source play, Verdi tried something new. All the principal characters – the Doge, his son Jacopo, Jacopo's wife Lucrezia, the Council of Ten – have distinctive characterizing themes, and are accompanied by them on most of the occasions when they appear on stage. The themes do not entirely do away with the need for the standard types of scene-setting prelude, and they are several times used where no change of scene is involved; nor was this an experiment Verdi ever felt disposed to repeat. But the *Foscari* preludes, in their over-schematic way, do perhaps mark a further stage in Verdi's conception of an operatic totality in which orchestral preludes (and postludes and interludes) depict not merely the scene, but the way the characters move within the scene, and the personality of the characters who do the moving.

Quite early in his career Verdi came to prefer starting his operas with a *preludio* rather than a *sinfonia* (see note 1), making the instrumental music an integral part of the drama rather than a detachable synopsis of it, or a kind of sounding proscenium arch behind which it could be set. In several of his ripest operas, beginning as early as *Il trovatore*, and then in *Don Carlos*, *Simon Boccanegra* II, *Otello*, and *Falstaff*, the prelude has all but disappeared, absorbed entirely into the opening scene of the opera, its function served by just a few measures which plunge the spectator *in medias res*. Between this extreme and the full-length *sinfonia*, the *preludio* might serve to plant in the mind a motif that is to play a crucial dramatic part in the opera (*Ernani*, *Rigoletto*), or to provide a musical portrait of one or more of the principal characters (*Macbeth*, *La traviata*).

The Act I prelude of *Un ballo in maschera* is one of Verdi's most substantial and sophisticated. As far as rehearsal figure 1 it is a transcription of the opening of the *introduzione*, "Posa in pace," an expression of the people's devotion to their governor. (The gentle drops of dominant which introduce it suggest a dewy awakening amid the first stirrings of birdsong.) As in the *introduzione*, this is followed directly by the music of the conspiracy that is to destroy this Eden, and this in turn by love music. The closing phrases of the prelude also match exactly those of the *introduzione*. This Eden–Conspiracy–Eros world is mapped out in the following form:

A Eden: 15 measures of rich, diatonic, almost hymnic harmony.
B Conspiracy: 10 measures of fugato, laid out in the manner of a regular fugal exposition.
C Eros: 26 measures, based on Riccardo's song of love for Amelia; first stated, then, with evident symbolic intent, elaborated in duet form; but the duet is boldly dissonant (bold beyond the measure of Verdi's purely vocal duets) and from rehearsal figure 3 overshadowed by a sighing motif in the cellos.
B′ Conspiracy: 8 measures, canonic restatement and extension of B.
Coda 9 measures, in which the love music is reduced to a single resonating motif sinking down through the woodwind.

This opening is a prelude rather than an overture because its material is drawn exclusively from the first scene of the opera, and continues to be developed during the course of it. In Riccardo's aria the conspiracy theme provides a menacing undercurrent to the coda; as the scene closes for Renato's entrance, intertwining fragments of Conspiracy and Eros only gradually clear. Incidentally, the three themes provide an almost absurdly pat glossary of connotations: Eden = harmony, Conspiracy = counterpoint, Eros = lyricism.

Several of Verdi's scene-opening preludes are in effect miniature tone poems, or rather tone paintings. And tone painting is even more evidently the aim in such orchestrally accompanied spectacles as battle scenes, sunrises, and storms.

Foresto's *scena* and aria in the prologue of *Attila* is adorned by both a storm and a sunrise. The storm is built on a series of tortuous approaches to a series of G cadences, some struggling up to the G, some folding in on the G. In the first section both the harmony, entirely built on various diminished-seventh chords, and the orchestral texture, dominated by brass and woodwind, are noteworthy; as in the *Otello* tempest, decades later, the general grimness of the sound is intensified by a throbbing pedal note. But what most surprises the ear accustomed to the orchestral storms of the German Romantics is how the young Italian composer hopes to capture the sublime disorder of Nature in a musical design of such orderliness.

The sunrise music, which provoked much enthusiasm at the early performances of *Attila*, is a piece of even more elemental simplicity. One rhythmic figure is reiterated, filled out harmonically, intensified, until with a solemn horn call (omitted from the vocal score) all is light and C major blazes forth. Doubtless the inspiration for this episode comes from Félicien David's *Le désert*, which was enjoying a successful run of performances in Milan in June and July 1845. But the character of Verdi's music is quite different. Compared with David's sumptuous scoring and his slow progressions of harmonies firmly anchored within a tonic framework, Verdi's music has a more glistering color. For the role of the strings is reduced and the rhythms of the woodwind figures sharpened, and it derives a certain tense dynamism from being built entirely over a dominant pedal.

In *Attila* storm and sunrise are not free-standing movements, but form integral parts of the *scena* sung by the principal tenor. Spaced out through Verdi's long career there followed a series of comparable movements that tended to blur the frontiers between one medium of operatic expression and another. In the storm in *Rigoletto* the dehumanized wailing of the tenor chorus forms a crucial element of color and texture, while the *burrasca* in *Aroldo* is supplied with an elemental choral commentary from off-stage voices. The final development of these tendencies comes in the hurricane scene which opens *Otello*. The ebb and flow of the dynamic levels, the flexible intermingling of orchestral and vocal textures, and the way these textures change in the space of a few measures from huge tuttis to ominous emptinesses, and the culmination, nevertheless, in full-throated song: these things amount to as vivid an illustration as one could find of Verdi's capacity for transforming the appearance of Italian opera beyond recognition while in fact preserving its fundamental values intact.

No less resourceful in their manipulation of the possibilities of the operatic medium are Verdi's battle scenes. That in *I lombardi* is his most remarkable essay in a kind of theatrical stereophony in which the orchestra, representing the Crusaders, is pitted against a stage band, representing the Saracens. Both play marches heard earlier in the opera, but now in fragmentary, antiphonal form. Tuttis with no specific connotation lead to a climax; and after the Crusaders' victory the stage band representing the enemy plays only a series of slow sigh figures. Similar spatial effects are heard in *La forza del destino*, Act III, where realistic offstage trumpet signals evolve into an instrumental battle, which serves in turn as the supporting background for a foreground *parlante*.

One of the novelties of the 1865 *Macbeth* is the fugal battle music with which Verdi replaced the banal quick march (little but reiterated fanfare themelets) of 1847. I know of no evidence that Verdi ever studied Mendelssohn's Scottish Symphony, but several passages in the revised score suggest that it may have served as a model for music in a Scottish-Ossianic spirit. The idea of a fugal battle scene is only one of several features common to both. Verdi's fugue is carefully coordinated with the stage action: its first climax at rehearsal figure 29 comes with a *coup de théâtre* that reveals Birnam wood;[6] the reestablishment of the tonic (a passage thick with strettos) comes with Macduff's challenge to Macbeth, "Carnefice de' figli miei," and it turns to the minor as he reveals that he was not "of woman born." That climactic moment, on an internal tonic pedal, is followed by cries of distress from the female chorus, and the sounds of warfare die away over another tonic pedal. The fugal writing is not exactly regular: the exposition, instead of swinging to and fro between tonic and dominant, modulates widely to suggest the violence and energy of the scene. In the closing section, subject and countersubject are separated out as quasi-symphonic motifs and worked antiphonally in a purely harmonic-rhythmic texture.

Almost all Verdi's operas make use of stage music: marching armies are accompanied by military bands; religious ceremonies by organs (real or imitated); scenes of revelry have dance bands in attendance. Obviously such episodes are related to the "sounding décor" already remarked on in this essay. But they are also important in the interaction of the two synchronous time scales on which the art of opera had always depended: real time (the pace of the words and actions in a recitative, for example) and a kind of interior or psychological or suspended time (represented by an aria or duet).

In principle, stage music represents real time: the "real" march of an occupying army; the "real" ritual unfolding of a religious ceremony. But real time is accommodated without any lowering of the stylistic level from "full" to "half" music such as recitative had usually caused, and the coordination of real and interior time is managed with growing sophistication.[7] To observe that the *introduzione* of *La traviata* occupies something like two thirds of the first act (the rest is taken up by Violetta's *scena ed aria*) is to observe its almost total avoidance of recitative. Verdi achieves an unbroken musico-dramatic continuity, and the medium of that continuity is stage music: partly real stage music played by a backstage band (for the real dancing), partly a stylized evocation of a band by orchestral wind and brass (for the more informal partying). The whole scene is structured as a huge block of music in triple time (the dialogue of the protagonists), framed in sections in duple time (the social context in which the dialogue takes place).[8]

Instead of being designed in the customary *cantabile–cabaletta* fashion, the Alfredo-Violetta duet forms the waltz-like core of the *introduzione*, part *brindisi*, part genuine *valzer-duetto* with stage band. The *cantabile* of the duet, "Un dì felice, eterea," functions as a trio to the waltz, the rhythms of which continue, as it were in the subconscious, until they are finally obliterated in the cadenza. When the waltz proper resumes after the duet, the voices for a time resume a *parlando* manner. But in the closing bars, as the pizzicato strings of the orchestra are added to the waltz of the stage band, the "realistic" conversation gradually gives way to an outpouring of Alfredo's love, and the parallel worlds of real and psychological time are superimposed.

Besides the frequent use of dance as an integral part of the dramatic plot, several operas contain full-fledged ballet music: the French grand operas composed for Paris (*Jérusalem*, 1847; *Les vêpres siciliennes*, 1855; *Don Carlos*, 1867) and a number of operas which enjoyed particularly important revivals in Paris (*Il trovatore/Le trouvère*, 1857; *Macbeth* II, 1865; *Otello*, 1894). Ballet music forms an integral part of *Aida*, in effect an Italian grand opera.

The ballet music in *Les vêpres siciliennes* is not confined to the Act III *divertissement*, a depiction of the four seasons, but spreads itself into other parts of the score. Most importantly, the Act II finale is built, not round the customary *cantabile–stretta* pairing, but round a pair of dances, *tarantella* and *barcarolle*. Verdi gave much thought to how he could make the music typically Sicilian, seeking from his Neapolitan friend De Sanctis and the publisher Cottrau information about Sicilian popular festivals and traditional music. He was unimpressed by the specimens sent him, but later, as the opera was nearing completion, returned to the topic: "I should like a real *siciliana*... a song of the people, not a song made up by one of your composers; the most beautiful and the most characteristic one there is." When it materialized, this too disappointed him as "nothing outstandingly characteristic," and in the end he decided to distill from his unsatisfactory but somehow suggestive impressions of the repertory what Conati calls a "siciliana inventata."[9] Summer harvests the sheaves of corn; she begins to dance with her companions, but is soon overcome by the heat. The delicious languor of this opening movement of the third *ballabile* moved the critic of *La France musicale* to flights of rare eloquence: "Oh! this melody! It languishes, yields, swoons, it breathes all the softness of the siesta, all the sensual pleasures of the hot countries... the doves of Engadi cooed it to the Sunamite, when she swooned for love on the mountain of spices; Armide taught it to her enchantress-birds to bewitch Renaud; the satyrs of temptation played it on their pipes to the desert fathers, when they rolled themselves in the sand, thinking of the women of Rome and Alexandria."[10]

Historically what most distinguished the ballet music in *Les vêpres siciliennes* was the fact that it linked the classical French *ballet d'action* and the new Italian *danse aérienne* on points; it was performed half by French artists (Winter, Summer), half by Italian (the rest).[11] Winter contains some of Verdi's most startlingly graphic mime music: for shivering with cold, for striking fire from rock, and for the "sliding steps" of the 6/8 Allegro giusto.[12] In such passages Verdi fashioned new resources for his musical language that would enable him, in the revised *Macbeth*, to move easily backward and forward between the worlds of sung spectacle and danced spectacle.

The ballets of *Jérusalem* and *Les vêpres siciliennes* remained less than fully integral parts of the opera: in Italian revivals they could be, and regularly were, omitted. With *Macbeth* II there was no such option. When it was performed in Italy, it had to be done "without cutting or adding a note. The ballet, which is important, would have to be put on as well."[13] The explanation for this new attitude is that the ballet is based on "antimasques" of singing and dancing witches added to Shakespeare's own *Macbeth* early in the seventeenth century and therefore, from Verdi's perspective, as authentically Shakespearian as anything else in the play.

One distinctive dramatic quality of these antimasques is the differentiation between the dancing witches ("Double, double toil and trouble; / Fire burn and cauldron bubble") and the severe Hecate who presides over them. It is this separation that Verdi reinforces by writing a ballet score in which the principal character does not dance. "The appearance of Hecate... interrupts all those devilish dances and gives way to a calm and severe *adagio*. I don't need to tell you that Hecate should never dance, but only assume poses."[14] The music has a remarkable structure that reinforces its remarkable dramatic function: two dance movements in E minor, the one a wonderfully macabre rondo, its principal theme played by cornets and trombones, the other an "infernal" waltz, enclose a central movement in B flat major which is devoted to dramatic mime.[15] This *mimodramma* is itself in an entirely symmetrical form: A B C D C′ B A. It begins and ends with inchoate rumblings, flickerings, and crashes on diminished-seventh harmony (A) – in short, with storm music – for the appearance and disappearance of Hecate; within those passages come two statements of a flowing but grave series of string harmonies in Verdi's ripest 1860s style (B) as the witches pay their respects to Hecate. At the core of the scene is a ternary movement (C D C′), evidently conceived as a mimed parallel to Hecate's speeches in Shakespeare's III, v, and IV, i. The central minor key episode, for example, accompanies an inspection of the contents of the cauldron, while the grandiose restatement of the principal *cantabile* theme at rehearsal figure 16 marks the point where Hecate "announces that the king (Macbeth) will be coming to interrogate them about his destiny," and the flute obbligato that suddenly breaks out ten measures later signifies that "if the visions overwhelm too much his senses, [they] must invoke the spirits of air to reawaken and reinvigorate him." The scene "[strains] to breaking point the semantics of nineteenth-century ballet."[16]

Deeply experienced in the actualities of operatic performance, Verdi did not compose his music simply as an expression of the inner life of his characters. In his mind's eye he saw the drama unfolding on an ideal imaginary stage. In addition to the words the librettist gives the characters to sing and the steps the choreographer gives them to dance, their movements and gestures are captured in tiny instrumental interludes, often no more than a single motif. Such moments are conspicuous in Verdi's first Parisian opera, *Jérusalem*, and thereafter remain an integral element. When a *disposizione scenica* survives to amplify the particulars noted in the vocal score – as it does, for example, for *Simon Boccanegra* II – we can see that each and every stage action is composed into the score. In the prologue, at the close of the first conversation between Pietro and Paolo, there is a four-measure instrumental interlude to accompany Pietro's departure; a moment later "at the beginning of the *più mosso* Paolo, hearing footsteps, moves a little to the right and looks toward the back. Boccanegra enters quickly."[17] At the end of the conversation between Boccanegra and Paolo "the latter hears a distant noise"; even this little pantomime – for we must imagine Paolo gesturing "listen, someone is coming" – has its own fragment of instrumental music. At rehearsal letter E there is a relatively extended prelude to the next scene, vividly pantomimic, sharply articulated into several balanced phrases to accommodate the slow entrance, "a few at a time," of "sailors, artisans, citizens, forming groups of six to eight persons; some go forward to meet friends, shaking hands and seemingly asking for news…then little by little they gather in the centre of the square." Such instrumentally accompanied pantomimes continue throughout the opera. But they scarcely merit further discussion, beyond remarking that they exist, that they have no independent formal life of their own, and that they shed much light on Verdi's aesthetics of opera (especially taken in conjunction with the *disposizioni sceniche* and with the striking lack of stage movement recorded there during arias and ensembles). Verdi's operas consist in part of recitative, which is to be performed in as lifelike a way as possible, in part of pantomime, which needs to be carefully coordinated with the music, and in part of song. And when song is in the ascendant, stage action is virtually suspended.

One last matter warrants mention: the technique known as *parlante* can hardly be described as instrumental music pure and simple, but the orchestra does play the dominant role in some respects. A quasi-naturalistic declamation, commonly a dialogue, is set against statements, restatements, interludes, variations, and developments of an orchestral theme. Pioneered by the *opera buffa* masters of the late eighteenth century, the technique is commonly used in *tempi d'attacco* and *tempi di mezzo*. Verdi too began to practice *parlante* systematically in his own solitary *opera buffa*, the ill-fated *Un giorno di regno*, and he composed his first masterly example in the *tempo d'attacco* of the Abigaille-Nabucco duet in *Nabucco*. Thereafter he used it in a remarkable range of dramatic circumstances and pressed into service a remarkable variety of orchestral/instrumental backgrounds, quite often, as in the Act II finale of *La traviata*, in large-scale ensembles and on a very generous scale.[18] It is, however, to *Falstaff* that one must turn to observe *parlante* at its most refined, and woven most intricately into the texture of the score. A brief examination of some aspects of the opening scene of Act II will help draw together most of the strands of this essay.

When the curtain goes up at m. 15, Verdi begins what sounds as if it is to be the answering phrase to the lively, but repetitiously formal unison theme played as a miniature prelude to start the act. But exigencies of situation, character, comedy, and sheer musical invention transform it into something far more than a mere answering phrase: its *mf* unison opening is foreshortened; it suddenly sprouts lightly shifting harmonies; it is extended, not quite in sequence, but rather in fanciful variants on the *idea* of sequence. The same theme recurs in a further variant as Bardolfo begs leave to introduce Quickly. But instead of being highlighted in the manner of a *parlante*, it sinks away to become little more than a pattering on the surface of the chords that support his recitative. At rehearsal figure 2 the theme – at least its essential rhythmic character – is provided with a decisive final cadence for Bardolfo's exit. When it is repeated, with varied harmony, for his return with Quickly, a countermelody that appears at first sight to be nothing more than a resumption of the vigorous movement of the prelude is in fact – to remind us of the purpose of Quickly's visit – a scarcely disguised version of

Example 9.3 Verdi, *Falstaff*, II, i, related motifs

(a)

(b)

(c)

the orchestral theme that had framed the scene of the wives' conspiracy in Act I, scene ii.

Up to rehearsal figure 3 the Falstaff-Quickly scene is surely intended to sound like a minuet. But the thematic substratum of the minuet is not genuine instrumental dance music; instead it is provided by two deliciously witty examples of *parola scenica* ("Reverenza" and "Buon giorno, buona

Example 9.3 (continued)
(d)

(e)

donna"). The start of the scene with "Fontana" (figure 9 onwards) likewise begins with minuet-like courtesies. Here, however, the orchestral development arises not from *parola scenica* but from the equally characteristic Verdian habit of setting to music stage movement and gesture: a deep bow on either side. As far as figure 10 the music is a kind of *parlante*; but in the way that is so typical of *Falstaff*, it is a *parlante* without any of the old repetitions and transposed variants of the initial idea. Instead it unfolds as a long, spacious, single theme, contained and decorous, but dark with suppressed passion.

Another instrumental flowering springs from the "dalle due alle tre" motif at figure 4 (see example 9.3, a). In this case the *parola scenica* is the climactic cadential statement of an instrumental figure that has been latent in the texture for seven measures, from "Alice sta in grande agitazione d'amor per voi" (see example 9.3, b). From that turning point in the plot onward, it is rarely long absent, lurking in the rhythmic design of "Caro Sir John"; returning to the open four measures before figure 18 (see example 9.3, c); thereafter providing the motif of the orchestral accompaniment of the Agitato at "Quel tanghero, vedrai" (see example 9.3, d); ominously darkened in Ford's monologue at "L'ora è fissata" (see example 9.3, e).

One last *parlante* accompanies Falstaff's return to the stage, dressed to kill, at m. 13 of figure 24, a theme of witty and exquisite gracefulness, redolent of ballet in the sheer physical presence with which it moves. True to the comic formality of the episode, it is laid out in the most old-fashioned aria manner: *a a′ b b′ a″* Coda. The scene ends with a final orchestral idea, the return of the ritornello that had framed "Va, vecchio John" earlier in the act.

By the time of *Falstaff*, the traditional forms of Italian opera had been dissolved into a musically continuous fluidity in which few familiar landmarks remained. Instrumental music suffers the same fate as aria, ensemble, and chorus: it is no longer a simple matter to define its function, or even to determine unequivocally which sections of the score can sensibly be regarded as instrumental music. Under these circumstances *parlante* becomes one of Verdi's most prized resources, the medium in which his hard-won orchestral sophistication and his inexhaustible lyrical inventiveness can be most wittily, beguilingly, and movingly blended.

10 Verdi's non-operatic works

ROBERTA MONTEMORRA MARVIN

Though primarily an opera composer, Verdi also wrote a number of works in other genres. Only one of these, the *Messa da Requiem*, has assumed a significant place in the repertory. The remaining solo songs, instrumental music, and choral works, more-or-less ignored and virtually forgotten, are infrequently performed and have not been broadly discussed in print. Consequently, this chapter will provide an overview of their history, style, and sources.

Beginning as a young boy in Busseto, Verdi composed a variety of non-operatic works, both sacred and secular. In mid-career he attested to the diversity of his youthful compositional activities:

> From the age of thirteen to the age of eighteen (the time when I went to study counterpoint in Milan) I wrote a hodgepodge of pieces: hundreds of marches for band, perhaps just as many small *sinfonie* that were played in church, in the theatre, and at concerts; five or six concertos and variations for piano, which I myself played in concerts; several serenades, cantatas (arias, a lot of duets, trios), and diverse pieces for church, of which I remember only a *Stabat mater*. In the three years I was in Milan I wrote very few free compositions: two *sinfonie* which were performed in a private concert in the Contrada degli Orefici though I do not remember in whose house, a cantata which was performed at the home of Count Renato Borromeo, and a variety of pieces, most of them comic ones, which the *maestro* [Lavigna] had me write as exercises and which were not even orchestrated. After returning to my hometown I began to write marches, *sinfonie*, vocal pieces, etc., an *entire Mass* and an *entire Vesper service*, three or four *Tantum ergo* and other sacred pieces that I do not remember. Among the vocal pieces there were three-voice choruses from Manzoni's tragedies, and *Il cinque maggio* for solo voice. Everything is lost, and that is just as well, with the exception of a few *sinfonie* that they still play here [Busseto], but which I never again wish to hear, and the *Inni di Manzoni* which I have kept.[1]

Verdi wrote many of his earliest works for the Società Filarmonica in Busseto; others he probably composed for Pietro Massini's Società dei Filarmonici in Milan. Compositions for Busseto would have furnished music suitable in instrumentation, level of difficulty, and purpose for various civic, social, and religious functions, while the works composed in Milan would no doubt have served both artistic and commercial purposes, bringing the young composer before the public and promoting him in cultural circles. As Verdi's career progressed, however, the necessity to compose non-operatic music diminished. Thus, with the exception of the sacred choral compositions, the majority of these works responded to specific social, political, or cultural obligations more than to artistic whim, necessity, or opportunity.

By comparison with the prestige it accorded to opera, nineteenth-century Italy neither nurtured nor encouraged instrumental music and choral works, and solo song, while popular, remained of secondary importance. Nonetheless, musical traditions existed for these genres, and Verdi's secular and sacred works reflect the stylistic tendencies of the era while bearing his personal imprint. This chapter discusses the historical context and musical profile of many of Verdi's extant non-operatic compositions in three general categories: songs or *liriche da camera*, instrumental music, and choral compositions.

Songs and other vocal music

Written under various generic titles including "romanza," "arietta," and "lirica," and any number of specific names such as "barcarolle" and "stornello," Italian songs or *liriche da camera* in the Ottocento assumed a wide range of forms and characters from miniature operatic *scene* to brief folk-like settings. Musicians of both greater and lesser fame composed such works, which manifested the close marriage of text and music so highly valued in opera. Although Verdi's most concentrated output of songs appeared during the first decade of his career, the genre occupied him at other times as well.

An "aria" titled "Io la vidi" for two tenors and orchestra, believed to date from ca.1836, is, in all probability, the earliest surviving vocal work by Verdi.[2] The text is from Act I, scene iii, of *Il solitario di Eloisa* by Calisto Bassi, written originally for Stefano Pavesi in 1826. Much like an operatic *scena*, the piece opens with a lyrical Andante in E flat major, followed by an Allegro that serves as a lengthy transition to the second lyrical section also in E flat major, marked "Meno mosso." The vocal range is moderate, though at times the tessitura seems low for the tenor voice. Commentators have noted that this aria anticipates the style of Verdi's early operas in its clearly delineated phrasing and simple developmental techniques.

Verdi's earliest published work is a set of six *romanze* for solo voice with piano accompaniment, printed in Milan by Giovanni Canti in 1838 and

Example 10.1a Verdi, *Sei romanze* (1838), "In solitaria stanza"

Sal - va - te, o Dei pie - to - - si,

Example 10.1b Verdi, *Il trovatore*, I, 3, "Tacea la notte placida" (Leonora)

gli ac - cor - di d'un li - u - - to,

dedicated to Count Pietro Favagrossa. Four are settings of verse written by minor Italian poets (about whom little is known), while two use translations of poetry by Goethe:

1 Non t'accostare all'urna (Jacopo Vittorelli, 1749–1835)
2 More, Elisa, lo stanco poeta (Tomaso Bianchi)
3 In solitaria stanza (Vittorelli)
4 Nell'orror di notte oscura (Carlo Angiolini)
5 Perduta ho la pace (translation by Luigi Balestra, 1808–63, of Johann Wolfgang von Goethe's "Meine Ruh' ist hin")
6 Deh, pietoso, oh addolorata (translation by Balestra of Goethe's "Ach neige, Du Schmerzensreiche")

In each of these songs, the interest lies primarily in the melody, while the accompaniment is formulaic, consisting mostly of arpeggiated figures, punctuating chords, and melodic doublings. Designs range from simple strophic settings to through-composed sectional forms. All of the songs exhibit a competent handling of metrical accentuation resulting in natural declamation patterns. Budden (among others) has pointed out a number of traits in these songs that foreshadow the style of Verdi's operas; for example, in "Deh, pietoso, oh addolorata" the "ordered chaos of ideas" following the opening melody, which resembles the music Verdi wrote to portray Nabucco's madness; and in "In solitaria stanza" the triplet accompanimental rhythm and regular phrase lengths that are characteristic of the early works as well as a specific phrase that anticipates *Il trovatore* (see examples 10.1a and b).[3]

In the following year (1839) Canti published three more of Verdi's vocal works: "Notturno – Guarda che bianca luna," for soprano, tenor, bass, flute obbligato, and piano, with poetry by Vittorelli and a dedication (added by the publisher) to the tenor Cesare Sangiorgi; "L'esule" for solo voice and piano on verse by Temistocle Solera, dedicated to Pietro Minoia; and "La seduzione" for bass and piano with text by Luigi Balestra, also dedicated to

Minoia.[4] "Notturno" proceeds homophonically, for the most part, with its three voices closely spaced. Over the lyrical vocal melody the flute plays an obbligato evoking the nightingale.[5] "La seduzione" is a through-composed song with simple piano accompaniment, its vocal line resembling an early Verdian operatic *cantabile* melody. "L'esule," on the other hand, takes the form of an operatic *scena* comprising an opening piano prelude, recitative, slow movement, *tempo di mezzo*, and *cabaletta*. In contrast to the other two songs, the accompaniment is orchestrally conceived in both figuration and sonority, and the melody aptly expresses the exile's nostalgia for the homeland. Publication of these songs would have furnished a means for the young musician to position himself before the Milanese public as a professional composer while he was composing *Oberto, conte di San Bonifacio* in 1838 and 1839.

Following the success of *Nabucco* in 1842, Verdi was a sought-after guest in fashionable *salotti* both in Milan and in the cities he traveled to for the premieres of his operas. His attendance at these gatherings during the early and mid-1840s provided occasions for him to compose and dedicate music as gifts to the ladies of society and other prominent citizens. One song, dating from May 6, 1842, "Che i bei dì m'adduce ancora," surely originated this way. A Largo in 6/8 (E minor/major), setting Goethe's "Erste Verlust" in a translation believed to have been made by Balestra, it was found in the musical album of Countess Sofia de' Medici, Marchesa di Marignano.[6] Another song "Cupo è il sepolcro e mutolo" survives as an album leaf which belonged to Count Lodovico Belgioioso.[7] Dated Milan, July 7, 1843, and dedicated to the Count, the piece sets poetry by an unnamed author, though it is likely by Andrea Maffei (1798–1885).[8] The song opens with a nine-measure Grave followed by a six-measure recitative and concludes with a twenty-three-measure Largo in common time (A flat major) with an arpeggiated accompaniment; the vocal line in measures 21–27 is strikingly similar to a passage from the finale of *Ernani* (see examples 10.2a and b).

Two songs from 1844 were also written as album leaves. While in Rome for the premiere of *I due Foscari*, Verdi composed "È la vita un mar d'affanni," setting verse by an unidentified poet.[9] Dated November 5, 1844, the short (thirteen-measure), light-hearted piece for soprano and piano is preserved in an album of the daughters of the librettist Jacopo Ferretti.[10] Another song, "Era bella ancor più bella," a thirteen-measure Andantino in 6/8, bears the same date. Little is known about the song, though it was probably composed for a similar purpose.

In 1845 Verdi published a second set of six *romanze* with piano accompaniment, issued by Francesco Lucca in Milan.[11] The set consists of:

Example 10.2a Verdi, "Cupo è il sepolcro e mutolo" (1843)

Example 10.2b Verdi, *Ernani*, IV, 14, *scena e terzetto finale*

1   Il tramonto (Andrea Maffei)[12]
2   La zingara (Manfredo Maggioni)
3   Ad una stella (Maffei)
4   Lo spazzacamino (Maggioni)
5   Il mistero (Felice Romani)
6   Brindisi (Maffei)[13]

By the time he composed these pieces, Verdi had written several operas, and the songs indeed bear the marks of a composer who had gained experience in text setting and in shaping dramatic music. In comparison to the 1838 *romanze* the accompaniments to these songs are more pianistic, more varied within each song, and at times more independent of the melody; and the formal designs tend to take into account the "story" of the text.

Verdi wrote no further sets of songs after 1845, but he continued to compose individual melodies for specific occasions. "Il poveretto," issued by Lucca in 1847, sets verse by Maggioni, staff librettist at the Royal Italian Opera in London at the time.[14] In Italy the song was issued free to subscribers to Lucca's journal *L'Italia musicale*.[15] And in France it was published by the Escudiers (in 1848) with French text as "Le pauvre" in an album containing six songs by different composers (*Les astres*), which was distributed to subscribers to the publisher's journal *La France musicale*.[16] In 1849 Escudier issued another song titled "L'abandonnée" (with text by either Léon or Marie Escudier, or both), also as a musical supplement to *La France musicale*.[17] That the song was presumably composed for Giuseppina Strepponi is especially significant since it dates from the time when she and

Verdi began living together in Paris. The vocal line is characterized by florid writing with abundant *fioriture* and a wide pitch range, similar to the music Verdi composed for Abigaille in *Nabucco*, a role Strepponi created. Budden proposed that the song was intended as an exercise for Giuseppina's singing pupils.[18]

While in Trieste for the premiere of *Stiffelio* the following year (1850), Verdi, Piave, and Ricordi were guests at the villa of the tenor Giovanni Severi. During this time Verdi composed a lullaby on a text by Piave, "Al tuo bambino (Fiorellin che sorgi appena)," for the birth of Severi's son Gabriele.[19] A simple nineteen-measure Allegretto in 6/8, notated in the tenor clef, it was dated by the composer November 19, 1850. Verdi's Neapolitan visit in 1858 resulted in his composing at least two songs in tribute to colleagues. On April 20 he dedicated a song to the Neapolitan painter and caricaturist Melchiorre Delfico (1825–95). For the twenty-two-measure song, "Sgombra, o gentil," Verdi set the third strophe of the concluding chorus from Act IV, scene i, of Manzoni's *Adelchi* (the only surviving music by Verdi on this poet's verse).[20] In the autumn Verdi set "La preghiera del poeta" by the Neapolitan poet Nicola Sole (1821–59) and presented it to him as a memento.[21]

In the 1860s, in the wake of Italian independence and unification, nationalistic tendencies in music increased, among them adoption of traits from folk music. One manifestation of this technique can be found in musical settings of poems known as *stornelli*. A well-known form in folk poetry (and song), the *stornello* is characterized by vivid emotional expression, rustic language, and imagery and metaphors derived from everyday, often amorous, subjects. Authentic poems were gathered from the countryside, transcribed, and published in collections during the Ottocento; in addition, poets wrote their own texts based on folk models, either adopting traditional love themes or devising satirical or political topics.

Verdi composed two *stornelli*: "Il brigidino" (1861) and "Tu dici che non m'ami" (1869). He supposedly wrote the first of these pieces, a setting of one of Francesco Dall'Ongaro's "Stornelli politici" from his *Stornelli italiani* (a volume Verdi had recently received as a gift), shortly after he was appointed to the newly formed Italian parliament. The composer gave the song to Giacomo Piroli (as a gift for his daughter), who in January 1863 sent it to Giulio Cesare Ferrarini, director of the Conservatory in Parma (in response to the latter's request for a copy of it from Verdi).[22] Its first official performance is believed to have been given in that city by Isabella Galletti-Gianoli on February 24, 1863, in the Camera di San Paolo.[23] Despite the political undertones and patriotic flavor of the text, the music retains a lighthearted and serene character, typical of the composed *stornelli* of the era. Verdi again sought out a *stornello* in 1869 for his contribution to a volume of songs organized on his initiative and published by Ricordi for the benefit of the librettist Piave, who had suffered a stroke two years previously.[24] He found an appropriate text in Giuseppe Tigri's *Canti popolari toscani*, which he had received from Piroli in 1868. Verdi set the original Tuscan folk poem strophically with slight variations to accommodate the text; each strophe contains phrases of varying lengths imparting an improvisatory flavor.

Late in his career, Verdi composed a number of sacred works, including two for solo voice.[25] In 1880 he wrote an *Ave Maria* on what he believed to be a translation by Dante, for soprano and small string ensemble (two each of first and second violins and violas and four cellos *divisi*). Traditional in style, the song opens with a string introduction followed by chant-like vocal declamation on a single pitch in the minor key. It gradually becomes more lyrical and turns to the major key, eventually returning to the minor; and the strings close the piece as a final response to the prayer. The design is strikingly similar to the "Ave Maria" Verdi would write in *Otello* some years later.[26] (The song was intended as a companion to the *Pater noster*, discussed below.) Verdi's last known solo song was also a sacred one. The *preghiera*, "Pietà, Signor," dating from 1894, sets a text by Arrigo Boito. It served as Verdi's contribution to a publication titled *Fata Morgana*, issued to aid victims of earthquakes that occurred on November 16 of that year in Sicily and Calabria.[27]

Although Verdi's song output is small, it nonetheless constitutes a representative sampling of the types of serious and not-so-serious settings of poetry composed in mid-nineteenth-century Italy. These diverse works satisfied a variety of purposes for Verdi, helping him to ascend the commercial ladder, appease his "fans," honor his colleagues, and satisfy his own artistic whim.

Instrumental music

In the early nineteenth century original compositions for various instrumental ensembles or for piano were not nearly so common in Italy as arrangements of operatic music heard in transcriptions, fantasies, variations, and the like. Although the instrumental tradition was not an especially strong one, purely instrumental music by native Italian composers grew (albeit slowly) in quantity and in popularity. The genre eventually experienced a renaissance in Italy in the 1860s and 1870s, when the dissemination of and interest in German music, a by-product of the progressive cultural ideology of the time, took root in major Italian cultural centers.

Verdi composed instrumental works for orchestra, piano, and chamber ensembles throughout his life. Although he seems to have written a number of marches, *sinfonie*, and other types of instrumental works during his early years in Busseto, most of the extant instrumental music dates from the latter part of his career. However, a few early works have survived.

One early orchestral work, recently recovered, is a Sinfonia in D major that may date from the early 1830s (or before). It is a one-movement composition scored for a full complement of strings, pairs of woodwinds, horns, and trumpets, three trombones, and timpani. It begins with a sixteen-measure Maestoso introduction followed by a 274-measure Allegro constructed on sonata principles; its formal structure is strikingly similar in many respects to the archetypal Rossinian overture. The Sinfonia was never published during Verdi's lifetime, and there is no definitive record of a performance, although it is possible that the work was performed in Busseto or in Milan during the mid-1830s.[28] Two other works are extant: a Sinfonia in A major for orchestra and an Adagio for trumpet and orchestra.

While in Rome in 1844, Verdi composed not only songs for album leaves but also at least one piano piece for this purpose. His *Romanza senza parole*, also titled *Cielo d'Italia*, for solo piano dates from the time of the production of *I due Foscari* and is found in an album of the Princess Torlonia, Marchesa di Capranica. It was published in a collection issued by Canti in 1865 titled *Gioie e sospiri*.[29] Another solo piano work by Verdi, a *Walzer* in F major, may date from 1859.[30]

With the rise in popularity of German instrumental music in Italy in the latter half of the nineteenth century, string quartet societies began forming in major Italian cities. Perhaps influenced or scandalized by this trend, Verdi composed the String Quartet in E minor, his only known instrumental chamber composition. He composed the work in Naples in 1873 and arranged an informal, private first performance in his apartment. Although he claimed to attach little importance to his quartet and initially had no intention of publishing it, he allowed a public performance and eventually agreed to its execution by string orchestra. The work consists of four movements: Allegro, Andantino, Prestissimo, and Allegro assai mosso (Scherzo-Fuga). All four movements are written in a clearly idiomatic instrumental language. Indeed, they seem almost self-consciously instrumental in nature, as if Verdi had made a calculated effort to show that he could write music other than operas. The first movement moves quickly from one idea to another, alternating between homophonic and imitative textures, yet provides no textural or figurative differentiation of parts. The second movement develops its lengthy spun-out theme in a rondo-like pattern. Its harmonic adventurousness reflects Verdi's adroitness at manipulating keys to dramatic purpose. The third movement, a scherzo in form though not in title, has an almost Haydnesque style, especially in its folk-like theme played by solo cello in the contrasting middle section. The fourth movement, a fugue parody ("Scherzo-Fuga"), illustrates Verdi's mastery of fugal writing, the result of the rigorous contrapuntal study he had pursued in Milan under Vincenzo Lavigna.[31] Despite the idiomatic writing in the String Quartet, Verdi's lack of experience with "symphonic" developmental techniques is evident. Moreover, several writers have expressed the opinion that for Verdi the composition of this work may, in some way, have been a reaction against the infiltration into Italian music of the Teutonic tradition, a phenomenon against which he often railed during the latter part of his career.

Choral works

In Ottocento Italy sacred music flourished in provincial settings and was composed by local composers, though most of the major composers also made significant contributions to the genre. Much of this music was intended for religious services, but there were notable exceptions written specifically for concert performance. Verdi composed both sacred and secular choral works, the sacred works being far more important and better known. His sacred compositions span his entire career, from the surviving *Tantum ergo* (ca.1836) to the *Pezzi sacri* (1898).

Verdi composed a number of pieces as a youth in Busseto, including *I deliri di Saul* (1828), a cantata for baritone and orchestra on a text by Vittorio Alfieri, *Le lamentazioni di Geremia* (1829) for chorus, a *Stabat mater*, a Vesper service, and other *Tantum ergo* settings. Unfortunately, these works have been lost. Recently, however, a *Messa di Gloria* from the composer's youth was recovered. This work, believed to date from ca.1833, consists of a Kyrie and a Gloria (currently missing two sections), both of which were begun by Verdi's teacher Ferdinando Provesi and completed by Verdi.[32] Prior to the recovery of this Mass, the aforementioned *Tantum ergo* (in G major) for tenor and orchestra (with alternative organ accompaniment) was long known as Verdi's earliest extant sacred work. Its lengthy orchestral prelude is followed by a slow section which begins in recitative-like style and gradually takes on a lyrical character. This flows into an Allegro which is *cabaletta*-like in structure and flavor with its florid, wide-ranging tenor solo.

Although Verdi wrote religious music in many of his operas, he did not return to it as an independent genre until 1869 when he composed the "Libera me" movement for the collaborative *Messa da Requiem* to

honor Rossini (which was not performed as planned).³³ The "Libera me"
served as the basis for his *Messa da Requiem per l'anniversario della morte
di Manzoni* written in 1873–74, through which Verdi's sacred music is
best known today. The Requiem is scored for soprano, mezzo-soprano,
tenor, and bass soloists, chorus, and orchestra and consists of the following
movements:

1 "Requiem [Introit] e Kyrie," in two linked sections: the first is an ABA design with
   the antiphon "Requiem aeternam" surrounding the psalm verse; the second opens
   with a soloistic declamation of "Kyrie" and "Christe" in alternation followed by
   four sections ("Kyrie," "Christe," "Kyrie," "Christe").
2 "Dies irae," in ten sections: "Dies irae," "Tuba mirum," "Mors stupebit" (bass solo),
   "Liber scriptus" (mezzo-soprano solo in the definitive version, originally a four-
   part choral fugue), "Quid sum miser" (soprano, mezzo-soprano, and tenor trio),
   "Rex tremendae majestatis," "Recordare" (soprano and mezzo-soprano duet),
   "Ingemisco" (tenor solo), "Confutatis maledictis" (bass solo), and "Lacrymosa."
3 "Offertorio," in ABCBA' design.
4 "Sanctus," a fugue for double chorus.
5 "Agnus Dei," a theme and variations with coda, alternating soloists (soprano and
   mezzo-soprano in octaves with theme fragments) with choral responses.
6 "Lux aeterna," soloists and orchestra, in the design ABCB'DD'D"A'.
7 "Libera me," in five sections: a recitative-like solo for soprano, a choral passage
   including music from the "Dies irae" movement, an unaccompanied section for
   soprano solo and chorus with a reprise of the "Requiem aeternam" antiphon, a
   transition to the fugue for soprano solo and orchestra, and a closing fugue for
   soprano solo, chorus, and orchestra.³⁴

Verdi borrowed from himself twice in this work, in the "Libera me" and
in the "Lacrymosa" section of the "Dies irae." For the latter Verdi crafted
the primary melody from a duet he had composed for *Don Carlos* but
had suppressed before the 1867 premiere of the opera in Paris. In adapting it to his purposes in the Requiem, he revised it to accommodate the
new text, improve voice-leading, and emphasize cadences.³⁵ In recycling
the 1869 "Libera me," Verdi also made revisions, though none radical.
His alterations involved transposition, cadential placement, phrase expansion, redistribution of performing forces, modified voicing, and some new
music.³⁶ Moreover, he not only adopted the movement as a whole but also
appropriated passages from it for the "Requiem aeternam" and "Dies irae"
movements.

The Requiem had its first performance on May 22, 1874, in the church of
San Marco in Milan with soloists Teresa Stolz (soprano, the first Aida), Maria
Waldmann (mezzo-soprano, the first Amneris), Giuseppe Capponi (tenor),
and Ormondo Maini (bass); Verdi conducted. Although the Requiem was
first performed as part of a liturgical service, it soon moved to concert

halls and opera houses throughout Europe. Shortly after its premiere Verdi conducted it at La Scala in Milan, and on November 17, 1874, Verdi's former student Emanuele Muzio directed the authorized United States premiere at the American Academy of Music in New York. The version of the *Messa da Requiem* performed in these locations was the same as that heard today with a single exception. The "Liber scriptus" section of the "Dies irae," originally a fugue for four-part chorus and orchestra, was rewritten by Verdi for the London performance of 1875 (Albert Hall, May 15) as a mezzo-soprano solo that became the definitive version. Although by the end of 1875 the work had been heard in four Italian cities, elsewhere in Europe, and as far away as Argentina, Egypt, and the United States, the number of performances declined quickly in the following years.[37] It seems to have become established in the repertory no earlier than the 1930s.[38]

Some controversy concerning the "genre" of the Requiem has surrounded the work from its earliest years. Numerous writers have called attention to the "operatic," "dramatic," and "theatrical" qualities of the music. But the musical style of the Requiem differs in significant ways from Verdi's operas, as the composer himself implied when he commented on the manner in which the work must be performed: "one must not sing this Mass as one sings an opera, and therefore the *coloriti* [phrasing, attacks, dynamics] that may be good for the theatre will not be to my liking at all."[39] Above all, the Requiem has a "character," perhaps resulting in part from the musical systems imparting coherence to the work as a whole, as well as through reprises of music from the "Requiem aeternam" and "Dies irae" movements, subtle thematic connections within and across movements involving intervallic motion, motivic figuration, "harmonic mystification," and even tempo.[40] Verdi's work surely deserves its hallowed position in the sacred music repertory.

During his twilight years Verdi composed other sacred choral works: a *Pater noster* for five-part unaccompanied chorus, paired with an *Ave Maria* for solo voice (discussed above) and the *Pezzi sacri*. The *Pater noster* and the *Ave Maria*, on vernacular translations Verdi attributed to Dante, were completed in 1880. The first performance was given on April 18 of that year in a benefit concert at La Scala with Franco Faccio conducting. As Verdi noted, "My *Pater noster* is written in five parts without accompaniment in the style of Palestrina, of course with modern modulations and harmony, rather perhaps with too many modulations, especially in the beginning. Nevertheless, it is not difficult."[41]

Verdi's final works were the *Pezzi sacri*. Although not originally intended to be performed as a group, they were published together in vocal score in 1898.[42] They comprise the *Laudi alla Vergine Maria*, *Ave Maria*, *Stabat mater*, and *Te Deum*. The *Laudi* for four-part unaccompanied female chorus or four solo voices (SSAA) was completed ca.1890; its title does not originate with Verdi who simply referred to it as a "prayer."[43] Setting a text by Dante from the final canto of the *Paradiso*, it is characterized by a primarily homophonic texture with an occasional imitative phrase and close voicing. The *Ave Maria (sulla scala enigmatica)* for four-part (SATB) unaccompanied chorus was written in 1889 and revised for publication (with the other three pieces) in 1898. It is based on an irregular chromatic scale, apparently originally published as a "puzzle" in Ricordi's *Gazzetta musicale di Milano*, which appears as a slow-moving *cantus firmus* throughout the brief work. (The original version could be considered a contrapuntal exercise of sorts that Verdi may well have written for his personal amusement.) The *Stabat mater* for four-part (SATB) chorus and orchestra was completed in 1896–97. It is an "atmospheric" piece, its varied timbres enriched by unusual voicing, extensive chromaticism, and (at times) almost Puccinian orchestration and harmonic progressions. The *Te Deum* for double (SATB) chorus and orchestra, dating from 1895–96, is equally adventurous in its harmonic language and even more dramatic. It opens with a brief unaccompanied phrase of plainchant and proceeds through a homophonic chant-like passage, gradually building in intensity and exhibiting contrasting textures as well as masterful contrapuntal writing and colorful instrumentation. It is said that Verdi wanted the score to this powerful and highly dramatic *Te Deum* buried with him. Verdi apparently regarded all four of these pieces highly, for he provided numerous performance suggestions.[44]

Verdi also wrote secular choral works, though only the *Inno popolare* (1848) and the *Inno delle nazioni* (1862) appear to have survived. In 1836, however, he composed a *Cantata pel dì natalizio di S. M. Ferdinando Primo Imperatore e Re* for Massini's ensemble in Milan, which was performed on April 19. Only the text, by Count Renato Borromeo, is extant.[45] The *Inno popolare* ("Suona la tromba"), for male (TTB) chorus and piano, sets a text by Goffredo Mameli and remains a popular "tune" in Italy today.[46] The *Inno delle nazioni* (for solo voice, mixed chorus, and orchestra), titled "Cantica" in the autograph, resulted from an official commission for Verdi to compose an instrumental piece (a march) to represent Italy at the London International Exhibition of 1862.[47] Claiming to have been notified by Auber, one of the other contributors to the event, that he was writing a march, Verdi opted instead to compose a texted work, commissioning Boito to write the poetry. The organizers of the exhibition, however, refused to perform a work that was not what they had requested, and the cantata was not performed with the other works composed for the occasion. Instead, Verdi rewrote the original solo tenor part for soprano (the tenor evidently having been prohibited from singing in the piece) and had the work performed at Her Majesty's

Theatre on May 24. Originally intended as a piece of Italian patriotic propaganda, the *Inno delle nazioni* did not remain in the repertory, although it came to the attention of twentieth-century audiences when Arturo Toscanini performed it (again apparently as propaganda) during both World Wars.[48]

Verdi's compositional activities outside the operatic realm do not compare to his accomplishments within it. Nonetheless, throughout his career he produced a small corpus of compositions that, while reflecting his interests and inspirations, as well as the opportunities presented to him, provide us with a broader musical context within which to understand and appreciate more fully his dramatic art.

Since this book went to press, a number of claims have been made concerning the discovery of several other works by Verdi. Of the "new" works, only the following (a few of which have been mentioned in passing here) can be securely attributed to Verdi: Sinfonia in C major (1838), Variazioni per pianoforte (1837, piano part only extant), *Canto di Virginia*, Variazioni per oboe ed orchestra (oboe part by oboist Giacomo Mori), Sinfonia in A major (date unknown), and Adagio for trumpet and orchestra (date unknown). The others await authentication. (I wish to thank Roger Parker for furnishing some of the information about these works.)

PART THREE

Representative operas

11 Ernani: the tenor in crisis

ROSA SOLINAS

In accepting a commission from the Teatro La Fenice, Venice, in 1843, Verdi was breaking faith with La Scala, for which he had composed all his previous operas, and for which he had been approached to provide another for the following season. It proved a decisive departure: leaving aside *Giovanna d'Arco* (1845), arguably no more than a nostalgic gesture, and a revised version of *La forza del destino* (1869), the composer's grand homecoming to Milan would occur only after he felt secure enough to impose his own rules, with the revised *Simon Boccanegra* (1881), *Otello* (1887), and *Falstaff* (1893).[1] Moving to Venice meant more than adjusting to a smaller stage; it called for a kind of personal drama for which there had been no space in works such as *Nabucco* or *I lombardi*. This in turn deprived Verdi of the rich fund of reference associated with that specific theatrical milieu, forcing him to take on the personality, as it were, of a quite different establishment. Indeed, the imprint of La Fenice can be felt at all stages of the genesis of *Ernani*, from censorship of the libretto to the distinctive vocal style of the score.

The success of *Ernani* at its premiere on March 9, 1844 – in spite of the sets not being ready, and the tenor having lost his voice and the soprano her sense of pitch – seemed testimony that the opera would stand on its intrinsic qualities.[2] Confirmation came with its warm reception at many other opera houses, and *Ernani* greatly enhanced Verdi's reputation at the national and international level, establishing it as second only to Donizetti's among Italian opera composers.[3] Verdi's own theatrical instincts can plausibly take most of the credit: if the idea of the subject first came to Count Alvise Francesco (Nani) Mocenigo, director of La Fenice in 1843–44, it was Verdi who, exercising the right to choose his own libretto for the first time, rejected a series of suggestions (including *Catherine Howard*, *Cola di Rienzi*, *I due Foscari*, *The Bride of Abydos*, *King Lear*, *Cromwello*, and *Allan Cameron*) and became enthused only when Victor Hugo's *Hernani* was mentioned.[4] The choice of librettist also worked in his favor: *Ernani* was the first of nine librettos for Verdi by the then inexperienced Francesco Maria Piave.[5] Collaborating with a novice not only gave Verdi the opportunity to impose his own dramaturgical views, as has frequently been suggested, but also obliged him to develop them on his own, having no experienced collaborator to channel his artistic inspiration.[6]

Yet Verdi had to delegate certain responsibilities. Piave, for instance, sought "political approval" from police censors, an unenviable task, for at that time Venice was part of the Austrian Empire and *Hernani* had been considered sufficiently revolutionary to be banned in cities such as Milan.[7] Fortunately, the theatre authorities and director Mocenigo were sufficiently interested in the project (having put so much effort into finding a subject acceptable to Verdi) to send Piave detailed plans for adapting the source in such a way as to circumvent potential objections. This prospectus indicated, among other things, that Ernani should be a contralto, so that the popular and prestigious singer Carolina Vietti could be engaged. The other principals were to be Elvira (soprano), Carlo (tenor), and Silva (baritone), a timbral arrangement that was already rather old-fashioned.[8]

Verdi was so keen on the subject that he agreed at first to everything – only to change most of the original stipulations at a later stage.[9] Finalizing the libretto involved several readings by the authorities, during which Piave's initial poetry changed considerably, as documented in the different drafts; it is harder, though, to assess how readily Verdi abandoned or held on to his most prized ideas. Whether he gave serious thought to the role *en travesti* remains tantalizingly unclear, though he certainly recognized the perils of crossing a powerful *prima donna* (be she soprano or contralto).[10] At one point, he proposed, somewhat disingenuously, that Vietti be given the role of Carlo instead of Ernani, knowing full well that such an idea would be considered disrespectful. Mocenigo's guidelines made the King more honorable than in Hugo's model, free of undignified impulses and properly regal, not a potential vehicle for the eccentricities of a *prima donna*. Whatever Verdi's reasons, this proved to be the pivotal step that led, without lengthy wrangling, to the more up-to-date vocal distribution: tenor, soprano, baritone, and bass. Though Verdi's decisions have been credited to his progressiveness, growing autonomy, and those unfailing instincts, his choices may have been more practical than aesthetic.

Finding one's voice

The right cast seemed, as always, to be of paramount importance to Verdi, so much so that he threatened to break his contract with La Fenice if the premiere was not postponed until the Lent season, when Carlo Guasco would be available for the title role.[11] What might seem a control freak's whim was in fact dictated by exasperation: having discarded the contralto option, finding the tenor for Ernani was proving no easy matter.[12] Domenico Conti, the singer suggested by the theatre, had recently been involved in the notorious fiasco of *I lombardi* at La Fenice on December 26, 1843, and was therefore unlikely to find favor with a Venetian audience that had already proved itself exacting that season. Other composers, though established and popular, had failed to please: Giovanni Pacini's *La fidanzata corsa* had been booed off the stage, almost causing Mocenigo to resign.[13] These circumstances might well account for Verdi's anxiety, recorded in letters such as the following:

> I am writing this poor *Ernani* of mine and I am not unhappy. In spite of my apparent indifference, if it is a fiasco I will dash my brains out: I couldn't stand the idea, the more so as these Venetians are expecting I don't know what.[14]

Guasco, who had been highly successful in the Rossini-Bellini-Donizetti repertory and as Oronte in *I lombardi* at La Scala, seemed to be the only singer who could save the day.[15] Only a few weeks before the premiere, however, Guasco himself tried to get out of his *Ernani* contract, claiming exhaustion from previous performances. Eventually persuaded to reconsider by the threat of a police order, he shouted himself hoarse an hour before the beginning of the first performance, complaining about everything else not being up to his standards.[16]

It is perhaps too reductive to read the progress towards the premiere of *Ernani* as emblematic of the hero's reluctance to come out in full voice, but recognition of the fluid nature of Verdi's reasoning and decision making can provide both a deeper appreciation of musical detail and an insight into the complex and changing institutional world it reflects. Nowhere do the practicalities seem more complex – and more bound up in musical detail – than in the question of the title character's changed vocal type and his resulting identity crisis. The revolutionary potential in the matter of *Ernani* was not merely a political issue with the power to alarm the authorities but crucial to this particular stage in Verdi's career. Getting around the censorship and solving casting problems were only exercises along the way; whether or not the work would survive clearly depended on less tangible – but no less decisive – factors.

A self-centered hero

Ernani could be very briefly summarized as a love story with a vague political background and a tragic final twist. The bandit Ernani, who is actually Duke Don Giovanni d'Aragona on the run from the King, who killed his father, is in love with Elvira, who lives at the palace of her uncle (and fiancé) Don Ruy Gomez de Silva. The King himself, Don Carlo, is also interested in Elvira, and the three men spend half of the opera playing a kind of hide and seek with each other in and around Silva's castle. Eventually, the King takes Elvira away, leaving Ernani Silva's prisoner. Ernani rejects Silva's proposal of a duel and the two join forces in a conspiracy against the King. Silva thus spares Ernani's life, but only on condition that he would kill himself at once were Silva to blow his hunting horn. Don Carlo foils the conspirators, however, becomes Emperor and forgives everybody, including Ernani, giving the young lovers his blessing. But as their marriage is about to be consummated, Ernani hears the fatal horn: as agreed, he kills himself, while Elvira faints.[17]

The general structure is simple and repetitive: the action goes in circles across four acts that make use of similar narrative devices, above all that of a situation suddenly interrupted by a *coup de théâtre* – frequently a revelation of identity. At the beginning of Act I, after a short prelude, a male chorus introduces the tenor Ernani, living in the Pyrenees at the head of a band of outlaws. It is clear from the start that he is not quite one of them; indeed, it becomes increasingly obvious that it is his very inability to conform, to overcome his sense of alienation (and fit into, among other things, an unequivocal vocal category), that is the essence of his tragedy. This tendency is confirmed by the unfolding of events. In I, 1, while his companions extol the virtues of wine and their peripatetic lifestyle in a carefree song ("Evviva!... beviamo"), Ernani recruits them to help him kidnap Elvira, ostensibly to save her from an unwanted marriage. Not quite as heroic as he seems at first, in his "Mercè, diletti amici... Come rugiada al cespite" (I, 2) Ernani makes no secret of his vested interest:

Il vecchio Silva stendere	Old Silva dares to lay
Osa su lei la mano...	his hands upon her...
Domani trarla al talamo	Tomorrow the creature
Confida l'inumano...	hopes to drag her to the nuptial bed...
S'ella m'è tolta, ah misero!	If she is taken from me, woe is me!
D'affanno morirò!	I shall perish from anguish!

The real inhumanity of Silva's wedding plan is that it would kill Ernani himself. The subsequent *cabaletta*, syncopated as if to underline Ernani's impetuous nature, explains that Elvira's love is his only comfort, confirming his self-centered outlook.

If Ernani and his boys open the opera in keeping with their rough, self-consciously unsophisticated surroundings, singing rowdily about the sweetness of love and protesting (too much?) their desire for feminine presence, Elvira is introduced, by contrast, in the exclusive company of women, inside a castle boasting every comfort and luxury. The conventional change to lyrical strings for this scene anticipates the *cavatina* of the *prima donna* – and emphasizes that this is specifically female space. Like her lover, Elvira thinks the grass is greener on the other side of the fence (or mountain) and rejects the security offered by Silva in favor of the more adventurous

Example 11.1 Verdi, *Ernani*, I, 3, "Ernani!... Ernani, involami" (Elvira)

prospect of the "antri e lande inospite," set to uneasy leaps, promised by Ernani (see example 11.1).[18] But what she wants is hardly relevant, as *Ernani* is certainly not her story: she hardly sings on her own after this entrance aria, which begins, significantly, "Ernani!... Ernani, involami" ("Ernani, carry me off!"). The creator of Elvira's role, the soprano Sofia Loewe, desperately tried, right up to the rehearsal stage, to persuade Verdi to end the opera with a *rondò* for her, but the composer had definitively discarded the idea months earlier in an answer to Piave's first draft of the libretto: "For God's sake do not finish with the *rondò* but do the trio: and in fact this trio must be the best piece in the opera."[19] Verdi's patience with singers' egos seemed already in short supply.

Ernani, on the other hand, is allowed to define himself vocally, again and again, though mostly in short, impetuous spurts rather than in proper arias. Indeed, he shows up every time the possibility of action presents itself, making a cliché of his heroic status. When Don Carlo invades Elvira's cloister, and – notwithstanding the carefully censored text protecting his propriety and nobility of intentions – ends up trying to drag her away, Ernani comes to the rescue, or at least tries to. The main function of the hero's entrance at this point is to back up Elvira, musically speaking, and to blur her individuality: she now shares Ernani's style, plentiful concurrent syncopation suggesting the union of their youthful energy. Visually and dramatically the duet turns into a trio, but not musically, since Ernani and Elvira are singing mostly in unison, albeit to different texts (see example 11.2). Both antagonize Carlo without interacting with each other: they give differently gendered expression to the same melodic persona, one that is emphatically inflected toward the hero. What subsequently changes the course of events is a first revelation of identity – Ernani's – which distracts and

Example 11.2 Verdi, *Ernani*, I, 8, "No, crudeli" (Elvira, Ernani, Carlo)

engages Carlo far more deeply than his amorous pursuits, and from now on the whole story will revolve not so much around who will get Elvira, but who will get – and get rid of – Ernani.

The only other action presented on stage in which the King shows interest in Elvira involves the entrapment of Ernani: in II, 8, Don Carlo returns to Silva's castle on the outlaw's trail. Brushing aside Silva's protests, Carlo searches the castle, disarms Silva's men, and orders that his host be tortured until he reveals the bandit's hiding place. The sudden appearance of Elvira imploring for mercy takes him aback but brings about no more than a shift in strategy: Don Carlo takes her in Ernani's stead, only to use her as bait. With the sinuous line of "Ah vieni meco o sol di rose" (II, 9, reminiscent of his adulatory tone in the duet in I, 7, "Da quel dì che t'ho veduta"), the King returns to his seductive mode; but even more evident is his smug self-congratulation at his quick thinking. Except for a brief paternal tirade, Silva does nothing to stop Elvira from going; securing his real prize, Ernani, compensates for all his trouble.

Ernani, after all, has been Silva's nemesis for the entire second act. He had arrived at Silva's castle disguised as a pilgrim and disrupted his wedding an hour before the ceremony with the show-stealing gesture of revealing his identity and offering his own head, worth a handsome bounty from the King, as a wedding present. Furthermore, he had gone on to seek intimacy with the bride (in the unison *a due* "Ah morir potessi adesso") behind the groom's back. And as the King entered the castle, Silva was forced to jeopardize himself by hiding his troublesome guest behind a portrait of himself! So, when Don Carlo leaves with Elvira, Silva – who retains the authority of a bass, though diminished to the compass of a fifth – has nothing else in mind but revenge, and challenges Ernani to a duel, forgetting that the King is also a rival, in more senses than one. Frustratingly, Ernani declines to fight, not only out of respect for Silva's age (and for literary and operatic precedents), but to trump Silva with a more elaborate challenge of his own, one carrying more genuine risk for himself. It is Ernani who lays the groundwork for the tragic end, not only by devising the pact, but also by giving Silva the tools to reap the rewards, including the fatal horn.

Ernani, however, is not the only character whose attempts at defining his peculiar vocal self have the power to affect circumstances. Twice a change of perspective is forced on characters and audience alike by an official flourish announcing Carlo's presence and identity. In I, 10, the arrival of the equerry Don Riccardo hailing the King prevents Silva from killing both Ernani and Carlo, whom he had just found in his niece's room, and provokes the solemn ensemble "Vedi come il buon vegliardo," which underlines the swift change of atmosphere effected by the presence of real power. Similarly, in III, 6, Don Riccardo arrives once again in the nick of time to declare Carlo Holy Roman Emperor, when, on the day of the elections, he had been hiding inside Charlemagne's tomb to defeat the conspiracy led by Ernani and Silva. This announcement precipitates the finale; the conspirators are all condemned to imprisonment, or decapitation if of noble extraction, which prompts Ernani to make an announcement of his own: he is an aristocrat, Don Giovanni d'Aragona. Though Elvira begs Carlo for pity ("Virtù augusta è la pietà") it is

Ernani, with his totally unsolicited confession, who gives the new Emperor the opportunity to exercise the greatest privilege of his newly acquired status: clemency. Ernani thus comes to terms both with the competition provided by Don Carlo at different levels and with the fact that he himself is not the protagonist of what is arguably the finest act in the opera. Here Don Carlo not only takes central stage but seems truly to find his voice in "Oh, de' verd'anni miei," Verdi's first great baritone aria. While Carlo moves on from nostalgic reflections to positive, forward-looking resolutions, Ernani, recovering from the blow, finds a way of ensuring that the last act remains his own. After the impressive climax of Don Carlo's final exit, no other voice but that of a horn, called up by a frustrated bass, will silence Ernani the tenor for good.

Ernani clearly moves away from Verdi's large-scale epic operas, marking that turn from religious to secular works and from a public, choral rhetoric to the private, psychological one often noted by scholars.[20] But it also provides more continuity between previous and subsequent works than might at first appear. Though individual characters and their personal dramas push the chorus into the wings in *Ernani*, secular human issues had always been at the center of the "religious" operas as well. Moreover, in certain respects *Ernani* is more conventional than *Nabucco* or *I lombardi*, adhering to a *modus operandi* closer to *Oberto* and to *melodramma à la* Donizetti. It relies extensively on the *convenienze* and on closed set pieces: a succession of arias to introduce each character in the first act, standard-issue *cavatine* and *cabalette*, an opening chorus with drinking song, and a conventional layout of duets, ensembles, and finales. Yet in some sense *Ernani* does supersede these earlier works, if only in its felicitous control over the events that bring the characters into confrontation: as we have seen, concentration on personal conflict is achieved through a stringently monitored – if at times oversimplified – succession of dramatic moves, streamlining the overall structure and bringing the opera quickly to a plausible end.

Also indicative of Verdi's future development are the recurring melodic contours introduced in the opening phrases of significant numbers. One is a rising gesture, used with slight changes to signify different characters (an impetuous sixth for the young lovers, a fourth for the more mature Carlo; see example 11.3); another is a chromatic inflection involving a diminished third, often present in cadential passages, around the dominant pitch.[21] The "horn" theme, Ernani's fatal oath to Silva, "Se uno squillo intenderà / Tosto Ernani morirà," first heard in the prelude to Act I on solo trumpet and trombone, is a version of the latter motif (see example 11.4: the gb^1 is followed in the next measure by $e\natural^1$ in the first trumpet). The score is full of both of these distinctive melodic cells, making reminiscences of this kind much more prominent than in Verdi's previous operas, although they

Example 11.3 Verdi, *Ernani*, motifs based on a rising interval

Example 11.4 Verdi, *Ernani*, II, 12, "horn" theme

are not yet developed enough to carry dramatic weight or give the opera internal musical coherence, at least by comparison with the works of his maturity.

The recurring motives do, however, hold *Ernani* together at other levels. They have been read as representing "love" and "honor" respectively, on the assumption that the main issue in the opera is the conflict between the two.[22] But their inconsistent usage and varying associations suggest that they are not unequivocal signifiers. For example, "honor," like "love," could be replaced with something else – "natural law," for instance, particularly in the last appearance of this motif at the very end of the opera. In Act IV, when Elvira pleads for sympathy for her love for Ernani, Silva replies that Ernani dies *because* of this love ("per tale amor morrà"). Silva's code of honor carries even more weight when Ernani has apparently ceased to be a rebel: once he reveals his identity, is reintegrated socially and politically, and the troubling matter of class crossing is resolved, his love for Elvira loses its subversive luster as an affront to institutional authority and values. In a sense, on revealing his official identity at the end of Act III – "Io son conte, duca sono" – Ernani the bandit dies. But Silva's use of the name "Ernani" again in Act IV in conjunction with the "horn" theme seems to insist that no public revelations (or repudiations) of identity will alter the course of his implacable justice. Hence the absence of Don Carlo from the last act: he and all he represents have in the end nothing to do with Ernani's destiny. Silva, on the other hand, is not regal; his authority has little to do with political conventions; his strength comes from a law that is as unarguable and unforgiving as nature itself. He would have no power to make the ex-transgressor respect an oath made solemn entirely by the memory of a dead father were that memory not such a powerful lever. Ernani knew this only too well when he suggested the terms of the pact: it is his own obsessive pursuit of tragedy that finally undoes him.

Ernani's identity crisis

Verdi's insistence, in the face of official requirements, that Ernani should not be played by a contralto suggests that he, like the old Silva, was uncomfortable leaving Ernani and Elvira alone, away from the rest of the principals, whether on stage or in the dressing room.[23] This uncertainty regarding Ernani's gender identity is immediately evident in his entrance aria, where we suspect that all might not be well with the hero's sense of self. "Mercè, diletti amici . . . Come rugiada al cespite" is introductory in more than the usual sense: at the end of the recitative, he pauses, as if confused, over his own name, saying, "Forse per sempre Ernani fia perduto." This rather pompous unburdening is followed, in the *cabaletta* "O tu che l'alma adora," by two different settings of the concluding phrase "Gli stenti suoi, le pene, / Ernani scorderà" ("Ernani will forget his hardship, his pains"), both repeated, and the scene ends with his extended melismas on the word "Ernani" over the chorus singing (apparently without irony) "Le dolcezze dell'amor." Oddly enough, even by the standards of 1840s operatic rhetoric, the tenor continues bizarrely to refer to himself in the third person throughout. In the Act I finale he asks Elvira "Serba a Ernani la tua fe'" ("Keep faith with Ernani"); lastly, of course, there is that ringing pledge at the end of Act II, in which Ernani speaks of his own (but third-person) death at the sound of the horn. Vocally these references stand out from the rest of the music: especially at the beginning of the opera, they tend to be marked as slower than the surrounding tempo, they frequently incorporate the downward "sighing" figures that conventionally denote a troubled spirit, and they are quite often melismatic. Thus Ernani's self-consciousness is expressed both in the repetition of his name, almost as if wistfully addressing someone else, and in the peculiarly exposed music to which it is set. Significantly, almost every time he says it, the voice is at or near the "break," the joint between the middle and high registers, and the point at which singers may be most vulnerable. It seems that Ernani is (at the very least) a little uncomfortable with his role; bearing in mind the compositional history, the irresistible conclusion is that he is not a "real" tenor. As if in some disturbed Freudian nightmare, he fears emasculation. He worries that his voice will break – not down, but (much worse) *up* – and that Hugo's "beardless youth" will turn into the contralto she really is.[24]

Questions of identity are, after all, central to opera of this period. The situation envisaged by the original plan for La Fenice – a woman dressed up as Duke Don Giovanni d'Aragona masquerading as a bandit, entering a castle in yet another disguise – odd though it is to us, would have passed then as unremarkable. But one might nevertheless feel a special sympathy for Ernani, whose anxieties are probably exacerbated by the fact that his one-time enemy Carlo, the ex-tenor, has been allowed to retain a certain suave charm from his previous existence. His voice apart, he is a much more traditional character, the kind of gallant found throughout Mercadante and Rossini, and this is reflected in his proper *cavatina* "Oh, de' verd'anni miei." It is a classic mixture of public ambition and private feeling, with an equally classic "vocalità": the middle register carries the serious sentiments, while the top is reserved for mere ornamentation. Carlo the baritone, then, retains a great deal of the presence of Carlo the tenor. How peripheral to Verdi's aesthetics the remains of that particular kind of tenor would become is witnessed by the character of the Duke in *Rigoletto* (1851), an opera written only a few years later but in which the gallant tenor seems very deliberately set apart from the rest of the cast.

Similarly, then, it is difficult to think of Ernani the tenor without remembering Ernani the contralto. A trace of the cross-dressed *prima donna* remains, even if none of the music had been conceived by the time the character's vocal range changed. Despite the grown-up things Ernani does, there's something self-indulgent about him and his vocal persona. On the other hand, if he sometimes seems too eccentric, stamping his foot and constantly talking about himself in the third person, maybe it is no surprise. For in generic and stylistic terms he *is* rather immature: he represents the very first truly Verdian tenor. He is the first of a long line that ends with the title role in *Otello*: men who are all, in their different ways, exposed and vulnerable, tortured by inner conflict. In this light, Ernani's transgressive position within the plot (bandit, traitor, clandestine lover, etc.) seems a reflection of other kinds of lawlessness: his vocal origins and their confused gender, as we have seen, but also Verdi's experimentation with the rules then governing vocal roles. Ernani the outlaw, disguised, unsure about his own identity in the stifling confinement of those Pyrenean male-voice choruses, is himself a decoy, insinuating through his very uncertainty a new kind of voice. Though Ernani the contralto did not make it to the stage, what she left behind her would certainly endure. Over forty years later, in Milan, the vault of La Scala would resound to the outpourings of the Moor of Venice, his voice defiantly introducing itself in that dangerous *passaggio* zone, between middle and high register, going over the top even by comparison with normal tenor excesses, almost crossing the boundaries – temperamental as well as vocal – between the genders.[25]

If there is progress in the timbral distribution of *Ernani*, it is not, as Verdi himself disingenuously hinted, in the rejection of the trouser-role lead, but precisely in his temporary acceptance of it. Without Ernani's schizophrenia, with which Verdi called into question the tenor's role in more ways than one, it is difficult to see how the light "tenore di grazia" found in Donizetti and Bellini could have become the complex and profound vocal personality of the later nineteenth century. In other words, by reneging on La Scala, Verdi did no more than his hero: while Carlo, in "Oh, de' verd'anni miei," faces up to his responsibilities and answers the demands of tradition, Ernani and his creator instead go on the run from history, to hide – in the mountains of Aragon and the canals of Venice respectively – and plot momentous deeds.

12 "Ch'hai di nuovo, buffon?" or What's new with *Rigoletto*

CORMAC NEWARK

Set at the court of the Duke of Mantua in the sixteenth century, *Rigoletto* is the story of a jester whose situation is anything but funny. Ugly, with a hunched back, he is pitilessly derided by the courtiers. In his whole life he has known only one brief period of happiness, when – well before the time of the opera – a woman took pity on him, became his wife, and gave him a daughter. Now a widower, his only solace is that daughter, Gilda, whom he protects obsessively, hoping above all that the Duke (a notorious seducer) will not find her. Unfortunately this is precisely what happens: as the curtain rises, the Duke is preparing to make his move. Gilda is aware of her suitor (although not of his identity) but says nothing to her father. In Act I she enjoys her first few moments together with the Duke before being abducted by a group of courtiers intent on playing a trick on Rigoletto – they think Gilda is his mistress. Momentarily thwarted, the Duke is soon back on top of things: the courtiers can't wait to tell him about their exploits, and about the woman they are keeping prisoner in the palace. Exit the Duke to an adjoining room, to do what he does best. Rigoletto then arrives to quiz the courtiers, soon realizing that what he fears most is happening at that very moment. When Gilda comes back in to confess that she is no longer the emblem of unworldly purity he thought, he swears revenge on the Duke. This he will attempt through the services of a hired assassin, Sparafucile, whose pretty sister Maddalena is to lure the Duke to his death at their inn. Keen that Gilda should know her lover's faithlessness, Rigoletto has her secretly watch the Duke in action. Although dismayed, she still loves him, and, when Maddalena presses her brother to spare her admirer and earn the promised reward by killing somebody else, Gilda steps in. Disguised, she calls at the inn and is promptly murdered – it is *her* body that is bundled into a sack and delivered to Rigoletto as arranged. Unable to resist gloating over his powerful enemy brought low, Rigoletto opens the sack...

This compelling drama occupies a central position in Verdi's oeuvre: its premiere was in 1851, about halfway through both his life and his catalog of operas. With the possible exception of *Nabucco* (which has a rather particular performance history), it was the first never to drop out of the repertory, and it remains among his most popular.[1] Even within the composer's lifetime critics referred – sometimes nostalgically – to a glorious "trilogy" comprising *Rigoletto*, *Il trovatore* (1853) and *La traviata* (1853). Similarly, in surveys of music history *Rigoletto* marks the beginning of Verdi's maturity: a newly sophisticated mix of his characteristic musical energy and judicious formal experimentation, inspired by just the right theatrical setting. It has received especially lavish attention in the *Bollettino dell'Istituto di studi verdiani*, and was the first opera in the Verdi critical edition.[2] It is as good a candidate as any for the title of his best-loved work. What, then, makes it such a success?

Musical structure

Despite its subtle characterizations, *Rigoletto* has proved more susceptible than other Verdi operas to reductive approaches. In an analysis by Wolfgang Osthoff, for example, the opera is organized as a series of mirror symmetries, each confrontation showing sharply defined similarities and differences.[3] The duet with Sparafucile in Act I persuades Rigoletto there is little essential difference between jester and assassin.[4] Taking his cue from Rigoletto's own reflections, Osthoff shows how characters in the opera tend to assume monochromatic identities. "Sparafucile" means literally "shoot-gun." When the assassin asks his victim's name, Rigoletto does not hesitate to refer to both the Duke and himself in abstractions, as "Crime" and "Punishment" respectively.[5] These contrasts are at their most stark in the imagery surrounding father and daughter – one ugly and paranoid, the other beautiful and trusting. Rigoletto dwells bitterly on this striking difference after Gilda's bedroom encounter with the Duke: "That she might rise as far as I had fallen: near the gallows it is fitting there should be an altar!"[6] In this black-and-white picture of the drama, the protagonist is destroyed not by human mistakes but by essential identity. There can be no rapprochement; the tragedy is inevitable.[7]

Such a view of the plot neatly complements structuralist thinking about the musical setting: both strip the opera down to basic forces. Nowhere have the qualities of *Rigoletto* been more energetically expounded than in the detailed studies of Verdi's tonal planning, although precisely how it sums up the drama remains controversial. Among the most comprehensive interpretations is Martin Chusid's, in which the principal tonality is D flat, with important sidesteps into C (to denote tragic foreboding, especially in Act I) and D (the tragedy itself, heralded by the tempest in Act III).[8] In the broadest terms, the entire opera revolves systematically around chromatic approaches to the home key from above and below. David Lawton also privileges D flat, but for him only D is its complement.[9] Marcello Conati's

Example 12.1 Verdi, *Rigoletto*, beginning of the prelude

study assimilates both of these ideas, and introduces a third: G flat as tonal and dramatic antithesis of C. Rigoletto's favored pitch (in "Cortigiani, vil razza dannata" and intoned or quasi-recitative lines throughout the opera), C is tonally as far as can be from G flat (strikingly associated with the Duke in "Parmi veder le lagrime" at the beginning of Act II).[10] Rigoletto himself is, socially and temperamentally, correspondingly distant from the Duke.

These readings probably tell us more about the analytical enthusiasms of the 1970s, when most of them were conceived, than the coherence of the work. More historically situated approaches have concentrated on key associations: the E major of Gilda's love song "Caro nome" in Act I, for example, may be understood as having connotations of simplicity and innocence that were well established by the time of Mozart.[11] On the other hand, *Rigoletto* does seem to exhibit a slightly more systematic handling of keys than other Verdi operas – the problem is deciding whether, in a tradition where musical texts were notoriously unfixed, that is significant.[12] While trying to decide, the student of Verdi may be further disoriented to find even quite fundamental questions approached differently by different scholars: Julian Budden, for one, asserts baldly that pitch, and not key area, is the only real criterion of coherence.[13]

All this notwithstanding, *Rigoletto* keeps reminding us how musically integrated it is. Example 12.1 shows the distinctive gesture, first heard in the prelude, that recurs somewhat ostentatiously at melodramatic moments later in the opera. As Rigoletto's soliloquy reveals (see example 12.2), this gesture is associated with a pivotal moment in Act I, when Monterone, a courtier, interrupts the palace festivities to reproach the Duke for seducing his daughter. Rigoletto mocks the old man, bringing down upon himself Monterone's curse: "Tu che d'un padre ridi al dolore / Sii maledetto!"[14]

Example 12.2 Verdi, *Rigoletto*, I, 3, "Quel vecchio maledivami!" (Rigoletto)

Example 12.3 Verdi, *Rigoletto*, I, 7, "Ah! la maledizione!" (Rigoletto)

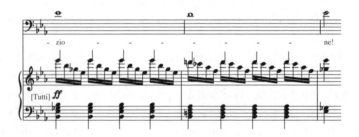

Whenever the jester remembers those troubling words, the musical accompaniment has a moment of reminiscence too. Thus the motif would appear to represent Rigoletto's brooding personality as much as the curse itself.[15] For the many Verdians who have homed in on it, however, the "curse motif" expresses more, the dramatic essence of the whole opera.[16] This is because Verdi, in a letter to his librettist Francesco Maria Piave, said as much: "the whole plot is in that curse."[17] His assertion is endlessly reiterated in references to the intermediate stages of composition, above all that at which the work was entitled "La maledizione."[18]

Rehearings of the motif in example 12.1 can easily be understood as a kind of commentary on the drama. As Monterone's curse is fulfilled, the portentous opening becomes closure (see examples 12.3 and 12.4) and the motif becomes more and more a part of the surrounding musical syntax. Harmonically, too, it is less obtrusive as time goes on: the piquant "German"

Example 12.4 Verdi, *Rigoletto*, III, 14, "Ah! la maledizione!" (Rigoletto)

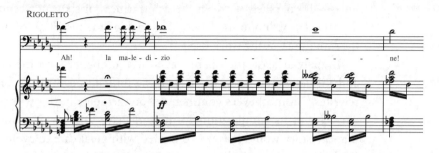

sixth (example 12.1, m. 2) gives way to the more familiar diminished chord (m. 8) even by the end of the first act.[19]

This metaphor alone cannot account for the generative role Verdi assigned to the curse. As the synopsis given earlier shows, it is possible to summarize the plot without mentioning Monterone, or the curse, at all.[20] The opening scenes tell us all we need to know: Sparafucile claims to loiter outside the jester's house most evenings, where he sees the Duke, who – for several months now – has also been coming there regularly. He has noted the Duke's keen interest in Gilda. Marullo, too, has been in the neighborhood, observing Rigoletto with Gilda. Rigoletto, self-absorbed to the point of blindness, has, despite his exaggerated vigilance, seen none of these spectators.[21] He is guarding something very precious to him, and he has numerous enemies, so the odds are already stacked against him at the outset. So much so that Monterone's melodramatic intervention makes the ensuing tragedy seem overdetermined – still more, perhaps, the story of the opera's genesis.

Genesis

The literary source for *Rigoletto* is a play by Victor Hugo, *Le roi s'amuse*, which had its first performance in 1832. Set at the court not of some anonymous duke but rather the glorious François I, it was promptly banned by the censor.[22] Hugo appealed, and there ensued a long dispute with the authorities, who claimed the piece was immoral. The context was highly politicized: the recent July Revolution (1830) had, after all, broken out over the matter of state censorship, and a future celebrated orator of the 1848 uprising, Odilon Barrot, spoke in defense of *Le roi s'amuse* at the appeal hearing. Although Hugo did not succeed in overturning the ban on performance of his play (in fact it was not seen again in Paris until 1882), he was free to publish the text – and with it a lengthy preface, as much concerned with the injustices his work was suffering as with aesthetic issues.[23] In it, Hugo draws sly (and not-so-sly) parallels between the arbitrariness of sixteenth-century court life and censorship in the 1830s, thus making the reception of the play tell the same story as the work itself.[24]

Initially at least, the opera was to fare no better with the authorities, and *Rigoletto* only reached the stage via difficult negotiations and several rewrites.[25] Almost every commentary on the opera begins with a standard narrative of its composition. Verdi and Piave were aware from the start that the story would have to be treated with great care to avoid incurring the Venetian censor's disapproval. So enthused by the subject was Verdi, however, that he apparently accepted Piave's soothing reassurances at face value and went ahead with working out the opera in some detail. When the inevitable crisis came, and the libretto was found unacceptable, he petulantly blamed Piave for his wasted effort.[26] In the end they arrived at a compromise whereby the most scandalous parts were removed but the essential ideas remained.[27] Doubtless Verdi knew all along that this was the most likely outcome.

Recounted this way, the censorship dispute over *Rigoletto* is significant for several obvious reasons. First, it provides clues to the composer's working methods. Describing his progress with the opera, he implies very strongly that it is fixed in his head well before he writes it down. Second, his wrangling with the Venetian authorities reveals precisely what he considers dramatically vital (and what, therefore, may be sacrificed to expediency). Third, and perhaps most interesting, it offers useful material to a wide range of interpreters hoping to find in those working methods and in that principled wrangling the reasons for the opera's eventual success. For prodigious creativity and artistic obstinacy are, naturally, signs of mature genius.[28] Conati, piecing together a mostly documentary account, feels that the creative impulse is responding to Hugo's text, above all to the jester Triboulet.[29] In Elizabeth Hudson's broader cultural analysis, it is the restrictiveness of both opera and nineteenth-century society that squeezes *Rigoletto* into its rich, densely expressive form.[30]

For Verdi himself, then, the opera's trials represent a process whereby *Rigoletto* is reduced to its essence. And that essence, he explicitly stated, is the curse. Hugo thought the same – or at least, when defending his play, claimed he did: "From this flows the entire play. The real subject of the drama is Saint-Vallier's curse."[31] The preface, paraphrased by the composer in the earlier letter to Piave already mentioned, claims for Saint-Vallier's (i.e. Monterone's) curse a justice more than merely poetic. This is not a scurrilous work, Hugo is saying; on the contrary, its values are entirely moral. When the jester is struck down, it is not just by the logic of the stage but by Providence.

But the curse, post-revolutionary cipher for divine intervention or not, is no more essential to *Le roi s'amuse* than it is to *Rigoletto*, and Hugo's defense is an obvious attempt to shift the basis of his tragedy from pitiless irony to the more respectable territory of implacable justice. Similarly, Verdi's interpretation of the plot is not (or not only) the expression of his characteristically unerring dramatic instinct but rather a preemptive defense based on Hugo's.

In musical studies of *Rigoletto* where the motif plays a similar generative role, it can be made to seem as moral as Verdi insisted the curse itself was: a moral not only of the story but of Verdi's creative process too. Rigoletto's inability to shake off the old man's warning could be a metaphor for Verdi's famously detailed intuition in matters of dramatic color – what he called "tinta." According to the composer himself, such inspiration would mysteriously come to him, fully formed and immutable, and set the tone for whole operas. In the sense that he is ambushed by worries that have their own, ready-made moral and musical identity, something similar happens to Rigoletto on his way home from the palace in Act I – but if that is what Verdi means when he says that the entire drama is contained in that moment, then he seems to be suggesting that his inspiration is the idea of inspiration itself. So intertwined are aesthetic pronouncement and defensive rhetoric in Verdi's correspondence, and so religiously do discussions of *Rigoletto* quote from it, that it is easy to end up with a sense of inevitability – that musical structure, dramatic shape, and moral complexion are all predetermined by Verdi's genius. But we should feel free to dissent: perhaps "Quel vecchio maledivami!" was not the vital catalyst in the making of *Rigoletto* Verdi implied it was. Perhaps, alternatively, its motif fades into the texture of the opera after Act I not because the curse has been fulfilled, nor because it is evolving into a yet more severe punishment, but because in the later stages of writing he simply got bored with it.[32] Either way – morally or musically – the curse works much better as a metaphor for Verdi's practice when setting a play to music than it does as a key to *Rigoletto*.

Novelty

If *Rigoletto* has a special aura, a unique place in the composer's oeuvre, what Verdi himself said helped give it that aura. No doubt commentary has over the years been to some extent self-propagating, with each successive critical generation fashioning its own tools to measure the opera's already established integrity and novelty. Much of the feeling of newness comes from a title role that introduces to the operatic stage a hitherto unheard-of kind of protagonist: complex, obsessive, and almost completely unsympathetic. Convinced that the outward deformities that make him the ideal buffoon have brought with them internal disfigurement as well, Rigoletto admits, in a frank summing-up as early as halfway through the first act, that he is jealous, resentful, and cruel.[33] And yet his sublime grotesqueness makes him all the more effective as a dramatic lead; indeed, Hugo went as far as declaring, in another famous preface, that ugliness was beauty.[34] In Italian opera, by 1851 still several steps behind Hugo's radical advances of the 1830s, the contradictions seemed even stronger: as Alessandro Roccatagliati puts it, "such vile things had never before been seen at the opera."[35]

Rigoletto's actions, none of them laudable, make his status as a hero highly problematic. His voice, moreover, does not quite fit into the categories of early nineteenth-century Italian opera: as a paternal figure he is rightly a baritone, like the other father, Monterone, whose destiny he shares.[36] As tragic protagonist, however, Rigoletto might more conventionally have been cast as a tenor. Most confusing of all, the actual tenor, the Duke, has eminently heroic music (carefree songs, tender expressions of love, vibrant calls for revenge) but no moral or emotional right to sing it. He is a character who makes a point of his own superficiality while at the same time singing some of the most subtle and moving pieces – largely in satisfyingly traditional forms – in the entire repertory. "Parmi veder le lagrime," in particular, has proved a peculiarly pleasant headache for scholars trying to understand the Duke's role, in the widest sense.[37] He and Rigoletto therefore share some of the characteristics of the traditional male lead. Not only do they both love the soprano, in their very different ways, but each loves her with an unforgivable selfishness. Similarly, each plays an indirect part in her death. How the Duke and his servant interact brings into question the then established hierarchies of opera – the relationship between noble and common characters and the style of music each should sing, their comic and tragic roles, and the voice types involved – with all the attendant connotations of dramatic function and performer status. No one refers to Rigoletto merely as "the baritone," and he is perhaps the first Verdian baritone (the first of many) who cannot at all usefully be identified by voice type.[38]

The scene which Rigoletto and the Duke have together (I, 2, set in the ducal palace) puts these various relationships in flux. Commentators have praised its tight organization of competing expositions, all held in perfect musical, textural, and narrative balance. Many have compared it to the Act I finale of Mozart's *Don Giovanni*, also set at a reception in a grand hall.[39] There, the dance music of the party is woven into the score of the opera, Mozart wittily juggling three on-stage groups of instruments in addition to the theatre orchestra. Verdi's scene is hardly less elaborate, the musical continuity sustained by two bands, one backstage and one on stage, and the orchestra in the pit. The comparison is apt in other respects because Don Giovanni is, of course, another unconventional protagonist. He and the Duke are both smooth-talking seducers. The former has a comic servant to introduce his exploits; the latter does it himself, rather engagingly, though he of course has a jester.[40] Both seducers are challenged by fathers of their conquests; and both, crucially, retain a great deal of vital charm. The difference is in the resolution. Mozart's two pairs of lovers can live happily ever after once Don Giovanni has been punished, thereby reasserting a familiar social structure. Verdi's Duke escapes altogether, leaving almost everyone else to punishment. Despite this, it is difficult to boo the Duke: if Rigoletto is not exactly a sympathetic hero, then his employer is far from being a typical villain. His immediate prototype, the King in Le roi s'amuse, even has moments of genuine comedy, while Triboulet and Rigoletto, the professional funny-men, never do.[41] Mozart's opera eventually saves its audience from disquieting amorality with the happy ending, Verdi's obviously not: in terms of the genre's stock roles (though not of tragic inevitability), ambiguities persist until the final curtain.

The sense of things not quite fitting, of people not behaving quite as expected, is pervasive: in Act III, to complete this most unpredictable of casts, we meet an honorable assassin and an amorous prostitute. This restlessness of purpose, so to speak, whereby the audience is never quite sure what it is supposed to think of the characters and their situation, is perhaps what compels critics to try to identify something completely new in Rigoletto. But the opera resists their attempts. It is not especially radical in formal terms: conventions are never precisely broken, merely held up to scrutiny. If there is a story to be told about Rigoletto, then – a neatly reductive approach – it is perhaps not so much that the opera fails to belong (to an older operatic aesthetic, or to Verdi's first period) as that it is *about* not belonging. Each of the three principals seems out of place. The very name of the protagonist – which seems in the play to derive from the Italian ("tribolare," to suffer) and in the opera from the French ("rigoler," to joke) – keeps reminding us not only of the paradox of his personal situation, but also that he is in transit between two different traditions.[42] Gilda's innocence, and lack of a strong musical presence, means she lives in a very different world from that of her father and the Duke.[43] Her tragic misjudgment of her suitor reflects this. And perhaps most clearly out on his own is the tenor, who sometimes seems a refugee (albeit a blissfully carefree one) from another opera entirely. Nowhere is he less concerned with surrounding events than in his solo in Act III, whose lightheartedness contrasts painfully with Gilda's impending sacrifice.

Example 12.5 Verdi, *Rigoletto*, III, 11, "La donna è mobile" (Duke)

"La donna è mobile"

With its incongruous style and remote key, "La donna è mobile" (see example 12.5) is the most out-of-place moment in the opera. Ironically, it is the best known: a showpiece from the first performance onward, it recently acquired a passport to a whole new realm of popularity through the influence of those operatic ambassadors the Three Tenors. Verdi, it seems, was well aware of the aria's propensity to steal the show. While rehearsing the premiere (the story goes), he withheld it until the last possible moment, eager to preserve as much as possible of its impact for the first night.[44] He was confident members of the audience would go home singing it, and in order to make a bigger impression, he is said to have asked Raffaele Mirate, who was to create the role of the Duke, not to practice it anywhere outside the theatre. If this account is true, "La donna è mobile" certainly justified the composer's confidence, having proved one of the catchiest tunes in the repertory.

But "La donna è mobile" would appear to be an unfortunate theme-song for the opera: it is brash where other parts of the work are subtle, cheerful where they are gloomy. The text is heavily ironic, too, because the women in this opera are anything but inconstant. On the other hand, its incongruity is not altogether surprising, for, rather than being direct self-expression, it is a stage song, musically and rhetorically distinct, as if marked off by inverted commas. That is, "La donna è mobile" sounds out of place because it is supposed to. It is mere apt quotation, a *canzone* the Duke sings for his own pleasure because the words fit his mood, though so exactly do they reflect his character that the audience has to keep reminding itself that those words are not, strictly speaking, his own. Musical details emphasize this discontinuity with the surrounding scenes: the empty measure at the start, for example, and the self-conscious vamping accompaniment before the voice enters. Most strikingly, snatches of the song return to the Duke's lips as he falls asleep later in the act, and, like that ideal audience imagined by Verdi, he too sings it to himself on the way home.[45] Although stage songs are common in nineteenth-century opera, few are presented so believably.

In the equivalent scene of *Le roi s'amuse* the King has a similar speech, also delivered in the form of a sung interlude. Again, the tune was probably catchy, and the text may even have been known to the audience as well as the other characters: the proverbial-sounding "Souvent femme varie / Bien fol est qui s'y fie" ("Woman is often changeable: he who trusts her is quite mad") is attributed to the real François I, whose theatrical stand-in performs the song.[46] So while in the opera the source of the Duke's wisdom about the opposite sex is another, more famous philanderer, in the play the King sings a song apparently quoting himself – they are his words after all. Their presence in the play rounds off what seems to be a whole series of metaphors of detachment. Apparently Hugo came across them inscribed on a window sash when he visited Chambord, the magnificent chateau of François I. No doubt from the best historicist motives, he broke off a piece, and carried the King's couplet home with him.[47] Hugo's vandalism of the physical patrimony nicely echoes his attack on its literary counterpart. But bound up in the story is also the idea of separation from historical source, of decontextualization; in other words, the same feeling of things being out of place. The image of the stolen fragment of wood ending up in the hands of the Duke of Mantua, as it were, not only lends an excitingly polyphonic quality to this simplest of songs, but seems to symbolize the uneasy coexistence in the opera's background of different political and aesthetic milieux.

On closer examination, then, "La donna è mobile" turns out to be the perfect operatic highlight, giving us the emotional core of the work and a glimpse of its literary and aesthetic background in one short song. So non-progressive in some respects, with its straightforward texture and strophic form, it is nonetheless emblematic of what makes *Rigoletto* such an uncomfortable masterpiece, the constant vague sense of anomaly. In this it is itself anomalous, especially for those surveying Verdi's oeuvre and trying to find convincing ways of making popularity in opera house and concert hall the consequence of compositional completeness, above all in works from the famous "middle period." The piece in *Rigoletto* that least fits that pattern was from the very beginning the most popular. Verdi's own pronouncements, couched as they are in an essentialist rhetoric that belies the work's complexity (he had his reasons, as we have seen), are in this respect unhelpful.

But perhaps it is a good thing if we can read him against the grain, and retain some suspicion of through-composed narratives, whether in the public relations surrounding composition, in the works themselves, or in the criticism that seeks to praise them. If Verdi's audiences over the past 150 years have chosen as their favorite work one that keeps shifting under the gaze, that is amenable to reduction but easily exhausts it, maybe that is a good thing too.

13 Verdi's *Don Carlos*: an overview of the operas

HAROLD POWERS

Philip II, King of Spain	Bass
Don Carlos, his son, Infante of Spain	Tenor
Elisabeth of Valois, his queen, originally betrothed to his son	Soprano
Roderick, Marquis of Posa, an aristocratic freethinker	Baritone
Princess Eboli, secretly in love with Carlos	Mezzo-soprano
The Grand Inquisitor of Spain	Bass
A monk, imagined to be the former Emperor Charles V	Bass
Thibault, Elisabeth's page	Soprano
The Count of Lerma, the King's chamberlain	Tenor
A herald	High baritone
A voice from above	Soprano
The Countess of Aremberg, the Queen's attendant	Silent
Woodcutters and their families	Mixed chorus
Cloistered monks	Men's chorus
Six deputies from Flanders	Basses
Inquisitors [of the Dominican Order]	Basses
Populace, courtiers	Mixed chorus

Don Carlos is the longest and most complex of Verdi's operas, not only in its dramatic, poetic, and musical design but also in the history of its composition, recompositions, abbreviations, and supplementations. It was not a great success in its first run at the Paris Opéra in 1867, and not much more so in revivals of the more familiar Italian versions from the 1880s. It is expensive to produce, and its many revisions make its status as a "work," finished once and for all, ambiguous. It began to move into its high place in the Verdian canon after the Second World War when it was revived in 1959 by Rudolf Bing for his debut as general manager of New York's Metropolitan Opera, conducted by Fritz Stiedry. By now *Don Carlos* can be seen as the greatest representative of the Parisian grand opera tradition of the middle two quarters of the nineteenth century. It is the most impressive of Verdi's operas as well, matched in grandeur only by *Aida* and in profuseness of melodic invention only by *Falstaff*. Neither they nor *Otello* could have been composed as they were without Verdi's experience with *Don Carlos*. But Verdi had to perform major amputations on his original conception twice: once in 1866–67 to shorten it for its original 1867 production in Paris, and again in 1882–83 to shorten it still further for a proposed production in Vienna that eventually took place in Milan in 1884. For that 1884 production he cut the original first act but reinstated some plot material cut from 1867, with new or revised text and new or recomposed music. For a production in Naples in 1872 he had undertaken some minor surgery to heal one of the worst injuries done five years previously in Paris, but that Naples 1872 revision was not used for the major repairs undertaken for the 1884 production.

The best full-scale account to date both of the opera and of the history of its composition and revisions is the *Don Carlos* chapter in volume III of Julian Budden's magisterial *The Operas of Verdi*, with its ninety musical examples, each with detailed notes on the instrumentation.[1] Gregory Harwood's *Giuseppe Verdi: A Guide to Research* lists individual studies published up to the mid-1990s.[2] The culmination of the research to date is the composite vocal score of all the versions in the so-called *Edizione integrale*.[3] Unavoidably it is not always easy to find one's way around in the *Edizione integrale*, but it is absolutely indispensable.

Notwithstanding its almost universal performance in Italian, *Don Carlos* was conceived as a French opera and composed on an original French libretto by Joseph Méry and Camille Du Locle, starting from a scenario sent to Verdi in July 1865.[4] Verdi composed the music in 1865–67 for the Paris Opéra, and the revisions of 1882–83 were also composed to French text.[5] Many passages were improved in that revision, but it is this writer's feeling that, considering the work as a whole, Verdi got it right the first time, as he had with *Macbeth* and *La forza del destino*.

Of the historical facts about the neurotic epileptic Infante Don Carlos, his father King Philip II of Spain, and the French Princess Elisabeth of Valois, the third of Philip's four queens, only King Philip's obsession with the Netherlands provinces given him by his father, the Holy Roman Emperor Charles V, is relevant to the libretto, which is based primarily on an adaptation of Friedrich Schiller's sprawling five-act verse play *Don Carlos*.[6] Schiller in turn drew his basic material from the seventeenth-century novel *"Dom Carlos": Nouvelle historique* by the Abbé César Vichard de Saint-Réal.[7] In adapting Saint-Réal's already unhistorical basic plot to his drama, Schiller dramatized Philip's obsession with Flanders by inventing a beloved friend for Don Carlos in the improbably freethinking Knight of Malta, Marquis Roderich von Posa – remotely based on Saint-Réal's historical Flemish patriots Egmont and Horn – who devotes himself to persuading Don Carlos to take up the cause of religious freedom for the Flemings, even more improbably becomes the King's confidant, and eventually sacrifices himself so that the young Prince may continue the fight to free Flanders from tyranny.

The Méry–Du Locle libretto is primarily derived from Schiller's play, probably with de Barante's 1861 translation into French prose at hand. Their first act, however, is based on a prologue separately titled "L'étudiant d'Alcala" – Alcala is mentioned as Don Carlos's university in Saint-Réal's novel and Schiller's play – with which Eugène Cormon (later the librettist for Bizet's *Les pêcheurs de perles*) had introduced his 1846 five-act play *Philippe II, roi d'Espagne... imité de Schiller*.[8] Cormon's prologue puts Don Carlos's unhistorical but compelling obsession with his young stepmother, talked of only in retrospect in Schiller's play, before the audience in the theatre, in the form of a rendezvous in a garden between Don Carlos, incognito, and his then presumed fiancée Elisabeth of Valois. In the scenario libretto Méry and Du Locle disposed of the impossibility of such an unchaperoned encounter by having the Princess and her page, out with a hunting party near the palace at Fontainebleau, momentarily lose touch with the hunters. They encounter Don Carlos, who has traveled with the Spanish embassy sent by his father King Philip to the court of Henry II of France to conclude a peace treaty by betrothing his son to the Princess; Carlos has been traveling incognito because he has defied his father's command to remain in Spain.

When Verdi received the scenario sent him by his librettists he asked that they add two scenes from Schiller's play that were not in the scenario (nor in Cormon's play), both of them dramatic dialogues involving King Philip: one with the Marquis of Posa from the last two scenes of Schiller's Act III; another with the Grand Inquisitor in the penultimate scene of Schiller's Act V.[9] Those two scenes were duly included in the verse libretto sent to Verdi and became two of the most impressive numbers in the opera. Though the King's confrontation with Posa was necessarily much shorter in the eventual libretto, the two essential elements in Schiller's scene – Posa's plea for religious freedom for the Flemings, and the King's improbable adoption of Posa as his domestic confidant – were retained and highlighted. In the scene from Act V of the play, however, though the King's confrontation with the Grand Inquisitor takes place *after* the King has had Posa shot, for the opera it was shifted back, to come *before* Posa's death. The order of the two basic divisions of Schiller's dialogue, which concern the King's relationship with the heretic Posa and his relationship with his rebellious son, was also reversed for the libretto. With the matter of the Prince disposed of first, then, the Inquisitor can accuse not only Posa but also King Philip of heresy; he can demand most dramatically that the King have his confidant done away with, rather than merely blame the King for having deprived the Inquisition of the chance to execute that prominent freethinker publicly.

Verdi also commented that there was no scene containing the sort of grand spectacle that was a prime feature of successful grand operas such as Meyerbeer's *Le prophète*.[10] The librettists responded by preceding and following the action of the Act III finale that was already present in their scenario with an *auto-da-fé*, complete with attending crowd, Inquisition monks in procession, and finally heretics sent to the stake, an event mentioned only in passing in Act I, scenes iii and vi, of Schiller's play. Using an *auto-da-fé* as a scene of grand spectacle was suggested to the librettists by Cormon's play, where an *auto-da-fé* is actually taking place throughout Act III. It is going on offstage but was to be represented to the audience audibly and visibly; among Cormon's stage directions one reads, for scene vi, "le son des cloches, toujours lent et sombre, continue" and for scene vii, "une lueur rougeâtre brille à travers les vitreaux."

Particular aspects of nineteenth-century French *livrets* contribute mightily to the uniqueness of Verdi's *Don Carlos*, on three different levels. In the large, whole musical numbers often reflect one of two basic designs described succinctly in a letter of 1832 from Meyerbeer to Scribe that was unearthed by Steven Huebner: either they were to be shaped "à l'italienne" with the (verse) rhythm of the medial and the final lyric movements different; or "à la française" with the (verse) rhythm (and sometimes even the verses themselves) of the medial lyric movement returning in the final one.[11] Aspects of both these fundamental aspects of the design of whole musical numbers are found in Verdi's *Don Carlos*. Beyond that, some numbers have the form of *couplets*, a pair of stanzas each concluding with the same refrain. In the discussions that follow, musical numbers are identified according to their enumeration in the first published vocal score.[12]

On the level of individual movement design, the strong contrast between verse for recitative and verse for lyric movements, a contrast that characterizes Italian libretto verse and is correlated with the internal structure of musical numbers in Italian opera of the "Great Tradition," does not exist in French libretto verse. Italian recitative verse has variable line lengths, is essentially unrhymed, and sense and syntax are often enjambed from one line to the next. Italian lyric verse, to the contrary, is rhymed, in stanzas of equal line length, and individual lines are usually end-stopped syntactically and/or semantically. French libretto verse is normally end-stopped too, but it is always rhymed, and line lengths are not consistent in the way they are in Italian libretto verse. That being so, individual stanzas of French verse intended for a lyric number often enough have lines of varying lengths, while a passage for *récit* may be uniform in its line lengths, with rhymes, and is usually end-stopped. As a consequence, the sharp distinctions between recitative, declamation, *parlante* texture, and formal melody that characterize operas composed to Italian verse are often rather more blurred in French opera.

On the level of the individual musical phrase, finally, French verse led Verdi into approaches to melodic line often quite different from his way with Italian libretto verse, arising from an essential rhythmic difference between the languages: Italian has strong stress, French weak. Thus while individual lines of French verse are reckoned by syllable count with a principal stress at the end of the line, like Italian verse lines, overall stress patterns can be quite inconsistent from one line to the next.[13] Maintaining parallelism in musical phrases of equal length where the internal stresses do not correspond from one line to the next, even in lines of verse with the same syllable count, can lead to interesting variation in detail from one melodic idea to the next. More than that: what stress there is in French is on the final sounded syllable of a word, and yet the *e caduc* that is not sounded in speech is sounded in verse and music; some words end, so to speak, trochaically, that is, strong–weak, so that not all melodic motifs will have a strong arrival point but rather may tail off after a downbeat arrival. And since most words have two or three syllables, the weak final stress leads to frequent pseudo-dactylic or pseudo-anapestic three-syllable patterns in the accentuation of words within a line of verse; that is, a minimally strong final syllable of a word is as often as not followed or preceded by two slightly weaker syllables. That in turn leads to frequent use of triplet afterbeats or triplet upbeats in a melodic line.

As noted above, there are two basic versions of Verdi's *Don Carlos*, each with variants. Verdi worked on the original five-act version, composed to the French *livret* by Méry and Du Locle, beginning at the end of 1865; it was first performed at the Paris Opéra on March 11, 1867. The second version, in four acts with the original first act eliminated, was created in 1882–83, with some new French text by Du Locle; it was first performed at La Scala in Milan on January 10, 1884, in Italian based on the 1867 translation by Achille de Lauzières, with emendations of old verse as well as new verse for the replacements by Angelo Zanardini.

Each of these two basic versions has its own variants (described in detail in Ursula Günther's preface to the *Edizione integrale*). For the *second* performance of the 1867 *Don Carlos*, on March 13, 1867, the entire Act IV finale (no. 20) after the death of Posa (no. 19) was deleted. But even before the premiere several substantial passages had been deleted or replaced with abbreviated versions. Between the dress rehearsal on February 24, 1867, and the premiere, the entire opening scene (no. 0) and portions of two duets involving the Marquis of Posa in Act II (nos. 5 and 11) were eliminated to ensure that the opera would finish in time for suburban patrons to catch the last train home. Some significant passages composed for no. 17 in Act IV (the quartet) and no. 22 in Act V (the third Carlos-Elisabeth duet) had been eliminated even *before* the dress rehearsal, for other reasons. The slow *concertato* in the Act IV finale (no. 20) had also already been eliminated – Verdi recomposed it later as the "Lachrymosa" for his Requiem – and the rest of the Act IV finale had been shortened. Finally, for a production in Naples in 1872 Verdi reinstated the plot content of the last half of no. 11, the Philip-Posa duet in Act II, with entirely new music composed to Italian verse – it is the only part of any version of *Don Carlos* not composed to French verse – and a part of no. 22 was deleted. Otherwise, Naples 1872 = Paris 1867 as performed at the premiere.

The second version of the opera, performed in 1884, involved very substantial changes, described in detail by Budden; the grossest was the elimination of the entire original Act I, with text and music of Carlos's aria (no. 1 bis) revised and inserted between what corresponds to nos. 4 and 5 of the original Act II. Much of the Act II Carlos-Posa duet (no. 5) and most of no. 11 (the Philip-Posa duet) was recomposed; the opening scene of Act III (no. 12) was eliminated altogether and replaced by an orchestral prelude based on the melody of Carlos's Act I *romance* (no. 1 bis). In the first set of Act IV, parts of the quartet (no. 17) were recomposed in condensed form, and plot content in no. 18 (*scène* and Eboli's aria) that had been eliminated before the 1867 premiere was reinstated, with new text and music. The rebellion that had ended the Act IV finale in 1867 (no. 20) before it was dropped altogether was reinstated, though drastically shortened. In Act V the concluding composite number (nos. 22–23) was partly recomposed (no. 22), and drastically shortened (no. 23). Then in 1886 a five-act *Don Carlo* was produced in Modena that was simply the four-act version with the 1867 first act restored and Don Carlos's displaced *romance* returned to its original place there. Otherwise, Milan 1884 = Modena 1886.

The overview of the opera that follows is intended to help the reader find a way among the various forms in which the opera is currently being produced and recorded. As already noted, the overview is broken up into individual musical pieces numbered according to the first vocal score; the titles come from that first vocal score and/or Verdi's autograph.[14] It is a *précis*, with somewhat fuller summaries of only two of its twenty-three numbers. Numerals headed "JB" following the title of each musical number are page numbers in volume III of Julian Budden's *The Operas of Verdi*; numerals headed "EI" are page numbers in the *Edizione integrale*. The first and largest of the episodes deleted before the premiere has been designated "0."

Within whole musical numbers outlined in more than minimal detail the internal articulations are marked 0 through 4: 0 designates preparatory material; 1 and 3 designate action or dialogue segments; 2 and 4 designate formally constructed lyric movements. One threefold set of duet scenes – nos. 2–3, no. 9, and nos. 22–23 – highlights three phases of the emotional relationship between the doomed lovers, Don Carlos and Elisabeth of Valois, daughter of Henry II of France. A pair of duet scenes points up two dramatic confrontations for King Philip: one (no. 11) is with the historically inconceivable freethinking Marquis of Posa; the other (no. 16) is with the all too conceivable, terrifyingly orthodox Grand Inquisitor. Asterisks mark places where fragmentary musical examples from no. 11 and nos. 22–23 have been appended (see pp. 229–35 below). At the end of the overview are annotations on the contents of two CD recordings of *Don Carlos* in French.

Act I: The forest at Fontainebleau; the castle in the distance; winter.

0 Woodcutters, later Elisabeth and entourage.
JB 39–44. EI 1–29.
This scene was replaced after the dress rehearsal of February 24, 1867, by no. 1 below.
For the rest of the Fontainebleau act 1867 = 1872 = 1886.

1 **Introduction. Choeur des chasseurs**.
JB 45. EI 30–34.
This replaced no. 0 above at the premiere on March 13, 1867.

1-bis **Récit et Romance.** Carlos.
JB 45–47. EI 35–39.
In the 1884 *Don Carlo*, in which the Fontainebleau act was suppressed, this one-movement aria, transposed and with new text, was patched in between the equivalents of no. 4 (the monks' chorus) and no. 5 (the Carlos-Posa duet). In the 1886 *Don Carlo*, the revised four-act version with the Fontainebleau act reinstated, Carlos's aria returned to this, its original position, with its original text and in its original key.

The rest of the Fontainebleau act is identified as a single item in Verdi's autograph: "scene [sic] et duo." In the headings of the 1867 Escudier vocal score Verdi's "scene et duo" is broken up into no. 2, "Scène et duo" (plus "duo"), and no. 3, "scène et morceau d'ensemble final" (plus "suite de final"). It is the first of three duet scenes for Carlos and Elisabeth that tell the story of their doomed love: initial rapture followed by despair (nos. 2–3); medial desolation (no. 9); final transcendence (nos. 22–23). In the large, Verdi's single "scene et duo" here is shaped *à l'italienne*, where the medial and final ensembles are different, like a slow movement and *cabaletta* or *stretta* in the Italian tradition. The two lyric movements themselves, however, are shaped internally *à la française*, with the same music at the beginning and end; the second has two contrasted musical subjects, one for the two principals and another for the chorus, which are combined at the end.[15]

2 **Scène et Duo.** Carlos, Elisabeth.

JB 47–52. EI 40–67.

The rapturous phase of the relationship is set forth in the first half of Verdi's "scene et duo."

3 **Scène et morceau d'ensemble final.**

JB 52–55. EI 68–94.

In the second half of Verdi's "scene et duo" rapture is replaced by despair.

Acts II through V of the Paris 1867, Naples 1872, and Modena 1886 versions of *Don Carlos* correspond with Acts I through IV of the Milan 1884 version. Verdi composed the passages substituted for Naples 1872 directly to an Italian text by Antonio Ghislanzoni. He composed the revised music for the 1884 = 1886 version to Du Locle's French text but until the appearance of the 1985 Deutsche Grammophon recording conducted by Claudio Abbado it was heard internationally only in the Italian translation of Achille de Lauzières, supplemented and revised by Angelo Zanardini. French text is quoted hereafter for everything that survived revisions unchanged, Italian text for Naples 1872 and for the revised portions in Milan 1884 = Modena 1886.

Act II, set A: The monastery of St. Juste, with the tomb of Emperor Charles V.

4 **Introduction, Choeur, prière et scène.** Monks' chorus offstage, Carlos, a monk.

JB 55–59. EI 95–105 (1867 = 1872 = 1886) :: 95–101 + 126–132 (1884).

5 **Scène et Duo.** Carlos, Posa.

JB 60–66. EI 106–125 + 140–147 (1867 = 1872) :: 126–147 (1884 = 1886).

The elimination of Posa's tale of a visit to Flanders in division 1 of the 1867 version of the duet after the dress rehearsal had no effect on the design *à l'italienne* of the overall sequence; individual lyric movements were shaped *à la française*. The original design was lost in the revision of 1884 = 1886.

From here to the end of the set, 1867 = 1872 = 1884 = 1886.

Act II, set B: A delightful open garden adjoining the monastery.

6 **Choeur des dames d'Honneur.**

JB 66–68. EI 148–156.

7 **Chanson du Voile.** Eboli's *couplets* (with choral refrain).
   JB 68–69. EI 157–166.

8 **Scène et Ballade.** Posa, Eboli, Elisabeth.
   JB 68–71. EI 167–181.

9 **Duo.** Carlos, Elisabeth. The desolation phase of the relationship.
   JB 71–78. EI 182–197.

   Unlike the rapturous love duet in the Fontainebleau act and the transcendent farewell duet in the last act, most of this duet is dialogue. At the end of the coda of the central portion of the number there are a few measures of singing *a due*, but everywhere else musical passages succeed one another without repetition or recurrences. Aspects of both the French and the Italian ensemble designs are nevertheless evident, at different formal and aesthetic levels. After (1) a series of confrontational episodes, (2) an extended central division, the first moment of static calm, follows the pattern *à la française* in that its opening music returns at the end, before (3) the action resumes. And while the two successive brief episodes of (4) the final fast-tempo division in no way follow any kind of traditional *cabaletta* design, they contrast with all that has come before in their sudden violence, with all the vigor and agitation of a closing *cabaletta*.

10 **Scène et Romance**. Elisabeth's *couplets*.
   JB 79–80. EI 198–205.

11 **Duo.** Philip, Posa.[16]
   JB 80–98. EI 206–231 + 232–254 (1867) :: 255–276 (1872) :: 277–294 (1884 = 1886).

   This number has the most complex compositional history of the entire opera. It was not called for in Méry and Du Locle's original scenario and was one of the two duets for King Philip added to the libretto at Verdi's request. Between the dress rehearsal on February 24, 1867, and the first performance on March 11, most of division 3 below – in which the King tells Posa of his suspicions of his wife and son and asks him to spy on them – was eliminated as part of the shortening needed to see the opera finished by midnight. But this leaves an important aspect of the drama unexplained, in that the reason for the King to involve Posa in his private life was left unspecified, so that the King's suspicions that burst forth in his dialogue with the Queen in Act IV (no. 18) lack preparation. Verdi remedied the defect for the Naples production he supervised in 1872 by composing new versions of divisions 3 and 4, to Italian text supplied by Antonio Ghislanzoni (who later wrote the libretto for *Aida*). The duet was almost entirely recomposed to mostly new French text when *Don Carlos* was revised in 1882–83, eventuating in the 1884 Milanese production in Italian. Its new shape was almost entirely in dramatic order, one episode following another, with perhaps a faint trace of the original design *à l'italienne* surviving only in the presence of the brief *a due* at the end. If Verdi had his 1867 or 1872 music for the originally deleted part of the duet at hand in 1882–83 he made no use of it. Text from the deleted episode was reinstated in the 1884 = 1886 version of the duet, but the music was all new.

0 (a) *Allegro assai moderato, 4/4, a*

As the Queen and her entourage leave the stage the King commands Posa to remain. He wants to know why such a brave and loyal soldier asks nothing from him and has left military service.

1867 = 1872	1884 = 1886
(b) *Allegro sostenuto, 4/4, E♭ and*	[*Allegro assai moderato*], E♭ to
modulations	V/d
Posa will serve Spain but	Posa will serve Spain, but wants
leaves butchery to others. He	nothing for himself.
rejoices that chance or God has put it	
in his way to bring the truth to his	
King. The King bids him speak.	The King bids him speak.

1 (a) Posa's Flanders narrative.

Allegro moderato, 4/4, d

In the first three of four quatrains Posa tells the King of the horrors he has seen in Flanders; in the fourth quatrain he thanks God for the chance to report these terrible things to his King. The fourth quatrain was cut altogether in Naples 1872; its text was restored in 1884 = 1886, with the same musical ideas recomposed.

(b) The King's response: the goal of religious conformity justifies even extreme means. (See example 13.1.)

1867	1872	1884 = 1886
Meno mosso, 4/4, E♭	*Meno mosso, 4/4, A*	[♩ = 92], 4/4, B♭
* Philippe: "J'ai de ce	* Filippo: "Col sangue	* [again the same text,
prix sanglant payé	sol potei la pace	with yet again
la paix du monde /	aver del mondo /	completely new music]
... La mort, entre	... Il ferro in	
mes mains, peut	questa man può	
devenir féconde."	devenir fecondo."	

(c) Posa's reaction and the King's rejoinder. Henceforth both text and music in 1884 = 1886 are completely new (except for a few words of text as noted)

1867	1872	1884 = 1886
Allegro agitato, 4/4, Eb to *V/F*	*[stringendo],* 4/4, *a* to *V/F*	*Più mosso,* 4/4, Bb to *f*
Rodrigue: "Quel bras a jamais arrêté / La marche de l'humanité?"	Rodrigo: "Quel braccio fermar mai potrà / Nel suo cammin l'umanità?"	Rodrigo: "Che! voi pensate, seminando morte, / Piantar per gli anni eterni?"
		Db to *f*
Philippe: "Le mien!..."	Filippo: "Il mio!..."	Filippo: "Volgi un guardo alle Spagne/...La pace istessa io dono alle mie Fiandre!"

The formal design of the Philip-Posa duet in the Paris 1867 and Naples 1872 productions continues *à l'italienne,* with a static movement reflecting on matters to date, followed by the introduction of new dramatic matter, and a concluding *cabaletta* reflecting on that new matter. Though the music for the Naples production was completely new the design was the same. In Verdi's recomposition of 1884 = 1886, to the contrary, almost all traces of any such design were lost; Verdi's music goes on as it has begun, simply following events in the new dramatic texts moment by moment. Only in the final *a due* is there some remnant of the *cabaletta* tradition. (See example 13.2.)

1867	1872	1884 = 1886
		to *e*
		R: "Orrenda, orrenda pace! la pace dei sepolcri! / O Re, non abbia mai / Di voi l'istoria a dir: Ei fu Neron!"
2 *Meno mosso,* 4/4, F/*f*	[as in 1867]	*Allegro,* 4/4, *a* to E
* (a) R: "Un souffle ardent a passé sur la terre /...Donnez à vos enfants, [Sire] la Liberté!"	* [the same text (in Italian) and the same music]	* R: "Quest'è la pace che voi date al mondo! /... Come un Dio redentor l'orbe inter rinovate /... Date la Libertà!"

* (b) P: "Je n'avais jamais écouté / Cette inconnue ayant pour nom, la Vérité!"	* [the same text (in Italian) and the same music]	* F: "O strano sognator! / Tu muterai pensier, se il cor dell'uom / Conoscerai qual Filippo il conosce."
a 2 (a′) R, P: [text as in (a) above]	[the *a 2* was cut]	
	bb: i and Gb: I	E to C (= V/F)
3 P: "Plus un mot!... Levez-vous! votre tête est bien blonde / Pour que vous invoquiez le fantôme imposteur /...	F: "Taci ormai né invocare il fantasma impostor!"	F: "Or non più. Ha nulla inteso il Re /...non temer!
Allez! et gardez-vous / De mon Inquisiteur!"		Ma ti guarda dal Grande Inquisitor."

The King, struck by Posa's honest and independent spirit, changes his mind, asks him to stay, and proposes to confide in him.

1867 = 1872	1884 = 1886
Allegro, 4/4, F to C	*C, ad libitum*
P: "Non! reste, enfant! j'aime ton âme fière / La mienne à toi va s'ouvrir tout entière."	F: "Tu resti in mia regal presenza / E nulla ancor hai domandata al Re / Io voglio averti a me d'accanto."

As Verdi first composed the duet, the King then went on to hint strongly of his suspicion that the Queen, his wife, was unfaithful to him with the Prince, his son, a notion that Posa vehemently rejects on behalf of both. The King concluded by granting Posa permanent access both to himself and to the Queen, placing complete trust in him. This whole passage was cut after the dress rehearsal of February 24, 1867. The music for the King's first speech was adjusted to lead directly into the *cabaletta*, division 4 below, and thus it was performed at the premiere on March 11, 1867. For Naples 1872, and again for the later revising, Verdi wanted the King's suspicions replaced for clarification of the drama, and he composed new music, to Ghislanzoni's Italian text for Naples. For the revised version first produced in 1884 he composed new music to Du Locle's French text, shown below in Angelo Zanardini's Italian version. (See example 13.3.)

[cut after dress rehearsal] a, modulations, V/D♭	1872 e♭ to V/D♭	1884 = 1886 Allegro moderato, 4/4, ƒ
* P: "Tu m'as vu sur mon trône et non dans ma maison! / Tout y parle de trahison /	* F: "Ma tu che alzasti il guardo al trono mio / Nella mia reggia / Perchè non guardaresti?"	* F: "Osò lo sguardo tuo penetrar il mio soglio,/ Dal capo mio, che grava la corona, / L'angoscia apprendi e il duol! / …"
	R: "A te dappresso un figlio / E un angelica donna, altro non veggo."	R: "Sire, che dite mai?"
La reine … un soupçon me torture / Mon fils…"	F: "Né un murmure sinistro udisti mai? / … Le prove in mio poter."	F: "La Regina …un sospetto mi turba… / Mio figlio!…"
R: "Son âme et noble et pure."		R: "Fiera ha l'alma insiem e pura."
P: "Rien ne vaut sous le ciel le bien qu'il m'a ravi."		F: "Nulla val sotto il ciel il ben che tolse a me."
R: "Qu'osez vous dire?!"	R: "Chi osato avrebbe?"	
	F: "L'Eboli… il Duca d'Alba… il sacerdote"	*ancora più mosso*
	R: "Son lor nemici!"	"Il lor destin affido a te / …"
P: "Ami, sois nôtre juge… Je veux mettre mon coeur en tes loyales mains."	F: "Ma un cor leal scerner potrebbe il ver / D'un uom m'è d'uopo, e scelgo voi."	"Tu che sol sei un uom … Ripongo il cor nella leal tua man."
R: "C'est un rêve…"	R: "Me! Sire!"	

The *cabalette* of the Paris 1867 and Naples 1872 duets then follow, but the *cabeletta* as sung at the 1867 premiere – that is, after the cuts – was preceded only by the King's brief transitional lines, shown again below. As noted above, the brief *a due* in F major at the end of the 1884 = 1886 duet is a faint echo, as it were, of the *cabaletta* function and style. (See example 13.4.)

[1867]	1872	1884 – 1886

[as performed at the premiere]

[*Allegro, 4/4, F to V7 /Db*]

[P: "Non! reste, enfant! j'aime ton âme fière / La mienne à toi va s'ouvrir tout entière."]

Allegro, 4/4, Db	*Allegro giusto, 4/4, Db*	[*Allegro moderato, 4/4, F*]
4 * P: "Enfant! à mon coeur éperdu / Rends la paix dès longtemps bannie."	* F: "Di lei, di Carlo in core / Lo sguardo tuo discenda."	* R: "Inaspettata aurora in ciel appar! / S'apri quel cor che niun potè scrutar."
* R: "Quel rayon du ciel descendu / M'ouvre ce coeur impitoyable?"	* R: "O Carlo, Carlo mio! / Se a te vicin sarò / …"	* F: "Possa cotanto dì la pace a me tornar."
P: "Le marquis de Posa peut entrer désormais / … à toute heure au palais."		
	F: "Ma bada al vecchio Inquisitor."	*lo stesso movimento*
a 2 R: "O dieu puissant c'est un rêve …"	*a 2* F: "Un detto tuo …" R: "Questo non piangerò …"	*a 2* F: "Possa tal dì la pace a me tornar."
P: "Je trouve à cette heure … l'homme attendu …"		R: "O sogno mio divin, o gloriosa speme."
		F: "Ti guarda dal Grande Inquisitor!"

Act III, set A: The Queen's gardens; a fête is going on in the distance.

(1867 = 1872)   (1884 = 1886)

12 **Introduction, Choeur, Scène.**   **Preludio.**
Eboli, Elisabeth.   Orchestra
JB 98–100. EI 295–310 (1867).   JB 105–106. EI 350–351.

The deletion of the scene for Eboli and the Queen for 1884 dramatically weakens Eboli's subsequent encounter with Don Carlos (no. 13). In the 1867 version Eboli's appearance in the Queen's cape, necklace, and mask strongly supports Carlos's assumption that the lady in the garden, who sent the note, is indeed his beloved Elisabeth (no. 13 below). Also lost is a reference, both verbal and musical, to Eboli's *couplets* in Act II (no. 7), whose theme is a lady in disguise who turns out to be the real Queen. Without this reference, Eboli's Veil Song in 1884 = 1886 is only an attractive showpiece; it has lost its musico-poetic link to the drama.

Le ballet de la Reine. "La Pérégrina."
JB 100–105. EI 311–346.

13 **Duo et Trio.** Carlos, Eboli, then Posa.
JB 106–110. EI 352–376.
Beginning with this number and until the middle of Act IV – nos. 13 through 16 inclusive – the opera was performed, in French or in Italian as the case may be, as Verdi had first composed it in 1866–67.

Act III, set B: A public square, church to the right, palace to the left.

14 **Choeur, Marche, Final.**
JB 111–120. EI 377–433.
This magnificent internal finale – formed *à la française* in that it begins and ends with the same music – along with its unforgiving priests, its processionals, and its central slow ensemble led off by baritone voice(s) following an intervention by the principal tenor, is the template for the triumphal scene in that most French of Verdi's purely Italian operas, *Aida* (whose scenario was by Camille Du Locle).[17]

Act IV, set A: The King's chamber.

15 **Scène et cantabile de Philippe.**
JB 120–123. EI 434–441.

16 **Scène. Le Roi et l'Inquisiteur.**
JB 123–126. EI 442–453.
This confrontational dialogue of State and Church in alexandrine couplets is the second Schillerian scene added to the libretto at Verdi's request, like no. 11. But Verdi never saw any reason to redo his extraordinary initial conception here. The most striking feature of the music is the alternation of a slow contrabassoon melody accompanying King Philip with a series of sustained brass chords accompanying the Inquisitor, in the first division of the scene and again at the close.

17 **Scène et Quatuor.** Elisabeth, Philip, later Posa and Eboli.
JB 125–132. EI 454–478 (1867 = 1872) :: 504–521 (1884 = 1886).

There are many changes in detail from the 1867 = 1872 to the 1884 = 1886 version. Zanardini replaced some lines in de Lauzières's Italian translation. In the *scène* Verdi replaced one of Elisabeth's two lyric passages completely and adjusted details elsewhere, and he condensed the quartet from fifty-five measures to forty-five with only minor changes in its melodic content.

18 **Scène et Air.** Eboli, Elisabeth.

JB 132–137. EI 479–503 (1867 = 1872) :: 522–532 (1884 = 1886).

A lovely duet, in which the Queen forgives Eboli for trying to betray her to the King out of frustrated passion for Don Carlos, was cut even *before* the dress rehearsal of February 24, 1867. Also eliminated before the dress rehearsal was Eboli's second confession, that she herself had committed, with the King, the crime of adultery of which she had accused the Queen. With that passage gone, however, the Queen appears to be banishing Eboli from the court merely in response to her confession of love for Don Carlos – a motive suspicious indeed! – so for 1884 = 1886 similar text for Eboli's confession of adultery was supplied, for which Verdi composed new music.

Act IV, set B: A prison cell.

19 **Scène et Air.** Posa, Carlos.

JB 138–140. EI 533–546.

20 **Scène et Final.**

JB 140–144. EI 547–584 (1867 including passages cut before the second performance on March 13, 1867) :: 585–594 (1884 = 1886).

The *concertato* movement of this finale had been eliminated prior to the dress rehearsal of February 24, 1867. Between the premiere on March 11, 1867, and the *second* performance on March 13 the *entire* finale was dropped, so that from then until the 1884 production Act IV concluded with the murder and death of Posa (no. 19). In the revision for 1884 the action that had been cut by ending the act with the death of Posa was reinstated, with mostly old text considerably compressed, and with new music, except for the music from the Grand Inquisitor's entrance to the end of the act, retained from 1867.

Act V: The monastery of St. Juste, night.

21 **Stances.** Elisabeth alone, in six quatrains of alexandrine verse.[18]

JB 144–147. EI 595–605.

22 **Duo.** Carlos, Elisabeth. The transcendent final phase of the relationship.

JB 147–151. EI 606–618 + 626–633 (1867) :: 606–633 (1872) :: 652–667 (1884 = 1886).

Like the duet and finale of the Fontainebleau act (nos. 2–3) – the unitary "scene et duo" of Verdi's autograph – nos. 22–23 that conclude

the opera are also best construed as a single composite number. Like
Verdi's Fontainebleau "scene et duo," the 1867 conclusion of the opera
begins with (1) an extended stretch of dialogue, continues with (2)
a lovely static slow movement, then (3) is interrupted by action. To
that extent it seems as though it would be shaped *à l'italienne*, but
instead of concluding with another and more agitated set piece it ends
with the interrupting action, following a grand opera convention of
finishing with violent action. But this is also a pattern Verdi himself
had sometimes deliberately adopted for finales, preparing for a *stretta*
but ending with the act curtain instead. Verdi first composed this sort
of finale for Act I of *Luisa Miller*, perhaps even under the influence
of his then recent acquaintance with Parisian practice. The same
musico-dramatic design is used for the Act II finale of *Il trovatore*,
the Act II finale of *Un ballo in maschera*, the Act I finale of the
revised *Simon Boccanegra* (the Council Chamber scene), the Act III
finale of *Otello*, and the Act II finale of *Falstaff* (the laundry basket scene).
For the 1884 production of *Don Carlo*, division 1(a) of no. 22 was
completely recomposed, divisions 1(b) and 2 were transposed up a half
step, and the orchestral décor was touched up in a number of places.

0 *Allegro moderato, 4/4, modulations*
  Carlos, en route to Flanders, arrives for a last farewell. Seeing his
  still beloved Elisabeth his resolve wavers, but she encourages him to
  remember Posa's self-sacrifice. Carlos will build him a magnificent
  monument in Flanders.

  For the first sixteen measures the music is the same in 1867 = 1872
  and 1884 = 1886, then different for the next eight, and again the same
  for Elisabeth's final soaring line: "Les fleurs du Paradis réjouiront son
  ombre!"

  (See examples 13.5 and 13.6)

	1867 = 1872	1884 = 1886
1 (a)	*Allegro, 3/4, E to V/C*	[*The Allegro moderato continues*]
	* Carlos: "J'avais fait un beau rêve...	* [In the revision the first part of
	il fuit... et le jour sombre / Me	Carlos's dream is sung to the
	montre un incendie illuminant les	nostalgic melody of "Ô bien
	airs. / Un fleuve tent de sang, des	perdu... trésor sans prix" from
	villages déserts, / Un peuple	division 2 of the garden duet
	agonisant, et qui vers moi s'addresse	(no. 9). The new music then starts
	... à lui j'accours... / Vous chantez	getting increasingly agitated as
	mon triomphe, ou pleurez sur ma	Carlos begins describing his
	mort."	vision of the condition of Flanders
		under present Spanish tyranny. He
		will triumph or die.]

(b) *Allegro marziale, 4/4, C*
   [this passage was cut for Naples 1872]
   Élisabeth: "Oui, voilà l'héroisme
      . . . L'amour digne de nous . . . Qui
      font de l'homme un Dieu . . ."
   Carlos: "Oui, c'est par votre voix
      que le peuple m'appelle / . . ."

Allegro marziale, 4/4, C
[Text and music from
1867 remained in the 1884
production, intensified here and
there in the vocal lines, more
subtly instrumented, and with
a different concluding
modulation.]

(c) *un peu moins vite, c*
   C: ". . . vous pleurez?"
   É: ". . . Ce sont les pleurs . . . Que les
      femmes toujours accordent aux
      héros!"

moins vite, c#
[The same as in 1867 = 1872,
but transposed a half step higher,
anticipating the transposed
tonality of the slow movement
that follows.]

2   *Andante assai sostenuto, 4/4, B♭*
   É: "Au revoir dans un monde où la
      vie est meilleure / . . ."

a 2   * C: "Au revoir dans un monde . . ."
        * É: "Au revoir dans un monde . ."
        É: "Au moment solennel point
           d'indigne faiblesse / Oublions
           tous les noms de profane
           tendresse."

   [Elisabeth sings a countermelody
   against the main melody in the
   strings]

Assai sostenuto, 4/4, B
[Words and vocal lines are the
same, in the new key, with some
revised instrumentation, with
subdued new figuration in the
cellos.]

[In the revised version Elisabeth
sings the main melody, doubling
the strings, and Carlos joins her
for the second quatrain.]

a 2   C, É: "Donnons-nous ces noms
           chers aux plus chastes
           amours"
        C: "Adieu, ma mère!"
        É: "Adieu / Mon fils!"
        C, É: "Et pour toujours!"

[The closing cadential gesture is
slightly different but still climaxes
with the high notes.]

23   **Final.** Carlos, Elisabeth, Philip, the Grand Inquisitor and his inquisi-
torial Dominicans; later the monk from the cloister and the chorus of
monks offstage, as in no. 4.
JB 151–152. EI 634–651 (1867 = 1872) :: 667–669 (1884 = 1886).
Unlike the preceding duet movements (no. 22), where the revised
version is very close to the original, the action in the revised finale
was drastically shortened and the music removed, replaced, or
recomposed.

	1867 = 1872	1884 = 1886

3 (a) *Allegro assai sostenuto, 4/4,*   *Allegro agitato, 4/4, modulations*
          modulations

Philippe: "Oui, pour toujours! Il   Filippo: "Sì, per sempre! Io voglio
    faut un double sacrifice / Je   un doppio sacrificio! / Il dover
    ferai mon devoir..."   mio farò!..."
L'Inquisiteur: "Le Saint-Office /   L'Inquisitore: "Il Santo Uffizio /
    Fera le sien!"   Il suo farà!"

The threefold series of accusation, justification, and condemnation that follows in the 1867 finale is a classic Noskean "ritual" scene: the same music heard thrice, starting a half step higher each time.[19] It was not used in 1884 = 1886. (See example 13.7.)

(b) *Allegro assai sostenuto, 4/4, sequence*

d♭ to d♮
* Philippe: "À vous l'indigne fils
    que de moi Dieu fit naître! /
    Un détestable amour le
    brûle... à vous ce traître!"
* Élisabeth, Carlos: "Dieu le/me
    jugera!"
* Les Dominicains: "Dieu l'a
    dit! / Que le traître soit maudit!"

d♮ to e♭
Inq: "À vous... ce parjure
    hérétique!"
É, C: "Dieu le/me jugera!"
Dom: "Dieu l'a dit! / L'hérétique
    soit maudit!"

e♭ to e♮
P: "À vous... ce rebelle!"
É, C: "Dieu le/me jugera!"
Dom: "Dieu l'a dit! / Le rebelle
    soit maudit!"

(c) *a / A*

P, Inq, Dom: "Sois maudit artisan
    d'une oeuvre détestée... /
    Chassé du lieu céleste... Sois
    maudit!"
É: "De nos chastes adieux ces
    bourreaux font des crimes."

C: "Pour voyeurs de la mort il
  leur faut deux victimes."

f#, ensemble
P, Inq, Dom: "Chassé du lieu
  céleste…"
É: "De nos chastes adieux…"
C: "Pour voyeurs de la mort…"

From here to the end the dramatic action is the same in both versions, with mostly the same text. The music was recomposed, and where the opera ends softly in A major in 1867 = 1872, in 1884 = 1886 it ends *fortissimo* in B major. The monk's speech and the monks' chorus, reprised from no. 4 in Act II, are the same in both versions of the finale, transposed to the new key in 1884 = 1886, and a revised stage direction in 1884 = 1886 makes it clear that the monk really is supposed to be Charles V, not just some sort of mass hallucination. In 1884 = 1886 the music for the monks' chorus before the end is heard only in the orchestra. (See example 13.8.)

1867 = 1872	1884 = 1886
Carlos draws his sword: A to B♭	*D to C*
C: "Ah! Dieu me vengera ce tribunal de sang!"	C: "Dio mi vendicherà / Il tribunal di sangue sua mano spezzerà!"
(d) *Largo, g to V/V/a*	*Largo, a to V/V/b*
* Le moine: "Mon fils, les douleurs de la terre / Nous suivent encore dans ce lieu, / La paix que votre coeur espère / Ne se trouve qu'auprès de Dieu."	Il monaco: "Il duolo della terra / Nel chiostro ancor ci segue, / Solo del cuor la guerra / In ciel si calmerà."
Allegro to a / A	*Allegro agitato come I^a to b / B*
Inq: "La voix de l'Empereur!"	Inq: "La voce di Carlo!"
Dom: "C'est Charles Quint!"	Dom: "È Carlo Quinto!"
P: "Mon père!"	F: "Mio padre!"
É: "Grand Dieu!"	E: "O ciel!"
The monk takes Don Carlos into the cloister	*The monk takes Don Carlos into the cloister*
Monks offstage, *pianissimo*: "Charles Quint, l'auguste Empereur / N'est plus que cendre et que poussière."	[In 1884 = 1886 the *pianissimo* music of the monks' offstage chorus is heard in the orchestral brass instead, *fortissimo*.]

Reflecting its existence in multiple versions, Verdi's *Don Carlos* is performed and recorded in diverse ways. Most common is the 1886 five-act version in Italian, though the four-act 1884 version is often produced as well, while performances in French on the international circuit are beginning to appear at last. At the time of writing there are two first-rate recordings in French available. In 1985 Deutsche Grammophon released a studio record-ing conducted by Claudio Abbado with a stellar cast. In 1996 EMI released a live recording of a performance at the Théâtre du Châtelet, conducted by Antonio Pappano and directed by Luc Bondy; there is a corresponding videotape released by Kultur. The stage décor is too sparse, but, apart from a few eccentricities, the directing and acting is superb, and there is some fine singing by the principals Karita Mattila, Roberto Alagna, Thomas Hampson, and José van Dam.

The Abbado recording is of the 1886 version, to the French text of Méry and Du Locle as revised by Du Locle (which was what Verdi set but which was always sung in the Italian translation). The recording is supplemented, however, with six bands of material from the 1867 version in an Appendix on CD 4. The Châtelet production is of the 1867 version, with a number of omissions and alterations; fortunately some of them are available in Abbado's Appendix.

Number 0 (the woodcutters' scene) is not on the Châtelet sets but it can be heard on CD 4.4 of the Abbado set. It can be seen as well as heard, but in Italian, on the 1983 Metropolitan Opera videotape conducted by James Levine. Both the Châtelet and the Metropolitan Opera productions include the rest of the Fontainebleau act (nos. 1–2–3).

In Act II the Châtelet production omits the *à deux* of the Carlos-Posa duet (no. 5). Posa's duet with King Philip (no. 11), moreover, is a mixture of the first half (divisions 0–1–2) from 1867 and the second half (corre-sponding with divisions 3–4) from 1884 = 1886, with two measures from 1872. An ingenious and hardly noticeable transposition is used to help the transition.[20]

The Elisabeth-Eboli scene opening 1867 Act III (no. 12) is complete on CD 4.5 of Abbado's Appendix, as well as the ballet music, on CD 4.6. In the Châtelet production the exchange of capes, necklace, and mask in no. 12 is omitted, probably necessitated by the minimal staging for all of Act III; there are some cuts in the chorus music, and there is no ballet.

In the Philip-Elisabeth scene before the quartet in Act IV, set A (no. 17), the Châtelet production uses the 1884 = 1886 version of the Queen's second lyrical passage, in which she reminds the King that she was once affianced to his son and hence keeps his portrait among her jewels. The lovely duet in the first part of no. 18, after Elisabeth has forgiven Eboli her theft of the jewel coffer out of thwarted love for Don Carlos, is absent from the Châtelet production; just that portion of the scene, however, is fortunately available in Abbado's Appendix, on CD 4.7.

The Abbado recording has divisions 1 and 2 of the original Act IV finale on CD 4.8, including the *concertato* that was cut before the dress rehearsal and that Verdi later recomposed as the "Lachrymosa" for his Requiem. This much is also included in the Châtelet production, which then continues with a jumble of bits from various redactions of the aborted rebellion that ends the act.[21]

In the Châtelet production of Act V there are two cuts in the composite number 22–23, the duet and finale. Division 1(b), Elisabeth's Allegro marziale that was cut in 1872 and restored with improvements in 1884 = 1886, is omitted; also omitted are divisions 3 (b) and 3 (c), the Noskean ritual accusations and the ensemble that follows. Fortunately, again, this latter omission is remedied by CD 4.9 of Abbado's Appendix.

Many years ago a fine complete performance of the 1867 *Don Carlos* was broadcast by the BBC, under the auspices of Julian Budden. A recording of this broadcast was once briefly available on a set of LP discs put out by Voce Records, their no. 23; a re-release of that performance on CD would be most welcome. Still better would be a new recording of all the music Verdi composed in 1866–67, including the passages cut before and after the premiere, with perhaps a couple of supplementary bands with the replacement passages for Naples in 1872 – a *desideratum* indeed, if only (so to speak) for the record.

Example 13.1 Verdi, *Don Carlos*, II, 11, Duo (Philip, Posa), three versions of a passage in division 1(b): Philip's response to Posa's Flanders narrative (see p. 218).

(a) Paris 1867

(b) Naples 1872

(c) Milan 1884 = Modena 1886

Example 13.2 Verdi, *Don Carlos*, II, 11, Duo (Philip, Posa), two versions of a passage in division 2 (slow movement): Posa's plea to Philip and Philip's reaction (see p. 219–20)

(a) Paris 1867 = Naples 1872

(b) Milan 1884 = Modena 1886

Example 13.3 Verdi, *Don Carlos*, II, 11, Duo (Philip, Posa), three versions of a passage in division 3: Philip wants Posa to be his domestic confidant (see pp. 220–21).

(a) Paris 1867

(b) Naples 1872

(c) Milan 1884 = Modena 1886

Example 13.4 Verdi, *Don Carlos*, II, 11, Duo (Philip, Posa), three versions of a passage in division 4 (see pp. 221–22)

(a) Paris 1867: Philip believes Posa can bring him peace of mind, and Posa wonders what has opened Philip's heart

(b) Naples 1872: Philip wants Posa to keep an eye on Elisabeth and Carlos, and Posa welcomes the chance to be near his friend

(c) Milan 1884 = Modena 1886: Posa wonders what has opened Philip's heart, and Philip looks forward to peace of mind

Example 13.5 Verdi, *Don Carlos*, V, 22, Duo (Carlos, Elisabeth), settings of corresponding French and Italian texts from division 1(a) of the opera's finale: Carlos's dream (see pp. 225–26)

(a) Paris 1867

(b) Milan 1884 = Modena 1886

Example 13.6 Verdi, *Don Carlos*, V, 22, Duo (Carlos, Elisabeth), from division 2 of the opera's finale: Carlos and Elisabeth say farewell (see pp. 225–26).

Paris 1867; in Milan 1884 = Modena 1886, a half step higher

Example 13.7 Verdi, *Don Carlos*, V, 23, Final (Carlos, Elisabeth, Philip, Grand Inquisitor, Dominican monks, cloistered monks), from division 3(b) of the opera's finale: stage 1 of the ritual of accusation (see pp. 227–28)

Paris 1867 only

Example 13.8 Verdi, *Don Carlos*, V, 23, Final (Carlos, Elisabeth, Philip, Grand Inquisitor, Dominican monks, cloistered monks); from division 3 (d) of the opera's finale: the monk (Charles V?) takes Carlos into the cloister (see p. 228).

Paris 1867; in Milan 1884 = Modena 1886, a whole step higher

14 Desdemona's alienation and Otello's fall

SCOTT L. BALTHAZAR

In an oft-quoted assessment of Shakespeare's Desdemona, Verdi described her as "not a woman, but a type. She is the type of goodness, resignation, self-sacrifice. They are creatures born for others, unconscious of their own egos."[1] Shakespeare's play, of course, provides ample material for this sort of interpretation, as characters extol her beauty, virtue, selflessness, and other merits. And as James Hepokoski has documented, in recreating Desdemona for their own *Otello* (1887) Verdi and his librettist Arrigo Boito were probably influenced by nineteenth-century critical traditions represented by August Wilhelm Schlegel and by Victor Hugo, who viewed Desdemona as "saintly" and as "a spiritualist and almost a mystic," and also seem to have drawn upon such late nineteenth-century literary themes as *decadentismo* devotional iconology and the *femme fragile*.[2] Of course devout heroines in peril were nothing new to Verdi, the Leonoras in *Il trovatore* and *La forza del destino* being prime examples, while heroines falsely accused had long been stock-in-trade, and Violetta (*La traviata*) provided a precedent for the physically fragile heroine. So by emphasizing Desdemona's purity, naïveté, and vulnerability, Verdi and Boito adhered to an aesthetic involving the cathartic destruction of a sympathetic female lead with which their audience could readily identify.

As Joseph Kerman and others have observed, Verdi and Boito expanded Desdemona's presence on stage, and many of her added scenes, as well as other adaptations of her role, contribute to her idealized image and encourage the audience to empathize with her.[3] This orientation is most apparent in two of the principal non-Shakespearean pieces – she is beatified by her companions in the Act II homage chorus and caught in prayer in the Act IV "Ave Maria" – as well as in the elimination of dialogue with Iago during the opening storm scene, through which Shakespeare had portrayed her as childishly self-absorbed and nonchalant about Othello's safety. It also occurs, sometimes more subtly, in other aspects of her characterization. For example, Verdi and Boito fueled sympathy for Desdemona by making her more articulate about her distress and her supporters more attentive to it, a shift evident in the Act III finale in which Otello abuses her before the Venetian ambassadors.[4] As Kerman has noted, "after Otello has insulted her in front of them and thrown her to the ground, Verdi's Desdemona, instead of escaping, rises to the occasion with another long, explicit song of

[237]

self-expression. In fact a huge ensemble in the old style, with seven soloists and two choruses, is constructed downwards from her superb lament."[5] Apart from Cassio's self-interested response and Jago's secretive advice to Otello and Roderigo, reaction focuses on Desdemona's humiliation. Otello is virtually ignored, except as the cause of his wife's misery, and literally side-lined, according to the blocking diagram and stage directions.[6] In contrast, Othello had taken center stage in Shakespeare's version of the scene. Desdemona and the others had barely responded before she exited, and Othello's continued accusations were the only sustained attention she received. There Lodovico treated the incident primarily as a social gaffe ("this would not be believed in Venice," IV, i, 264) that called into question Othello's character and fitness to command: "Is this the noble Moor whom our full senate / Call all in all sufficient?" (IV, i, 290–96).[7]

Just as the operatic Desdemona is more sympathetic than that of the play, Otello is more menacing and less heroic. Hepokoski has proposed that Verdi and Boito's conception of the title character was influenced by the interpretations of two Italian Shakespeareans: Ernesto Rossi, who played Othello as an enraged primitive, and Tommaso Salvini, whose Othello was more heroic and idealistic.[8] Hepokoski suggests that "Verdi tends to depict Otello in two different modes ... roughly analogous to the Salvini–Rossi polarity," showing Otello's nobility in Acts I and IV, his savagery in Acts II and III.[9] But as Hepokoski acknowledges, this dichotomy is hardly clear cut. And while Boito and Verdi may have been aware of this critical and theatrical polarity, their tilt toward the "savage" interpretation is evident in all four acts. Unlike some other passages from the discarded Venetian Act I of the play that were saved and relocated in the opera, Othello's scene before the senators, which had introduced him as the only viable savior of Cyprus, was eliminated. Instead, in the opera he appears first during the opening storm as the fortuitous beneficiary of its destruction of the Turkish fleet. Musical inflation of his brief entrance – as a "demigod," according to Hepokoski – only underscores the insubstantiality of his presumed heroism.[10] Although Boito claimed that Otello acts rationally in the opera immediately following the duel, he abuses his power – as Hepokoski has also noticed – demoting Cassio for personal rather than professional reasons, acting only after Desdemona has been awakened, and seems "musically violent" here.[11] In the love duet, music for Otello's account of his exploits is also inflamed rather than temperate, and later he exclaims that his joyous love "m'innonda / Sì fieramente ... che ansante mi giacio" ("engulfs me so fiercely ... that I lie breathless").

Kerman's assertion that Otello's "nobility, as well as his degradation" is established in Act III is also debatable.[12] Because Verdi and Boito had previously emphasized his manipulation by Iago to the exclusion of his heroism, the fanfares that announce the ambassadors' arrival to begin Act III and its finale, as well as the "Lion of St. Mark" choruses in that finale, sound hollow. To the audience they trumpet the expedient misjudgment of his character by the Venetians instead of attesting to his former grandeur.[13] Deletion of Shakespeare's "It is the cause" speech (V, ii, 1–22) when Otello enters Desdemona's bedroom in Act IV allows Verdi's music, as Kerman has skillfully shown, to speak at a crucial moment and, no doubt, to reclaim some of the content of the original text.[14] Yet it effectively eliminates Otello's disturbed rationalization and "ennoblement" of the crime he is about to commit that had partly vindicated his actions in the play. Though perhaps overstated, Hepokoski's contention that "in the opera there is not a single bar of music that so much as hints at that aspect of the play's hero that stood calm and self-controlled" in battle seems true to the spirit of Verdi's interpretation.[15]

As well as eviscerating Otello's nobility, Verdi and Boito systematically eliminated mitigating factors that helped Shakespeare's audience to pity Othello's behavior. They cut Brabantio's curse and his insinuations about his daughter's deceptiveness, indications that Desdemona might betray her foreign husband to regain her former Venetian status, and Othello's perceived sacrifice of masculine independence for his marriage ("But that I love the gentle Desdemona / I would not my unhoused free condition / Put into circumscription and confine / For the sea's worth," I, ii, 26–29). In particular, despite their emphasis of Otello's choleric side, Verdi and Boito made less of his race than Shakespeare – or various Ottocento actors – had. Hepokoski considers "Verdi and Boito's handling of the racial question . . . commendably understated," and Kerman asserts bluntly that in the opera "there is no reason for Otello to be black."[16] Boito may have wanted an African or Turkish Otello, but Verdi won out, prohibiting "any stage-costume that suggested the exotic or the primitive instead of the noble Venetian."[17] Gone are the pervasive references in the play to "the Moor," Otello's given name appearing mostly in the opera instead. And racial slurs are confined to a scant few passages: Jago's comments to Roderigo immediately after Otello's entrance in Act I and a line for the Venetian knights ("Quell'uomo nero è sepolcrale" ("That black man is tomblike") hidden in the *largo concertato* of the Act III finale, where Otello is otherwise repeatedly feted (as noted above). Compare, for example, Emilia's "O, more the angel she, / And you the blacker devil," "The Moor has killed my mistress," "O thou dull Moor," etc., in Shakespeare (V, ii, 157–58, 200, and 265) to her "Otello has killed Desdemona" in the final scene of the opera.

By pushing ethnicity into the background, Verdi deflected any impulse to regard "primitiveness" as an excuse for "inevitably" violent behavior, and forced his audience to judge Otello on his actions rather than as a racial stereotype.[18] Given his adoration by Desdemona and, apparently, by Venetian society, Otello's racial insecurity smacks of self-pity. And his attempt in the Act II duet/quartet to link his ethnicity to his lack of social sophistication and his inability to trust his own intuitions or to believe the abundant evidence that vindicates Desdemona seem unconvincing:[19]

Forse perchè gl'inganni	Perhaps because I do not understand
D'arguto amor non tendo,	the deceits of sly love,
Forse perchè discendo	perhaps because I am declining
Nella valle degli anni,	into the valley of my years,
Forse perchè ho sul viso	perhaps because on my face
Quest'atro tenebror...	there is this darkness...
Ella è perduta e irriso	she is lost and I am mocked
Io sono e il core infrango.	and my heart breaks.

In short, Verdi and Boito made Otello anti-heroic, an emotional weakling and abusive dupe who irrationally disregards his wife's loyalty.[20]

Otello's suspicion that his wife will stray seems all the more preposterous in the opera because she lacks the independent identity of the play's heroine. Shakespeare's Desdemona was, and clearly considered herself, the "deserving woman" of Iago's homily (II, i, 168–89): intelligent, articulate, assertive. A woman of boundless potential, she entered her marriage from a position of strength and, according to Emilia, gave up countless opportunities: "Hath she forsook so many noble matches, / Her father and her country, all her friends, / To be called whore?" (IV, ii, 146–48). The noted Shakespearean scholar Jane Adamson has observed that "in the first three acts [of the play, Desdemona] ... seems active, resolute, confident – as decisive as Othello at the beginning,"[21] a characteristic seen in the way she reassures Cassio with machismo and some vanity as late as III, iii, 22–31:

> My lord shall never rest;
> I'll watch him tame and talk him out of patience;
> His bed shall seem a school, his board a shrift;
> I'll intermingle everything he does
> With Cassio's suit. Therefore be merry, Cassio,
> For thy solicitor shall rather die
> Than give thy cause away.

In fact, Shakespeare's Desdemona coveted the opportunities afforded only to men. Othello boasted to the Venetian senate that he had attracted her partly because she could experience his career vicariously: "My story being done... / She wished she had not heard it; yet she wished / That heaven had made her such a man" (I, iii, 174–79). Later she seemed to agree (I, iii, 277–81):

> So that, dear lords, if I be left behind,
> A moth of peace, and he go to the war,
> The rights for which I love him are bereft me,
> And I a heavy interim shall support
> By his dear absence.

Though Verdi and Boito made Desdemona more articulate in certain respects than her Shakespearean counterpart, she also assumes a more dependent and vulnerable persona, arousing the audience's protective instincts.[22] Unlike Shakespeare, they avoided characterizing her as sophisticated, self-reliant, vicariously thrill-seeking, and potentially conflicted about her life choices. And while their Desdemona is hardly passive, the vigor, tenacity, and obliviousness to Othello's moods with which she had championed Cassio's cause in the play – and unwittingly supported Iago's – is largely absent. Her submissiveness in the opera is underscored in the operatic Willow Song (Act IV), which differs considerably from Shakespeare's in its focus on Desdemona's wifely subordination – "'Egli era nato per la sua gloria, / Io per amar…Io per amarlo e per morir'" ("'He was born for his glory, I to love…I to love him and to die'") – rather than her incomprehension of infidelity. In contrast to Shakespeare's spitfire, she sees herself as a traditional wife: dutiful, supportive, and completely devoted.

This dissimilarity in marital roles is apparent in the different way the two Desdemonas handle their men. Shakespeare's heroine seemingly had manipulated Othello largely through ego massaging and dogged (albeit well-intentioned) nagging. Shakespeare alluded to her ability also to nurture only once, during the lovers' reunion in Cyprus (II, i, 212–30), when Othello tells her:

>   O my soul's joy!
> If after every tempest come such calms,
> May the winds blow till they have wakened death!
> …
> My soul hath her content so absolute
> That not another comfort like to this
> Succeeds in unknown fate.

In the opera, however, Otello's dependence on Desdemona's knack for subduing his frenzies and restoring his balance becomes central to their relationship.[23] The love duet (Act I) draws on the passage cited above in casting love as an antidote to violence, but employs more active imagery ("furious heart," "war thunder[s]," "the world [is] engulfed," "immense wrath"), emphasizing Otello's violence and the importance of Desdemona's healing presence:

Già il mio cor fremebondo	Already my furious heart
S'ammansa in quest'amplesso e si risensa.	is soothed by this embrace and grows calm.
Tuoni la guerra e s'inabissi il mondo	Let war thunder and the world be engulfed
Se dopo l'ira immensa	if after such immense wrath
Vien questo immenso amor!	comes this immense love!

In the opera's love scene (but not in the play) love fuels but also exhausts Otello's frenzy, an image that Hepokoski notes is underscored by the stage directions, which call for Desdemona to support him as he staggers: "Ah! la gioia m'innonda / Sì fieramente...che ansante mi giacio" ("Ah! Joy engulfs me so fiercely...that I lie breathless").[24]

Verdi and Boito later created a new context for Shakespeare's "If she be false, O, then heaven mocks itself" (III, iii, 313), locating it in the coda of the Act II homage chorus. In Shakespeare, Othello's remark had followed Desdemona's unheralded entrance with Emilia, but it could easily be construed as an affirmation of his own privileged status, which precludes such betrayals. In the opera, by adding a line for Otello acknowledging the chorus in which Desdemona is deified – "Quel canto mi conquide. / S'ella m'inganna, il ciel sé stesso irride!" ("That song conquers me. If she is betraying me, heaven is mocking itself!") – Verdi and Boito provided a non-ambiguous interpretation of Shakespeare's words, attributing a comforting power to the purity of Desdemona's musical image.[25] Shortly thereafter, in the slow movement of the Act II quartet with Jago and Emilia (again, a passage not found in Shakespeare), Desdemona blunts Otello's anger by adopting a subservient stance and empowering him to pardon her ("La tua fanciulla io sono / Umile e mansueta" – "I am your maiden, humble and obedient") and by playing a nursing role: "Vien ch'io t'allieti il core, / Ch'io ti lenisca il duol" ("Come, let me gladden your heart, let me ease your suffering"). In the corresponding scene, Shakespeare's Desdemona had made no such effort, only offering dryly "I am very sorry that you are not well" (III, iii, 327). In Verdi, Desdemona's preoccupation with Otello's mood continues to the end (as in Shakespeare) when she prepares for bed in Act IV:

| EMILIA Era più calmo? | Was he calmer? |
| DESDEMONA Mi parea. | He seemed so to me. |

Significantly, Desdemona answers Emilia's question, whereas in Shakespeare she had ignored his mood, responding "He says he will return incontinent [immediately]."

Verdi and Boito's treatment of the handkerchief in itself reflects the operatic Desdemona's greater presence and modified persona. In the play it had been associated primarily with Othello as "my first gift" (III, iii, 488), "my handkerchief" (IV, i, 174), and a magical heirloom (III, iv, 63–84). Shakespeare's Iago had treated it as a fortuitous enhancement of his plot, Cassio as a meaningless *billet-doux* (III, iv, and IV, I), and Desdemona (and Othello, for that matter) as inconsequential before Iago made it an issue. In the opera, however, it is less Otello's appendage: he initially refers to it (Act II duet with Jago) as his "first pledge of love" ("pegno primo d'amor"), emphasizing its importance for his marriage rather than his ownership of it, he alludes only briefly to its magical powers – though with arresting music – when demanding its return in Act III ("Una possente maga ne ordia lo stame arcano. / Ivi è riposta l'alta malìa d'un talismano" – "A mighty sorceress disposed its secret weave. It contains the lofty magic of a talisman"), and he ignores its familial importance almost entirely.

Having weakened the handkerchief's ties to Otello, Verdi and Boito made it an iconic representation of Desdemona. She offers it to her husband in Act II with greater solicitude than in the play. Shakespeare's Desdemona had responded to Othello's "pain upon my forehead" offhandedly, "Faith, that's with watching; 'twill away again. / Let me but bind it hard, within this hour / It will be well." In the opera, however, she acknowledges Otello's illness ("that troublesome burning"), emphasizes her own role in healing ("if *my* hand bandages you"), and offers to bandage Otello with soft cloth rather than "bind it hard":

Quell'ardor molesto	That troublesome burning
Svanirà, se con questo	will disappear if my hand bandages you
Morbido lino la mia man ti fascia.	with this downy linen.

The affection with which the operatic Desdemona tenders her handker-chief makes it a physical embodiment of her nurturing persona, an associa-tion reinforced for the audience by Cassio's raptures in a substantial lyrical movement that serves as the centerpiece of the Act III trio. For Cassio it not only promises a new, mysterious liason; he describes it in terms that echo Desdemona's image in the Act II homage chorus – rays, whiteness, lightness, snow, clouds, breezes, and miracles – and reveal his repressed love. Conse-quently, as Otello watches Cassio produce the handkerchief, the possibility that she has given it away is itself a betrayal apart from any sexual infidelity it might divulge, because it symbolizes giving herself away, playing her nurs-ing role for another man. Earlier, Otello's rejection of the handkerchief – "Non ho d'uopo di ciò" ("I do not need that"), which is more decisive than in Shakespeare ("Your napkin is too little," III, iii, 325) – marked a water-shed in their relationship, the point at which he first rejected her calming intervention, neutralizing her ability to manipulate him, control him, and keep his anger in check. Once "Duce del nostro Duce" ("Commander of our Commander," Act II), like Cassio she has been demoted, having lost the tug-of-war with Jago for Otello's allegiance. That is why Jago (in the Act III trio) compares it to a cobweb, the whole of the trap he has set, indicating tangentially the importance of dissolving Desdemona's control for the success of his plot. Invested with these layers of meaning, the handkerchief becomes more than Jago's serendipity. When it falls, it opens the path to Otello's alliance with Jago in their Act II duet and to Desdemona's concession in her Act III duet with Otello that his moods are beyond her comprehension and consequently her control: "In te parla una Furia, la sento e non l'intendo" ("A Fury speaks in you; I hear it and don't understand it").[26] In telling her, "I do not need that," Otello might as well have said, "I do not need you." Desdemona's defeat is, of course, Jago's victory: in the absence of her influence – and of a rational, heroic side to her husband's character – Otello's fragile equilibrium is easy prey to Jago's wiles.

So by presenting Otello as volatile from the very start, Verdi and Boito changed the dynamics of the story line and elevated Desdemona's importance within it. Adamson has argued that in Shakespeare both Othello and Desdemona undergo significant transformations and consequently play equally meaningful structural roles. While Othello becomes more and more obsessive, Desdemona loses confidence in herself and withdraws, becoming increasingly dependent on her idealized image of her husband and increasingly alienated from him and the realities of his behavior. According to Adamson, the tragedy of *Othello* hinges equally on Othello's festering distrust and Desdemona's debilitating self-doubt. In contrast, we have seen that the operatic Otello's "nobility" is minimized, his intemperance dominates from the beginning, and his characterization remains relatively uniform and his reactions out of proportion throughout. As Hepokoski has remarked, "one might be hard put to demonstrate a careful gradation of emotion [in Otello's responses] from the first to the last."[27] Otello's transformation having been neutralized, Desdemona's declining ability to blunt her husband's rage almost exclusively determines the trajectory of their relationship and the structure of the opera.

One of the most important ramifications of French influence for Verdi's late style is his adoption of a motif-dominated musical language in both the voices and the orchestra as a counterpoint to more traditional Italianate lyricism, an approach which begins in the middle-period operas shortly after his first Parisian sojourn.[28] In *Otello* the network of related motives is extremely dense, involving a much more sophisticated elaboration of this technique than in *Aida* or in the French operas that had influenced Verdi originally. Here relationships among motifs not only unify the score but also define roles. Hepokoski has argued, for example, that Desdemona is musically distinct, her "pure, guiltless passivity" allowing Verdi "the opportunity to permit 'naïve' melodic lyricism to counterpoint with an otherwise relentless, pointed declamation and motivic symphonism" more typical of the other characters.[29] This "motivic" orientation is particularly evident in Jago's music. His Credo, while perhaps overdrawn in its text – Budden and others have tended to dismiss it[30] – is nonetheless essential along with the preceding *scena* in linking him both to a discontinuous, anti-lyrical vocal style and to an extensive repertory of motifs that characterize him. His diverse musical vocabulary, which is presented in the Credo and the preceding *scena* as a freely juxtaposed series of thematic units, many of which are developed immediately, includes: his signature triplet rhythms (see example 14.1, a); sawtooth melodic contours and large melodic leaps (see example 14.1, b); trills and harsh grace notes (see example 14.1, b); staccato or *marcato* articulation, particularly of repeated chords or rapid passagework (see example 14.1, c); unstable harmony involving chromatic half steps and tritone-oriented dissonance, especially diminished-seventh chords (see example 14.1, b); and the inevitable daemonic low brass scoring.[31] Once Jago's ownership of this repertory is established, his musical presence is evident in all of the scenes of Act I, not only those in which he participates actively (the drinking song), but also in those that foreshadow his later devastation: the opening storm, a precursor to Otello's psychological "storm" in the postlude of his confrontation duet with Desdemona (Act III, after "quella vil cortigiana che è la sposa d'Otello"); the bonfire chorus, in which fire is compared to love that exhausts itself; and several of Otello's agitated passages in the love duet. And more obviously, exposition of Jago's motifs in the Credo allows their increasing dominance of Otello's music to be heard as Jago's corrupting influence, the cause of the jealousy that poisons him.

But Jago's motifs corrupt Desdemona's music as well. The point of departure for this process is the love duet, in which Desdemona first sings and

Example 14.1 Verdi, *Otello*, II, "Credo in un Dio crudel" (Jago), motifs
(a) mm. 13–15

(b) mm. 45–56

(c) mm. 81–82

in which she defines her preferred "naïve lyricism" and self-protectively soothing affect. In contrast to Jago's music, Desdemona's boasts demurely radiant melodies but no distinctive motifs. Her conjunct vocal lines consist primarily of scales and repeated notes set in declamatory rhythms, avoiding the expressive leaps and high notes that stock the expressive arsenals of operatic heroines. Also unlike Jago, whose musical portrait in the Credo is an irregularly periodic patchwork, Desdemona adheres to a more traditional framework of predictable two- and four-measure phrases. The "girlish" side of Desdemona's musical language is particularly evident in the "reminiscence" episode of the duet (beginning "Quando narravi") in which she and Otello relive their courtship as a prelude to intimacy. Here Desdemona summons the innocent persona that won Otello originally and apparently keeps him in tow. "Poi mi guidavi," for example, demonstrates for the first time the calming role of Desdemona's music, as she counteracts Otello's unexpectedly fervid account of his exploits ("Pingea dell'armi"). Desdemona's docile purity in these passages is reinforced later in the homage chorus, which together with the love duet frames Jago's Credo, emphasizing the stylistic disparity between the two characters, and again reassures Otello by providing a calming antidote to his unstable temperament.

As others have suggested, Verdi's Desdemona is not immaculate.[32] And her sensuousness – the womanly maturity that commentators have noted – is conveyed by chromaticism even in her initial *risposta* ("Mio superbo guerrier"). However, unlike Jago, who embraces the potential anarchy of chromaticism wholeheartedly, hiding only deceptively behind diatonic music, Desdemona seems more ambivalent about it. Her tonal digressions initially seem innocuous and inconsequential, "excused" as direct responses to the text: the mixed-mode circle of fifths sequence for "quanti tormenti" ("how many torments") and rising scale to "soavi abbracciamenti" ("tender embraces"); the gliding parallel sixth chords, tinged by chromaticism at the end, for "mormorare insieme" ("whisper together"), possibly foreshadowing Jago's later "whisperings"; the dream-like harp arpeggio for "Te ne rammenti" ("Do you remember"). Similar inflections occur later in the piece, also in response to specific phrases, such as at "gli spasimi sofferti" ("the torments suffered"). Apart from these "madrigalisms" and the secondary dominants that turn the ends of Desdemona's solos to different keys, her language is remarkably diatonic at a local level, particularly by comparison with Jago's (and her husband's as the opera progresses).

While the angelic cast of Desdemona's music charms the audience, reinforcing the textual adaptations discussed earlier, the subtle duality of her style displayed in the love duet, in which ingenuous "impurities" tinge her naïve lyricism, charts her downfall. To a great extent she loses control of Otello by gradually abandoning her girlish style, which represents constancy to him, and by relying increasingly on the womanly, sensual style that agitates him. Jago aggravates the problem by encouraging Otello to associate Desdemona's sexuality with potential infidelity and to hear her womanly music as an echo of Jago's own motivic repertory and accusations.

This shift is first observed in the Act II duet/quartet. In the opening section her petition for Cassio and proffer of the handkerchief is tinged with Jago-like chromaticism and dissonance through modal mixture (for example, in her opening line "D'un uom che geme"), chromatic passing and neighbor notes (particularly following "Perchè torbida suona"), and non-functional, tritone-laced harmony and sequential progressions (at "Lui stesso"). Jago's triplets and scurrying sixteenths also appear in her vocal line and accompaniment. And after Otello's rebuke, her melody leading the *largo concertato* of the quartet ("Dammi la dolce e lieta parola"), though modest, also departs from her "girlish" style in its disjunct contours (including the initial major-seventh chord), pentatonicism, unconventional three-measure opening phrases, triplets, and climactic B♭s (B♮s in the original version).[33] Though her music may sound innocent enough to the audience, Otello's suspicions lead him to measure it against the idealized purity of her music at their courtship and to hear in it a disingenuous sophistication that echoes and seems to substantiate Jago's insinuations.

Otello's increasing distrust of and unresponsiveness to Desdemona's "corrupted" womanly persona is even more evident in the confrontation duet in Act III ("Dio ti giocondi"). At the beginning he toys with her, putting her off guard by trading phrases of a melody in her ingratiating, naïvely lyrical voice, and by returning deceptively to that melody at the end. By mocking her calming style, he dispossesses her of it, forcing her to tack in a direction that makes matters worse. Responding to his first outburst, her attempt to calm him ("Tu di me ti fai gioco"), while diatonic and regularly periodic, is more disjunct, seventh-oriented, and sequential than anything she has sung previously. And after reaching a climax on the Neapolitan of the tonic G major she veers in defeat to C minor, a tonal center that later plays into Jago's hands, as discussed below. Following Otello's next assault ("Pel cielo! l'anima mia si desta!"), her music goes even farther awry. Her reply ("Esterrefatta fisso") begins with declamation underpinned by ominous open tritones, a passage that Jago himself might have sung. And her attempt at soothing stepwise diatonic lyricism ("io prego il cielo") is structured sequentially and infected by large leaps and chromaticism in the accompaniment. Though poised at first, pacing herself in symmetrical four-measure phrases that allude to the opening phrases of a standard lyric-form melody, she soon loses her composure as she leaps to a climactic B♭ in her second medial phrase (again, B♮ in the original version, at the second "Guarda le prime lagrime"). Thus her attempt to gain credibility through convention is undermined by her apparent recourse to sensuality and histrionics. After Otello dismisses her, the transformation of her style is complete. Abandoning traditional melodic form entirely, she whispers three brief, irregular, chromatically tinged phrases, then without further preparation impatiently blurts a climactic phrase ("E son io l'innocente cagion") that compresses the range of "io prego il cielo" into a single desperate f^1 to bb^2 leap ("di tanto pianto"). This disjointed assemblage of ill-advised gestures serves only to confirm Jago's portrait of Desdemona as a seductive, insincere adulteress: she seals her own fate by abandoning the musical language that had won Otello's love.

The shift of Desdemona's musical language is consolidated in her Act IV Willow Song, which symbolizes her capitulation to Jago's plot and her recasting from Otello's emotional handler to his victim. Though ostensibly a folk song – Desdemona dissociates herself from her own situation by reenacting Barbara's song, which had been sung to her by her mother – Verdi's setting is not folk-like. Paralleling the metrical complexity of Desdemona's text, her music consists of an idiosyncratic, unsymmetrical series of disconnected phrases and motifs of different lengths that fragments its poem about betrayed love.[34] Although the song alludes to strophic form, suggesting stanzas preceded by the same ritornello and framed by refrains, its second and third stanzas introduce new ideas (at "E dalle ciglia" and "Scendean l'augelli") and rearrange old ones. This tendency is especially pronounced in the extended third stanza (beginning "Scorreano i rivi"), in which references to the motifs of the song are interspersed with Desdemona's reactions, the disintegration of the internal stanzaic structure suggesting her bewilderment, lost self-confidence, and resignation. Madrigalistic vocal gestures and accompaniments for "Salce" (musical sighs), "Scorreano i rivi" (murmuring sixteenth notes), "Cantiamo" (the return to lyricism), and "Scendean l'augelli" (bird-like chirping) mimic art song rather than folk song. And Desdemona's idiosyncratic vocalism – her chilling arpeggiation of the diminished-minor-seventh (half-diminished) chord ("Piangea cantando"), octave leaps ("Cantiamo"), and frequent pentatonicism – further suggests a sophistication embodying Jago's motivic orientation that is removed from the folk tradition.[35] So Desdemona's capitulation through retreat from the naïve lyrical style that Otello had trusted is completed in the scene with which her role is most identified as she provides her final assessment of their relationship.

Immediately afterward, even in prayer ("Prega per chi adorando"), she is unable to regain fully her purity of musical language. Although the piece opens in a diatonic lyrical style, it includes many of the "corruptions" from earlier pieces: unconventional phrase structure characterized by three-measure phrases, chromaticism, and Jago's triplets – significantly at her reference to suffering "oltraggio" (outrage) – and a non-symmetrical return of the opening melody. Desdemona's death scene demonstrates her literally fatal loss of musical control over her husband. Later, her final moments are an operatic screaming match dominated by Jago's chromatic sixteenth

			series I	series II	series III
Act I					
Storm		"Vittoria! Sterminio!"	e–E		
Bonfire song		"Fuoco di gioia!"	e/E		
Drinking song		"Inaffia l'ugola!"	b/D/A	b/D/A	
Love duet		"Già nella notte"			Gb
		"Quando narravi"		F	
		"Venga la morte"			Db
Act II					
Credo		"Credo in un Dio"		f–F	
Homage chorus		"Dove guardi"	E		
Duet/quartet		"D'un uom che geme"	E		
		"Dammi la dolce"	B		
Alliance duet		"Ora per sempre"	Ab (G♯)		
		"Era la notte"		C	
		"Sì pel ciel"		A	
Act III					
Confrontation duet		"Dio ti giocondi"	E		
Scena		"Ma o pianto"	Eb		
Trio		"Essa t'avvince"	Ab (G♯)		
		"Questa è una ragna"		C	
Finale		Fanfare		C	
		"Viva! Evviva"		F–C	
		"A terra"	Ab (G♯)		Ab (G♯)
		"Viva! Viva!"		C	
Act IV					
Willow Song		Prelude			c♯
		"Piangea cantando"			F♯/f♯
Prayer		"Ave Maria"			Ab
Murder		"Chi è là?"	E		

Figure 14.1 Keys in Verdi's *Otello*

notes, which Otello has internalized. No longer the "captain's captain" in her music, she falls defenseless, Jago having fulfilled his vow in the homage chorus: "Beltà ed amor in dolce inno concordi! / I vostri infrangerò soavi accordi" ("Beauty and love united in sweet song! I will interrupt your tender chords").

Just as the transformation of Desdemona's musical persona is critical to the dramatic structure of *Otello*, she plays an integral role in its tonal organization. That is, Desdemona's fatal inability to maintain a "safe" style in which she can control Otello has parallels in the treatment of her keys. Although many features of Verdi's tonal plan cannot be discussed in detail here, a brief overview provides a necessary context for examining keys in Desdemona's scenes with her husband.[36] The primary tonics of lyric movements as well as the vast majority of secondary tonics may be viewed profitably as contributing to three long-range, interwoven series that arpeggiate triads or move by fifths (see figure 14.1, in which the three columns correspond to the three series of tonics). These series proceed alternately throughout the opera, accompanying scenes that present the deterioration of the relationship from different perspectives.

The first series is a closed arpeggiation of E major – E–B–G sharp (A flat)–E – that accompanies the erosion of Venetian normalcy, Otello's growing jealousy, and ultimately his recognition of Desdemona's innocence. E major is established as a starting point in Act I in the victory chorus of the storm scene, the bonfire song, and the "bacio" motif of the love duet, and in Act II in the homage chorus and the opening of the duet/quartet in which Desdemona first petitions for Cassio's reinstatement. B minor opens each verse of the drinking song, which draws Cassio into Jago's scheme. And B major was the original key for the *largo concertato* of the Act II quartet, in which Desdemona is first rebuked and the handkerchief taken by Jago.[37] Otello acknowledges the end of his career in A flat (G sharp) ("Ora per sempre") in the Act II alliance duet. The same key serves the first lyric movement of the Act III trio as Cassio belittles his new love (assumed by Otello to be Desdemona) and the *largo concertato* of the finale, where Desdemona's murder is planned. Although the opera's last scene is tonally unstable, it starts in E, emphasizes E minor at important points surrounding the murder, and ends the opera in E major as Otello kisses Desdemona for the last time.

The second series is an open-ended arpeggiation of F major – F–A–C – that accompanies the disintegration of Otello's bond with Desdemona, his realignment with Jago, and Jago's domination of Otello, which again is facilitated by duping Cassio. Battle lines between Desdemona and Jago for control of Otello are drawn in the central F major of the love duet and in Jago's Credo in F minor/major. Otello's new allegiance to Jago is affirmed in A major in the *cabaletta* of their Act II duet (a key prefigured in the drinking song in which Cassio is discredited). Otello spies Cassio with the handkerchief in the C major *stretta* of the Act III trio, and Jago proclaims victory ("Ecco il Leone!") in C major, which frames the Act III finale.

A third series moves by a circle of fifths from G flat to A flat and back again – G flat–D flat–A flat–C sharp (D flat)–F sharp (G flat) – to mark Desdemona's betrayal and disillusionment. The first two keys frame the love duet, A flat coincides with her public humiliation in the *largo* of the Act III finale, and the return to F sharp (G flat) through C sharp (D flat) occurs in the Willow Song and its prelude, where it is associated with Desdemona's unjustified abandonment.

The love duet provides a tonal embodiment of the central problem of Otello and Desdemona's relationship, that of passion leading to violence. The fifth F–C is associated with Desdemona's ability to calm and ennoble Otello through her sympathy and is "safe" as long as she directs C back to its tonic F, as she does initially at "Te ne rammenti" ("Do you remember"). In contrast, the fifth G flat–D flat is connected at the beginning and ending of the duet with the sensual side of their relationship. It is inherently

"dangerous" because it agitates Otello and because Desdemona has little
success controlling it (in harmonic terms because her preferred key F functions as the unstable third within D flat). And it initiates the progression
to A flat that brings her humiliation in the Act III finale and eventually
her bewildered withdrawal and reinterpretation of F sharp (G flat) in the
Willow Song.

Desdemona's hold on F – and on her husband's loyalty – is slippery at
best. She clings tenaciously to it through the first half of the duet, retreating
to the past in that key at "Quando narravi" and leading Otello back to
it several times before "E tu m'amavi," where it becomes a primary key.
In the process, she unwittingly opens the way to D flat, a digression she
would best avoid. She does so by introducing its dominant A flat at "Poi
mi guidavi" ("Then you led me") when she refers to Otello's sufferings, the
wellspring of her pity that made Otello love her. Her misstep is innocent: in
an effort to guide Otello back to F from C major, in which Otello becomes
agitated as he recounts his exploits, she naïvely chooses A flat as the mediant
in her arpeggiation. Unfortunately, Otello seizes A flat (at "e il labbro di
sospir," again referring to Desdemona's pity) and, her sympathy inflaming
his passion, moves to D flat. Desdemona quickly returns to the safety of F
for their affirmation of love ("E tu m'amavi"). Significantly, she alludes to
Otello's savage side – his "tempie oscure" ("dark temples") – in D flat and
to his noble side – the "eterea beltà" ("ethereal beauty") of his genius – as
F is reached. Otello again turns to D flat (and away from F) as he invites
death to take him in the ecstasy of their embrace ("mi colga nell'estasi / Di
quest'amplesso") – again associating D flat with the physical side of their
relationship. Desdemona's second mistake comes when she herself turns
from E to C sharp (D flat) minor in inviting Otello to her bed ("Tarda è
la notte") and to the radiant D flat in which the duet ends, initiating the
disastrous long-range progression to A flat.

The opening section of the Act II duet/quartet presents the last substantial
occurrence of E before the extended downward arpeggiation of that key
from B begins in the quartet slow movement and initiates the reorientation
of E from "normalcy" toward Desdemona's murder and Otello's eventual
epiphany at the end of the opera. Desdemona first petitions for Cassio's
reinstatement ("D'un uom che geme") in E major (and in A minor, alluding
to the drinking song that begins his trials), and responds to Otello's initial
irritation briefly in that key ("Perchè torbida suona") followed by chromatic
music. Otello rejects the handkerchief – and her – in E minor in the original
version of the scene, and her apology (at "Se inconscia") arpeggiates that
triad through G sharp minor to B major for the quartet movement (also in
the original version of the scene). As in the love duet, Desdemona acquiesces
tonally, allowing a key that had signified safety and stability at the beginning

of the opera to slip away and making herself responsible for instigating yet another perilous long-range progression.

In the opening duet scene of Act III, G flat, associated with affection in Act I, reappears as a more sinister F sharp minor, the key in which Desdemona will later mourn her abandonment in the Willow Song. It appears in the prelude of the scene, which presents its ominous motif in three variations that prefigure Otello's entrance prior to the murder in Act IV in their stealthiness (mm. 1–10), deliberative quality (the fughetta, mm. 11–20), and rage (mm. 21–34). F sharp also appears as Otello urges Jago to resume plotting their surveillance of Cassio ("Continua"). Thus G flat/F sharp is reoriented from love to jealousy.

E also takes on negative connotations in this scene. Framed by passages in F sharp, the herald's E major announcement of the arrival of the ambassadors, a reminder of Venetian normalcy, seems intrusive and unconvincing. Furthermore, at the start of the duet, Desdemona's effort to shore up that key is undercut by Otello's coopting of it and of her melody to lead her on. His poisoning of E is even clearer later in the duet, as he curses her in E minor ("Giura e ti danna") within a progression that includes A minor and F major, tonics that serve the long-range arpeggiation associated with Jago's control of Otello. And at the end of the scene, Otello returns to Desdemona's opening melody with obvious irony (at "Datemi ancor l'eburnea mano") before calling her a whore and driving her from the room in E minor music that recalls both the final variation of the prelude and the storm that had opened the opera.

F major – the key on which Desdemona originally depended to calm Otello's rages, but which Jago has usurped to exert his own control over Otello – and the related tonics A and C also gain perilous meanings in this piece. F is the key in which Desdemona realizes that Otello regards the lost handkerchief as proof of her infidelity ("Che?! l'hai perduto forse?"). A cadence in C minor punctuates the line in which she initially recognizes her peril ("nella tua voce v'è un grido di minaccia" – "in your voice there is a menacing cry"). She pleads with him and defends herself for the first time in A minor and F major ("Il volto e l'anima ti svelo"). And in the latter key she acknowledges incredulously that she has lost her power to heal ("E son io l'innocente cagion di tanto pianto" – "And I am the innocent cause of such weeping"). Once Desdemona relinquishes F major, Jago owns the opera's keys. Two scenes later, in the Act III finale, Desdemona and Otello are humiliated in A flat and C, Jago triumphing through his corruption of the F–C and G flat–D flat fifths that had originally signified their love.

Verdi waited until late in the compositional process to choose a title, he and Boito apparently vacillating between *Otello* and *Jago* until January of

1886. Theatrical convention demanded consideration for Rossini, whose *Otello* loomed over their own project, and Jago's importance as an instigator suggested that he be featured.[38] With the title up for grabs, and in light of the preceding discussion, one might wonder why *Desdemona* was not also considered. While Otello "loves, is jealous, kills and is killed," as Verdi pointed out in the famous letter that established the definitive title,[39] Desdemona is Jago's real adversary, as we have seen, and it is her defeat that turns love to jealousy, fury, and murder. Shakespeare's play, of course, centers on Othello's transformation – the erosion of his heroic stature – and its outcome for Desdemona, who is little more than his target. At the end, concerned more about his posthumous reputation than about Desdemona ("I pray you, in your letters, / When you shall these unlucky deeds relate, / Speak of me as I am," etc.), Othello kills himself because he realizes how unnecessarily he has lost everything, and his kiss is a final self-magnifying gesture. In contrast, Verdi and Boito gave more evenhanded treatment to the decline of Desdemona's powers and situation. Appropriately, in dying Otello attends more to Desdemona than to himself: "E tu . . . come sei pallida! e stanca, e muta, e bella, / Pia creatura nata sotto maligna stella" ("And you . . . how pale you are! And weary, and silent, and beautiful, sainted creature born under a malign star").[40] Unlike Shakespeare's hero, Otello kills himself primarily because he recognizes that despite her sensuality Desdemona is blameless. His kiss represents the maturation of his love for Desdemona, and his death aims at an almost Wagnerian spiritual reunion. So despite Verdi's idealized and perhaps dismissive characterization of Desdemona as "a type," his and Boito's recomposition of Shakespeare, in their text and music, ultimately made Desdemona's rejection, humiliation, and destruction the focus of the audience's empathy – and of Otello's at the end. From this perspective, Desdemona's fall – not Otello's – is the real tragedy of the opera.

PART FOUR

Creation and critical reception

15 An introduction to Verdi's working methods

For each of his operas, Verdi employed a complicated process that included many phases of creation and involved other individuals. Some aspects of this process remained remarkably consistent across his career. For example, despite changing conceptions of orchestration that emphasized families of instruments, Verdi continued the tradition of scoring primarily by pitch, putting violins and violas at the top of the page, cellos and basses at the bottom, other instruments in between generally in descending order of pitch range, and voices immediately above the cello line.[1] Other procedures changed considerably over time and even from opera to opera. Consequently, any general discussion of Verdi's working methods quickly involves many exceptions, and scholars have understandably focused on the creation of single works while hesitating to postulate broad theories. In attempting this overview, I shall limit my discussion to the changes in Verdi's compositional circumstances across his career and the changes in his treatment of seven creative stages through which his works normally progressed.[2]

Periods of composition[3]

From the perspective of working conditions and methods, Verdi's operas fall into four basic groups: 1) early: *Oberto* (1839) through *La battaglia di Legnano* (1849); 2) middle: *Luisa Miller* (1849) through *Un ballo in maschera* (1859); 3) "modern":[4] *La forza del destino* (1862) through *Aida* (1871); and 4) late: *Simon Boccanegra* (revised 1881) through *Falstaff* (1893). The coincidence of these groups with traditional stylistic groupings is striking and underscores the importance of considering working conditions and methods when providing an overview of his operas.[5] Changes from one period to another involve his pace of composition; association with different librettists, theatres, cities, and performers; the degree of interference from censors; changes in political life and other factors external to the opera business; and Verdi's own growth and maturity.

Verdi's first ten years of opera composition produced fourteen works, a prodigious accomplishment by any standard. During this period, he worked to secure his reputation in the eyes of the public and his peers and to gain financial security. With each new production he looked for unqualified success that would carry the work to other theatres. And with each subsequent agreement he sought to improve his standing. Verdi thus endeavored to conquer the world of the opera industry. Overlapping subgroups are needed to understand the variations in working conditions that Verdi experienced during his early period. For example, the first four operas and *Giovanna d'Arco* comprise his early Milanese works; *Ernani, I due Foscari, Alzira,* and *Macbeth* form the first group of works for other important Italian cities; *I masnadieri* and *Jérusalem* comprise the first group of works for foreign capitals; and so on. Operas with texts by Temistocle Solera, Francesco Maria Piave, Salvatore Cammarano, or Andrea Maffei form a different set of groups overlapping the first.[6] Most scores were owned and published by Ricordi, but three, *Attila, I masnadieri,* and *Il corsaro,* belonged to Francesco Lucca, and one, *Jérusalem,* involved Verdi's primary publisher in France, Escudier, from the beginning.

The 1848–49 revolutions and their aftermath played a significant role in the transition from Verdi's early works to his middle ones. *La battaglia di Legnano* reflects the enthusiasm of early Italian victories, while Italy's defeat influenced his turn to smaller, more domestic themes, beginning with *Luisa Miller.* It was also at this time that Verdi and Giuseppina Strepponi set up home together, first in Busseto, then in the villa at Sant'Agata.

Verdi's pace of composition slowed from fourteen operas in the first ten years to nine in the following decade. This second group can also be viewed as a web of overlapping subsets, but more salient characteristics tend to indicate two chronological subgroups. The first, from *Luisa Miller* to *La traviata,* consists completely of works written for Italian theatres. The impact of a repressive political regime affected the financial health of many cultural institutions, including opera theatres. The heightened activity of various censors affected the internal workings of publishers and opera houses, and even more substantially influenced the choice of opera subjects and their development as librettos. Despite these adverse conditions, Verdi's stature as an opera composer grew with each successive work, and although he might concede ground on financial remuneration, he became increasingly demanding about other aspects of his contracts.

Then there was Paris. *Les vêpres siciliennes* was the first of Verdi's works to begin life as a French opera, *Jérusalem* having been a revision of *I lombardi.* Verdi sought to exploit the grandiosity preferred in the French capital, and incorporated formal techniques from French opera into his vocabulary. Although *Les vêpres siciliennes* enjoyed a respectable success, Verdi won more favor in Paris by adapting his Italian works, which he did during this period by producing *Le trouvère* in 1857.

The Italian works in this second subset are characterized by revisions perhaps occasioned by Verdi's work in France and an uneasiness in returning to older Italian models. By the mid-1850s, composers had exhausted the potential of *primo Ottocento* style and Italy was in the midst of a musical crisis. Verdi produced *Simon Boccanegra* for Venice but was immediately dissatisfied with the result. He tinkered with it for a production in Reggio Emilia that took place shortly after the premiere, but more thoroughgoing revisions would have to wait for his late period and collaboration with Boito. Verdi also revised *Stiffelio* as *Aroldo* at this time, before returning to a subject that had fired his imagination on several previous occasions, *King Lear*. After working with Antonio Somma for months on a suitable libretto, he abandoned the project in favor of an Italian version of Scribe's libretto *Gustave III – Una vendetta in domino*.[7] Problems with the censors led Verdi to deny Naples the premiere of his twenty-third opera in favor of Rome, but even there the problem of censorship forced changes that resulted in *Un ballo in maschera*.

Shortly after *Un ballo in maschera*, Italy finally achieved its goal of becoming an independent nation. Verdi and Strepponi formalized their personal relationship in marriage. The composer was drafted into politics, first by representing Busseto in the Parma delegation requesting annexation to the Kingdom of Piedmont, and later through election to the first Italian parliament. In this third period of opera composition, Verdi's pace slowed even further. With land, wealth, and position firmly established, his approach to opera composition did not have the same urgency as in his earlier years, a period he referred to as his "anni di galera" ("galley years"). He took more time for each work, insisting on working at his own pace, and labored over revisions.

Following *Aida*, Verdi announced his retirement as a composer, though produced his String Quartet and the Requiem dedicated to Manzoni. Gentle yet persistent prodding by Strepponi and Giulio Ricordi, combined with the talent and ingenuity of Boito, brought Verdi back to produce his final operas. Indeed, his collaboration with Arrigo Boito is the defining feature of the late period. It consists of the 1881 *Simon Boccanegra*, *Otello*, and *Falstaff*, and includes the revision of *Don Carlos* for the Italian stage, an undertaking that did not involve Boito. The collaborative nature of these works goes beyond the relationship between composer and librettist, however. Giulio Ricordi worked alongside them, enlisting help preparing scores, parts, and librettos for performances and additional materials for sale to the general public, and (very likely) designing the staging. Moreover, Verdi himself participated in decisions about details such as set and costume designs.

The seven stages of Verdi's working methods

Verdi's compositional process involved at least seven stages which in their chronology overlapped increasingly as the process developed. They are: 1) a subject, cast, and contract; 2) the libretto; 3) sketches and continuity drafts; 4) the skeleton score, orchestration, and rehearsals; 5) staging, set and costume designs; 6) publications and other printed sources; and 7) revisions.

Subject, cast, and contract

Little is known of the transformation of *Rocester* into Verdi's first performed opera, *Oberto*, but it is safe to assume that he undertook this transformation to satisfy key individuals, among them the Milanese impresario Bartolomeo Merelli. Following the success of *Oberto*, Merelli contracted Verdi for three other operas. The first, *Un giorno di regno*, was forced on the composer and failed miserably. The second, *Nabucodonosor*, later known as *Nabucco*, truly excited Verdi and he set about composing right away; but questions arose regarding the timing of the premiere and the cast. The soprano Giuseppina Strepponi championed the composer and helped to convince Merelli to produce the opera in March 1842 when she was included in the roster of performers. *Nabucco*'s immediate and widespread success is legendary.

Following *Nabucco*, a subject, a cast, and a contract formed the initial step toward a completed work. Though agreement was not necessarily reached on all three at once, Verdi needed to believe that an accord would be found in each case before developing a project to the point where it could be performed. The subject needed to excite his imagination and strike him as stageworthy. The performers needed to possess the qualities Verdi imagined for the characters, and he consequently exercised great control over the cast. In the case of *Alzira*, Verdi's desire to have his preferred cast may have led him to 'prolong' an illness so that the opera would be performed during the Neapolitan season when the preferred artists would be on the roster.[8] In many cases, Verdi had particular performers in mind from the initial choice of a subject. For example, he thought immediately of Felice Varese for the title role in *Macbeth* and consulted him extensively during its composition. In addition to the subject (or conditions under which the subject would be chosen) and the cast, the contract spelled out issues surrounding the creation of the libretto, the timing of the first performances, the involvement of a publisher, and remuneration. Early in his career, Verdi accepted three contracts for multiple works. These include the Milanese agreement with Merelli mentioned above, a contract with Lucca that resulted in *Attila*, *I masnadieri*, and *Il corsaro*, and an understanding with the management of the Neapolitan theatres that gave rise to *Alzira* and *Luisa Miller*. In each case, disputes erupted that sometimes involved legal wrangling. For the Milanese contract, Verdi attempted to sell Lucca the publication rights which Merelli had already guaranteed to Ricordi, a conflict eventually settled by the Milanese Mercantile Tribunal, with Ricordi and Lucca splitting the performance rights.[9] Verdi's disappointment with Ricordi over the treatment *Giovanna d'Arco* received in the *Gazzetta musicale di Milano*, the house journal of Ricordi's publishing operation, prompted the composer to accept a contract with Lucca for three operas. This relationship ended in ill feeling created by Lucca's insistence on the timely completion of the third work, *Il corsaro*. Once Verdi had complied with this demand he uncharacteristically played no significant role in the first production. Verdi's negotiations with the Neapolitan management were the most complex. An opera for Naples was clearly a step forward in Verdi's career; guardian of a venerable tradition, the San Carlo theatre boasted the best orchestra in the Italian peninsula. Verdi began negotiations with Vincenzo Flaùto, who was acting on behalf of a group of shareholders, but Ricordi was instrumental in closing the deal, which included promises for subsequent works. *Alzira* was the first product of those negotiations; Verdi's middle period begins with the other, *Luisa Miller*.[10]

For insight into Verdi's deliberation over opera subjects, the most interesting surviving document is one labeled *argomenti d'opere* (opera subjects) and is found in one of his *copialettere* (large ledgers used mostly to draft correspondence). Although there has been some debate about the date of this document, a detailed analysis of both its contents and its position within the large bound volume unquestionably places its origin in 1849, at the beginning of Verdi's middle period.[11] Various analyses of this list have been published, but the most important point is that it exists at all. After an early career in which he was working constantly, Verdi appears to have wanted to proceed in a more organized fashion by laying out his options and weighing their potential before beginning a new project. It is also significant that he only completed one item on the list, *Le roi s'amuse*, which became *Rigoletto*; but another, *Re Lear*, would also preoccupy him.

In Verdi's middle period, an appropriate cast continued to be an essential ingredient for an acceptable contract. Sometimes Verdi depended on his increased stature to command first-rate performers and allowed final decisions to be delayed, an approach that worked in casting the role of Azucena in *Il trovatore*, but not for Violetta in *La traviata*. Poor casting could scuttle an entire project. Indeed, *Re Lear* fell apart when the Neapolitan management failed to sign Maria Piccolomini to sing the role of Cordelia.[12]

Verdi's experience with French publishers was the most important influence on contracts in his middle period. He introduced the more evolved French model of authors' rights and royalties, including the percentage a composer received for subsequent performances, the rights of the librettists, and other legal issues surrounding the opera business. Over time these concepts came to provide a more secure and stable model for the rights of all Italian composers, and brought Italy and Italian opera to the forefront of legal thinking and practice regarding intellectual property.

After his *anni di galera* (from *Oberto* through *Un ballo in maschera*), Verdi insisted on composing at his own pace, and only when a subject truly excited him. The result is that from 1860 though 1871 he composed only three new works, *La forza del destino*, *Don Carlos*, and *Aida*. Bringing a subject, a cast, and a contract together was no longer a problem for Verdi but rather one for those who wanted him to compose. After *Aida*, even convincing him to pick up the pen became difficult. Giulio Ricordi, Giuseppina Strepponi-Verdi, and Arrigo Boito had to join forces to make arrangements for the final operas to fall into place.[13] Casting these late works was also critical to the compositional process. Verdi's faith in the baritone Victor Maurel helped him formulate many details for both Jago and Falstaff. Conversely, his dissatisfaction with Romilda Pantaleoni may explain the many revisions to the part of Desdemona (or perhaps Verdi's idealistic conception of the role would have left him dissatisfied with any soprano). After hearing Giuseppina Pasqua, Verdi reshaped the role of Quickly in *Falstaff* and expanded it considerably.[14]

The libretto

The process of developing a libretto began with the choice of a subject and ended only with the final revisions of an opera. Important phases include a general outline, a detailed scenario broken down into individual scenes and numbers, and the actual poetic text. Verdi always collaborated with a librettist for this work, but he actively participated in – and sometimes dominated – the collaboration. There might be interventions from the opera house management, such as the objections to the use of Silva's horn in *Ernani*; or the state or the Church might take steps to change certain aspects, as in attempting to ban the baptismal scene in *I lombardi* or to remove its "Ave Maria," which Verdi turned into a "Salve Maria."

The manner in which Verdi interacted with librettists depended in part on his view of a particular individual's abilities. For example, Francesco Maria Piave, whose background had been primarily as a stage manager, began his career as a librettist with *Ernani*. Though Verdi found him adequate, Piave was definitely the junior partner. For *Macbeth*, however, Verdi was far from satisfied and turned to Andrea Maffei to complete Piave's text. Although Piave eventually produced the texts for major works including *Rigoletto*, *La traviata*, and *La forza del destino*, Verdi's treatment of him was often condescending. Salvatore Cammarano represents the other extreme.

Having written the librettos for such celebrated operas as Donizetti's *Lucia di Lammermoor*, Mercadante's *La vestale*, and Pacini's *Saffo*, Cammarano had experience that Verdi valued and their collaboration bolstered the composer's reputation. Verdi's deference waned as his own stature increased and as he began to view the poet as a pawn of the Neapolitan theatre management. By the time of *Il trovatore*, Verdi was asserting his primacy, and a more balanced working relationship ensued.

Although censorship played a role in Verdi's early period, it was most acute for his middle works, affecting textual details and major aspects of the plot, and even impeding the choice of a subject. *Rigoletto* and *Un ballo in maschera* are the two most celebrated cases because Verdi battled with the censors right up to the final completion of the works. On the other hand, Verdi may have chosen *Luisa Miller* rather than *L'assedio di Firenze* in part to avoid problems with the censors.[15] Other operas suffered censorship following the premiere, examples being *Stiffelio*, which circulated in a bowdlerized version titled *Guglielmo Wellingrode*, for which the central premise of a Protestant clergyman who forgives his erring wife was erased, and *La traviata*, sometimes performed as *Violetta*, in which the status of the lead character as a courtesan is obscured.

Sketches and continuity drafts

Until recently, this phase, which constitutes the core of the compositional process, had been poorly documented for Verdi's works. For decades scholars relied on bits of sketch materials for *Il trovatore*, *La traviata*, *Un ballo in maschera*, *Aida*, *Otello*, and *Falstaff* published by Carlo Gatti,[16] and a reproduction of the *abbozzo* (a sketch, or outline) for *Rigoletto* which he published separately.[17] The bulk of the *abbozzo* for *Rigoletto* consists of a continuity draft which plots the score by means of a bass line and a vocal or principal melody line for the entire opera, usually on one or two staves. Verdi added staves as necessary for multiple characters or for melodic ideas in the orchestra. This *abbozzo* also contains a few sketch fragments which extend chronologically from before the draft to after it.[18] Gatti reported that he saw *abbozzi* similar to the one for *Rigoletto* for each of Verdi's operas from *Luisa Miller* through *Falstaff*.

On the basis of this scant information, some postulated that Verdi began to use continuity drafts with *Luisa Miller* and continued for the remainder of his career. Manuscripts that have recently surfaced call these assumptions into doubt, however. For example, sketch fragments for *I due Foscari* and *Alzira* indicate that Verdi used continuity drafts for at least sections of these operas.[19] And the bundle of sketch material for *La traviata* provided by the Carara-Verdi family for the critical edition indicates that he did not make a continuity draft for all of that opera.[20]

Skeleton score, orchestration, and rehearsals

Verdi began his autograph full score by first entering the bass line and the vocal or principal melody lines. Where a continuity draft exists, we can confirm that Verdi primarily transferred the information from the draft into what became the orchestral score. Scholars have dubbed this phase a "skeleton score." Once this task was completed, singers' parts were extracted so that they could begin learning their roles, and Verdi then proceeded to orchestrate. Rather than being a simple mechanical task, however, this phase served as an opportunity to rethink and refine the draft.

During the negotiations for *Ernani*, Verdi declared that it was his custom to orchestrate during the rehearsals.[21] While this continues to be a general rule for his early and middle works, documentation demonstrates that he strayed from this habit by completing some of the orchestration before traveling to the city of the first performance for *I due Foscari, Macbeth, Il corsaro, La battaglia di Legnano, Il trovatore*, and probably *Stiffelio*.[22] Because the skeleton score eventually became the final autograph, this phase of composition became clear to scholars only as discarded pages from skeleton scores were discovered. The earliest of these to have surfaced come from the concluding section of *I due Foscari*. Differences between the discarded pages and the final version show that Verdi reconsidered melodic shape, dynamics, and key.[23] For his modern and late works, the role of orchestration became more complex and integral to the compositional process, but Verdi continued to take advantage of rehearsals to refine orchestral details.

For most of Verdi's career, the autographs were working documents that the composer used through the first performances; for the late operas, however, Verdi submitted his completed autograph score, generally in sections, before rehearsals began. A printed full score was prepared together with a full set of parts for the rehearsals, work continuing and changes being made in the printed score up to the opening night. The autographs of the late works thus represent an ongoing process and may not reflect in all respects the composer's thinking at the time of the first performance.[24]

Staging, set and costume designs

Although information on the degree of Verdi's involvement with visual presentation varies considerably from one work to another, over time his attention to this aspect increased tremendously. For the early operas, it primarily involved casting. He repeatedly expressed concern about how a particular singer appeared on stage, whether she or he looked the part or could act. By the end of his career, he involved himself to a greater or lesser degree in all matters, including the blocking, set and costume design, and lighting and special visual effects. Verdi's exposure to French stagecraft was the single most important factor in boosting his interest in visual presentation.

Of the early works, the most material regarding Verdi's participation in visual presentation survives for *Macbeth*. The abundant correspondence reproduced in *Verdi's "Macbeth": A Sourcebook* is replete with references to staging for the initial production.[25] It ranges from conversations between individuals in the circle of people involved, such as the complaints of the impresario Alessandro Lanari to the librettist Piave ("As for the notes on the staging you sent me for *Macbeth*, they are too concise"), to comments by Verdi himself ("Note that Banquo's ghost must make his entrance from underground; it must be the same actor that played Banquo in Act I. He must be wearing an ashen veil, but quite thin and fine, and just barely visible; and Banquo must have ruffled hair and various wounds visible on his neck").[26]

There also exists abundant documentation of contemporary set and costume design, and even a manuscript staging manual for *Jérusalem*, Verdi's revision of *I lombardi* for Paris.[27] Although Verdi cannot be tied directly to much of this early material, it seems probable that he at least tacitly approved of some of it, such as the costume designs Ricordi published in full color lithographs.[28]

With *Les vêpres siciliennes* Verdi became better acquainted with the French tradition of staging manuals. Although they vary in their level of detail, these booklets provide instructions for stage movement, from specific gestures made by individual characters to the positioning and movement of large choral bodies. Occasionally they provide information that is absent from the score, as for the episode in Act II of *Otello* when a group of women and children serenade Desdemona. The number of singers, their positioning, and gestures between Otello and Jago described in the staging manual are details not provided by other sources.[29] Frequently referred to in Italian as "disposizioni sceniche," staging manuals initially served as internal documents for particular theatres, but over time they were published for use by other theatres. Evidence of Verdi's involvement varies from case to case. For example, the *disposizione scenica* for *Un ballo in maschera* was published after the premiere in Rome and was written by Giuseppe Cencetti, *direttore di scena* for that production. For *Aida*, the *disposizione scenica* was published by Giulio Ricordi after the first production at La Scala, but a tantalizing phrase in a letter he wrote to Verdi, "compensation for your stage direction of the opera," suggests that Verdi was the true author of the manual.[30]

Commercial publications and other printed sources

Verdi's operas were made available to the public through librettos and a wide variety of scores. Verdi himself prepared sections of the piano-vocal scores for *Oberto*, *Un giorno di regno*, *I due Foscari*, *Alzira*, and *La battaglia di Legnano*, but these should be seen not as a regular part of his working method but as anomalies that arose from unique circumstances and were essentially tacked onto his usual working habits. The publisher generally contracted other musicians to prepare these publications, which included arrangements that sold by the dozens. They provide a window on reception history and patterns of dissemination by chronicling operatic numbers that circulated in various transcriptions, paraphrases, souvenirs, and so on in a variety of instrumental combinations.[31]

Other printed sources include materials that were prepared and rented out for specific productions. These rental materials generally consisted of printed parts for the strings and chorus and manuscript parts for everyone else. Publishers must have found it more economical to print parts for multiple players but to have single parts copied by hand. Indeed, Ricordi's house ledgers indicate that his plate numbers 8001–8300 were assigned to the "copisteria," probably a division within the company that housed all rental materials, both printed and manuscript. For the early and middle works, a manuscript copy of the full score generally accompanied the rental parts to any new production. Where there was insufficient room on a page for all performing parts, certain parts were copied into the score at the end of the number. This and the general cleanliness of these scores confirm their use as reference rather than conducting scores, particularly since most Italian theatres did not employ conductors (in the modern sense) until after 1860.[32] There are also many extant copies of parts prepared for the "violino principale e direttore d'orchestra" that included the cues necessary for the first violinist to hold the ensemble together.[33]

Of the middle works, Ricordi printed a full score only for *La traviata*, perhaps in reaction to the huge demand for *Il trovatore*, which immediately preceded it, and thinking that printing the full score would allow rapid production of materials for multiple stagings. Late in Verdi's career, however, printed sources became an essential part of the process. Work progressed in the usual manner through sketches, drafts, skeleton score, then autograph, but continued after Verdi had submitted his autograph to Ricordi, as the publisher immediately printed the score and all the parts. Verdi would review the prints, attend rehearsals, then make changes and corrections on the printed score, at times inserting the changes into his autograph, but not always. For these works the printed score was central to Verdi's working method.[34]

Revisions

The revisions Verdi made after the premiere are the final step in his compositional process.[35] They generally fall into two categories: definitive – those seen as permanent replacements – and non-definitive – those understood as discretionary alternatives to the earlier version. Where Verdi revised an opera extensively, scholars frequently list the different versions as separate works, a relatively simple task in some cases, such as *I lombardi/Jérusalem*, *Stiffelio/Aroldo*, and the 1847 and 1865 versions of *Macbeth*. These examples include definitive revisions, such as *Aroldo*, which Verdi intended to replace *Stiffelio*, and non-definitive revisions, such as *Jérusalem*, a French work that coexisted with its Italian original *I lombardi*. Distinguishing revisions as separate works is more complicated for operas such as *La forza del destino* and *Don Carlos*, for which several versions survive. Criteria include not only the number of revisions but also the relative value placed on them, which involves research into Verdi's thoughts about them and, to a certain extent, aesthetic judgments on the part of scholars.

Revisions were frequently related to specific performances or artists. The prime example is *Oberto*, which Verdi altered considerably for a revival in Milan, performances in Turin, and a production in Genoa for which he rewrote the title role for baritone. Add to this list an insert aria for the first Oberto, Ignazio Marini, to perform in Spain.[36] Although this opera is unique because of the rapid succession of revisions precipitated by the needs of specific productions, and because it was swept aside by the success of *Nabucco*, it illustrates the futility of our efforts to segregate all revisions into definitive and non-definitive categories and forces us to acknowledge the fluidity of these works during Verdi's lifetime. Nonetheless, most revisions in Verdi's early period are thought to be non-definitive.[37] Besides *Oberto* and *I lombardi/Jérusalem*, examples from the early period include revisions of *Nabucco* for a production in Venice and most of the insert arias Verdi wrote, usually reluctantly.

During his middle period, revision almost became a habit for Verdi. He may have been motivated by the lukewarm receptions of *La traviata* and *Simon Boccanegra*, which he immediately revised for subsequent productions. In the case of *Stiffelio*, censorship eviscerated the drama and Verdi replaced it with *Aroldo*. Verdi had Paris in mind for other revisions, as in his extensive discussions about transforming *Luisa Miller* for the French stage. A simple translation of the text from Italian into French spoiled his plans for a more thoroughgoing revision.[38] He transformed *Il trovatore* into *Le trouvère*, which has recently been recognized as a version different enough to merit its own place in the list of Verdi's works.[39]

Revisions are also a central feature of the modern works. Following the premiere of *La forza del destino* in St. Petersburg, Verdi revised it for Madrid and again for Milan; he transformed *Macbeth* for the French stage; and he revised *Don Carlos* numerous times beginning prior to the opening night. For the 1880 production of *Aida* in Paris, Verdi enlarged the ballet music, which was later incorporated into the Italian original. Revised late works begin with the second *Simon Boccanegra* and include the Milanese version of *Don Carlos*. Nor were the two final operas left untouched. Both *Otello* and *Falstaff* had touring companies supervised by Verdi, and many small revisions were made as they traveled from theatre to theatre. For *Otello*, the most important were for Paris, where Verdi provided a ballet that is almost never performed today, and where he made significant revisions to the third act finale. The Parisian production of *Falstaff* also motivated Verdi to make some final significant changes.

16 Verdi criticism

GREGORY W. HARWOOD

The earliest Verdi criticism, chronicling the successes and failures of his first operas, appeared in music journals, at first on the Italian peninsula and eventually throughout Europe and the Americas.[1] *La gazzetta musicale di Milano* held a particularly important position as the house journal of Verdi's principal publisher, Ricordi. As early as 1846, the *Gazzetta* reprinted a series of reviews by B. Bermani, hailing the young composer – who at the time had written only half a dozen operas – as a major figure who stood out among his contemporaries through his "exquisite taste, an untiring elegance, and [a] marvelous instinct... for effect." During the following decade, Florentine music critic Abramo Basevi wrote an extensive series of articles about Verdi's operas, which he collected and republished in 1859 as *Studio sulle opere di Giuseppe Verdi*. Basevi's detailed and systematic discussion of the early and middle operas (through *Aroldo*) has exerted considerable influence on modern Verdi criticism.[2] Notably, Basevi was the first critic to suggest two different styles or "maniere" in the composer's works, with *Luisa Miller* as the decisive turning point.

Verdi enjoyed a reputation as the undisputed living master of Italian opera during the latter part of the nineteenth century, and during this period the quantity of critical writings about his music continued to expand prodigiously. New and fertile territory for music criticism included such diverse topics as his changing musical style, historical position, and the relationship of his music and aesthetic ideals to those of Richard Wagner and the new *verismo* composers.[3] These topics engendered lively debate that was not always favorable to Verdi, since many critics, particularly outside Italy, held fast to the belief that Wagnerian aesthetics were intellectually superior to the "popular entertainment" of Italian opera.

Overall, modern Verdi scholarship has only begun to scratch the surface in assessing the scope, content, and significance of music criticism from nineteenth-century periodical literature. The journals themselves are scarce and not well indexed. Both problems are gradually being addressed through the ongoing publications of *RIPM*, the *Répertoire internationale de la presse musicale*.[4] In the meantime, published anthologies, such as Marcello Conati's exemplary *Interviste e incontri con Verdi* (1980), have made some nineteenth-century journalistic criticism more widely available to modern readers, while other studies have provided preliminary assessments of

[269]

the reception of Verdi's music during the Ottocento in specific geographic regions.[5] Fabrizio Della Seta's "Gli esordi della critica verdiana" (2000) provides a useful overview of this area of scholarship at the end of the twentieth century and makes a strong case for the need for more intensive research in this area in the future. Della Seta's article points to Alberto Mazzucato as a central figure deserving more scrutiny and analyzes Mazzucato's use of the term "quadro" in his critical writings.

Biographical studies of Verdi began, like the criticism of his works, in nineteenth-century periodicals. French music critic Arthur Pougin penned the most widely circulated of these early accounts, which was initially serialized in several European music journals. Pougin later issued his work as a monograph (1881), with additional material contributed by Giacomo Caponi writing under the pen name Folchetto. Pougin's anecdotal approach proved popular, as witnessed by a series of successive works in the same vein.[6] Over the course of time, however, biographical episodes have been shown to be colored, if not factually inaccurate. It is now clear that Verdi himself was an active instigator in this process, shaping the view of himself as a self-made genius, who rose to greatness despite the obstacles of poverty, illiteracy, and jealous machinations and who, through his music, shaped the soul of the modern Italian nation. This bias pervades the composer's statements to Michele Lessona that formed the basis for a chapter in his *Volere è potere* (1869), a moralizing collection of inspirational biographies. It also colors Verdi's autobiographical reminiscences, recorded by Giulio Ricordi and published in the sixth chapter of Pougin's *Vita aneddotica*.[7] Neither the degree of hyperbole nor the composer's active participation in this process is unique to Verdi among nineteenth-century composers. Nevertheless, much of later twentieth-century Verdi biography, starting particularly with Frank Walker's *The Man Verdi* (1962), has taken as a major goal the weeding out of romanticized legends from his life story.

Verdi's death in 1901 and the centenary of his birth only twelve years later prompted a new burst of scholarly activity, including an interest in assessing both the entirety of his work and his historical position. This new focus can be seen in Luigi Torchi's "L'opera di Giuseppe Verdi e i suoi caratteri principali," a feature article in the 1901 commemorative issue of *La rivista musicale italiana,* as well as in monographs such as Oreste Boni's *Giuseppe Verdi: L'uomo, le opere, l'artista* (1901) and the *Biographie critique* (1905) by Camille Bellaigue, a close personal friend of the composer and music critic for the influential *Revue des deux mondes* in Paris. Interest in Verdi as a historical figure at the dawn of the twentieth century also led to the first publication of primary source materials, particularly correspondence and iconographies, and reference materials, such as bibliographies. Luigi Torri published the first major bibliography on Verdi in the 1901 commemorative issue of *La rivista musicale italiana*. Even though he excluded many articles from "familiar" periodicals, such as the *Gazzetta musicale di Milano* and *L'illustrazione italiana*, Torri's bibliography boasts roughly 250 items concerning Verdi's life and nearly 100 critical assessments of his compositions. These numbers more than doubled in Carlo Vanbianchi's 1913 revision of this bibliography. A sixty-eight-page bio-bibliography by Stefano Lottici, now extremely rare, also appeared in 1913 in commemoration of the centenary of the composer's birth.[8]

While snippets of Verdi's prolific correspondence had appeared in periodicals since the late nineteenth century, the pioneering publication in this field was *I copialettere*, a hefty 759-page volume issued in 1913 by Gaetano Cesari and Alessandro Luzio. It contained drafts, copies, and summaries of some of the composer's correspondence from his "letter books," supplemented by a large number of letters and documents from other sources. Although flawed by omissions, fragmentary reproductions, suppressed passages, errors in transcription, and inaccurate ordering, *I copialettere* represents a major milestone in Verdi research. In the following decades, the four volumes of *Carteggi verdiani* edited by Luzio (1935–47) provided an additional 1,300 pages of correspondence, documents, and essays. Other documentary collections, published both in periodicals and as monographs, usually focused on a particular correspondent or group of correspondents, or, in later years, on a particular opera. Most of these publications continued to be marred to a greater or lesser extent, however, by the same editorial problems as the *Copialettere*.

Giuseppe Bocca's "Verdi e la caricatura" of 1901 offered the first major iconographic study of Verdi's life and career. It reproduced caricatures and drawings, some of the composer and some drawn by Verdi himself, as well as set and costume designs from a number of his operas. Twelve years later, Gino Monaldi issued his *Saggio di iconografia verdiana*, the first full-length iconographic study of the composer. It emphasized illustrations of scenography, costume designs, and early interpreters, but also incorporated portraits and caricatures of the composer, his family, and associates. No other full-length iconography appeared until 1941, when Carlo Gatti published *Verdi nelle immagini*, an important volume that included facsimile reproductions of selected pages from the composer's working drafts.

In addition to a continuation of the Verdi–Wagner controversy during the early decades of the twentieth century, a new debate emerged over the merits of Verdi's middle- and late-period works.[9] Supporters of the earlier works lauded their directness, clarity, and tunefulness, accusing the composer of becoming tainted with "Wagnerism" in his later years. Their opponents viewed Verdi's career as a creative ascent from a somewhat crude vigor in his early works to the pinnacle of sophistication in the final operas.

Alfredo Parente identified this debate and the related question of stylistic integrity as the central problem of Verdi criticism in his probing essay of 1933, "Il problema della critica verdiana." This controversy continued to engage critics during most of the twentieth century, leading to a recent new appraisal by Gilles de Van in his *Verdi: Un théâtre en musique* (1992, published in English as *Verdi's Theater: Creating Drama through Music*, 1998). De Van argues that the composer's dramaturgical principles were cohesive across his entire career. Individual works, however, drew on the contrasting poles of melodrama and music drama in various proportions, with a general trend toward music drama in his later works.

While Verdi's musicological fortunes generally waxed stronger in the early decades of the twentieth century, the popularity of his operas waned in some locations, particularly in Germany and England. For the most part, however, they never fell into total disfavor. The New York Metropolitan Opera, for example, staged productions of *Aida* every season from 1898 to 1945! Works from the trio of middle-period favorites (*Rigoletto*, *Il trovatore*, and *La traviata*) frequently dominated its playbills during the 1910s and 1920s, but the Met also mounted productions of *Forza* from 1918 to 1923, *Don Carlos* from 1920 to 1923, and *Ernani* from 1921 to 1924 and again in the 1928–29 season.[10] A renewed interest in Verdi's music, often called the "Verdi Renaissance," started in Germany in the mid-1920s and eventually spread to other countries, particularly England.[11] A major figure in this revival was Franz Werfel, whose historical novel *Verdi: Roman der Oper* (1923) quickly spread through many editions and translations. Werfel's edition of Verdi's correspondence soon followed (1926), the first major collection of Verdi's letters to be published in German. 1932 saw a significant new German biography by Herbert Gerigk, and new biographies were published in English by Francis Toye and Dyneley Hussey in 1930 and 1940 respectively. Italian musicologist Carlo Gatti prepared the most significant new biography from this period (1931). Longer and more detailed than earlier accounts, Gatti incorporated information from primary source materials preserved at Sant'Agata that had previously been unavailable to researchers. A quarter century later, Franco Abbiati also gained access to privileged materials, which he integrated into his mammoth four-volume biography that totaled well over 3,000 pages (1959). Less carefully prepared than Gatti's account, Abbiati tacitly abridged many documents, and his study includes both faulty transcriptions and factual misstatements. Nevertheless, it remained the standard Verdi biography in Italian for several decades. Another Italian scholar, Massimo Mila, offered thoughtful new critical discussions of Verdi's music starting with *Il melodramma di Verdi* (1933) and culminating many years later in two books that collected, updated, and amplified his earlier critical writings. *La giovinezza di Verdi* (1974, rev. 1978) presents a particularly welcome emphasis on the composer's early life and career, while *L'arte di Verdi* (1980) is broader in scope and includes a valuable bibliography with useful references to "older" periodical articles from the early and middle part of the century.[12]

The 1960s saw the beginning of a new age for Verdi in both musicological studies and performance. Traditional biases against Italian opera as being simplistic, formulaic, and void of substance gradually began to break down. New investigations of Italian opera and its composers laid important historical and cultural background for Verdi scholars, who began an intensive period of self-examination and reevaluation and established priorities for future work. Elvidio Surian's "Lo stato attuale degli studi verdiani" (1977), an appraisal of Verdi research up to the mid-1970s, includes a topically organized bibliographic essay that offers an excellent overview of important publications that appeared from 1960 to 1975.

Without a doubt, the central events marking the start of this new period of Verdi criticism were the founding of two national institutes for the study of Verdi, one in Italy and one in America. The institutes provided the stimulus, either directly or indirectly, for most important initiatives in Verdi research and criticism during the final decades of the twentieth century: international congresses, many new publications devoted to Verdi and his music, source-critical editions of Verdi's music and his correspondence, important new doctoral dissertations about Verdi, and more frequent performances of all of Verdi's operas, even his most obscure ones.

Verdi scholars and enthusiasts established the Istituto di Studi Verdiani in 1960 with headquarters in Parma (the name changed to L'Istituto Nazionale di Studi Verdi during the 1980s to reflect official sponsorship by the Italian government). Among its major initiatives were the dissemination of Verdi research through a series of international congresses and publications, including conference reports, the *Quaderni*, and the *Bollettini*. In 1982, *Studi verdiani* superseded the *Bollettini*, offering scholarly articles on all areas of Verdi's life, work, and legacy. Since 1983, the Parma Institute, together with the Rotary Club of Parma, has sponsored a biennial international competition that allows researchers to pursue studies at the Institute and publish their results in a special series. The wide range of creative new directions in the winning proposals attests to the vitality of current Verdi scholarship (see table 16.1).

In the mid-1970s, the American Institute for Verdi Studies was founded with headquarters at New York University. Its main publication was an annual newsletter (at first called the *AIVS Newsletter*, but later the *Verdi Newsletter* and most recently the *Verdi Forum*). Over the next decades, the American Institute sponsored conferences, international congresses, lectures, and summer seminars for college teachers, as well as performances

Table 16.1 Winners of the Premio Internazionale Rotary Club di Parma "Giuseppe Verdi"

Year	Author	Title	Published
1983	Markus Engelhardt	*Verdi und Andere: "Un giorno di regno," "Ernani," "Attila," "Il corsaro" in Mehrfachvertonungen*	1992
1985	Roger Parker	*"Arpa d'or dei fatidici vati": The Verdian Patriotic Chorus in the 1840s*	1997
1987	Marco Beghelli	*Atti performativi nella drammaturgia verdiana* (the tentative title for the published volume is *La retorica del rituale nel melodramma ottocentesco*)	
1989	Knud Arne Jürgensen	*The Verdi Ballets*	1995
1991	Roberta Montemorra Marvin	*Verdi the Student – Verdi the Teacher*	
1993	Dino Rizzo	*Verdi filarmonico e maestro dei Filarmonici bussetani*	
1995	Olga Jesurum	*Le scenografie verdiane tra due secoli: "ieri e oggi"*	
1997	Damien Colas	*Verdi et le rythme de la langue française, des "Vêpres siciliennes" à "Don Carlos"*	
1999	Gloria Staffieri	*Il "grand opéra" di Meyerbeer e la produzione verdiana degli anni '40–'50: Le tentazioni europee del melodramma italiano di metà Ottocento*	
2001	Alessandro Di Profio	*Verdi al Théâtre Lirique di Parigi (1863–1869): "Rigoletto," "Violetta," "Macbeth," "Le bal masqué"*	

of little-known works and early versions of works that Verdi later revised, such as *Macbeth* and *Forza*. Several of these conferences produced important publications: the 1977 conference in Danville, Kentucky, engendered *Verdi's "Macbeth": A Sourcebook*, edited by David Rosen and Andrew Porter (1984), while the 1993 conference in Belfast, Northern Ireland, led to a significant new volume entitled *Verdi's Middle Period*, edited by Martin Chusid (1997).

Both Institutes have made their greatest contribution to Verdi scholarship through systematically gathering and cataloging primary source materials, including printed and manuscript scores and parts, librettos, letters, and other documents, as well as secondary materials such as books and monographs, periodicals, and sound recordings. The assembly, organization, and evaluation of this material allowed Verdi studies to leap forward by initiating the publication of complete scholarly, source-critical editions of both the composer's music and his correspondence. This venture was particularly daunting in the case of the music: orchestral scores for a half-dozen operas had either never been published or could only be rented by opera houses, and available editions were full of errors and inconsistencies. As scholars laid plans to start the critical editions, two important reference works appeared: Martin Chusid's *A Catalog of Verdi's Operas* (1974) and Cecil Hopkinson's *A Bibliography of the Works of Giuseppe Verdi, 1813–1901* (1973–78). These volumes provide crucial information about autograph manuscripts and early editions of Verdi's music respectively, and together they offer much information that will be found in a definitive thematic catalog, which has yet to be prepared.

The *Works of Giuseppe Verdi* (*WGV*), co-published by the University of Chicago Press and Casa Ricordi, began with the publication of *Rigoletto* in 1983; by the beginning of the Verdi commemorative year 2001, editions of nine operas and the Requiem had been issued. This source-critical edition follows a "middle-of-the-road" editorial philosophy, intended to present a text based on a primary source that is clear and easy to read for both performers and scholars.[13] Many volumes rely on the composer's autograph score as the primary source. In his later operas, however, Verdi often made revisions in proofs for the printed orchestral score and parts after completing the autograph score; for these works, therefore, the first printed full score typically supersedes the autograph score as the primary source. In the case of *Don Carlos*, where the composer made numerous excisions and revisions during rehearsals preceding the premiere, the editor has opted to reconstruct the version presented at the first performance as the primary source.[14] The *WGV* provides references to alternative readings from qualified secondary sources, corrects errors that crept into earlier editions, and standardizes discrepancies from part to part in such areas as articulation, rhythm, and dynamics. Each volume contains a historical introduction and a discussion of editorial issues relating to that particular work, published in both English and Italian, and a critical commentary, published as a separate volume in English alone.

The need for authoritative source-critical editions of Verdi's correspondence was a task equal in importance to the musical scores, for the composer's voluminous exchange of letters contains invaluable insights relating to the genesis and aesthetic conception of his works, compositional process, performance practice, reception, and business transactions with theatres, publishers, and others. Mario Medici and Marcello Conati issued the Verdi–Boito correspondence in 1978 as the first complete letter exchange to be published in a source-critical edition. A multi-volume edition of the Verdi–Ricordi correspondence started in 1988, and editions of correspondence with other significant figures, such as librettists Salvadore Cammarano and Antonio Somma and the French music publisher Escudier, have recently been or soon will be published.

The 1970s initiated a marked increase in both the quantity and the quality of Verdi dissertations, and in many cases their authors subsequently became leading authorities on their topic. These include, among others, David Lawton's investigation of tonality and drama in early Verdi (Berkeley, 1973), David Rosen's examination of the source materials for the Requiem (Berkeley, 1976), James Hepokoski's analysis of the autograph score of *Falstaff* (Harvard, 1979), and Roger Parker's study of Verdi's early career (London, 1981). This trend has continued in recent years with important new dissertations on individual works – for example, Roberta

Montemorra Marvin's investigation of the genesis and reception of *I mas-nadieri* (Brandeis, 1992) – as well as dissertations that focus on broader historical or analytical issues: Markus Engelhardt's examination of choruses in Verdi's early operas (Würzburg, 1986), Elizabeth Hudson's investigation of narrative in Verdi's dramaturgy (Cornell, 1993), Teresa Klier's analysis of Verdi's orchestration (Würzburg, 1995), David Gable's inquiry into mode mixture and lyric form (Chicago, 1997), and Andreas Giger's analysis of the role of French influences on the development of Verdi's melodic style (Indiana, 1999). This stream of new research by doctoral students provides solid evidence of a rising new generation of Verdi scholars. A similar trend, especially during the last decade, can be seen in *tesi di laurea* from Italian universities.

During the last two decades, the musicological literature on Verdi has grown by leaps and bounds, both quantitatively and qualitatively. Nowhere can this be better seen than in the ongoing bibliographies published by Marcello Conati in each issue of *Studi verdiani*. These annual bibliographies have sometimes featured well over 200 items, encompassing books, articles, theses and dissertations, and scholarly essays written for performances. For researchers who need more detailed information about the most significant secondary literature, I have provided a selective annotated bibliography of more than 1,000 sources published to ca. 1993 in my *Giuseppe Verdi: A Guide to Research* (1998). The *Verdi Handbuch*, an important new reference work edited by Anselm Gerhard and Uwe Schweikert, appeared in 2001. Short chapters cover a broad range of topics, including individual works, convention and innovation in Verdi's work (including a discussion of librettos, versification, voice and role types, compositional process, visual aspects, and performance practice), and reception. Each chapter includes a substantial bibliography, supplemented by a more general, selective bibliography at the end of the volume.

The preceding chapters in this *Companion* illustrate the main areas of current research about Verdi and summarize recent thinking by scholars in each of those areas. Among biographies and surveys of his life and works, Julian Budden's *The Operas of Verdi*, first published between 1973 and 1981, has become the standard survey of Verdi's operas in English for musical connoisseurs, as well as an important point of departure by researchers probing more deeply into issues of musical style. Budden has also provided a concise single-volume generalist biography in the *Master Musician* series. John Rosselli's *Verdi*, published in 2000, deftly interweaves biography with historical and cultural issues such as the changing conception of the opera composer as an artist, the shift toward performing repertory works rather than new or recent operas, new publishing practices, and issues regarding copyright and censorship. Mary Jane Phillips-Matz, author of the biographical chapter in this *Companion*, has furnished the most imposing new biography (1993), encompassing nearly 1,000 pages. Her volume amasses a plethora of new details culled from archives or little-known sources about Verdi's life and business affairs, particularly during his early years. A richly illustrated but scarcer volume by the same author, *Verdi: Il grande gentleman del Piacentino* (1992), reproduces in Italian translation Hercules Cavalli's 1867 biography of the composer, now extremely rare. Two recent winners of the Parma Rotary Club Prize will soon publish valuable studies that focus on Verdi's early life and career: *Verdi the Student – Verdi the Teacher* by Roberta Montemorra Marvin and *Verdi filarmonico e maestro dei Filarmonici bussetani* by Dino Rizzo. Several important studies have focused on Verdi's cultural milieu, among them David Kimbell's *Verdi in the Age of Italian Romanticism* (1981), Marzio Pieri's lavishly illustrated *Verdi: L'immaginario dell'ottocento* (1981), and Daniele Tomasini's splendid *La cultura umanistica e letteraria di Giuseppe Verdi* (1997). As shown in the second and third chapters of this *Companion*, Verdi's cultural, musical, and political milieu offers particularly fertile ground for future study.

An even greater explosion has occurred among historical and analytical studies devoted to individual works, fueled in part by preparations for the complete critical edition of the music. Significant milestones include the *Bollettini* issued by the Parma Institute, each volume of which devotes hundreds of pages to a single opera: *Ballo, Forza, Rigoletto*, and *Ernani*. The Institute's *Quaderni* offer more modest contributions, mostly on lesser-known works: *Il corsaro, Jérusalem, Stiffelio*, the Mass for Rossini, and *Aida*. Several international congresses have focused on individual operas, including *Don Carlos, Les vêpres siciliennes, Simon Boccanegra, Ernani*, and *Stiffelio*. While Verdi's operas have dominated both performances and critical studies of his music, during the last decades researchers have turned more frequently to his non-operatic compositions (see chapter 10 of this *Companion*). The Requiem has commanded the most attention, primarily due to the fine research of David Rosen. With little published about other non-operatic compositions, this area will remain an important and fruitful field for scholars in the future.

Analysis has been one of the most rapidly growing and influential areas of Verdi research in recent years, and the four chapters in this volume devoted to case studies of representative operas illustrate the wide variety of approaches that have been taken. Investigations of normative expectations in Ottocento opera as a whole have laid an important foundation for analytical studies of Verdi's music, and the chapters by Scott Balthazar and Emanuele Senici in this *Companion* provide an excellent overview of research in this area. Harold Powers's influential article from 1987, "'La solita forma' and the 'Uses of Convention,'" outlined a methodology for a historical approach to analysis based on the writings of Abramo Basevi and nineteenth-century versification practices. Pierluigi Petrobelli, director of the Parma Institute, has proposed a comprehensive analytical methodology based on mutual interaction among the "systems" of dramatic action, verbal organization, and music.[15] Coupling this approach with historical evidence from Verdi's writings, he has argued that musico-dramatic unity, embracing all of the constituent elements of opera, was as significant to Verdi as it was to Wagner.[16] Other analytical approaches have focused on tonality, sonority, Schenkerian analysis, and semiotics.[17]

Many scholars have scrutinized Verdi's dramaturgy and issues relating to his librettos and their sources in recent years. Especially significant are the contributions of Gilles de Van, whose writings have elucidated many aspects of Verdi's dramaturgy and aesthetics. Other areas of exploration have included narrative techniques, the interplay of tragic and comic elements (both in individual works and in the operas as a whole), the influence of French and wider European culture, the relationship of the composer to his librettists, performance gestures in operatic staging, and linguistic features of the libretto.[18] A specialist in the last field, Daniela Goldin Folena, has made a particularly valuable contribution with her "Lessico melodrammatico verdiano" (1995), which evaluates the meaning of terms such as "soggetto," "argomento," "dramma," "programma," "schizzo," "selva," "poesia," "versi," and "situazione" that the composer used in reference to his own creative process. Feminist approaches to Verdi's dramaturgy date at least as far back as A. G. Corrieri's "Le donne nelle opere di G. Verdi," published in the *Gazzetta musicale di Milano* in 1895. Feminism has lately been seen in studies related to individual female characters, such as Elizabeth Hudson's "Gilda Seduced: A Tale Untold" (1992–93), and in broader surveys, such as dissertations examining Verdi's writing for lower women's voices (Naomi Andre, Harvard, 1996) and heroines' deaths in Verdi's operas (Michal Grover, Brandeis, 1997). A wide range of more general studies exploring feminism in Ottocento opera have also touched on Verdi.

The composer's working methods have been an important area of recent inquiry (see chapter 15 of this *Companion*), despite the fact that the earliest layer of primary source material – Verdi's sketches and continuity drafts – have largely remained unavailable to scholars. A notable exception is *Rigoletto*, for which a facsimile of Verdi's early working manuscript was published in 1951. During the 1990s, Verdi's heirs released autograph sketch materials for *Stiffelio*, *La traviata*, and *Un ballo in maschera*. In each case, these materials provided editors of the critical edition with invaluable new information. Materials for *Stiffelio* helped resolve many questions that could not be answered by the autograph full score, which the composer cannibalized when he revised the work as *Aroldo*. The *Traviata* materials surprised researchers by showing that Verdi did not always prepare a continuity draft of the entire work, as had been assumed from materials for *Rigoletto* and *Stiffelio*: in this case, he worked in smaller, discrete units, generally individual numbers. The Parma Institute and Casa Ricordi have launched a new facsimile series with the sketches for *Traviata*, published with a transcription, critical apparatus, and commentary by Fabrizio Della Seta (2000). A second volume, featuring the composer's drafts for *Un ballo in maschera*, is in preparation. The Institute also published in cooperation with La Scala facsimiles and transcriptions of all Verdi autograph manuscripts (except the Requiem) conserved at the Museo Teatrale alla Scala (2000).

Performance practice studies have also flourished, particularly in the realm of staging and scenography. Researchers have examined a wide variety of archival sources, including engravings in contemporary periodicals, and sketches and paintings by scenery and costume designers. Sources habitually overlooked by scholars until the 1970s were the staging manuals (*disposizioni sceniche* or *livrets de mise-en-scène*) prepared under the direction of the composer for premiere productions of most of his later operas. Michaela Peterseil has provided the most thorough overview of these sources to date, including a comprehensive catalog of all of Ricordi's staging manuals and their known locations, in her article "Die 'Disposizioni sceniche' des Verlags Ricordi: ihre Publikation und ihr Zielpublikum" (1997).

In 1994, the Parma Institute sponsored an international congress devoted to issues of staging and scenography. Essays in the congress report, *La realizzazione scenica dello spettacolo verdiano* (1996), cover subjects such as Verdi's work as scenographer, the influence of French and Italian traditions on staging, staging practices at several individual theatres, assessments of major scenographic designers associated with Verdi's operas, and issues relating to theatrical lighting, costuming, and ballet. In the first essay, "L'esperienza teatrale verdiana e la sua proiezione sulla scena," Pierluigi Petrobelli passionately argues that the visual aspect of Verdi's operas was as important to his conception of a work as the aural aspect. Two essays in the report adopt a practical tone, suggesting ways in which modern producers can utilize historical information about staging and choreography in contemporary productions.[19] More recently, Marcello Conati has provided further evidence for the primacy of Verdi's visual conception of his operas in "Prima le scene, poi la musica" (2000), which focuses on the first version of *Simon Boccanegra*.

William Weaver's *Verdi: A Documentary Study*, published in 1977 and reissued in several translations, was the first important iconographic study of the later twentieth century. It was in the 1990s, however, that Verdi iconography truly blossomed. Foremost among these is the beautifully illustrated catalog that accompanied a traveling exhibition sponsored by Parma Institute entitled *"Sorgete! Ombre serene!": L'aspetto visivo dello spettacolo verdiano* (1996). During the 1990s, the Ricordi firm led an important initiative in this area with a series entitled *Musica e spettacolo.* Sumptuously illustrated volumes on *Otello, Simon Boccanegra,* and *Un ballo in maschera* each include facsimile reproductions of the staging manuals, color reproductions of set and costume designs from important early productions, and engravings first published in nineteenth-century periodicals. An additional volume on *Un ballo in maschera* is in preparation.[20]

Scholars have begun to probe more deeply into issues of performance practice involving the solo voice, the chorus, and the orchestra. Topics have included singing technique, style, and ornamentation; the size, makeup, and function of the chorus; the size and seating arrangement of the orchestra; the practice of using the *primo violino* as a dual performer-conductor in Verdi's early operas and the gradual transition to a baton-wielding conductor in the later ones; the adoption of standardized pitch; the types of individual instruments used (particularly in the low brass); and stage bands.[21] These studies will no doubt exercise a significant influence on performances in years to come. John Eliot Gardiner has already released a recording of the Requiem and the *Quattro pezzi sacri* with the Monteverdi Choir and the Orchestre Révolutionnaire et Romantique using historical instruments and performance techniques.

Recent studies that challenge conventional thinking provide a significant indication that at the beginning of the twenty-first century Verdi criticism has reached an important new plateau. For example, several authors have questioned the traditional notion that Verdi's contemporaries read overt political interpretations into his early operas. Roger Parker has proposed that the true political significance of the early operas came not at their premieres but retrospectively, at the end of the nineteenth century, as nostalgic reminiscences of political struggle.[22] In his "*Ottocento* Opera as Cultural Drama" (1997), James Hepokoski has challenged the traditional analytical goal of searching for unity or coherence, suggesting that issues of heterogeneity and inner tension might be equally or more important in understanding Verdi's operas. Fabrizio Della Seta (1994) has proposed that the composer may have intended the term "parola scenica" to express a particular idea at a specific moment to his librettist, Antonio Ghislanzoni, rather than as a general principle, as it has often been interpreted. He suggests incorporating conventional thinking about *parola scenica* into a broader conception of *musica scenica.* These and other revisionary studies will no doubt exert a powerful influence on future Verdi criticism by stimulating debate and establishing new paradigms.

Pierluigi Petrobelli recently referred to the many live and recorded performances of Verdi's music that emerged during the last decades of the twentieth century, noting the extremely varied cultural contexts in which this phenomenon occurred.[23] At the same time, musicological activity has rivaled the complexity and energy of a Verdian *stretta* as researchers have opened new avenues of investigation, reassessing and challenging traditional thinking about the composer and his music. Both branches of activity testify to the richness and vitality of Verdi's music and his lasting legacy as a cultural icon. At the dawn of the twenty-first century, the future of Verdi studies shines brightly indeed.

Notes

For complete citations of frequently referenced works, see the bibliography of this volume, pp. 312–28.

1 Verdi's life: a thematic biography

1. My chapter is based on original research in dozens of Italian archives and on the works of many authors. I recommend the following: Julian Budden, *The Operas of Verdi*, David R. B. Kimbell, *Verdi in the Age of Italian Romanticism*; George Martin, *Verdi: His Music, Life, and Times* (New York: Dodd Mead, 1963); Charles Osborne, *Verdi* (New York: Knopf, 1987); Andrew Porter, "Giuseppe Verdi," in *The New Grove Masters of Italian Opera* (New York: Norton, 1983), pp. 191–308, especially pp. 193–202; and William Weaver, *Verdi: A Documentary Study* (London: Thames and Hudson, 1977).

2 The Italian theatre of Verdi's day

1. From a confidential document sent by the papal legate to the municipality of Ferrara on July 20, 1833, preserved in the Archivio Storico Comunale di Ferrara, series "XIX secolo – Teatri e spettacoli."

2. The best study of Italian opera production in this period is John Rosselli, *The Opera Industry in Italy from Cimarosa to Verdi: The Role of the Impresario* (Cambridge University Press, 1984). For the budgetary information given here, see pp. 52–54.

3. "I cannot sign a contract without knowing who will be in the company." So Verdi wrote with regard to *La traviata*, letter of February 4, 1852, in Marcello Conati, *La bottega della musica*, p. 272.

4. Letter to Francesco Maria Piave, February 9, 1857, and document signed by G. B. Tornielli, February 24, 1857, in Conati, *La bottega della musica*, pp. 402 and 406.

5. Letter to Cesare De Sanctis, May 26, 1854, in Alessandro Luzio (ed.), *Carteggi verdiani*, vol. I, pp. 24 ff.

6. The four operas were given the new titles *Viscardello* (and also *Lionello* and *Clara di Perth*), *Violetta*, *Guglielmo Wellingrode*, and *Giovanna di Guzman*, respectively.

7. It is neither easy nor historiographically appropriate to attempt to determine which elements were "causes" and which "effects," primary versus secondary. See Carl Dahlhaus, *Foundations of Music History* (Cambridge University Press, 1983), particularly the chapter "Thoughts on Structural History," pp. 129–50.

8. See Piero Weiss, "Verdi and the Fusion of Genres," *Journal of the American Musicological Society* 35 (1982), 138–56.

9. See David Rosen, "The Staging of Verdi's Operas," in *Report of the Twelfth Congress [of the International Musicological Society]*, pp. 239–45.

10. Letter to Jacovacci, June 5, 1859, in Gaetano Cesari and Alessandro Luzio (eds.), *I copialettere di Giuseppe Verdi*, pp. 575 ff.

11. See Conati, *La bottega della musica*, pp. 358–63.

12. Letter of October 28, 1854, in Cesari and Luzio (eds.), *I copialettere*, pp. 154 ff.

13. For French influences on Verdi's style, see chapter 7 below.

14. For an insightful discussion of this subject, see Adriana Guarnieri Corazzol, "Opera and Verismo: Regressive Points of View and the Artifice of Alienation," *Cambridge Opera Journal* 5 (1993), 39–53.

15. From Verdi's letter to Tito Ricordi, November 17, 1868, issued to all main newspapers in Italy, in Cesari and Luzio (eds.), *I copialettere*, pp. 210 ff.; see Frank Walker, *The Man Verdi* (London: Dent; New York: Knopf, 1962), pp. 350 ff.

16. Letters from Giulio Ricordi to Verdi, June 27, 1883, in Franca Cella *et al.* (eds.), *Carteggio Verdi–Ricordi 1882–1885*, pp. 117 ff., and January 19, 1886, in Franca Cella and Pierluigi Petrobelli (eds.), *Giuseppe Verdi–Giulio Ricordi: Corrispondenza e immagini 1881–1890*, p. 65.

17. See letters dated March 1, 1869, and February 20, 1871, in Luzio (ed.), *Carteggi verdiani*, vol. III, pp. 62 and 68–70.

18. See letters dated August 29, 1872, and December 29, 1872, in Cesari and Luzio (eds.), *I copialettere*, pp. 685 ff.

19. See Verdi's letter, October 18, 1886, in Cella and Petrobelli (eds.), *Giuseppe Verdi–Giulio Ricordi*, p. 51.

3 Verdi, Italian Romanticism, and the Risorgimento

1. Antonio Gramsci, *Quaderni del carcere*, ed. Valentino Gerratana, 4 vols. (Turin: Einaudi, 1975), vol. III, 14/72, p. 1739; trans. in David Forgacs and Geoffrey Nowell-Smith (eds.), *Antonio Gramsci: Selections from the Cultural Writings*, trans. William Boelhower (Cambridge, Mass.: Harvard University Press, 1985), pp. 204–5.
2. Gramsci, *Quaderni*, vol. III, 14/19, pp. 1676–7; Forgacs and Nowell-Smith (eds.), *Selections*, pp. 379–80.
3. See Carlo Calcaterra (ed.), *I manifesti romantici del 1816, e gli scritti principali del "Conciliatore" sul Romanticismo* (Turin: Unione Tipografico-Editrice Torinese, 1951), pp. 261–331; and Gary Tomlinson, "Italian Opera and Italian Romanticism: An Essay in Their Affinities," *19th-Century Music* 10 (1986–87), 43–60.
4. Alessandro Manzoni, "Sul Romanticismo. Lettera al Marchese Cesare D'Azeglio," in *Opere*, vol. III: *Opere varie*, ed. Guido Bezzola (Milan: Rizzoli, 1961), p. 455.
5. Giuseppe Mazzini, *Filosofia della musica* (1836), cited passage trans. in "From the *Philosophy of Music*," in Ruth A. Solie (ed.), *Source Readings in Music History: The Nineteenth Century* (New York and London: Norton, 1998), p. 46.
6. See Tomlinson, "Italian Opera and Italian Romanticism," 50–51.
7. See Stefano Castelvecchi, "Walter Scott, Rossini, e la *couleur ossianique*: il contesto culturale della *Donna del lago*," *Bollettino del Centro rossiniano di studi* 23 (1993), 57–71; and Gary Tomlinson, "Opera and *Drame*: Hugo, Donizetti, and Verdi," in *Music and Drama* (New York: Broude Brothers, 1988), pp. 171–92.
8. For a thorough discussion of Verdi's compositional engagement with Romantic writers, see David R. B. Kimbell, *Verdi in the Age of Italian Romanticism*, pp. 460–515.
9. Mary Ann Smart, "'Proud, Indomitable, Irascible': Allegories of Nation in *Attila* and *Les vêpres siciliennes*," in Martin Chusid (ed.), *Verdi's Middle Period*, pp. 227–56.
10. Letter to Francesco Maria Piave, April 21, 1848; trans. in Mary Jane Phillips-Matz, *Verdi*, pp. 230–31.
11. Letter of October 18, 1848; Gaetano Cesari and Alessandro Luzio (eds.), *I copialettere di Giuseppe Verdi*, p. 469; trans. in Phillips-Matz, *Verdi*, p. 237.
12. In this case the colonial oppressor was France (ruling thirteenth-century Sicily), which presented something of a diplomatic problem for Verdi since *Vêpres* was destined for the Paris Opéra, a constituency he particularly wished to please. On the inflections of patriotism in *Vêpres*, see Anselm Gerhard, *The Urbanization of Opera: Music Theater in Paris in the Nineteenth Century*, trans. Mary Whittall (University of Chicago Press, 1998), pp. 342–87, especially pp. 378–83; and Andrew Porter, "*Les vêpres siciliennes*: New Letters from Verdi to Scribe," *19th-Century Music* 2 (1978), 95–109.
13. George Martin, *Aspects of Verdi*, pp. 93–116; Paul Robinson, *Opera and Ideas: From Mozart to Strauss* (New York: Harper and Row, 1985), pp. 155–209.
14. Some of the material that follows appeared in a different form in my article "Liberty on (and off) the Barricades: Verdi's Risorgimento Fantasies," in Albert Russell Ascoli and Krystyna von Henneberg (eds.), *Making and Remaking Italy: The Cultivation of National Identity around the Risorgimento* (Oxford and New York: Berg, 2001), pp. 103–18.
15. Textbooks of nineteenth-century music, for example, unanimously take the political angle as a starting point, and descriptions of the 1840s audiences who "roared [with] approval" for Verdi's early choruses too often stand in for observations about the sound of the music (Leon Plantinga, *Romantic Music*, New York and London: Norton, 1984, p. 300). Even Carl Dahlhaus, usually impressive for the caution with which he treats links between works of music and social context, is seduced by the Risorgimento narrative. He characterizes Verdi as "a popular composer before he was a significant one," and repeats the familiar idea that Verdi's early choruses "were received as musical symbols of the Risorgimento by a torn and disrupted nation whose ardor flared up in opera." See Dahlhaus, *Nineteenth-Century Music*, trans. J. Bradford Robinson (Berkeley and Los Angeles: University of California Press, 1989), p. 206.
16. Philip Gossett recounts one typical tale involving an 1846 performance of *Ernani* in Bologna during which the name of the baritone character, the sixteenth-century Spanish king Charles V, was replaced throughout the entire last act by that of Pope Pius IX, yielding lines such as "Sia lode eterna, Pio, al tuo nome." See Gossett, "Becoming a Citizen: The Chorus in Risorgimento Opera," *Cambridge Opera Journal* 2 (1990), 41–64.

17. For a classic version of this classic story, see George Martin, "Verdi and the Risorgimento," in William Weaver and Martin Chusid (eds.), *The Verdi Companion*, pp. 13–41.

18. The story of the "Va pensiero" encore appears in most standard biographies. Franco Abbiati actually went as far as to manufacture journalistic "evidence" for the encore in his *Giuseppe Verdi*. As Parker has shown, Abbiati's account of the *Nabucco* premiere fuses together two separate reviews so as to make it appear that the number encored was "Va pensiero." The initial correction of Abbiati's massaged quotation is published in "Historical Introduction," *Nabucodonosor*, ed. Roger Parker, *The Works of Giuseppe Verdi*, series I, vol. III (University of Chicago Press; Milan: Ricordi, 1987), p. xvi. Since then Parker has undertaken more detailed discussions of the musical content and popular reception of "Va pensiero" in chapter 2 of his *Leonora's Last Act*, pp. 20–41, and in a monograph entirely devoted to the question of Verdi's pre-1848 reception, *"Arpa d'or dei fatidici vati": The Verdian Patriotic Chorus in the 1840s* (Parma: Istituto Nazionale di Studi Verdiani, 1997).

19. Parker has also debunked the anecdote about the insertion of Pius IX's name into *Ernani*, tracing the story to an item in the theatrical journal *Teatri, arti e letteratura*, which reported that at an 1846 performance of Donizetti's *Roberto Devereux* a chorus from *Ernani* with new words honoring Pius IX was inserted between the acts, in a manifestation that was officially planned and announced in advance (*Leonora's Last Act*, p. 137).

20. I owe this information to a personal communication from David Rosen.

21. Parker, *"Arpa d'or dei fatidici vati"*, p. 110. Parker's monograph reproduces a facsimile of the Cornali chorus in an appendix.

22. Studying another manifestation of Verdi's presence in the popular imagination, Birgit Pauls has shown that school textbooks from the last quarter of the nineteenth century rarely mention Verdi in connection with the Risorgimento (or, indeed, mention him at all). It was not until the 1920s that the acronym "Viva VERDI" and Verdi's folk-popular connections began to feature in elementary school books. See Pauls, *Giuseppe Verdi und das Risorgimento: Ein politischer Mythos im Prozess der Nationenbildung* (Ph.D. dissertation, University of Frankfurt am Main, 1996; Berlin: Akademie Verlag, 1996), pp. 301–10.

23. Parker, *"Arpa d'or dei fatidici vati"*, pp. 48–82.

24. On the circumstances of the *Battaglia* commission and premiere, see Budden, *The Operas of Verdi*, vol. I (New York, 1973), pp. 389–95.

25. In his nuanced discussion of this and other historical subjects revived by Risorgimento artists, Lyttelton emphasizes that the Oath of Pontida episode celebrated the role of the Catholic Church in uniting the Lombard towns, and thus was a particularly popular subject during the early, Giobertian phase of the Risorgimento. Lyttelton speculates that the strong Catholic overtones that became attached to the Oath may be a reason for the omission of this episode from *Battaglia*, which was not premiered until January 1849 after serious disillusionment with Pius IX had set in. See Lyttelton, "Creating a National Past: History, Myth and Image in the Risorgimento," in Ascoli and von Henneberg (eds.), *Making and Remaking Italy*, pp. 27–74.

26. Pauls, *Verdi und das Risorgimento*, pp. 199–200, speculates that Verdi and Cammarano may have chosen Méry's play over a Risorgimento drama as the source for *Battaglia* because the French play better met the tastes of the intended audience and because it gave more weight to its love interest than did any contemporary Italian patriotic drama.

27. Solie (ed.), *Source Readings*, p. 43.

28. I am thinking of such oft-reproduced works as Vincenzo Cabianca's *La partenza del volontario* (1858), Odoardo Borrani's *Le cucitrici di camicie rosse* (1863), and Gerolamo Induno's *Il ritorno del soldato* (1867), all admittedly from a later phase of Risorgimento activity than Verdi's 1840s images of warrior women. Before 1848, images of contemporary women are almost non-existent, perhaps excluded by the dominant neo-classical idiom. For an overview of styles and subject matter in Italian painting of the period, see Albert Boime, *The Art of the Macchia and the Risorgimento: Representing Culture and Nationalism in Nineteenth-Century Italy* (University of Chicago Press, 1993), and Roberta J. M. Olsen (ed.), *Ottocento: Romanticism and Revolution in Nineteenth-Century Italian Painting* (New York: American Federation of Arts, 1992).

29. Mazzini, *Filosofia*; trans. in Jean-Pierre Barricelli, "Romantic Writers and Music: The Case of Mazzini," *Studies in Romanticism* 14 (1975), 109.

4 The forms of set pieces

1. Abramo Basevi, *Studio sulle opere di Giuseppe Verdi*, p. 191. The implications of Basevi's comments are discussed by Harold Powers in "'La solita forma' and 'The Uses of Convention'," *Acta musicologica* 59 (1987), 65–90. Roger Parker, "'Insolite forme,' or Basevi's Garden Path," in Martin Chusid (ed.), *Verdi's Middle Period*, pp. 129–46, cautions against relying excessively on Basevi for evidence of Verdi's formal practices.

2. Carlo Ritorni, *Ammaestramenti alla composizione d'ogni poema e d'ogni opera appartenente alla musica* (Milan: Pirola, 1841), pp. 40–58, discussed in Scott L. Balthazar, "Ritorni's *Ammaestramenti* and the Conventions of Rossinian Melodramma," *Journal of Musicological Research* 8 (1989), 281–311.

3. Scott L. Balthazar, "Evolving Conventions in Italian Serious Opera: Scene Structure in the Works of Rossini, Bellini, Donizetti, and Verdi, 1810–1850" (Ph.D. dissertation, University of Pennsylvania, 1985).

4. This process as exemplified by the arias of Rossini's predecessor Simon Mayr is discussed in Scott L. Balthazar, "Mayr and the Development of the Two-Movement Aria," in Francesco Bellotto (ed.), *Giovanni Simone Mayr: L'opera teatrale e la musica sacra* (Bergamo: Stefanoni, 1997), pp. 229–51.

5. This characteristic has been noted elsewhere. See, for example, Martin Chusid, "Toward an Understanding of Verdi's Middle Period," in Chusid (ed.), *Verdi's Middle Period*, p. 11. Verdi's engagement with French grand opera beginning in the 1840s also produced arias modeled on French *couplets* and da capo forms which occur in both his French and his Italian works. See chapter 7 below, pp. 113–17.

6. For Verdi's response to French melody, see chapter 7 below, pp. 128–38.

7. For an explanation of the lyric prototype, see chapter 6 below, pp. 92–93.

8. See chapter 6 below, pp. 93–98, for extended discussion of this movement and a score.

9. For the development of the duet from Rossini to Verdi, see Scott L. Balthazar, "The *Primo Ottocento* Duet and the Transformation of the Rossinian Code," *Journal of Musicology* 7 (1989), 471–97, and Balthazar, "Analytic Contexts and Mediated Influences: The Rossinian *Convenienze* and Verdi's Middle and Late Duets," *Journal of Musicological Research* 10 (1990), 19–45.

10. For a seminal discussion of Rossini's finales, see Philip Gossett, "The 'candeur virginale' of *Tancredi*," *Musical Times* 112 (1971), 327–29.

11. For the early development of the serious finale, see Scott L. Balthazar, "Mayr, Rossini, and the Development of the Early Concertato Finale," *Journal of the Royal Musical Association* 116 (1991), 236–66.

12. Ritorni, *Ammaestramenti*, p. 51. The most thorough discussion of Verdi's openings is David Rosen's "How Verdi's Operas Begin: An Introduction to the Introduzioni," in Giovanni Morelli (ed.), *Tornando a Stiffelio: Popolarità, rifacimenti, messinscena, effettismo e altre "cure"* (Florence: Olschki, 1987), pp. 203–21.

13. For Rossini's *introduzioni*, see Philip Gossett, "Gioachino Rossini and the Conventions of Composition," *Acta musicologica* 42 (1970), 52–56.

14. These terms are adapted from David Rosen, "How Verdi's Serious Operas End," in Angelo Pompilio *et al.* (eds.), *Atti del XIV Congresso della Società internazionale di musicologia*, vol. III, pp. 443–50, which discusses Verdi's final scenes in detail. My discussion diverges from Rosen's on some points.

15. For a recent discussion of Verdi's choruses, see Markus Engelhardt, "'Something's Been Done to Make Room for Choruses': Choral Conception and Choral Construction in *Luisa Miller*," in Chusid (ed.), *Verdi's Middle Period*, pp. 197–205.

16. For covert meanings in Verdi's patriotic choruses, see Philip Gossett, "Becoming a Citizen: The Chorus in *Risorgimento* Opera," *Cambridge Opera Journal* 2 (1990), 41–64.

17. See also James A. Hepokoski's discussion of form in *Otello* in *Giuseppe Verdi: "Otello"* (Cambridge University Press, 1987), chapter 7.

5 New currents in the libretto

1. See Fabrizio Della Seta, "The librettist," in Lorenzo Bianconi and Giorgio Pestelli (eds.), *Opera Production and Its Resources* (University of Chicago Press, 1998), pp. 229–89. The best history of the Italian opera libretto is found in Giovanna Gronda and Paolo Fabbri (eds.), *Libretti d'opera italiani dal Seicento a Novecento* (Milan: Mondadori, 1997), pp. 9–54.

2. See, for example, Mario Lavagetto, *Quei più modesti romanzi: il libretto nel melodramma di Verdi: Tecniche costruttive funzioni poetica di un genere letterario minore* (Milan: Garzanti,

1979); Guido Paduano, *Noi facemmo ambedue un sogno strano: Il disagio amoroso sulla scena dell'opera europea* (Palermo: Sellerio, 1982); John Black, *The Italian Romantic Libretto: A Study of Salvadore Cammarano* (Edinburgh University Press, 1984); Daniela Goldin, *La vera Fenice: Libretti e librettisti tra Sette e Ottocento* (Turin: Einaudi, 1985); Carl Dahlhaus, "Drammaturgia dell'opera italiana," in Lorenzo Bianconi and Giorgio Pestelli (eds.), *Teorie e tecniche, immagini e fantasmi, Storia dell'opera italiana*, vol. VI (Turin: EDT/Musica, 1988), pp. 77–162; Guido Paduano, *Il giro di vite: Percorsi dell'opera lirica* (Scandicci: La Nuova Italia, 1992); Alessandro Roccatagliati, *Felice Romani librettista* (Lucca: Libreria Musicale Italiana, 1996); Luigi Baldacci, *La musica in italiano: Libretto d'opera dell'Ottocento* (Milan: Rizzoli, 1997). The best and most recent discussion of the role of the libretto in Verdi's dramaturgy is Gilles de Van, *Verdi's Theater*, particularly chapter 3.
3. Letter of November 15, 1843, cited in *Ernani*, ed. Claudio Gallico, *The Works of Giuseppe Verdi*, series I, vol. V (University of Chicago Press; Milan: Ricordi, 1985), p. xvii.
4. See Friedrich Lippmann, *Versificazione italiana e ritmo musicale* (Naples: Liguori, 1986); Wolfgang Osthoff, "Musica e versificazione: funzioni del verso poetico nell'opera italiana," in Lorenzo Bianconi (ed.), *La drammaturgia musicale* (Bologna: Il Mulino, 1986), pp. 125–41; Paolo Fabbri, "Istituti metrici e formali," in Bianconi and Pestelli (eds.), *Teorie e tecniche, immagini e fantasmi*, pp. 163–233; Roccatagliati, *Felice Romani librettista*, pp. 129–59; Robert Moreen, "Integration of Text Forms and Musical Forms in Verdi's Early Operas" (Ph.D. dissertation, Princeton University, 1975; Ann Arbor, Mich.: University Microfilms, 1976).
5. Letter of April 22, 1853, cited in Alessandro Pascolato (ed.), *"Re Lear" e "Ballo in maschera": Lettere di Giuseppe Verdi ad Antonio Somma* (Città di Castello: Lapi, 1902), p. 4.
6. See Luigi Dallapiccola, "Words and Music in Italian Nineteenth-Century Opera," in William Weaver and Martin Chusid (eds.), *The Verdi Companion*, pp. 183–215; Piero Weiss, " 'Sacred Bronzes': Paralipomena to an Essay by Dallapiccola," in *19th-Century Music* 9 (1985–86), 42–49; Baldacci, *La musica in italiano*, pp. 91–117.
7. See Carlo Matteo Mossa (ed.), *Carteggio Verdi–Cammarano, 1843–1852* (Parma: Istituto Nazionale di Studi Verdiani, 2001), pp. 104–61.

8. See Piero Weiss, "Verdi and the Fusion of Genres," *Journal of the American Musicological Society* 35 (1982), 138–56, especially 146 ff.
9. Letter of December 17, 1847, in Mossa (ed.), *Carteggio Verdi–Cammarano*, p. 15; as cited in Weiss, "Verdi and the Fusion of Genres," 148.
10. Mossa (ed.), *Carteggio Verdi–Cammarano*, pp. 105–9.
11. *Ibid.*, pp. 110–11.
12. Letter of May 22, 1849, in Mossa (ed.), *Carteggio Verdi–Cammarano*, pp. 112–18; as cited in Weiss, "Verdi and the Fusion of Genres," 149.
13. *The Aeneid of Virgil*, trans. Allen Mandelbaum (Berkeley: University of California Press, 1981), p. 239; Ludovico Ariosto, *Orlando furioso (The Frenzy of Orlando)*, trans. Barbara Edwards, vol. I (Harmondsworth: Penguin, 1975), p. 573.
14. Letter of October 20, 1853, cited in *La traviata*, ed. Fabrizio Della Seta, *The Works of Giuseppe Verdi*, series I, vol. XIX (University of Chicago Press; Milan: Ricordi, 1997), p. xiii.
15. See Weiss, "Verdi and the Fusion of Genres," 151 ff.
16. All are published and translated in Hans Busch (ed. and trans.), *Verdi's "Aida"*, pp. 440–71, 483–93, and 499–553.
17. See Philip Gossett, "Verdi, Ghislanzoni, and *Aida*: The Uses of Convention," *Critical Inquiry* 1 (1974–75), 291–334.
18. Letter of August 17, 1870, trans. in Busch (ed. and trans.), *Verdi's "Aida"*, p. 50.
19. Letter of September 30, 1870, trans. *ibid.*, p. 72.
20. Letter of November 13, 1870, trans. *ibid.*, p. 103.
21. Letter of January 4, 1870, trans. *ibid.*, p. 92. Dante's *Divine Comedy* is written entirely in tercets of *endecasillabi*.
22. See Harold S. Powers, "Boito rimatore per musica," in Giovanni Morelli (ed.), *Arrigo Boito* (Florence: Olschki, 1994), pp. 355–94.
23. Letter of August 20, 1889, cited in William Weaver (trans.), *The Verdi–Boito Correspondence*, p. 150. On the genesis of the opera, see also Hans Busch (ed. and trans.), *Verdi's "Falstaff"*. For a critical discussion, see James A. Hepokoski, *Giuseppe Verdi: "Falstaff"* (Cambridge University Press, 1983), pp. 19–34.
24. Letter of July 7, 1889, in Weaver (trans.), *The Verdi–Boito Correspondence*, p. 126.
25. Letter of July 7, 1889, trans. *ibid.*, p. 141; letter to Giulio Ricordi, December 12, 1892, trans. in Busch (ed. and trans.), *Verdi's "Falstaff"*, p. 341.

26. Letter of July 7, 1889, in Weaver (trans.), *The Verdi–Boito Correspondence*, p. 121.
27. See Wolfgang Osthoff, "Il sonetto nel *Falstaff* di Verdi," in Giorgio Pestelli (ed.), *Il melodramma italiano dell'ottocento: Studi e ricerche per Massimo Mila* (Turin: Einaudi, 1977), pp. 157–83.

6 Words and music
1. For reasons of space I cannot include a discussion of Verdi's recitatives, nor a treatment of his setting of French texts. For the latter, however, see chapter 7 below, pp. 128–38. I would like to thank Suzie Clark, Karen Henson, Roger Parker, David Rosen, and Mary Ann Smart for reading previous versions of this chapter and offering invaluable comments and suggestions.
2. Parker, *Leonora's Last Act*, p. 186.
3. Letter from Verdi to Antonio Somma, August 30, 1853, in Alessandro Pascolato (ed.), *"Re Lear" e "Ballo in maschera": Lettere di Giuseppe Verdi ad Antonio Somma* (Città di Castello: Lapi, 1902), p. 53; trans. in Philip Gossett, "Verdi, Ghislanzoni, and *Aida*: The Uses of Convention," *Critical Inquiry* 1 (1974–75), 292.
4. See the statistics compiled by Rita Garlato, *Repertorio metrico verdiano* (Venice: Marsilio, 1998), pp. 193–230.
5. *Luisa Miller, melodramma tragico in tre atti di Salvadore Cammarano, musica del Maestro Giuseppe Verdi* (Milan: Ricordi, 1850), p. 23; translations for this text and for "Tu puniscimi, o Signore" have been adapted from William Weaver's translations for the booklet accompanying the CD reissue of the 1965 RCA Victor recording (GD86646).
6. The superscript *s* indicates a *verso sdrucciolo*; the superscript *t* indicates a *verso tronco*.
7. The concept of the lyric form was introduced in relation to Bellini's arias by Friedrich Lippmann, *Vincenzo Bellini und die italienische Opera seria seiner Zeit: Studien über Libretto, Arienform und Melodik, Analecta musicologica* 6 (Cologne: Böhlau, 1969), rev. Italian ed., "Vincenzo Bellini e l'opera seria del suo tempo. Studi sul libretto, la forma delle arie e la melodia," in Maria Rosaria Adamo and Friedrich Lippmann, *Vincenzo Bellini* (Rome: ERI, 1981), pp. 313–555 (see especially pp. 427–29). Robert Moreen has applied it to early Verdi in his dissertation "Integration of Text Forms and Musical Forms in Verdi's Early Operas" (Ph.D. dissertation, Princeton University, 1975),

while Joseph Kerman has investigated its modifications in middle Verdi, "Lyric Form and Flexibility in *Simon Boccanegra*," *Studi verdiani* 1 (1982), 47–62, and Scott Balthazar its Rossinian genealogy, "Rossini and the Development of the Mid-Century Lyric Form," *Journal of the American Musicological Society* 41 (1988), 102–25. Steven Huebner has focused on issues of tonality and cadential articulation, paying special attention to the different types of expansion and tonal/thematic return, "Lyric Form in *Ottocento* Opera," *Journal of the Royal Musical Association* 117 (1992), 123–47. See also Gary Tomlinson, "Verdi after Budden," *19th-Century Music* 5 (1981–82), 170–82, especially 174–77. Scott Balthazar has investigated Verdi's practice in setting kinetic movements (*tempi d'attacco* and *tempi di mezzo*) in "Music, Poetry, and Action in Ottocento Opera: The Principle of Concurrent Articulations," *Opera Journal* 22 (1989), 13–34.
8. See Giorgio Pagannone, "Mobilità strutturale della *lyric form*. Sintassi verbale e sintassi musicale nel melodramma italiano del primo Ottocento," *Analisi* 7/20 (May 1997), 2–17, who cites Emanuele Bidera, *Euritmia drammatico-musicale* (Palermo: Stabilimento tipografico dell'Armonia, 1853), pp. 82–89, and Abramo Basevi, *Studio sulle opere di Giuseppe Verdi*, p. 24.
9. See James A. Hepokoski, "*Ottocento* Opera as Cultural Drama: Generic Mixtures in *Il trovatore*," in Martin Chusid (ed.), *Verdi's Middle Period*, pp. 147–96. Since it is still occasionally cited, it seems necessary to point out how far from Verdi's practice is Luigi Dallapiccola's suggestion that in arias the climax corresponds to the third line of text; see Dallapiccola, "Parole e musica nel melodramma."
10. Basevi comments that in this movement Verdi did not follow convention, but composed a melody almost entirely independent from the initial theme. See *Studio sulle opere di Giuseppe Verdi*, p. 168.
11. On mixed forms in middle-period operas, see James A. Hepokoski, "Genre and Content in Mid-Century Verdi: 'Addio, del passato' (*La traviata*, Act III)," *Cambridge Opera Journal* 1 (1989), 249–76; and Hepokoski, "*Ottocento* Opera as Cultural Drama."
12. The version of the text given here is transcribed from the current Ricordi piano-vocal score; the translation is adapted from William Weaver, *Seven Verdi Librettos* (New York and London: Norton, 1975), p. 205.

13. Strictly speaking, lines 1 and 3 do not rhyme, since the consonant sound is different: "*-ide*," "*-ite*"; in Italian this is called an "assonanza".

14. See Huebner, "Lyric Form," 137–38.

15. This is Kerman's position ("Lyric Form and Flexibility," 57–58).

16. Roger Parker and Matthew Brown, "Motivic and Tonal Interaction in Verdi's *Un ballo in maschera*," *Journal of the American Musicological Society* 36 (1983), 243–65, especially 249–53.

17. Letter from Verdi to Giulio Ricordi, July 10, 1870, in Abbiati, *Giuseppe Verdi*, vol. III, p. 348; date and translation given in Busch (ed. and trans.), *Verdi's "Aida"*, p. 31, and Gossett, "Verdi, Ghislanzoni and *Aida*," 296. The expression reappears in two other letters from the summer of 1870 to Antonio Ghislanzoni, the librettist of *Aida* (letters of August 14 and 17, 1870, published in Gaetano Cesari and Alessandro Luzio (eds.), *I copialettere di Giuseppe Verdi*, pp. 639 and 641, and trans. in Busch (ed. and trans.), *Verdi's "Aida"*, pp. 47 and 50), and more than ten years later in a letter to Arrigo Boito about the reworking of *Simon Boccanegra*, January 15, 1881, published in Mario Medici and Marcello Conati (eds.), *Carteggio Verdi–Boito*, vol. I, pp. 31–32, trans. in Weaver (trans.), *The Verdi–Boito Correspondence*, p. 30. The concept is adumbrated in a letter to Antonio Somma of November 6, 1857 (see Pascolato (ed.), *"Re Lear" e "Ballo in maschera"*, pp. 79–81).

Three of the most recent and detailed discussions of *parola scenica* do not mention the letter to Ricordi, even though they comment on the letter to Somma. See Harold S. Powers, "*Simon Boccanegra* I.10–12: A Generic-Genetic Analysis of the Council Chamber Scene," *19th-Century Music* 13 (1989–90), 101–28, appendix 3; Fabrizio Della Seta, "'Parola scenica' in Verdi e nella critica verdiana," in Fiamma Nicolodi and Paolo Trovato (eds.), *Le parole della musica I: Studi sulla lingua della letteratura musicale in onore di Gianfranco Folena* (Florence: Olschki, 1994), pp. 259–73; and Daniela Goldin Folena, "Lessico melodrammatico verdiano," in Maria Teresa Muraro (ed.), *Le parole della musica II: Studi sul lessico della letteratura critica del teatro musicale in onore di Gianfranco Folena* (Florence: Olschki, 1995), pp. 227–53.

18. Powers, "*Simon Boccanegra* I.10–12," 128.

19. Della Seta, "'Parola scenica'."

20. "La parola che scolpisce e rende netta ed evidente la situazione" (letter to Ghislanzoni of August 17, 1870; see note 17 above).

21. See Powers, "*Simon Boccanegra* I.10–12," 128. Strictly speaking, Nabucco's words do not launch the *stretta*, but provoke the lightning that strikes him. It is to this scenic event that the *stretta* responds.

22. See Harold S. Powers, "Making *Macbeth* Musicabile," in *Giuseppe Verdi: "Macbeth"*, English National Opera Guide 41 (London: Calder; New York: Riverrun, 1990), pp. 13–36; Pierluigi Petrobelli, "Verdi's Musical Thought: An Example from *Macbeth*," in Petrobelli, *Music in the Theater*, pp. 141–52.

23. Other instances of *parole sceniche* placed immediately before a set piece and not mentioned by Powers are Leonora's "M'avrai, ma fredda, esanime spoglia" and Luna's "Colui vivrà" before the *cabaletta* of their duet in Act IV of *Il trovatore*; Leonora's "Son tua, son tua col core e con la vita" before the *cabaletta* of the Leonora-Alvaro duet in Act I of *La forza del destino*; and Amonasro's "Non sei mi figlia! Dei Faraoni tu sei la schiava" before the "non-*cabaletta*" of the Aida-Amonasro duet in Act III of *Aida*. For the last example, see Petrobelli, "Music in the Theater (Apropos of *Aida*, Act III)," in Petrobelli, *Music in the Theater*, pp. 116–17. Petrobelli considers "Dei Faraoni tu sei la schiava" as the *parola scenica*, but I would say that the situation is carved out by the opposition between "Non sei mia figlia" and "Dei Faraoni tu sei la schiava," and that therefore the *parola scenica* comprises the two lines shouted by Amonasro – an interpretation supported by Verdi's setting.

24. See David Rosen, "How Verdi's Serious Operas End," in Angelo Pompilio *et al.* (eds.), *Atti del xiv Congresso*, vol. III, pp. 443–50; reprinted in *Verdi Newsletter* 20 (1992), 9–15.

25. Notable exceptions by which Verdi might have been inspired are Rossini's *Otello*, in which the protagonist shouts "Punito m'avrà" and kills himself, all the other characters on stage exclaim "Ah!" and a few measures of the orchestra bring the curtain down; and especially Donizetti's revolutionary *Maria di Rohan*, which ends with the baritone Chevreuse's tensely declamatory "La morte a lui! . . . La vita coll'infamia a te, donna infedel." Words with similar potential had been available to Verdi earlier in his career – for example, Loredano's "Pagato ora sono!" (*I due Foscari*) – but he did not set them in musical relief: Loredano's exclamation is virtually inaudible.

26. Translation adapted from Hans Busch (ed. and trans.), *Verdi's "Otello" and "Simon*

Boccanegra", vol. II, pp. 443–44; *Disposizione scenica per l'opera "Simon Boccanegra" di Giuseppe Verdi* (Milan: Ricordi, [1883]), p. 16; facsimile ed. in Marcello Conati and Natalia Grilli (eds.), *"Simon Boccanegra" di Giuseppe Verdi* (Milan: Ricordi, 1993).

27. See Carl Dahlhaus, "Drammaturgia dell'opera italiana," in Lorenzo Bianconi and Giorgio Pestelli (eds.), *Teorie e tecniche, immagini e fantasmi, Storia dell'opera italiana*, vol. VI (Turin: EDT/Musica, 1988), especially pp. 102–4.

28. For a reading of Verdi's recurring themes, especially in *Aida*, in the light of their visual, bodily qualities, see Mary Ann Smart, "Ulterior Motives: Verdi's Recurring Themes Revisited," in Mary Ann Smart (ed.), *Siren Songs*, pp. 135–59.

29. Translation adapted from Busch (ed. and trans.), *Verdi's "Otello" and "Simon Boccanegra"*, vol. II, p. 604; *Disposizione scenica per l'opera "Otello"* (Milan: Ricordi, [1887]), p. 91; facsimile ed. in James A. Hepokoski and Mercedes Viale Ferrero (eds.), *"Otello" di Giuseppe Verdi* (Milan: Ricordi, 1990).

30. Marco Beghelli has investigated word painting in Verdi from a semiotic point of view, as one of the modes that performative musical acts can assume. See "Per un nuovo approccio al teatro musicale: l'atto performativo come luogo dell'imitazione gestuale nella drammaturgia verdiana," *Italica* 64 (1987), 632–53; "Performative Musical Acts: The Verdian Achievement," in Eero Tarasti (ed.), *Musical Signification: Essays in the Semiotic Theory and Analysis of Music* (Berlin and New York: De Gruyter, 1995), pp. 393–412; and "Semiotic Categories for the Analysis of *melodramma*," *Contemporary Music Review* 17/3 (1998), 29–42.

31. See Roger Parker, "'Infin che un brando vindice' e le cavatine del primo atto di *Ernani*," in Pierluigi Petrobelli (ed.), *"Ernani" ieri e oggi*, pp. 142–60.

32. I have discussed these examples more extensively in "Verdi's Luisa, a Semiserious Alpine Virgin," *19th-Century Music* 22 (1998–99), 144–68, especially 157–59, which includes musical examples.

33. See Budden, *The Operas of Verdi*, rev. ed. (Oxford, 1992), vol. II, p. 83.

34. See Marco Beghelli, "Lingua dell'autocaricatura nel *Falstaff*," in Gianfranco Folena *et al.* (eds.), *Opera e libretto II*, pp. 351–80.

35. In this context the term "madrigale" indicates early vocal music in general, including the vocalizing "excesses" of eighteenth-century opera, especially *opera seria*, so despised during the nineteenth century. In his setting of the *madrigale* "Sulla vetta tu del monte" in Act II of *Manon Lescaut* (premiered eight days before *Falstaff*) Puccini made ample use of gently ironic "madrigalisms," but, while (appropriately for a *madrigale*) the text pokes fun at sixteenth- and seventeenth-century Italian pastoral poetry, Puccini's music (adapted from a youthful Agnus Dei) parodies the style of eighteenth-century opera.

36. Letter from Boito to Verdi of July 12, 1889, in Medici and Conati (eds.), *Carteggio Verdi–Boito*, vol. I, p. 150; trans. in Weaver (trans.), *The Verdi–Boito Correspondence*, pp. 145–46.

7 French influences

1. Letter of April 21, 1868, trans. in Budden, *The Operas of Verdi*, rev. ed. (Oxford, 1992), vol. III, p. 26.

2. In reaction to a warning by the poet Giuseppe Giusti to shun foreign influences, Verdi responded, "If we want something that is at least effective, then we must, to our shame, resort to things that are not ours." Letter of March 27, 1847, trans. in Mary Jane Phillips-Matz, *Verdi*, pp. 207–8.

3. In Milan, where he spent much time between 1832 (the beginning of his studies with Vincenzo Lavigna) and 1847 (when he first traveled to Paris), Verdi may have had the opportunity to acquaint himself with French theatre. French was the language of the educated classes, and French plays, often presented in the style of the *mélodrame*, were much in vogue and frequently performed at the Teatro Re and the Teatro Carcano. These *mélodrames*, with their mixture of comedy and tragedy, speech and song, and acting and dancing, first became popular at the Parisian boulevard theatres. They soon began to leave their mark on the more serious genre of the *drame*, mainly in their overtures, music for scene changes, *entr'actes*, musical underpinning for stage action, and melodrama (that is, spoken dialogue over a musical background). In fact, the *mélodrame* became the most progressive theatrical genre and influenced the plays of Victor Hugo and Alexandre Dumas *père*, among others. Representative works of this genre often made their way across the Alps within a few weeks,

a period that included translation and rehearsals. It is unknown whether Verdi saw any of these works, serious or popular, in Milan. From the time of his first stay in Paris in 1847, however, we have evidence that he attended and enjoyed *mélodrames* at the boulevard theatres. See Marcello Conati, "Verdi et la culture parisienne des années 1830," in *La vie musicale en France au XIXe siècle*, vol. IV: *La musique à Paris dans les années mil huit cent trente*, ed. Peter Bloom (Stuyvesant: Pendragon Press, 1987), p. 214; Emilio Sala, "Verdi and the Parisian Boulevard Theatre, 1847–49," *Cambridge Opera Journal* 7 (1995), 190–91; and Piero Weiss, "Verdi and the Fusion of Genres," *Journal of the American Musicological Society* 35 (1982), 148.

4. *Giuseppe Verdi: "Macbeth"*, ed. Walter Ducloux (New York: Schirmer, 1969), p. 6. Misaccentuation is heard especially in the Act III chorus "Tre volte miagola la gatta in collera." In the section starting with "Tu rospo venefico," the weak final syllable of lines is often strongly accented.

5. His major periods of residence were July 1847 to early April 1848, May 1848 to December 1848, and January or February 1849 to the end of July 1849.

6. Letter to Cammarano of May 17, 1849, trans. in Weiss, "Verdi and the Fusion of Genres," 149. With regard to other Verdi operas, the influence of the boulevard theatres most likely went beyond the structure and content of the libretto, including details of musical dramaturgy and even melodic ideas. Emilio Sala ("Verdi and the Parisian Boulevard Theatre, 1847–49," 196 and 201) has recently attempted to show, for example, that a chorus from Alphonse Varney's music for Dumas and Auguste Maquet's *Le chevalier de maison-rouge* (1847) bears a strong resemblance to the opening chorus of *La battaglia di Legnano* (1849), while another *mélodrame*, Emile Souvestre and Eugène Bourgeois's *Le pasteur, ou L'évangile et le foyer* (1849), with music of uncertain authorship, may have provided musico-dramatic ideas for *Stiffelio* (1850).

7. Letter of May 8, 1850, to Piave; quoted in Franco Abbiati, *Giuseppe Verdi*, vol. II, p. 62. Verdi found dramatic inspiration not only in French plays but also in French operas. The most famous instance is the Act IV finale of *Les vêpres siciliennes*, modeled on the Act IV finale of Meyerbeer's *Le prophète* (1849).

8. "Di qual opera francese parla qui il periodico di Berlino? La vera fisonomia [*sic*] della melodia francese noi non la sapremmo ravvisare che nelle opere comiche. Nell'opera seria, il cui maggior tempio è il grand'*Opéra*, com'altri osservò, la musica francese è cosmopolita; ed infatti ben rado nelle grandi opere che si rappresentano a quel teatro ci viene fatto di scorgere i vizi inerenti alla melodia ed alla musica francese in generale." "Aristocrazie musicali," *Gazzetta musicale di Milano* 18 (1860), 57. See also Carl Dahlhaus, "Französische Musik und Musik in Paris," *Lendemains* 31–32 (1983), 6.

9. Julian Budden, "Aria," in Stanley Sadie (ed.), *The New Grove Dictionary of Opera*, 4 vols. (London: Macmillan, 1992), vol. I, p. 176. Both forms appear in Meyerbeer's earliest examples of grand opera, mainly *Robert le diable* (1831) and *Les huguenots* (1833).

10. James A. Hepokoski, "*Ottocento* Opera as Cultural Drama: Generic Mixtures in *Il trovatore*," in Martin Chusid (ed.), *Verdi's Middle Period*, pp. 157 and 161, suggests that Verdi seems to have associated stophic forms with middle- and lower-class subjects and characters, and lyric form with aristocratic ones. Abramo Basevi, the author of the first extended study of Verdi's works up to *Aroldo*, also alludes, though vaguely, to such an analogy. See Basevi, *Studio sulle opere di Giuseppe Verdi*, pp. 230–31.

11. Subscript numerals indicate the number of measures in a phrase.

12. For a discussion of lyric form, see Emanuele Senici's essay in chapter 6 above, pp. 92–93. The French repertory includes numerous examples of strophic arias with refrains. For possible models of Verdi's strophic songs with refrain, see James A. Hepokoski, "Genre and Content in Mid-Century Verdi: 'Addio, del passato' (*La traviata*, Act III)," *Cambridge Opera Journal* 1 (1989), 260–61; and Hepokoski, "*Ottocento* Opera as Cultural Drama," 150–66.

13. The early nineteenth-century French theorist Antoine Reicha discussed strophic songs under the category of "chansons et romances": "La *fraîcheur* et la *légèreté* du chant doivent faire le caractère principal de la Chanson et de la Romance. L'accompagnement doit par conséquent en être également frais et léger. Tout ce qui est *lourd* tue cette sorte de production." ("The *freshness* and *lightness* of the melody must make up the principal character of the *chanson* and *romance*. The accompaniment must consequently be equally fresh and light. Anything *heavy* kills this sort of

composition.") Antoine Reicha, *L'art du compositeur dramatique* (Paris: Farrenc, 1833), p. 31. The two strophic arias in *Rigoletto* (the Duke's "Questa o quella," I, 1, and "La donna è mobile," III, 2) lack a refrain.

14. Compare this approach with Angèle's "Chanson aragonaise" from Auber's highly popular *Le domino noir* (1837), where the effect also derives from the discrepancy between accompanimental and melodic accents and from the melody's irregular rhythmic groups. Henri's "La brise souffle" (V, 2) draws its effect at least in part from the discrepancy of prosodic and accompanimental accents. Verdi not only drew on French forms but occasionally also alluded to (or even borrowed) French melodies. See Julian Budden, "Verdi and Meyerbeer in Relation to *Les vêpres siciliennes*," *Studi verdiani* 1 (1982), 11–20.

15. Procida's "Et toi, Palerme" (II, 1) is also in ABA′ form.

16. "Quand il se trouve deux ou plusieurs de ces Choeurs en même temps sur la scène, et qu'ils chantent alternativement, le Compositeur imprimera à chacun le caractère qui lui est propre pour le distinguer des autres." ("If there are two or more of these choruses on stage at the same time, and if they sing in alternation, the composer imprints on each one the character that is appropriate to distinguish it from the others.") Reicha, *L'art du compositeur dramatique*, p. 64. Reicha considered it impossible truly to display different emotions simultaneously; nevertheless, examples of simultaneous but distinct emotions occur regularly in French grand opera. A particularly good example is provided by the triple chorus (Catholic women, Protestant soldiers, and Catholic men) in Act III of Meyerbeer's *Les huguenots*.

17. Markus Engelhardt, "'Something's Been Done to Make Room for Choruses': Choral Conception and Choral Construction in *Luisa Miller*," in Chusid (ed.), *Verdi's Middle Period*, p. 199.

18. For a useful description of this finale, see Markus Engelhardt, *Die Chöre in den frühen Opern Giuseppe Verdis* (Ph.D. dissertation, University of Würzburg, 1986; Tutzing: Schneider, 1988), pp. 215–17; and Budden, *The Operas of Verdi*, vol. I, pp. 412–14. In the prologue of *Giovanna d'Arco* (1845), Verdi juxtaposed a chorus of demons and a chorus of angels. The two choruses are combined for only a few measures, however, and lack the aspects of both continuity and grandeur.

19. "Nel principio, avanti il tempio di S. Ambrogio, vorrei unire insieme due o tre cantilene differenti: vorrei per esempio che i *preti* all'interno, il popolo al difuori, avessero un metro a parte e Lida un cantabile con un metro differente: lasciate poi a me la cura di unirli. Si potrebbe anche (se credete) coi preti mettere dei versetti latini ... fate come credete meglio, ma badate che quel punto deve essere d'effetto." Undated letter, in Cesari and Luzio (eds.), *I copialettere*, p. 56.

20. For an explanation of Italian syllable count and poetic accentuation, see chapter 5 above, pp. 70–72; see also Andreas Giger, "The Role of Giuseppe Verdi's French Operas in the Transformation of His Melodic Style" (Ph.D. dissertation, Indiana University, 1999), pp. 18–36 (French) and 52–58 (Italian).

21. "Le morceau qui a fait littéralement *furore* (jamais le mot n'a mieux été appliqué) est un double choeur chanté par des conjurés sur la scène, et par des dames et des seigneurs qui passent dans une barque. Ce beau chant s'élevant d'abord dans le lointain, se rapprochant, peu à peu, et s'éteignant *pianissimo*, produit un effet magique." *Le constitutionnel*, June 15, 1855; quoted in Hervé Gartioux (ed.), *Giuseppe Verdi, "Les vêpres siciliennes": Dossier de presse parisienne (1855)* (n.p.: Lucie Galland, 1995), p. 42.

22. Knud Arne Jürgensen, *The Verdi Ballets* (Parma: Istituto Nazionale di Studi Verdiani, 1995), p. 7.

23. *Ibid.*, pp. 83 and 87.

24. *Ibid.*, pp. 78–79.

25. "Nel terzo atto v'ha di nuovo il ballo che ha tutto il sapore della musica moderna: sono tre pezzi che corrispondono a tre capolavori di musica sinfonica." Quoted in Jürgensen, *The Verdi Ballets*, p. 88.

26. See William Edward Runyan, "Orchestration in Five French Grand Operas" (Ph.D. dissertation, University of Rochester, 1983), p. 4; and Teresa Klier, *Der Verdi-Klang: Die Orchesterkonzeption in den Opern von Giuseppe Verdi* (Ph.D. dissertation, University of Würzburg, 1995; Tutzing: Schneider, 1998), p. 205.

27. For Meyerbeer, see Runyan, "Orchestration in Five French Grand Operas," pp. 220 and 223.

28. The autograph shows rests for the ophicleide and crossed-out chords for the trombones. According to Ursula Günther ("La genèse de *Don Carlos*, opéra en cinq actes de Giuseppe Verdi, représenté pour la

première fois à Paris le 11 mars 1867," *Revue de musicologie* 60 (1974), 141), *pianissimo* chords for the ophicleide and the trombones were part of the original conception. They were removed in the course of the rehearsals and finally reinstated (with different spacing) for the 1884 version. My excerpt shows the version of the 1867 premiere.

29. See Alberto Mazzucato, "*Il profeta,*" *Gazzetta musicale di Milano* 13 (1855), 187.

30. See Scott L. Balthazar, "The Rhythm of Text and Music in 'Ottocento' Melody: An Empirical Reassessment in Light of Contemporary Treatises," *Current Musicology* 49 (1992), 6–9; see also Giger, "The Role of Giuseppe Verdi's French Operas," pp. 75–79.

31. Typical examples include "Merci, jeunes amies" and "La brise souffle au loin" (both from *Les vêpres siciliennes*, V, 2). Louis Benloew, *Précis d'une théorie des rythmes*, vol. I: *Rhythmes français et rhythmes latins* (Paris: Franck, 1862), pp. 20–24, encourages scanning when a composer wants to flatter the ear.

32. "[Le compositeur] fasse un chant *vague, sans caractère déterminé*, qui ne fasse pas trop sentir le rythme, et qui ne choque pas trop la prosodie." Quoted in A. Fleury, "Du rythme dans la poésie chantée," *Études religieuses, philosophiques* 60 (November 1893), 345. Castil-Blaze preferred French lines with regular accentual structures based on the most regular Italian models. Creating a "vague melody" thus presents only the least bad solution to a problem that could be avoided altogether by the choice of regularly accented verse.

33. A majority of the theorists argued for stress accent. In the eighteenth century, however, and again in the twentieth century, they predominantly argued for an accent of duration. See Giger, "The Role of Giuseppe Verdi's French Operas," pp. 21–23.

34. The French count up to the last accented syllable of their lines, the Italians up to the subsequent unaccented syllable, whether it is actually present or not. An Italian line of a specific length thus corresponds to the French type of one fewer syllable (e.g. a *settenario* is equivalent to a *vers de six syllabes*).

35. Another line type without a commonly used equivalent in Italian opera is the *décasyllabe* (the line of ten syllables according to the French system) with its customary caesura on the fourth syllable. The popular "Et toi, Palerme" (*Les vêpres siciliennes*, II, 1) belongs to this category, and the accentual structure indeed led to an unusual melodic rhythm in Verdi's setting. See Giger, "The

Role of Giuseppe Verdi's French Operas," pp. 227–30.

36. For the Italian concept, see, for example, Geremia Vitali, *La musica ne' suoi principj nuovamente spiegata* (Milan: Ricordi, 1847), pp. 11–12; for the French concept, see Aldino Aldini, "Premières représentations. Théâtre impérial italien: *Un ballo in maschera*, opéra en quatre actes, par. G. Verdi," *La France musicale* 25 (1861), 18, and the reviews of Meyerbeer's operas collected and annotated by Marie-Hélène Coudroy, *La critique parisienne des "grands opéras" de Meyerbeer: "Robert le diable" – "Les huguenots" – "Le prophète" – "L'africaine"* (Saarbrücken: Galland, 1988), *passim.*

37. "Che se non si frange si tramuta in diverso disegno, s'avvia per sentiero nuovo ed inatteso, a tale che la seconda parte di essa non sembra più avere regolare relazione colla prima." Mazzucato, "*Il profeta,*" 187.

38. Some critics saw in *Les vêpres siciliennes* a purely Italian work, Mazzucato positively, Basevi negatively.

39. "Fra i difetti notati in questo spartito è capitale quello che si riferisce alla mancanza di nesso e di relazione fra i pensieri melodici; di guisa che più presto che fusi appariscono cuciti fra loro, con danno del linguaggio musicale il quale, comunque composto di frazioni regolarissime in sè, sembra così procedere senza intendimento alcuno." Pietro Torrigianti, "*I vespri siciliani* a Parma," *L'armonia* 1/2 (1856), 6. The first typical examples of this procedure, which Budden (*The Operas of Verdi*, vol. III, p. 107) has called the *Aida* manner, occur in *Les vêpres siciliennes* (for example, in the Act II duet between Henri and Hélène, the beginning of which appears in example). For an analysis, see Giger, "The Role of Giuseppe Verdi's French Operas," pp. 224–25 and 253–60.

40. Translation by Andrew Porter.

8 Structural coherence

1. See Christensen's essay "Music Theory and Its Histories," in Christopher Hatch and David W. Bernstein (eds.), *Music Theory and the Exploration of the Past* (University of Chicago Press, 1993), pp. 9–39.

2. From an essay first published in 1972 and reprinted as "Toward an Explanation of the Dramatic Structure of *Il trovatore*," in Pierluigi Petrobelli, *Music in the Theater*, pp. 100–101.

3. Roger Parker, "Motives and Recurring Themes in *Aida*," in Carolyn Abbate and Roger Parker (eds.), *Analyzing Opera*, p. 228.

To be fair to Parker, it should be noted that this statement comes in the context of a discussion about the difficulty of attaching semantic labels to motivic transformations.

4. For the first issue see the warnings of Gary Tomlinson in "Musical Pasts and Postmodern Musicologies: A Response to Lawrence Kramer," *Current Musicology* 53 (1993), 23. For the second see Carolyn Abbate and Roger Parker, "Introduction: On Analyzing Opera," in Abbate and Parker (eds.), *Analyzing Opera*, p. 3.

5. James Webster, "To Understand Verdi and Wagner We Must Understand Mozart," *19th-Century Music* 11 (1987–88), 175–93. Webster prefers to separate "unity" from "coherence," whereas I see the former as one way of understanding the latter and both as subject to the interpretive agenda of the critic.

6. *Ibid.*, 191.

7. I borrow this use of the term "natural selection" from Leonard B. Meyer, "A Universe of Universals," *Journal of Musicology* 16 (1998), 4.

8. For a brief description of a semiological method that employs the neutral level, see Jean-Jacques Nattiez, *Music and Discourse: Toward a Semiology of Music*, trans. Carolyn Abbate (Princeton University Press, 1990), pp. 3–37.

9. The expression "authentic analysis" was coined by Peter Schubert in "Authentic Analysis," *Journal of Musicology* 12 (1994), 3–18.

10. Budden, *The Operas of Verdi*, rev. ed. (Oxford, 1992), vol. I, p. 15. Some today would argue that the case for tonal planning in Mozart is not as clear cut as Budden implies. See John Platoff, "Myths and Realities about Tonal Planning in Mozart's Operas," *Cambridge Opera Journal* 8 (1996), 3–15; Carolyn Abbate and Roger Parker, "Dismembering Mozart," *Cambridge Opera Journal* 2 (1990), 187–95; and James Webster, "Mozart's Operas and the Myth of Musical Unity," *Cambridge Opera Journal* 2 (1990), 197–218. It will become evident from my discussion in this chapter that I would question the use of the word "myth" – broadly speaking, something fictitious as opposed to something real – in this context.

11. Stanley Fish, *Professional Correctness: Literary Studies and Political Change* (Cambridge, Mass.: Harvard University Press, 1995), p. 29.

12. *Ibid.*, p. 128.

13. See his important article "Some Difficulties in the Historiography of Italian Opera," *Cambridge Opera Journal* 10 (1998), 3–13.

14. Inevitably there has been an immense amount of filling in, not always in the same way and with the same purpose.

15. Letter dated April 4, 1851, cited by Budden, *The Operas of Verdi*, vol. II, p. 61.

16. *Ibid.*, p. 62. It may be that Verdi presented extreme requirements to Cammarano not as a way to break down set pieces but to shake him out of conservative complacence. The score of *Il trovatore* ended up having relatively traditional numbering.

17. Cited by Marcello Conati, *Encounters with Verdi*, trans. Richard Stokes (Ithaca: Cornell University Press, 1984), p. 109. In my view such a remark should not be taken to mean that Verdi embraced Wagnerism, but rather as a signal that the Italian tradition could reform itself.

18. See Julian Budden, "Verdi and Meyerbeer in Relation to *Les vêpres siciliennes*," *Studi verdiani* 1 (1982), 14–15.

19. Scott Balthazar traces developments in "Aspects of Form in the *Ottocento* Libretto," *Cambridge Opera Journal* 7 (1995), 23–35.

20. "È probabilissimo che abbassi d'un mezzo tono il quartetto. Così strilla troppo, et tutti quei *si* di soprano et tenore sono troppo arditi." Letter to Giulio Ricordi postmarked October 21, 1886, cited in *Fine Printed and Manuscript Music: Friday 4 December 1998* (London: Sothebys, 1998), pp. 133–34. I am grateful to Emanuele Senici for this reference. The degree of emphasis to give to either "event" or "fixed work" in evaluating Verdi's remark is unclear: perhaps other singers might have performed the quartet without leaving an impression of "shrieking." Or perhaps Verdi felt this flaw was inherent in the way he had scored the piece (in B major) and would be irredeemable regardless of the cast.

21. See James Hepokoski, "Verdi's Composition of *Otello*: The Act II Quartet," in Abbate and Parker, eds., *Analyzing Opera*, pp. 143–49.

22. Powers's analysis of the components of "la solita forma" here has a good deal to recommend it, but for a warning about rigid applications of the Rossinian prototype after mid-century see Scott L. Balthazar, "Analytic Contexts and Mediated Influences: The Rossinian *Convenienze* and Verdi's Middle and Late Duets," *Journal of Musicological Research* 10 (1990), 19–45.

23. Harold S. Powers, "One Halfstep at a Time: Tonal Transposition and 'Split Association' in Italian Opera," *Cambridge Opera Journal* 7 (1995), 157. Powers is vague about the chronology of composition, however. In the initial continuity draft of *Rigoletto* the four statements of "Quel vecchio maledivami!" received three melodies in three different keys (F, D flat, and E flat). According to evidence presented by Martin Chusid, around the same time that Verdi composed the continuity draft for Act II he entered Act I into the autograph full score, a process during which he introduced the emphasis on pitch class C in the curse music. See "Introduction," *Rigoletto*, ed. Martin Chusid, *The Works of Giuseppe Verdi*, vol. XVII (University of Chicago Press; Milan: Ricordi, 1983), p. xix. Baritone c^1 might therefore already have been given a great deal of importance when Verdi came up with his *first* key scheme for the Act II Gilda-Rigoletto duet. This does not invalidate Powers's observation but does cause one to wonder why "resonances" with baritone c^1 "forced themselves irresistibly on Verdi's attention" at one time and not another.

24. Powers, "One Halfstep at a Time," 136.

25. Cited in "Introduction," *Il trovatore*, ed. David Lawton, *The Works of Giuseppe Verdi*, vol. XVIIIa (University of Chicago Press; Milan: Ricordi, 1992), p. xiii.

26. David Lawton, "Tonal Structure and Dramatic Action in *Rigoletto*," *Verdi: Bollettino dell'Istituto di studi verdiani* 3/9 (1982), 1559–81, which amplifies Lawton's doctoral dissertation, "Tonality and Drama in Verdi's Early Operas," 2 vols. (Ph.D. dissertation, University of California, Berkeley, 1973).

27. *Ibid.*, 1561. For further studies of double cycles, see David Lawton and David Rosen, "Verdi's Non-Definitive Revisions: The Early Operas," in Mario Medici and Marcello Pavarani (eds.), *Atti del III Congresso internazionale di studi verdiani*, pp. 216–19; Roger Parker and Matthew Brown, "Motivic and Tonal Interaction in Verdi's *Un ballo in maschera*," *Journal of the American Musicological Society* 36 (1983), 243–65; and David Lawton, "Tonal Systems in *Aida*, Act III," in Abbate and Parker (eds.), *Analyzing Opera*, pp. 262–75.

28. Lawton, "Tonal Structure and Dramatic Action in *Rigoletto*," 1565.

29. *Ibid.*, 1560. The piece that Lawton cites to substantiate his point is the opening duet in *Le nozze di Figaro*, in which "Every turn in the action is carefully reflected in the tonal structure." Though Lawton offers the point as self-evident fact, disagreements about this little piece in recent literature indicate that parallels (and tensions) between drama and music are mainly a matter of interpretation. For Abbate and Parker, "the point of *tonal* resolution [i.e. the recapitulation of this miniature sonata form] is temporally displaced from the moment of rapprochement implicit in the text and the action (Figaro at last takes notice of Susanna's hat)" ("Dismembering Mozart," 190). For James Webster, the dominant cadence (instead of recapitulation) when Figaro takes up Susanna's theme means that both are still speaking "past each other" ("To understand Verdi and Wagner," 183–84). Webster suggests a *process* of rapprochement that has several stages – an example of musico-dramatic coherence – whereas Abbate and Parker imply that the libretto calls for a normative musical response – a single point of rapprochement that would coincide with the recapitulation in a totally coherent musical setting – from which Mozart's music deviates.

30. For development of this aspect of the relationship between Gilda and her father, see Elizabeth Hudson, "Gilda Seduced: A Tale Untold," *Cambridge Opera Journal* 4 (1992–93), 229–51.

31. Martin Chusid has connected the transposition of "Caro nome" to the musical relationships between this piece and the E major Act III quartet ("Un dì, se ben rammentomi") in "The Tonality of *Rigoletto*," Abbate and Parker (eds.), *Analyzing Opera*, pp. 259–60.

32. Although listener perception is frequently invoked in analysis, it is important to distinguish between the "ideal" listener as the consumer of the analyst's vicarious recomposition, and real listeners. For consideration of what most listeners *really* hear when it comes to something even as basic as tonal closure in instrumental music, see Nicholas Cook, *Music, Imagination, and Culture* (Oxford University Press, 1990), pp. 43–70.

33. Chusid, "The Tonality of *Rigoletto*," p. 261. On this question see Edward T. Cone, "On the Road to *Otello*: Tonality and Structure in *Simon Boccanegra*," *Studi verdiani* 1 (1982), 72–98.

34. Siegmund Levarie, "Key Relations in Verdi's *Un ballo in maschera*," *19th-Century Music* 2 (1978–79), 143–47.

35. *Ibid.*, 144.

36. Joseph Kerman, "Viewpoint," *19th-Century Music* 2 (1978–79), 190. See also the response by Guy Marco, "On Key Relations in Opera," in *19th-Century Music* 3 (1979–80), 83–88, as well as Levarie's response to Kerman (same issue, 88–89).

37. Kerman, "Viewpoint," 190.

38. Levarie, "Key Relations in Verdi's *Un ballo in maschera*," 143.

39. In addition to the Petrobelli article already cited, William Drabkin elaborates this point in "Characters, Key Relations, and Tonal Structure in *Il trovatore*," *Music Analysis* 1 (1982), 143–53.

40. Scott L. Balthazar, "Plot and Tonal Design as Compositional Constraints in *Il trovatore*," *Current Musicology* 60–61 (1996), 51–77. Balthazar includes a critique of Petrobelli's influential analysis, but does not engage Levarie's observation about a "Neapolitan cadence." His methodology is premised on his own study of the evolution of the nineteenth-century Italian opera libretto in "Aspects of Form in the *Ottocento* Libretto."

41. Martin Chusid, "A New Source for *El trovador* and Its Implications for the Tonal Organization of *Il trovatore*," in Chusid (ed.), *Verdi's Middle Period*, pp. 207–25. See also "The Tonality of *Rigoletto*," "Drama and the Key of F Major in *La traviata*," in Medici and Pavarani (eds.), *Atti del III Congresso internazionale di studi verdiani*, pp. 89–121, and "Evil, Guilt and the Supernatural in Verdi's *Macbeth*: Toward an Understanding of the Tonal Structure and Key Symbolism," in David Rosen and Andrew Porter (eds.), *Verdi's "Macbeth": A Sourcebook* (New York: Norton, 1984), pp. 249–60.

42. Chusid, "A New Source for *El trovador*," p. 217.

43. Parker and Brown, "Motivic and Tonal Interaction in Verdi's *Un ballo in maschera*," 256–62.

44. Ibid., 262–63, 264.

45. See Harold S. Powers, "The 'Laughing Chorus' in Contexts," in *Giuseppe Verdi: "A Masked Ball"/ "Un ballo in maschera"*, English National Opera Guide 40 (London: Calder; New York: Riverrun, 1989), pp. 23–38.

46. See Cone, "On the Road to *Otello*," 95–98.

47. To contextualize fully the shift from E flat harmony to the key of E major at this point in *Macbeth* it should be noted that the former emerges from a strong articulation of D flat major. The play between D flat and E major (or F flat) is an important recurring tonal element in this opera.

9 Instrumental music in Verdi's operas

1. *Sinfonie* (the Italian term for full-length overtures) were composed for the following operas: *Oberto* (Milan, 1839); *Un giorno di regno* (Milan, 1840); *Nabucco* (Milan, 1842); *Giovanna d'Arco* (Milan, 1845); *Alzira* (Naples, 1845); *La battaglia di Legnano* (Rome, 1849); *Luisa Miller* (Naples, 1849); *Stiffelio* (Trieste, 1850); *Les vêpres siciliennes* (Paris, 1855); *Aroldo* (Rimini, 1857); *La forza del destino* II (Milan, 1869); *Aida* (Milan, 1871, discarded).

In the broadest terms Verdi gradually turned away from the full-scale overture in favor of the relatively brief *preludio*: of the first nine operas (those composed before the breakdown of his health following the premiere of *Attila* in 1846), five, including all of the first three, have *sinfonie*; of the last nine operas (those composed after 1858, the end of the *anni di galera*) only *Forza* II has such a *sinfonia*. Within this overall pattern there was an exceptional burst of new interest in the overture in 1849–50.

2. The Rossini overture is commonly designed as a sonata-form movement without development, preceded by a slow and in part *cantabile* introduction. Recurring standardized features within this overall pattern are described in Philip Gossett's essay "The Overtures of Rossini," *19th-Century Music* 3 (1979–80), 3–31.

3. The former, at rehearsal letter C, is taken from the priests' acclamation of Abigaille in Part 2 of the opera; the latter from the Hebrews' denunciation of Ismaelle in Part 1. The theme that might be taken for a "second subject" is from the Nabucco-Abigaille duet in Part 3.

References to printed editions of the music are to the following: *Nabucco*, vocal score (Milan: Ricordi, 1963, pl. no. 42312); *Un ballo in maschera*, vocal score (Ricordi, 1968, pl. no. 48180); *Les vêpres siciliennes*, vocal score (Ricordi, 1944, pl. no. 50278); *Macbeth*, vocal score (Ricordi, 1948, pl. no. 42311); *Attila*, vocal score (Ricordi, 1950, pl. no. 53700); *Simon Boccanegra*, vocal score (Ricordi, 1963, pl. no. 47372); *Falstaff*, vocal score (Ricordi, 1964, pl. no. 96000).

4. Budden, *The Operas of Verdi* (London, 1973–81), vol. II, pp. 188–91, supplies concordances.

5. In a letter to Antonio Somma, June 29, 1853, Verdi remarks that he would have composed more Shakespeare operas were it not for the frequency with which the scene changes. Otto Werner (ed.), *Giuseppe Verdi: Briefe*, trans. Egon Wiszniewsky (Berlin:

Henschelverlag 1983), p. 101; originally published in Pascolato (ed.), *"Re Lear" e "Ballo in maschera"*.

6. Letter from Verdi to Léon Escudier, March 11, 1865, in David Rosen and Andrew Porter (eds.), *Verdi's "Macbeth"*, p. 111.

7. See Luca Zoppelli, "'Stage Music' in Early Nineteenth-Century Italian Opera," *Cambridge Opera Journal 2* (1990), 29–39, for a discussion of this question.

8. The topics touched on in this section were first fully expounded in Fabrizio Della Seta, "Il tempo della festa. Su due scene della *Traviata* e su altri luoghi verdiani," *Studi verdiani 2* (1983), 108–46.

9. The quotations are from the Verdi–De Sanctis correspondence, April 10, 1855, and April 29 (?), 1855, quoted in Marcello Conati, "Ballabili nei *Vespri*. Con alcune osservazioni su Verdi e la musica popolare," *Studi verdiani 1* (1982), 39, 41.

10. June 24, 1855, quoted in Knud Arne Jürgensen, *The Verdi Ballets* (Parma: Istituto Nazionale di Studi Verdiani, 1995), p. 40.

11. Conati, "Ballabili nei *Vespri*," 32–33.

12. "The orchestra shivers, the flute blows on its fingers, the bows skate over the strings, the notes snow down." *La France musicale*, June 24, 1855, quoted in Jürgensen, *The Verdi Ballets*, p. 37.

13. Letter from Verdi to Tito Ricordi, September 23, 1865, in Rosen and Porter (eds.), *Verdi's "Macbeth"*, p. 123.

14. Letter from Verdi to Léon Escudier, January 23, 1865, in *ibid.*, p. 90.

15. Full details of plot and spectacle are given in Jürgensen, *The Verdi Ballets*, pp. 89–92.

16. Budden, *The Operas of Verdi*, vol. I, p. 301.

17. All quotations from the *disposizione scenica* are from Hans Busch (ed. and trans.), *Verdi's "Otello" and "Simon Boccanegra"*, pp. 430–31.

18. There are in fact three *parlante* episodes in this finale, the first depicting the guests at Flora's party chatting against a garishly colored *allegro brillante* in much the same style as the party music in Act I; a second, *allegro agitato*, accompanying the gambling scene; a third, *allegro agitato assai vivo*, the argument between Violetta and Alfredo. The instrumental material around which the second of these is fashioned is heard in the first eight measures, and is laid out in the characteristically symmetrical form *a a b b′ a*. The second phase commences as a major-key variant, more brightly scored; but after the *b b′* passage an extended transition brings the music back to the minor key (*a′ a′ b b′ c*). A third phase assumes the shape *a a″ c*, and the fourth and final phase *a b b′ a*, where *a* is a

fading coda. The whole *parlante* is notable for its breadth and regularity; it is the musical embodiment of the outwardly calm, inwardly fraught mood of the dramatic setting.

10 Verdi's non-operatic works

1. This statement is taken from a paragraph Verdi appended to a *prospetto* of his works compiled by Isidoro Cambiasi (1811–53, co-founder of Ricordi's *Gazzetta musicale di Milano*). It was reprinted in facsimile and in transcription in *Nel I centenario di Verdi 1813–1913: Numero unico illustrato* (Milan: Pirola, 1913), pp. 4–5.

While a few of Verdi's earliest compositions have been known for some time, most of them are believed to be lost; in recent years a few have been recovered (discussed below).

2. The autograph is in the Mary Flagler Cary Collection at the Pierpont Morgan Library in New York; I am grateful to J. Rigbie Turner for allowing me to study the manuscript. Aldo Oberdorfer, "Elenco delle opere di G. Verdi," in his *Giuseppe Verdi: Autobiografia dalle lettere*, 2nd ed., ed. Marcello Conati (Milan: Rizzoli, 1981), p. 484, placed the work in 1833; Pietro Spada, *Giuseppe Verdi: Inediti per tenore* (Milan: Suvini Zerboni, 1977), p. 4, dated it 1835; more recent publications date it ca.1836.

3. Julian Budden, *Verdi* (London: J. M. Dent, 1985), pp. 303–5.

4. "L'esule" and "La seduzione" were initially issued together. The latter song was also published separately, but Cecil Hopkinson, *A Bibliography of the Works of Giuseppe Verdi, 1813–1901*, 2 vols. (New York: Broude Brothers, 1973–78), vol. I, pp. 41 and 46, found no evidence that the former piece had been issued independently.

5. In addition to the flute part published in the piano score, the autograph has an additional page apparently inserted by the publisher with an alternative, much extended, and even more virtuosic variant of Verdi's flute obbligato part written, in all likelihood, by the famous flutist Giuseppe Rabboni. For information about the added flute part and Rabboni, see the introduction to Marco Marica (ed.), *Giuseppe Verdi, "Notturno"* (Milan: Museo Teatrale alla Scala; Parma: Istituto Nazionale di Studi Verdiani, 2000), especially pp. 28–29 and 34–35. If Verdi originally composed this piece for the Società Filarmonica di Busseto, he may have intended the flute part for his father-in-law Antonio Barezzi, who played in the ensemble.

6. See Frank Walker, "Goethe's 'Erste Verlust' Set to Music by Verdi: An Unknown

Composition," *Music Review* 9 (1948), 13–17, the first publication of the song; the piece is also discussed by Franco Schlitzer in *Mondo teatrale dell'Ottocento* (Naples: Fausto Fiorentino, 1954), pp. 125–27. Walker believed that one lengthy phrase in this song prefigures the "Di quell'amor" passage from *La traviata* ("Goethe's 'Erste Verlust'," 15).

7. The title of the song was printed incorrectly in Hopkinson, *Bibliography*, vol. I, p. 85, as "Cupa e il sepolcre mutolo," as was the date of its composition, as July 7, 1873. The worklist compiled by Andrew Porter for Stanley Sadie (ed.), *The New Grove Dictionary of Music and Musicians*, 20 vols. (London: Macmillan, 1980), lists it as "Cupo è il sepolcro mutolo," with the incorrect year. For additional information, see the introduction to Antonio Rostagno (ed.), *Giuseppe Verdi, "Cupo è il sepolcro e mutolo" per canto e pianoforte* (Milan: Museo Teatrale alla Scala; Parma: Istituto Nazionale di Studi Verdiani, 2000).

8. Rostagno convincingly argues for Maffei's authorship in the introduction to his edition of the song, *ibid*.

9. Since Piave was in Rome with Verdi and had attended Ferretti's *accademie* for several years, it is altogether possible that he was the author of the poetry. Of course, since Ferretti was also a librettist, it could be his.

10. Ferretti apparently had three daughters – Cristina, Chiara, and Barbara – and the literature on this piece contains conflicting attributions for the dedicatee of the album. See Pietro Spada, "Verdi in un salotto romano," in Adrian Belli and Ceccarius (eds.), *Verdi e Roma: Celebrazione verdiana 27 gennaio 1951* (Rome: Teatro dell'Opera di Roma, 1951), pp. 41–48.

11. According to Hopkinson, *Bibliography*, vol. I, p. 33, the first Italian edition of the songs bore a dedication to "Don Giuseppe de Salamanca, Gentiluomo di S. M. G. Donna Isabella IIa."

12. In the autograph Verdi originally titled the song "La sera." There is also an autograph copy of a slightly different setting of the first two stanzas of Maffei's poem, dated June 1, 1845, at the Pierpont Morgan Library in New York. Verdi and Maffei enjoyed a fairly close personal and professional relationship during this time, collaborating on a number of projects including, above all, *Macbeth* and *I masnadieri*.

13. Two versions of this song exist. Both are in F major and are 118 measures long. Variants occur primarily in the opening strophe, which recurs at the close of the song.

14. It is possible that Verdi composed this song while he was in London in spring and summer 1847 preparing for the premiere of *I masnadieri*, the opera he had created expressly for Her Majesty's Theatre and the publisher Lucca.

15. Hopkinson, *Bibliography*, vol. I, p. 62. He also noted that "Il poveretto" was used as an aria ("Prends pitié de sa jeunesse") for Maddalena in *Rigoletto* for a French performance. See also Patrick Schmid, "Maddalena's Aria," *AIVS Newsletter* 5 (June 1978), 4–7, and Budden, *Verdi*, pp. 306–7, who also reported that the performance took place at the Théâtre de la Monnaie in Brussels where the singer who portrayed Maddalena insisted on an aria.

16. Frank Walker referred to "Il poveretto" in "'L'abandonnée': A Forgotten Song," *Verdi: Bollettino dell'Istituto di studi verdiani* 2 (1960), 787.

17. The identification and history of the publication of the work is discussed by Walker in *ibid*., 785–89.

18. Budden, *Verdi*, p. 307.

19. A facsimile of the autograph was published and the piece discussed in Nullo Musini, "Giuseppe Verdi a Trieste. Una 'berceuse' inedita del Maestro," *Aurea Parma: Rivista di lettere, arte, e storia* 35 (1951), 199–202, and in Giuseppe Stefani, *Verdi e Trieste* (Trieste: Editore il Comune, 1951), pp. 64–68.

20. The composition is discussed by Fortunato Ortombina in "'Sgombra, o gentil': un dono di Verdi all'amico Delfico," *Studi verdiani* 8 (1992), 104–17, including a facsimile of the autograph and a transcription.

21. Paolo De Grazia, "Una musica di Giuseppe Verdi," *Rivista musicale italiana* 45 (1941), 230–32, brought this song to light in 1941. De Grazia also noted that in 1858 Sole asked Verdi to set his recently published poem "Il viggianese"; he believes there may also have been a plan for Verdi to set a libretto by Sole, *Il mercato di Smirne*.

22. The text Verdi set was the first of Dall'Ongaro's *stornelli*, written on August 4, 1847, and published in his *Stornelli italiani* of 1848, reissued in the early 1860s. Although Mario Cantù reported in his "'Il brigidino': così Verdi musicò il Tricolore," in Giuseppe Dall'Ongaro, *I tordi e il professore* (Rome: Altana, 1997), p. 103, that the song was composed in March 1861, the autograph he reproduced, i.e. the one Verdi presented to Piroli, was written on the embossed stationery of "La Camera dei Deputati" with

hand-drawn staffs and signed "G Verdi Torino 24 maggio 1862." "Il brigidino" is also discussed in Cantù's introduction to the score issued in Milan by Sonzogno in 1948, and by Gustavo Marchesi in "Le liriche da camera di Giuseppe Verdi," *La civiltà musicale di Parma* (Parma: Fondazione Verdi, 1989), p. 185.

23. Budden, *Verdi*, p. 308, gave the singer's surname as "Galli."

24. The *Album per canto a beneficio del poeta F. M. Piave* (Milan: Ricordi, 1869) contains six songs in all. In addition to the *stornello* by Verdi there are works by Auber ("L'esultanza," a *melodia* with poetry by Achille de Lauzières), Antonio Cagnoni ("Pensiero d'amore," a *romanza* with poetry by Giuseppe Torre), Federico Ricci ("Lamento"), Ambroise Thomas ("Sola! Canzone danese" with poetry by de Lauzières), and Saverio Mercadante ("L'abbandonata," a *romanza* dedicated to Giuseppina Strepponi).

25. A set of sacred duets was discussed by Hans Redlich and Frank Walker, "'Gesù morì,' an Unknown Early Verdi Manuscript," *Music Review* 20 (1959), 232–43, who believed the music was by Verdi. This manuscript has, however, been shown to be a forgery; see David Stivender, "The Composer of *Gesù morì*," *AIVS Newsletter* 2 (December 1976), 6–7.

Another false attribution, though not of sacred music, should be noted here as well. A hymn titled "La madre e la patria" and a "Marcia funebre," reproduced in facsimile and discussed by George Martin, *Aspects of Verdi*, pp. 144–53, are not works by Verdi.

26. For further discussion of the song, see Pierluigi Petrobelli, "On Dante and Italian Music: Three Moments," *Cambridge Opera Journal* 2 (1989), 219–49, especially 237–38.

27. Walker, "Goethe's 'Erste Verlust'," 17. Correspondence between Verdi and Boito about this work can be found in Luzio (ed.), *Carteggi verdiani*, vol. II, pp. 185–87.

28. The Sinfonia in D Major is discussed in detail in Roberta Montemorra Marvin, "A Verdi Autograph and the Problem of Authenticity," *Studi verdiani* 9 (1993), 36–61. See also the facsimile of the autograph and published edition of the work, Roberta Montemorra Marvin (ed.), *Giuseppe Verdi: Sinfonia in re maggiore* (Milan: Museo Teatrale alla Scala; Parma: Istituto Nazionale di Studi Verdiani, 2000).

There is also some documentation of a youthful *sinfonia* titled "La capricciosa" which Verdi supposedly wrote when he was twelve years old. It was performed for the inauguration of the Teatro Verdi in Busseto on August 5, 1868. For more information on this piece, see Almerindo Napolitano, *Il teatro Verdi di Busseto* (Parma: La Nazionale, 1968).

29. Following the publication of the *Romanza*, Ricordi, in an unpublished letter dated December 16, 1865, responded to Verdi's inquiry concerning how the piece came to be published by reminding the composer that he had composed it while in Rome during the autumn of 1844 directing the rehearsals for *I due Foscari*.

30. A facsimile of the autograph was published and the waltz discussed in Gioacchino Lanza Tomasi, "Verdi al ballo del gattopardo," in *Discoteca*, March–April 1963, 18–19. The piece was brought to light by Luchino Visconti in his film *Il gattopardo* (*The Leopard*) of 1963; a performing edition was issued by Musica Obscura in 1986.

31. Biographers routinely discuss Verdi's early training in general, referring in particular to his autobiographical statement. A more detailed account of Verdi's musical education will be provided in my study titled *Verdi the Student – Verdi the Teacher* (Parma: Istituto Nazionale di Studi Verdiani, forthcoming).

32. This Mass is discussed by Dino Rizzo in "'Con eletta musica del Sig. Verdi da Busseto, fu celebrata la messa solenne'," *Studi verdiani* 9 (1993), 62–96.

33. Verdi's composition of this work is discussed by David Rosen in "La *Messa* a Rossini e il *Requiem* per Manzoni," in Michele Girardi and Pierluigi Petrobelli (eds.), *Messa per Rossini: La storia, il testo, la musica* (Parma: Istituto di Studi Verdiani; Milan: Ricordi, 1988), pp. 119–49. A facsimile of the autograph of the original "Libera me" was issued by the Istituto di Studi Verdiani in 1988.

34. The analytical details (and much of the present discussion) are adapted from David Rosen, *Verdi: Requiem* (Cambridge University Press, 1997).

35. The movement is discussed in detail in David Rosen, "The Operatic Origins of Verdi's 'Lacrymosa'," *Studi verdiani* 5 (1988–89), 65–84, and in Rosen, *Verdi: Requiem*, pp. 76–79.

36. All of these are discussed in Rosen, *Verdi: Requiem*, pp. 60–74.

37. Information concerning the genesis, performance, and reception of the *Messa da Requiem* can be found in *ibid.*, especially pp. 1–17.

38. *Ibid.*, p. 15.

39. Letter from Verdi to Giulio Ricordi, April 26, 1874, in Franco Abbiati, *Giuseppe Verdi*, vol. III, p. 688. Rosen discusses the controversy at length in *Verdi: Requiem*, chapter 12.

40. The coherence of the work, or its "unità musicale," is discussed by Rosen in *Verdi: Requiem*, chapter 11.

41. Letter to Ferdinand Hiller, January 7, 1880, in Luzio (ed.), *Carteggi verdiani*, vol. II, p. 333.

42. There is conflicting information concerning the dates of composition of these pieces.

43. This composition is discussed by Petrobelli in "On Dante and Italian Music," 238.

44. Little has been written about these pieces. The most extensive discussion can be found in Budden, *Verdi*, pp. 336–45.

45. The work is discussed in Roger Parker, "Verdi and the *Gazzetta privilegiata di Milano*: An 'Official' View Seen in Its Cultural Background," *RMA Research Chronicle* 18 (1982), 51–65.

46. A composition by Verdi known as *"La patria": Inno nazionale a Ferdinando II*, with poetry by Michele Cucciniello, published by Girard in Naples in 1847–48, is in reality the chorus "Si ridesti il Leon di Castiglia" from *Ernani* set to a different text. See also Gaetano Della Noce, "Un inno per Ferdinando II," *Musica* (Roma) 7/36 (November 13, 1913), 8.

47. Other works included in the program for the opening ceremonies were by Auber (France), Meyerbeer (Germany), and Sterndale Bennett (England).

48. Information on the *Inno delle nazioni* comes from George Martin, *Verdi: His Music, Life, and Times* (New York: Dodd Mead, 1968), pp. 394–95; Mary Jane Phillips-Matz, *Verdi*, pp. 446–49; and Abbiati, *Giuseppe Verdi*, vol. II, pp. 688–94.

11 Ernani: the tenor in crisis

1. The other Verdi operas composed specifically for La Fenice are *Attila* (1846), *Rigoletto* (1851), *La traviata* (1853), and *Simon Boccanegra* (1857).

2. See Verdi's letter to Giuseppina Appiani, Venice, March 10, 1844, in Gaetano Cesari and Alessandro Luzio (eds.), *I copialettere di Giuseppe Verdi*, p. 425. See also Giovanni Barezzi, letter from Venice dated March 10, 1844, in Luigi Agostino Garibaldi (ed.), *Giuseppe Verdi nelle lettere di Emanuele Muzio ad Antonio Barezzi* (Milan: Fratelli Treves, 1931), pp. 73–74.

3. For a list of theatres, in Italy and abroad, where *Ernani* was performed in its first three years, see Marcello Conati, "Appendix II: First Performances of *Ernani* 1844–1846," in Pierluigi Petrobelli (ed.), *"Ernani" Yesterday and Today*, 268–79.

4. Victor Hugo's *Hernani* was first performed at the Théâtre de la Comédie-Française in Paris on February 25, 1830. For a list of topics discarded by Verdi, see Conati, *La bottega della musica*, pp. 72–73.

5. The others are *I due Foscari* (1844), *Macbeth* (1847), *Il corsaro* (1848), *Stiffelio* (1850), *Rigoletto* (1851), *La traviata* (1853), *Simon Boccanegra* (1857), and *La forza del destino* (1862).

6. See in particular Gabriele Baldini, *The Story of Giuseppe Verdi: "Oberto" to "Un ballo in maschera"*, ed. and trans. Roger Parker (Cambridge University Press, 1980), p. 71.

7. Hugo's *Hernani* caused trouble in Paris, too: its premiere became known as the "bataille d'Hernani," recorded by Théophile Gautier in his *Histoire du romanticisme* (Paris: Éditions d'Aujourd'hui, 1978; originally published Paris, 1874) as the beginning of French Romanticism.

8. See a letter from the theatre secretary Guglielmo Brenna to Verdi of September 20, 1843, in Conati, *La bottega della musica*, pp. 79–80.

9. See Verdi's letter of September 22, 1843, in response to the letter from Brenna cited above, in Conati, *La bottega della musica*, pp. 84–85.

10. One change that Verdi seems to have counted on was the title: he referred to the opera as *Ernani* right from the beginning, despite having been urged to use something different in order to avoid problems with the censors. Piave and the theatre administration referred to it, at different stages, as *L'onore castigliano* and *Don Gomez de Silva*. See the letter of September 22, 1843, cited above.

11. See Verdi's letter of December 29, 1843, in Conati, *La bottega della musica*, pp. 109–10.

12. For an account of Verdi's casting attempts see Gustavo Marchesi, "The *Ernani* Years," in Petrobelli (ed.), *"Ernani" Yesterday and Today*, p. 42.

13. See Verdi's reference in his letter to Francesco Pasetti of January 12, 1844, in Conati, *La bottega della musica*, p. 117.

14. "Scrivo questo mio povero Ernani e non sono malcontento. Ad onta della mia apparente indifferenza, se facessi fiasco mi schiaccio le cervella: non potrei sopportare l'idea, tanto più che questi veneziani si aspettano non so che cosa." Letter to Luigi

Toccagni from Venice, undated but probably written between the end of January and the beginning of February 1844. See Franco Abbiati, *Giuseppe Verdi*, vol. I, pp. 481–82.

15. For the tenor's repertory and career history, see Giorgio Gualerzi, *Carlo Guasco: Tenore romantico fra mito e realtà* (Alessandria: Cassa di Risparmio di Alessandria, 1976).

16. Reference to the police order is in a letter written by Guasco's agent Vincenzo Giaccone, from Turin, February 14, 1844 (Conati, *La bottega della musica*, pp. 121–22). For an account of Guasco's behavior on the night of the premiere, see Giovanni Barezzi, letter dated March 10, 1844, from Venice, in Garibaldi (ed.), *Giuseppe Verdi nelle lettere di Emanuele Muzio ad Antonio Barezzi*, pp. 73–74.

17. Differently from Hugo's play, where all three die in the end (*Hernani*, V, vi).

18. Musical examples are adapted from *Ernani*, ed. Claudio Gallico, *The Works of Giuseppe Verdi*, series I, vol. V (University of Chicago Press; Milan: Ricordi, 1985).

19. "Per l'amor di Dio non finisca col Rondò ma faccia il terzetto: e questo terzetto anzi deve essere il miglior pezzo dell'opera." Letter of October 2, 1843, in Abbiati, *Giuseppe Verdi*, vol. I, pp. 474–75.

20. For an extensive critical list of works, see Paduano, *Noi facemmo ambedue un sogno strano*, pp. 22–23, n. 3.

21. See Roger Parker, "Levels of Motivic Definition in *Ernani*," *19th-Century Music* 6 (1982–83), 144–45.

22. See Budden, *The Operas of Verdi* (London, 1973), vol. I.

23. Verdi's objection to trouser roles was more or less consistent: the only one in his entire oeuvre is Oscar in *Un ballo in maschera* (1859).

24. "Le jeune amant sans barbe," as Don Carlos famously describes him in *Hernani*, I, i.

25. See the fifth chapter of my doctoral thesis, "Arrigo Boito: The Legacy of Scapigliatura" (University of Oxford, 1999).

12 "Ch'hai di nuovo, buffon?" or What's new with *Rigoletto*

1. Verdi wrote thirty-two operas (counting the major revisions), of which *Rigoletto* is the seventeenth. For more on *Nabucco*'s special status, see Roger Parker, *Leonora's Last Act*, chapter 2.

2. Ed. Martin Chusid, *The Works of Giuseppe Verdi*, series I, vol. 17 (University of Chicago Press; Milan: Ricordi, 1983); all references will be to this edition. The opera's first

performance in the new edition was marked by a conference; see Marisa Di Gregorio Casati and Marcello Pavarani (eds.), *Nuove prospettive nella ricerca verdiana: Atti del Convegno internazionale in occasione della prima del "Rigoletto" in edizione critica, Vienna, 12–13 marzo 1983* (Parma: Istituto di Studi Verdiani; Milan: Ricordi, 1987).

3. Wolfgang Osthoff, "The Musical Characterization of Gilda," *Verdi: Bollettino dell'Istituto di studi verdiani* 3/8 (1973), 1275–314.

4. See the beginning of the following *scena*, "Pari siamo," I, 4 (p. 77).

5. III, 13 (pp. 289–90); see Osthoff, "The Musical Characterization of Gilda," 1278–79. At one stage in the genesis, Sparafucile's name was Strangolabene – "strangle-well."

6. II, 10 (pp. 232–33). "Ch'ella potesse ascendere / Quanto caduto er'io . . . / Ah presso del patibolo / Bisogna ben l'altare!" All translations are my own.

7. For more along these lines, see Gilles de Van, *Verdi's Theater*, p. 342.

8. See Martin Chusid, "Rigoletto and Monterone: A Study in Musical Dramaturgy," *Verdi: Bollettino dell'Istituto di studi verdiani* 3/9 (1982), 1544–58, and Chusid, "The Tonality of *Rigoletto*," in Carolyn Abbate and Roger Parker (eds.), *Analyzing Opera*, pp. 241–61. The latter (pp. 242–46) gives a summary of the opera's tonal organization.

9. David Lawton, "Tonal Structure and Dramatic Action in *Rigoletto*," *Verdi: Bollettino dell' Istituto di studi verdiani* 3/9 (1982), 1559–81.

10. II, 8 (p. 165), and II, 9 (p. 216): tenuous, perhaps, but see Marcello Conati, *"Rigoletto": Un'analisi drammatico-musicale* (Venice: Marsilio, 1992), pp. 147–61, especially pp. 155–56.

11. I, 6 (p. 133); see Osthoff, "The Musical Characterization of Gilda," 1284 ff.; Lawton, too (in "Tonal Structure and Dramatic Action in *Rigoletto*," 1560), invokes Mozart. Not only the flutes accompanying this aria but also the walled garden in which Gilda sings it are familiar fixtures; see Parker, *Leonora's Last Act*, pp. 155–56.

12. Chusid, "The Tonality of *Rigoletto*," is an impressively detailed attempt to take account of Verdi's intentions at all stages of the composition process – but for a cautionary word, see Parker, *Leonora's Last Act*, p. 154.

13. Budden, *The Operas of Verdi* (Oxford, 1992), vol. I, p. 486; see also Harold S. Powers, "One Halfstep at a Time: Tonal Transposition and 'Split Association' in Italian Opera," *Cambridge Opera Journal* 7 (1995), 135–64,

especially 152–57. Although for Chusid,
Lawton, and Conati key area is by contrast
crucial, they sometimes make no distinction
between major and minor modes, or even
between pitch, pitch class, and key. See
Chusid, "Rigoletto and Monterone," 1552,
n. 10, and Chusid, "The Tonality of *Rigoletto*,"
p. 250, n. 5. See also Conati, "*Rigoletto*",
p. 156.
14. I, 2 (pp. 52–53): "A curse on you who
laugh at a father's pain!"
15. See Joseph Kerman, "Verdi's Use of
Recurring Themes," in Harold S. Powers
(ed.), *Studies in Music History: Essays for Oliver
Strunk* (Princeton University Press, 1968),
pp. 495–510; see also Alessandro
Roccatagliati, *Drammaturgia romantica
verdiana: "Luisa Miller" e "Rigoletto"* (Bari:
Associazione Musicale Il Coretto, 1989),
p. 57.
16. For some, it is the musical essence, too.
See Martin, *Aspects of Verdi*, and Conati,
"*Rigoletto*", p. 155 and n. 74, who points out
that the diminished chord of the curse
contains both C and G♭, in his interpretation
the cardinal pitches for the whole opera.
17. "Tutto il soggetto è in quella
maledizione." The letter in question is
reproduced in Franco Abbiati, *Giuseppe Verdi*,
vol. II, pp. 63–64.
18. For the details, see the introduction to
Rigoletto, ed. Chusid, p. xiii, and Conati,
"*Rigoletto*", pp. 20–21.
19. For other references to the curse, see pp.
44, 84, 273, 293.
20. There is a similar point in Roccatagliati,
Drammaturgia romantica verdiana, p. 56.
21. Rigoletto's obtuseness helps us
understand how Gilda's abduction succeeds
under his very nose, and how he needs a flash
of lightning to recognize her body at the end.
In Carmine Gallone's 1946 film of the opera, a
famous Rigoletto, Tito Gobbi, puts this across
effectively in "Pari siamo" by approaching the
camera and glaring myopically into it.
22. Victor Hugo, *Oeuvres complètes* (Paris:
Robert Laffont, 1985), vol. VIII (*Théâtre I*),
pp. 827–968. For a full account, see Anne
Ubersfeld, *Le roi et le bouffon: Étude sur le
théâtre de Hugo de 1830 à 1839* (Paris: Corti,
1974), especially pp. 139–56.
23. Hugo, *Le roi s'amuse*, pp. 829–36. Once he
had delivered his address to the Tribunal de
Commerce in December it also appeared with
the fifth and subsequent editions of the play
(*ibid.*, pp. 837–45).
24. Hugo, *Le roi s'amuse*, p. 830.
25. See Mario Lavagetto, *Un caso di censura:
"Rigoletto"* (Milan: Il Formichiere, 1979); see

also the introduction to *Rigoletto*, ed. Chusid,
pp. xi–xxii.
26. The letter is reproduced in Conati, *La
bottega della musica*, p. 209.
27. For a side-by-side comparison of play and
libretto, see Conati, "*Rigoletto*", pp. 102–19.
Among the first cuts was one to Act III,
scene ii, of the play, when the King produces,
with an indelicate flourish, the key to the
bedroom into which Blanche has just fled.
28. Chusid calls Verdi's rejection of Piave's
compromises "one of the most extraordinary
declarations of artistic integrity in the history
of music"; see *Rigoletto*, ed. Chusid, p. xvi.
29. Conati, "*Rigoletto*", especially pp. 75–91.
Verdi famously wrote to Piave that Triboulet
was "a creation worthy of Shakespeare!"; see
Abbiati, *Giuseppe Verdi*, vol. II, pp. 62–63.
Hugo shared Verdi's admiration for
Shakespeare; see Ubersfeld, *Le roi et le bouffon*,
especially pp. 79–85.
30. Elizabeth Hudson, "Gilda Seduced: A Tale
Untold," *Cambridge Opera Journal* 4
(1992–93), 229–51, glides provocatively
between what it is possible for
Hugo/Piave/Verdi to say on stage, what the
characters themselves choose, or allow each
other, to say, and how musical structure and
operatic convention reflect and nuance these
suppressions.
31. Hugo, *Le roi s'amuse*, p. 831. "De ceci
découle toute la pièce. Le sujet véritable du
drame, c'est la malédiction de Saint-Vallier."
32. See Martin, *Aspects of Verdi*, pp. 166–75.
33. I, 4 (pp. 77–81).
34. See the 1827 preface to *Cromwell* (which
became something of a Romantic manifesto)
in Hugo, *Oeuvres complètes*, vol. XII (*Critique*),
pp. 3–39.
35. Roccatagliati, *Drammaturgia romantica
verdiana*, p. 61. It is worth remembering that
Quasimodo, the hunchback of Notre-Dame,
is an exact contemporary of Triboulet; for a
physical description, see Victor Hugo,
Notre-Dame de Paris 1482 (Paris:
Garnier-Flammarion, 1967; first published
1831), pp. 75–78.
36. Some have seen in Rigoletto and
Monterone an even closer relationship; see
Martin, *Aspects of Verdi*, p. 164, and Chusid,
"Rigoletto and Monterone," 1552.
37. II, 8 (p. 165), when the Duke regrets the
disappearance of Gilda; see Budden, *The
Operas of Verdi*, vol. I, p. 499, and Hudson
(who cites the judgments of Joseph Kerman
and Gary Tomlinson), "Gilda Seduced," 251.
38. See Martin, *Aspects of Verdi*, p. 158.
39. See Pierluigi Petrobelli, "Verdi and *Don
Giovanni*: On the Opening Scene of *Rigoletto*,"

in Petrobelli, *Music in the Theater*, pp. 34–47;
Kimbell, *Verdi in the Age of Italian Romanticism*,
pp. 625–26; Budden, *The Operas of Verdi*,
vol. I, p. 489.

40. I, 2 (pp. 12–17): "Questa o quella."

41. In the opera (I, 4, pp. 101–2), the Duke
gains access to the garden simply by throwing
a purse to Giovanna, Gilda's governess; in the
play (II, iv) there is a lengthy comic scene as
the King has to keep offering the governess
money (and when that runs out jewelry) to
encourage Blanche.

42. For more, especially on the role of
operatic adaptations in importing European
literary fashions into Italy, see de Van, *Verdi's
Theater*, p. 73; on stylistic synthesis, not only
in *Rigoletto*, see Piero Weiss, "Verdi and the
Fusion of Genres," *Journal of the American
Musicological Society* 35 (1982), 138–56, and
Roccatagliati, *Drammaturgia romantica
verdiana*, p. 69.

43. As Roger Parker, discussing "Caro nome,"
puts it, "perhaps this heroine is so innocent of
life 'out there', has been protected from the
world so thoroughly by her walled garden,
that she doesn't know what a cabaletta is"
(*Leonora's Last Act*, p. 156).

44. This possibly apocryphal tale is recounted
by Arthur Pougin in *Giuseppe Verdi: Vita
aneddotica* (Florence: Passigli, 1989; first
published 1881), p. 70.

45. III, 13 (p. 293), and III, 14 (pp. 333–34).

46. Hugo, *Le roi s'amuse*, IV, ii.

47. See Léon Guichard, "Victor Hugo and *Le
roi s'amuse*," *Verdi: Bollettino dell'Istituto di
studi verdiani* 3/7 (1969), 433.

13   Verdi's *Don Carlos*: an overview of the operas

1. Budden, *The Operas of Verdi* (rev. ed.,
Oxford, 1992), vol. III, pp. 3–157.

2. Gregory Harwood, *Giuseppe Verdi: A Guide
to Research*, pp. 193–206. Many of the entries
in Harwood's *Guide* are to be found in his
item no. 225 (p. 75), the published report of
the *Atti del II Congresso internazionale de studi
verdiani . . . 1969* (Parma: Istituto di Studi
Verdiani, 1971). For the genesis and revisions
of the opera, see the essays by Ursula
Günther, Andrew Porter, and David Rosen.
Rosen on *Don Carlos* is represented in print by
just one brilliant essay on the Philip-Posa
duet in Act II, but it was his discoveries in
Paris, reported orally at the 1969 Verdi
conference, that launched the subsequent
reconstructive researches.

3. *Giuseppe Verdi, "Don Carlos": Edizione
integrale delle varie versioni*, ed. Luciano
Petazzoni and Ursula Günther, 2 vols. (Milan:

Ricordi, 1980), vol. I, pp. v–xliv, 1–294;
vol. II, pp. 295–669. At present the eagerly
awaited critical edition of the full score is still
in preparation.

The complete French libretto of the original
production (including portions deleted
before the premiere), with Italian translation
and an English version by Andrew Porter,
along with Italian text from the 1884 revision
in an Appendix, is available in *Giuseppe Verdi:
"Don Carlos"/"Don Carlo", English National
Opera Guide* 46 (London: Calder; New York:
Riverrun, 1992), pp. 29–156. "I libretti di *Don
Carlos*" (ed. Eduardo Rescigno), in the
programma di sala of a production of the opera
at La Fenice in Venice in December 1991
(pp. 17–125), is a composite libretto based on
the *Edizione integrale* with the various texts in
parallel columns. It can be extremely helpful
as a guide, but unfortunately, like so much
useful Italian work on individual operas, it
was published in an ephemeral program
book.

4. The scenario Méry and Du Locle sent to
Verdi was published by Ursula Günther in
L'avant-scène opéra 90–91(September–October
1986), 28–35.

5. An account of Verdi's comments on the
scenario, and a complete outline of the
subsequent wrestling over text and drama,
may be seen in Günther's prefatory essay in
the *Edizione integrale*, and in the *Don Carlos*
chapter of Budden's book. Günther's and
Budden's essays also cover the gradual
evolution of the libretto revisions by Du Locle
for the new version of the opera undertaken
by Verdi in 1882–83.

6. Friedrich Schiller, *Werke*, vol. I, ed. Herbert
Krafft (Frankfurt am Main: Insel Verlag,
1966); the English verse translation by
Charles E. Passage (New York: Ungar, 1959) is
used in Budden's account. Among currently
available English verse translations is one by
A. Leslie and Jeanne R. Wilson, in *Friedrich
Schiller: Plays*, vol. XV of *The German Library*
(New York: Continuum, 1983).

7. A good modern edition of the novel, with
French text and Italian translation on facing
pages, is *Saint-Réal: "Don Carlos," novella
storica*, ed. Luciano Carcereri (Venice:
Marsilio, 1997), with copious notes on the
text, an account of the historical sources for
the novel, and a very useful introduction by
Giorgio Giorgetti.

8. Eugène Cormon, *Philippe II / Roi d'Espagne /
drame en cinq actes / imité de Schiller et précédé
de / L'étudiant d'Alcala . . .* (Paris: Lange Lévy,
[1846]). This important source, also reflected
elsewhere in the finished libretto, was

discovered by Marc Clémeur; see his "Eine neu entdeckte Quelle für das Libretto von Verdis *Don Carlos*," *Melos/Neue Zeitschrift für Musik* 6 (1977), 496–99.

9. Verdi's letter to Émile Perrin, director of the Paris Opéra, was published by Ursula Günther, "La genèse de *Don Carlos*," *Revue de musicologie* 58 (1972), 30.

10. Letter from Léon Escudier to Perrin, *ibid.*, 24.

11. Meyerbeer's "Remarques générales" (1832) on a prose draft by Scribe for *Les huguenots*; see Steven Huebner, "Italianate Duets in Meyerbeer's Grand Operas," *Journal of Musicological Research* 8 (1989), 208–9; the French text of the letter is on p. 251, n. 20.

12. *Don Carlos / Grand Opéra en Cinq Actes / Représenté sur le Théâtre Impériale de l'Opéra / poème de / M. M. Méry & C. DuLocle / Musique de G. Verdi* (Paris: Léon Escudier, [1867]; pl. no. L.E.2165).

13. Another letter of Meyerbeer's unearthed by Steven Huebner neatly epitomizes this problem; see Huebner's "Italianate Duets," 204–5 (French text on pp. 249–50, n. 7).

14. Autograph headings are cited after Martin Chusid, *A Catalog of Verdi's Operas* (Hackensack, N.J.: Joseph Boonin, 1974), pp. 42–50; Chusid also includes a convenient conspectus of the materials eliminated in connection with the Paris 1867 production, with references to the original studies reporting their discovery.

15. For a close analysis of Verdi's "scene et duo," see pp. 41–44 of my essay "Cormon Revisited: Some Observations on the Original *Don Carlos*," *Verdi Forum* 26–27 (1999–2000), 39–52.

16. Volume I of the *Edizione integrale* concludes with four printings of the duet in full: (1) as Verdi originally composed it, before the cut made after the dress rehearsal of February 24, 1867 (pp. 206–31); (2) as it was at the first performance on March 11 (pp. 232–54); (3) the Naples version of 1872 (pp. 255–76); (4) the 1884 = 1886 Milan/Modena version (pp. 277–94). The summary below is modeled on David Rosen, "Le quattro stesure del duetto Filippo-Posa," in *Atti del II Congresso internazionale de studi verdiani*, pp. 368–88. Rosen's essay includes the first thorough account of the two Paris versions and the Naples version and an exemplary comparative analysis of the piece in all its versions, showing the gradual dissolution of the original formal structure. See also Budden, *The Operas of Verdi*, vol. III, pp. 80–98; both Rosen's and Budden's

discussions are copiously illustrated with musical examples.

17. For a close analysis of this finale, see Powers, "Cormon Revisited," 45–50.

18. For a perceptive postmodern portrayal of this aria, along with much of its music, and with comments on other aspects of the opera as well as on feminine roles and the female voice, see Roger Parker, "Elizabeth's Last Act," in Smart (ed.), *Siren Songs*, pp. 93–117.

19. For a full discussion of this kind of threefold rising sequence, its musico-dramatic uses, and its music-historical origins and development, see Frits Noske, *The Signifier and the Signified* (The Hague: Nijhoff, 1977), chapter 10.

20. For anyone attempting to follow from the *Edizione integrale*, the pages are 206–19 (1867); 267 bottom–268 top (1872); 221 (1867, with the first two systems transposed down a whole step); 290–94 (1884 = 1886).

21. For anyone attempting to follow from the *Edizione integrale*, the pages are 564 (two measures); 586–90; 571–75; 578–80; and finally 580–84 from the Grand Inquisitor's entrance to the end of the act, which was reinstated from 1867 for 1884 = 1886.

14 Desdemona's alienation and Otello's fall

1. Letter to Giulio Ricordi, April 22, 1887, trans. in Busch (ed. and trans.), *Verdi's "Otello" and "Simon Boccanegra"*, vol. I, p. 301; see also the characterization of Desdemona in the production book compiled by Ricordi, translated in the same publication, vol. II, p. 486.

2. Hepokoski has made this argument in *Giuseppe Verdi: "Otello"* (Cambridge University Press, 1987), pp. 178–79. Hepokoski's monograph is the most comprehensive study of *Otello* to date.

3. Kerman's chapter "*Otello*: Traditional Opera and the Image of Shakespeare," in *Opera as Drama* (New York: Random House, 1956; first published 1952), pp. 129–67, is a landmark essay in Verdi studies. Kerman discusses the expansion of Desdemona's role on pp. 160–62. See also pp. 9–12.

4. *Ibid.*, p. 160.

5. *Ibid.*, p. 152.

6. See Busch (ed. and trans.), *Verdi's "Otello" and "Simon Boccanegra"*, pp. 587–89.

7. Quotations from the play are from William Shakespeare, *The Tragedy of Othello, the Moor of Venice*, ed. Louis B. Wright and Virginia A. LaMar (New York: Simon and Schuster, 1957). Quotations from and translations of the libretto are adapted from William Weaver

(trans.), *Seven Verdi Librettos* (New York: Norton, 1975; first published 1963).

8. Hepokoski, *Giuseppe Verdi: "Otello"*, pp. 166–69.

9. *Ibid.*, p. 172.

10. *Ibid.*, p. 173.

11. *Ibid.*, p. 174.

12. Kerman, *Opera as Drama*, p. 161.

13. Kerman, *ibid.*, p. 152, has noted the "ironic" quality of the fanfares. Significantly, Verdi and Boito rejected the possibility of ending Act III with a Turkish invasion, to which Otello would have responded heroically. See Hepokoski, *Giuseppe Verdi: "Otello"*, p. 36.

14. Kerman, *Opera as Drama*, pp. 9–12. In my view this argument is not incompatible with Hepokoski's suggestion (*Giuseppe Verdi: "Otello"*, p. 173) that Verdi's music may have mimicked Salvini's stage movements.

15. Hepokoski, *Giuseppe Verdi: "Otello"*, p. 172.

16. *Ibid.*, p. 171; Kerman, *Opera as Drama*, p. 160.

17. Hepokoski, *Giuseppe Verdi: "Otello"*, p. 171.

18. Here Verdi may have been trying to head off the stereotyping evident in Schlegel's and Hugo's interpretations, which are discussed in Hepokoski, *Giuseppe Verdi: "Otello"*, pp. 165–66 and 169–70.

19. Compare the corresponding passage in Shakespeare (III, iii, 290–302).

20. My interpretation challenges Hepokoski's assertion that "the tone and feel of the relatively recent ironic and ruthlessly objective critique of Othello was quite unknown to Verdi and Boito" (*Giuseppe Verdi: "Otello"*, pp. 170–71), and at least raises the possibility that the opera may have played a role in the "modern attack on Othello-as-hero" led by T. S. Eliot and others.

21. Jane Adamson, *"Othello" as Tragedy: Some Problems of Judgment and Feeling* (Cambridge University Press, 1980), p. 220.

22. On this point, see also Hepokoski, *Giuseppe Verdi: "Otello"*, pp. 179–80.

23. Verdi's first Iago, Victor Maurel, in his *Dix ans de carrière*, noticed this aspect of their relationship in connection with her entrance following the Act I duel: "The appearance of this white and beautiful creature, whose love he feels, disarms the Moor; his anger melts like ice under the beneficent rays which the eyes of his sweet and consoling wife shed upon this scene of violence ... About to strike the man who has failed in his duty, he lowers his arm, his anger appeased as if by magic."

24. Busch (ed. and trans.), *Verdi's "Otello" and "Simon Boccanegra"*, p. 636.

24. Hepokoski, *Giuseppe Verdi: "Otello"*, p. 175; according to the production book, "at the peak of emotion Otello feels weak. Desdemona moves to the left, and while he steps backwards, she follows him, supporting him" (*ibid.*). The kiss follows. Hepokoski points out that Otello's rhyme – "giacio" ("lie down" or "collapse") / "bacio" ("kiss") – both here and at the end of the opera emphasizes the connection.

25. The homage chorus was added and the line "that face conquers me" changed to "that song conquers me" after the first draft of the libretto (see Hepokoski, *Giuseppe Verdi: "Otello"*, p. 31), indicating that the authors considered this point crucial.

26. Compare her incomprehension of Otello's moods, which she normally controls, in Verdi with her incomprehension of jealousy itself in Shakespeare (III, iv, 112–15).

27. Hepokoski, *Giuseppe Verdi: "Otello"*, p. 176; Kerman, *Opera as Drama*, pp. 140–42, also discusses Otello's accelerated anger.

28. See chapter 7 above, pp. 128–38.

29. Hepokoski, *Giuseppe Verdi: "Otello"*, p. 179.

30. Budden, *The Operas of Verdi*, vol. III (New York, 1981), p. 318.

31. Citations of the score refer to Giuseppe Verdi, *Otello* (New York: Schirmer, 1962, pl. no. 43686).

32. Maurel commented that although pure, "this heroine is not a Holy Virgin, she is a woman" (Busch (ed. and trans.), *Verdi's "Otello" and "Simon Boccanegra"*, p. 636). See also Kerman, *Opera as Drama*, p. 161.

33. See Hepokoski's discussion of the transposition of this duet, done apparently to suit the first Desdemona, Romilda Pantaleoni, in "Verdi's Composition of *Otello*: The Act II Quartet," in Carolyn Abbate and Roger Parker (eds.), *Analyzing Opera*, pp. 143–49. See also Hepokoski, *Giuseppe Verdi: "Otello"*, pp. 53–55 and 67–68.

34. In "Verdi's First 'Willow Song': New Sketches and Drafts for *Otello*," *19th-Century Music* 19 (1995–96), 213–30, Linda B. Fairtile's transcriptions of Verdi's sketches for the Willow Song show that his music became less "folk-like" as the compositional process proceeded. See especially pp. 223, 224, and 228. For another important discussion of this piece, see Brooks Toliver, "Grieving in the Mirrors of Verdi's Willow Song: Desdemona, Barbara and a 'feeble, strange voice'," *Cambridge Opera Journal* 10 (1998), 289–305.

35. Desdemona's chilling upbeat arpeggiation was a late revision. See Hepokoski, *Giuseppe Verdi: "Otello"*, p. 72.

36. More detail will be given in "Cross-References in Context: Long-Range and Local Key Relations in Verdi's *Otello*," in preparation. Two important existing studies of motivic and tonal relationships in *Otello* are David Lawton, "On the 'Bacio' Theme in *Otello*," *19th-Century Music* 1 (1977–78), 211–20, and Roger Parker and Matthew Brown, "'Ancora un bacio': Three Scenes from Verdi's *Otello*," *19th-Century Music* 9 (1985–86), 50–62.

37. See Hepokoski, "Verdi's Composition of *Otello*," pp. 146–49, for an interpretation of Verdi's transposition of the quartet movement to B flat.

38. Budden, *The Operas of Verdi*, vol. III, p. 319.

39. Letter to Boito, January 1, 1886, quoted *ibid*.

40. Kerman, *Opera as Drama*, p. 161, has observed that "at the end, Verdi sacrificed the tragedy of Otello for the pathos of Desdemona." In revising the libretto, the authors cut an extended solo piece for Otello that would have given him more emphasis. See Hepokoski, *Giuseppe Verdi: "Otello"*, p. 35.

15 An introduction to Verdi's working methods

1. The piccolo is an exception and appears immediately below the first flute.

2. This discussion needs to be understood as an outline from which many details have necessarily been omitted. Examples are employed as highly selective representatives.

3. My focus is the operas. See chapter 10 for a discussion of his works in other genres.

4. This term was employed by Verdi and Giuseppina for these works. See Martin Chusid, "Toward an Understanding of Verdi's Middle Period," in Chusid (ed.), *Verdi's Middle Period*, p. 2.

5. Indeed, this reasoning supports including the 1847 *Macbeth* firmly within the early group even though some have used its stylistic differences as reason to advance a new group subdividing the early operas. Because the works that follow, *I masnadieri*, *Jérusalem*, *Il corsaro*, and *La battaglia di Legnano* all clearly belong with the early works, and because the general conditions and methods remained the same throughout, the 1847 *Macbeth* is perhaps best understood as a remarkable stylistic anomaly.

6. Antonio Piazza and Felice Romani fill out this group of librettists for the early works.

7. George Martin, "Verdi, *King Lear* and Maria Piccolomini," *Columbia Library Columns* 21 (1971), 12–20.

8. Budden, *The Operas of Verdi*, vol. I (New York, 1973), pp. 229–30.

9. Luke Jensen, *Giuseppe Verdi and Giovanni Ricordi with Notes on Francesco Lucca: From "Oberto" to "La traviata"* (New York: Garland, 1989), pp. 31–33.

10. For a discussion, see Jensen, *Giuseppe Verdi and Giovanni Ricordi*, pp. 125–48 and 189–206.

11. Facsimile in Gaetano Cesari and Alessandro Luzio (eds.), *I copialettere di Giuseppe Verdi*, table 11, pp. 419–23. For an analysis, see Chusid, "Toward an Understanding of Verdi's Middle Period," pp. 1–15.

12. Martin, "Verdi, *King Lear* and Maria Piccolomini."

13. It is a telling detail that the two new works in this group, *Otello* and *Falstaff*, are both based on plays by Shakespeare. This confirms Verdi's lifelong interest in and love for the works of the English bard. The revision of *Simon Boccanegra* is frequently cited as a warm-up for *Otello*, but it should also be seen as representative of the faith Verdi had in certain of his less successful efforts, which led him to return to them. In addition, his fashioning of *Don Carlos* for the Italian stage in this period is emblematic of his lifelong attribute of being a practical man of the theatre.

14. James A. Hepokoski, "Verdi, Giuseppina Pasqua, and the Composition of *Falstaff*," *19th-Century Music* 3 (1979–80), 239–50.

15. See Piero Weiss, "Verdi and the Fusion of Genres," *Journal of the American Musicological Society* 35 (1982), 138–56.

16. Carlo Gatti, *Verdi nelle immagini* (Milan: Garzanti, 1941).

17. Carlo Gatti (ed.), *L'abbozzo del "Rigoletto" di Giuseppe Verdi* (Edizione Fuori Commercio a cura del Maestro della Cultura Popolare, 1941).

18. See Pierluigi Petrobelli, "Remarks on Verdi's Composing Process," in *Music in the Theater*, pp. 48–74. Petrobelli's essay was originally published as "Osservazioni sul processo compositivo in Verdi," *Acta musicologica* 43 (1971), 125–43.

19. David Lawton, "A New Sketch for Verdi's *I due Foscari*," *Verdi Newsletter* 22 (1995), 4–16. Pierluigi Petrobelli, "Pensieri per *Alzira*," in Casati and Pavarani (eds.), *Nuove prospettive*

nella ricerca verdiana, pp. 110–24; trans. Roger Parker as "Thoughts for *Alzira,*" in *Music in the Theater,* pp. 75–99. As sketch materials currently held by the Verdi heirs become available, this area of inquiry will burgeon. Occasionally, materials may be found elsewhere. For example, while working with the Toscanini collection housed at the New York Public Library, Linda Fairtile found just such materials relating to the Willow Song in *Otello.* See "Verdi's First 'Willow Song': New Sketches and Drafts for *Otello,*" *19th-Century Music* 19 (1995–96), 213–30.

20. *La traviata,* ed. Fabrizio Della Seta, *The Works of Giuseppe Verdi,* series I, vol. XIX (University of Chicago Press; Milan: Ricordi, 1997), pp. xvi–xvii and l–li.

21. Letter from Verdi to Mocenigo dated April 9, 1843. Conati, *La bottega della musica,* p. 39.

22. Jensen, *Giuseppe Verdi and Giovanni Ricordi,* p. 2.

23. Petrobelli, "Remarks on Verdi's Composing Process," pp. 48–74.

24. For a discussion of this process for *Falstaff,* see James A. Hepokoski, "Overriding the Autograph Score: The Problem of Textual Authority in Verdi's *Falstaff,*" *Studi verdiani* 8 (1992), 13–51.

25. Rosen and Porter (eds.), pp. 1–125.

26. Letters dated November 23, 1846, and December 22, 1847. *Ibid,* pp. 17 and 27.

27. An introduction to the variety of extant materials can be gleaned from Martin Chusid, Luke Jensen, and David Day, "The Verdi Archive at New York University: Part II," *Verdi Newsletter* 9–10 (1981–82), 3–52.

28. Ricordi occasionally offered these lithographs as a "gift" for subscribers to the house journal, *La Gazzetta musicale di Milano.* The "figurini" or costume designs for *Macbeth* constituted part of the supplement for 1847. See Luke Jensen, *La Gazzetta musicale di Milano, 1842–1862,* 5 vols., *Répertoire international de la presse musicale* (Ann Arbor: University Microfilms International, 2000), vol. I, pp. 180, 183, and 184.

29. Budden, *The Operas of Verdi,* vol. III (New York, 1981), pp. 363–64.

30. Letter from Giulio Ricordi to Verdi dated September 6, 1871, as published by Busch (ed. and trans.), *Verdi's "Aida",* p. 218.

31. The scholar can determine not only how this music was performed in salons and parlors of the day, but also which specific numbers gained the widest currency. For example, in 1848 Ricordi resurrected the tenor *romanza* for Riccardo in Act II of *Oberto,*

"Ciel che feci," long after the opera had been forgotten. This occurred when Ricordi began re-releasing Verdi's works in "chiave di sol" (treble clef). This number was likely the only part of *Oberto* Italians knew in the late 1840s and for some time thereafter. See Jensen, *Giuseppe Verdi and Giovanni Ricordi,* p. 253.

32. See Luke Jensen, "The Emergence of the Modern Conductor for Nineteenth-Century Italian Opera," *Performance Practice Review* 4/1 (Spring 1991), 34–63, and 4/2 (Fall 1991), 223–25.

33. See Linda B. Fairtile, "The Violin Director in *Il trovatore* and *Le trouvère*: Some Nineteenth-Century Evidence," *Verdi Newsletter* 21 (1993), 16–26. Also note that Ricordi printed a part for "violino principale" for *Un ballo in maschera.*

34. James Hepokoski has brought this into view in various essays. In particular, see his "Overriding the Autograph Score."

35. Changes made during rehearsals would generally not be considered revisions, but certain exceptions can be made, as in the case of *Don Carlos,* when Verdi excised materials before the opening night because the opera ran too long.

36. This aria, "Infin che un brando vindice," was later associated with *Ernani.* See Roger Parker, "'Infin che un brando vindice': From *Ernani* to *Oberto,*" *Verdi Newsletter* 12 (1984), 5–7, and the critical edition prepared by Claudio Gallico (University of Chicago Press; Milan: Ricordi, 1985), in which the aria is discussed on pp. xxi–xxii and xlv–xlvi. The aria is on pp. 427–46.

37. See David Lawton and David Rosen, "Verdi's Non-Definitive Revisions: The Early Operas," in Mario Medici and Marcello Pavarani (eds.), *Atti del III Congresso internazionale di studi verdiani,* pp. 189–237.

38. Jensen, *Giuseppe Verdi and Giovanni Ricordi,* pp. 193–202.

39. Since this was recognized after the plan for the critical edition had been finalized, *Le trouvère* will be assigned the volume number XVIIIb. See Gregory Harwood, *Giuseppe Verdi: A Guide to Research,* p. 328.

16 Verdi criticism

1. Roger Parker has demonstrated that even general periodicals, such as *La gazzetta privilegiata di Milano,* may also contain valuable information about the composer's career; see his "Verdi and the *Gazzetta privilegiata di Milano*: An 'Official' View Seen in Its Cultural Context," *RMA Research Chronicle* 18 (1982), 51–65.

2. See Roger Parker's "'Insolite forme,' or
Basevi's Garden Path," in Martin Chusid
(ed.), *Verdi's Middle Period*, for a recent
assessment of Basevi's writings, their rising
fortune in contemporary Verdi criticism, and
their inherent biases and weaknesses. For an
earlier judgment of Basevi, see Alfredo
Parente, "Il problema della critica verdiana,"
Rassegna musicale 6 (1933), 199–200.
3. See, for example, Antonio Ghislanzoni's
"Le trasformazioni di Verdi," *Gazzetta
musicale di Milano* 22 (1867), 209–10,
which defends Verdi's musical style in
Don Carlos.
4. For the most current information on
volumes issued and forthcoming, see *RIPM*'s
home page at http://www.nisc.com/ripm/.
RIPM has recently released their materials in
digital format in addition to the traditional
hardbound volumes.
5. An exemplary survey of the early French
criticism is Raoul Meloncelli's "Giuseppe
Verdi e la critica francese," *Studi verdiani* 9
(1993), 97–122. Klaus Horschansky provides
an overview of criticism in the German
press in "Die Herausbildung eines
deutsch-sprachigen Verdi-Repertoires im 19.
Jahrhundert und die zeitgenössische Kritik,"
in Friedrich Lippmann (ed.), *Colloquium
"Verdi–Wagner" Rom 1969: Bericht, Analecta
musicologica* 11 (Cologne: Böhlau, 1972),
pp. 140–84, while Danièle Pistone offers a
different approach to analyzing critical
writings through linguistic analysis in "Verdi
et la critique musicale française: aspects et
évolution de 1860 à 1993," in Maria Teresa
Muraro (ed.), *Le parole della musica II: Studi sul
lessico della letteratura critica del teatro musicale
in onore del Gianfranco Folena* (Florence:
Olschki, 1995), pp. 295–305.
6. Another significant early volume was
Italo Pizzi's *Ricordi verdiani inediti* (Turin:
Roux e Viarengo, 1901). Its final chapter
contains many stories and anecdotes
collected in and around Busseto, in large
part by Verdi's brother-in-law Giovanni
Barezzi.
7. This volume was updated and rearranged
by Augusto Alfani as *Battaglie e vittorie: Nuovi
esempj di volere è potere* (Florence: G. Barbèra,
1890); Verdi also appears as a moral example
in A. Sicchirollo's *L'anima di Giuseppe Verdi, ai
giovanetti italiani* (Milan: Casa Editrice del
Risveglio Educativo, 1901). See also Roger
Parker's *"Arpa d'or dei fatidici vati": The Verdian
Patriotic Chorus in the 1840s* (Parma: Istituto
Nazionale di Studi Verdiani, 1977), as well as
two addition articles published in his
Leonora's Last Act: "'Va pensiero' and the

Insidious Mastery of Song" (a concise version
of *"Arpa d'or"*) and "*Falstaff* and Verdi's Final
Narratives."
8. This author is sometimes listed as Stefano
Lottici Maglione.
9. Gilles de Van provides an excellent
overview of these conflicts in the first chapter
of *Verdi's Theater*.
10. See William H. Seltsam, *Metropolitan
Opera Annals* (New York: Wilson, 1947) and
Thomas G. Kaufman, *Verdi and His Major
Contemporaries* (New York and London:
Garland Publishing, 1990), with additional
indexes by Linda Fairtile published in the
Verdi Newsletter 20 (1992), 16–21.
11. See Gundula Kreuzer's recent study of
this revival of Verdi's fortunes in Germany,
"Zurück zu Verdi: The 'Verdi Renaissance'
and Musical Culture in the Weimar
Republic," *Studi verdiani* 13 (1998), 117–54.
12. The two volumes have recently been
republished in a single volume as *Verdi*, ed.
Piero Gelli (Milan: Ricordi, 2000).
13. For discussions of editorial philosophy,
see Casati and Pavarani (eds.), *Nuove
prospettive nella ricerca verdiana*, particularly
the overview by Philip Gossett on pp. 3–9.
David Lawton offers a concise rationale for
the new edition in "Why Bother with the New
Verdi Edition?," *Opera Quarterly* 2 (Winter
1984–85), 43–54. See also statements by
individual editors in each volume of the
series.
14. For a further discussion of these issues,
see Ursula Günther, "*Don Carlos*: Edizione
integrale – Critical Edition," in Casati and
Pavarani (eds.), *Nuove prospettive nella ricerca
verdiana*, pp. 29–48; David Lawton, "The
Autograph of *Aida* and the New Verdi
Edition," *Verdi Newsletter* 14 (1986), 4–14;
and James A. Hepokoski, "Overriding the
Autograph Score: The Problem of Textual
Authority in Verdi's *Falstaff*," *Studi verdiani* 8
(1992), 13–51.
15. Petrobelli, "Music in the Theater
(Apropos of *Aida*, Act III)" and "More on the
Three 'Systems': The First Act of *La forza del
destino*," in Petrobelli, *Music in the Theater*, pp.
113–26 and 127–40.
16. Petrobelli, "The Music of Verdi: An
Example of the Transmission and Reception
of Musical Culture," trans. Roger Parker,
Verdi Newsletter 15 (1987), 3–6.
17. The following recent studies of *Il trovatore*
illustrate the wide variety of analytical
methodologies employed by scholars: Martin
Chusid, "A New Source for *El trovador* and Its
Implications for the Tonal Organization of *Il
trovatore*," in Chusid (ed.), *Verdi's Middle*

Period, pp. 207 25; William Drabkin, "Characters, Key Relations, and Tonal Structure in *Il trovatore,*" *Music Analysis* 1 (1982), 143–53; Joanna Greenwood, "Musical and Dramatic Motion in Verdi's *Il trovatore,*" *Jahrbuch für Opernforschung* 2 (1986), 59–73; and Pierluigi Petrobelli, "Per un'esegesi della struttura drammatica del *Trovatore,*" in Medici and Pavarani (eds.), *Atti del III Congresso internazionale di studi verdiani,* pp. 387–407.

18. For examples of notable studies in these areas, see Marco Beghelli, "Per un nuovo approccio al teatro musicale: l'atto performativo come luogo dell'imitazione gestuale nella dramaturgia verdiana," *Italica* 64 (1987), 632–53; Fabrizio Della Seta, "Verdi: la tradizione italiana e l'esperienza europea," *Musica/realtà* 32 (August 1990), 135–58; Daniela Goldin, "Il *Simon Boccanegra* da Piave a Boito e la drammaturgia verdiana," in Goldin, *La vera fenice: Libretti e librettisti tra Sette e Ottocento* (Turin: Einaudi, 1985), pp. 283–334; Gerardo Guccini, "La drammaturgia dell'attore nella sintesi di Giuseppe Verdi," *Teatro e storia* 4 (1989), 245–82; Pierluigi Petrobelli, "Boito e Verdi," in Giovanni Morelli (ed.), *Arrigo Boito: Atti del Convegno internazionale di studi* (Florence: Olschki, 1994), pp. 261–73; Gilles de Van, "Notes sur Verdi humoriste," in *Omaggio a Gianfranco Folena,* 3 vols. (Padua: Editoriale Programma, 1993), vol. II, pp. 1739–48; and Piero Weiss, "Verdi and the Fusion of Genres," *Journal of the American Musicological Society* 35 (1982), 138–56.

19. Knud Arne Jürgensen, "Come affrontare i balletti verdiani nella mise en scène di oggi?," in Pierluigi Petrobelli and Fabrizio Della Seta (eds.), *La realizzazione scenica dello spettacolo verdiano: Atti del Congresso internazionale di studi, Parma, 28–30 settembre 1994* (Parma: Istituto Nazionale di Studi Verdiani, 1996), pp. 367–71; and Roger Parker, "Reading the 'livrets' or the Chimera of 'Authentic' Staging," in Petrobelli and Della Seta (eds.), *La realizzazione scenica dello spettacolo verdiano,* pp. 345–66. The same argument is presented in Parker, "The Sea and the Stars and the Wastes of the Desert," *University of Toronto Quarterly* 67 (Fall 1998), 750–60.

20. Hepokoski and Ferrero (eds.), *"Otello" di Giuseppe Verdi* (1990); Conati and Grilli (eds.), *"Simon Boccanegra" di Giuseppe Verdi* (1993); David Rosen, *"Un ballo in maschera" di Giuseppe Verdi* (in preparation).

21. See, for example, Linda B. Fairtile, "The Violin Director and Verdi's Middle-Period Operas," in Chusid (ed.), *Verdi's Middle Period,* pp. 413–26; Roberta Montemorra Marvin, "Aspects of Tempo in Verdi's Early and Middle-Period Italian Operas," in Chusid (ed.), ibid, pp. 393–411; and two articles by Renato Meucci, "Il cimbasso e gli strumenti affini nell'Ottocento italiano" and "I timpani e gli strumenti a percussione nell'Ottocento italiano," *Studi verdiani* 5 (1989–90), 109–62, and 13 (1998), 183–254.

22. See *"Arpa d'or dei fatidici vati"* and "'Va pensiero' and the Insidious Mastery of Song." See also Birgit Pauls, *Giuseppe Verdi und das Risorgimento: Ein politischer Mythos im Prozess der Nationenbildung* (Ph.D. dissertation, University of Frankfurt am Main, 1996; Berlin: Akademie Verlag, 1996).

23. Petrobelli, "The Music of Verdi," 5.

Verdi's works

Title	Primary Librettist	Primary Source	Premiere
Luisa Miller	Cammarano	Schiller, *Kabale und Liebe*	Naples, San Carlo, Dec. 8, 1849
Stiffelio	Piave	E. Souvestre and E. Bourgeois, *Le pasteur*	Trieste, Grande, Nov. 16, 1850
Rigoletto	Piave	Hugo, *Le roi s'amuse*	Venice, La Fenice, Mar. 11, 1851
Il trovatore	Cammarano	A. García Gutiérrez, *El trovador*	Rome, Apollo, Jan. 19, 1853
La traviata	Piave	A. Dumas *fils*, *La dame aux camélias*	Venice, La Fenice, Mar. 6, 1853
Les vêpres siciliennes	E. Scribe and C. Duveyrier	Scribe and Duveyrier, *Le duc d'Albe*	Paris, Opéra, June 13, 1855
Simon Boccanegra	Piave	Gutiérrez, *Simón Boccanegra*	Venice, La Fenice, Mar. 12, 1857
Aroldo	Piave	Piave, *Stiffelio*	Rimini, Nuovo, Aug. 16, 1857
Un ballo in maschera	A. Somma	Scribe, *Gustave III*	Rome, Apollo, Feb. 17, 1859
La forza del destino	Piave	A. de Saavedra, *Don Alvaro*	St. Petersburg, Imperial, Nov. 10, 1862
Macbeth II	Piave (trans. C. Nuitter and A. Beaumont)	Piave, *Macbeth*	Paris, Lyrique, Apr. 21, 1865
Don Carlos	Méry and C. Du Locle	Schiller (poem, 1787)	Paris, Opéra, Mar. 11, 1867
La forza del destino II	Piave (rev. A Ghislanzoni)	Piave, *La forza del destino*	Milan, La Scala, Feb. 27, 1869
Aida	Ghislanzoni	A. Mariette (scenario)	Cairo, Opera, Dec. 24, 1871
Simon Boccanegra II	Piave (rev. A. Boito)	Piave, *Simon Boccanegra*	Milan, La Scala, Mar. 24, 1881
Don Carlo	Rev. Du Locle	Méry and Du Locle, *Don Carlos*	Milan, La Scala, Jan. 10, 1884
Otello	Boito	Shakespeare, *Othello*	Milan, La Scala, Feb. 5, 1887
Falstaff	Boito	Shakespeare, *The Merry Wives of Windsor* and *King Henry IV*	Milan, La Scala, Feb. 9, 1893

Other major works

Sei romanze, 1838

Inno delle nazioni (A. Boito), London, Her Majesty's, May 24, 1862

"Libera me" (from collaborative Requiem for Rossini), 1868–69; incorporated in
   Messa da Requiem, 1874

String Quartet in E minor, 1873

Messa da Requiem, Milan, San Marco, May 22, 1874

Ave Maria (Dante?), 1880

Pater noster (Dante?), 1880

Ave Maria, 1889

Laudi alla Vergine Maria (Dante), ca.1890, Paris, April 7, 1898

Te Deum, 1895–96, Paris, April 7, 1898

Stabat mater, 1896–97

Pezzi sacri, published together 1898

Select bibliography and works cited

GREGORY W. HARWOOD AND SCOTT L. BALTHAZAR

Abbate, Carolyn, and Roger Parker. "Dismembering Mozart." *Cambridge Opera Journal* 2 (1990), 187–95.

Abbate, Carolyn, and Roger Parker (eds.). *Analyzing Opera: Verdi and Wagner*. Berkeley and Los Angeles: University of California Press, 1989.

Abbiati, Franco. *Giuseppe Verdi*. 4 vols. Milan: Ricordi, 1959.

Adamson, Jane. *"Othello" as Tragedy: Some Problems of Judgment and Feeling*. Cambridge University Press, 1980.

Alfani, Augusto. *Battaglie e vittorie: Nuovi esempj di volere è potere*. Florence: G. Barbèra, 1890.

Andre, Naomi Adele. "Azucena, Eboli, and Amneris: Verdi's Writing for Women's Lower Voices." Ph.D. dissertation, Harvard University, 1996.

Baldacci, Luigi. *La musica in italiano: Libretto d'opera dell'Ottocento*. Milan: Rizzoli, 1997.

Baldini, Gabriele. *The Story of Giuseppe Verdi: "Oberto" to "Un ballo in maschera"*. Ed. and trans. Roger Parker. Cambridge University Press, 1980.

Balthazar, Scott L. "Analytic Contexts and Mediated Influences: The Rossinian *convenienze* and Verdi's Middle and Late Duets." *Journal of Musicological Research* 10 (1990), 19–45.

"Aspects of Form in the *Ottocento* Libretto." *Cambridge Opera Journal* 7 (1995), 23–35.

"Evolving Conventions in Italian Serious Opera: Scene Structure in the Works of Rossini, Bellini, Donizetti, and Verdi, 1810–1850." Ph.D. dissertation, University of Pennsylvania, 1985.

"Mayr and the Development of the Two-Movement Aria." In Francesco Bellotto (ed.), *Giovanni Simone Mayr: L'opera teatrale e la musica sacra*. Bergamo: Stefanoni, 1997, pp. 229–51.

"Mayr, Rossini, and the Development of the Early Concertato Finale." *Journal of the Royal Musical Association* 116 (1991), 236–66.

"Music, Poetry, and Action in Ottocento Opera: The Principle of Concurrent Articulations." *Opera Journal* 22 (1989), 13–34.

"Plot and Tonal Design as Compositional Constraints in *Il trovatore*." *Current Musicology* 60–61 (1996), 51–77.

"The *Primo Ottocento* Duet and the Transformation of the Rossinian Code." *Journal of Musicology* 7 (1989), 471–97.

"The Rhythm of Text and Music in 'Ottocento' Melody: An Empirical Reassessment in Light of Contemporary Treatises." *Current Musicology* 49 (1992), 5–28.

"Ritorni's *Ammaestramenti* and the Conventions of Rossinian Melodramma." *Journal of Musicological Research* 8 (1989), 281–311.

"Rossini and the Development of the Mid-Century Lyric Form." *Journal of the American Musicological Society* 41 (1988), 102–25.

Barricelli, Jean-Pierre. "Romantic Writers and Music: The Case of Mazzini." *Studies in Romanticism* 14 (1975), pp. 95–117.

Basevi, Abramo. *Studio sulle opere di Giuseppe Verdi*. Florence: Tofani, 1859; repr., Bologna: Antiquae Musicae Italicae Studiosi, 1978.

Beghelli, Marco. "Lingua dell'autocaricatura nel *Falstaff*." In Gianfranco Folena, Maria Teresa Muraro, and Giovanni Morelli (eds.), *Opera e libretto II*. Florence: Olschki, 1993, pp. 351–80.

"Per un nuovo approccio al teatro musicale: l'atto performativo come luogo dell'imitazione gestuale nella drammaturgia verdiana." *Italica* 64 (1987), 632–53.

"Performative Musical Acts: The Verdian Achievement." In Eero Tarasti (ed.), *Musical Signification: Essays in the Semiotic Theory and Analysis of Music*. Berlin and New York: De Gruyter, 1995, pp. 393–412.

La retorica del rituale nel melodramma ottocentesco. Parma: Istituto Nazionale di Studi Verdiani, forthcoming.

"Semiotic Categories for the Analysis of *melodramma*." *Contemporary Music Review* 17/3 (1998), 29–42.

Bellaigue, Camille. *Verdi: Biographie critique*. Paris: Librairie Renouard, 1905; repr., Paris: Henri Laurens, 1912.

Benloew, Louis. *Précis d'une théorie des rhythmes*. Vol. I: *Rhythmes français et rhythmes latins*. Paris: Franck, 1862.

Bermani, B. *Schizzi sulla vita e sulle opere del maestro Giuseppe Verdi (estratto dalla "Gazzetta musicale di Milano")*. Milan: Ricordi, 1846.

Bidera, Emanuele. *Euritmia drammatico-musicale*. Palermo: Stabilimento Tipografico dell'Armonia, 1853.

Black, John. *The Italian Romantic Libretto: A Study of Salvadore Cammarano*. Edinburgh University Press, 1984.

Bocca, Giuseppe. "Verdi e la caricatura." *Rivista musicale italiana* 8 (1901), 326–59.

Boime, Albert. *The Art of the Macchia and the Risorgimento: Representing Culture and Nationalism in Nineteenth-Century Italy*. University of Chicago Press, 1993.

Boni, Oreste. *Giuseppe Verdi: L'uomo, le opere, l'artista*. Parma: Luigi Battei, 1901; repr., Parma: Luigi Battei, 1980.

Budden, Julian. *The Operas of Verdi*. 3 vols. London: Cassell, 1973–81. Also published in the United States: vol. I, New York: Prager, 1973; vol. II, New York: Oxford University Press, 1979; vol. III, New York: Oxford University Press, 1981. Rev. ed., Oxford: Clarendon Press, 1992.

Verdi. London: J. M. Dent, 1985; rev. ed., London: J. M. Dent, 1993; repr., New York: Schirmer, 1996.

"Verdi and Meyerbeer in Relation to *Les vêpres siciliennes*." *Studi verdiani* 1 (1982), 11–20.

Busch, Hans (ed. and trans.). *Verdi's "Aida": The History of an Opera in Letters and Documents*. Minneapolis: University of Minnesota Press, 1978.

Verdi's "Falstaff" in Letters and Contemporary Reviews. Bloomington: Indiana University Press, 1997.

Verdi's "Otello" and "Simon Boccanegra" (Revised Version) in Letters and Documents. 2 vols. Oxford: Clarendon Press; New York: Oxford University Press, 1988.

Calcaterra, Carlo (ed.). *I manifesti romantici del 1816, e gli scritti principali del "Conciliatore" sul Romanticismo*. Turin: Unione Tipografico-Editrice Torinese, 1951.

Casati, Marisa Di Gregorio, and Marcello Pavarani (eds.). *Nuove prospettive nella ricerca verdiana: Atti del Convegno internazionale in occasione della prima del "Rigoletto" in edizione critica, Vienna, 12–13 marzo 1983*. Parma: Istituto di Studi Verdiani; Milan: Ricordi, 1987.

Castelvecchi, Stefano. "Walter Scott, Rossini, e la *couleur ossianique*: il contesto culturale della *Donna del lago*." *Bollettino del Centro rossiniano di studi* 23 (1993), 57–71.

Cavalli, Hercules. *José Verdi*. Madrid: J. M. Ducanzal, 1976. Trans. Riccarda Baratta, Riccardo Baratta, and Enrica Baratta. "Giuseppe Verdi." In Mary Jane Phillips-Matz, *Verdi: Il grande gentleman del Piacentino*. Piacenza: Banca di Piacenza, 1992, pp. 80–121.

Cella, Franca, and Pierluigi Petrobelli (eds.). *Giuseppe Verdi–Giulio Ricordi: Corrispondenza e immagini 1881–1890*. Milan: Teatro alla Scala, 1981.

Cella, Franca, Madina Ricordi, and Marisa Di Gregorio Casati (eds.). *Carteggio Verdi–Ricordi 1882–1885*. Parma: Istituto Nazionale di Studi Verdiani, 1996.

Cesari, Gaetano, and Alessandro Luzio (eds.). *I copialettere di Giuseppe Verdi*. Milan: S. Ceretti, 1913; repr., Bologna: Forni, 1987.

Christensen, Thomas. "Music Theory and Its Histories." In Christopher Hatch and David W. Bernstein (eds.), *Music Theory and the Exploration of the Past*. University of Chicago Press, 1993, pp. 9–39.

Chusid, Martin. *A Catalog of Verdi's Operas*. Hackensack, N.J.: Joseph Boonin, 1974.

"Drama and the Key of F Major in *La traviata*." In Mario Medici and Marcello Pavarani (eds.), *Atti del III Congresso internazionale di studi verdiani, Milano, 12–17 giugno 1972*. Parma: Istituto di Studi Verdiani, 1974, pp. 89–121.

"Evil, Guilt and the Supernatural in Verdi's *Macbeth*: Toward an Understanding of the Tonal Structure and Key Symbolism." In David Rosen and Andrew Porter (eds.), *Verdi's "Macbeth": A Sourcebook*. New York: Norton, 1984, pp. 249–60.

"A New Source for *El trovador* and Its Implications for the Tonal Organization of *Il trovatore*." In Chusid (ed.), *Verdi's Middle Period, 1849–1859: Source Studies, Analysis, and Performance Practice*. University of Chicago Press, 1997, pp. 207–25.

"Rigoletto and Monterone: A Study in Musical Dramaturgy." *Verdi: Bollettino dell'Istituto di studi verdiani* 3/9 (1982), 1544–58.

"The Tonality of *Rigoletto*." In Carolyn Abbate and Roger Parker (eds.),

Analyzing Opera: Verdi and Wagner. Berkeley and Los Angeles: University of California Press, 1989, pp. 241–61.

"Toward an Understanding of Verdi's Middle Period." In Chusid (ed.), *Verdi's Middle Period, 1849–1859: Source Studies, Analysis, and Performance Practice*. University of Chicago Press, 1997, pp. 1–15.

Chusid, Martin (ed.). *Verdi's Middle Period, 1849–1859: Source Studies, Analysis, and Performance Practice*. University of Chicago Press, 1997.

Chusid, Martin, Luke Jensen, and David Day. "The Verdi Archive at New York University: Part II: A List of Verdi's Music, Librettos, Production Materials, Nineteenth-Century Periodicals, and Other Research Materials." *Verdi Newsletter* 9–10 (1981–82), 3–52.

Chusid, Martin, John Nádas, and Luke Jensen. "The Verdi Archive at New York University (as of May 1979): Part I: A Brief History and Description." *Verdi Newsletter* 7 (1979), 3–23.

Clémeur, Marc. "Eine neu entdeckte Quelle für das Libretto von Verdis *Don Carlos*." *Melos/Neue Zeitschrift für Musik* 6 (1977), 496–99.

Conati, Marcello. "Ballabili nei *Vespri*. Con alcune osservazioni su Verdi e la musica popolare." *Studi verdiani* 1 (1982), 21–46.

La bottega della musica: Verdi e La Fenice. Milan: Il Saggiatore, 1983.

"Prima le scene, poi la musica." In Sieghart Döhring and Wolfgang Osthoff (eds.), in collaboration with Arnold Jacobshagen, *Verdi-Studien: Pierluigi Petrobelli zum 60. Geburtstag*. Munich: Ricordi, 2000, pp. 33–58.

"*Rigoletto*": Un'analisi drammatico-musicale. Venice: Marsilio, 1992.

"Verdi et la culture parisienne des années 1830." In *La vie musicale en France au XIXe siècle*. Vol. IV: *La musique à Paris dans les années mil huit cent trente*. Ed. Peter Bloom. Stuyvesant: Pendragon Press, 1987, pp. 209–25.

Conati, Marcello (ed.). *Interviste e incontri con Verdi*. 2nd ed. Milan: Emme Edizioni, 1981. Trans. Richard Stokes. *Interviews and Encounters with Verdi*. London: Victor Gollancz, 1984. *Encounters with Verdi*. Ithaca: Cornell University Press, 1984.

Conati, Marcello, and Natalia Grilli (eds.). "*Simon Boccanegra*" di Giuseppe Verdi. Milan: Ricordi, 1993.

Cone, Edward T. "On the Road to *Otello*: Tonality and Structure in *Simon Boccanegra*." *Studi verdiani* 1 (1982), 72–98.

Cook, Nicholas. *Music, Imagination, and Culture*. Oxford University Press, 1990.

Corazzol, Adriana Guarnieri. "Opera and Verismo: Regressive Points of View and the Artifice of Alienation." *Cambridge Opera Journal* 5 (1993), 39–53.

Corrieri, A. G. "Le donne nelle opere di G. Verdi." *Gazzetta musicale di Milano* 50 (1895), 589–90.

Coudroy, Marie-Hélène. *La critique parisienne des "grands opéras" de Meyerbeer: "Robert le diable" – "Les huguenots" – "Le prophète" – "L'africaine"*. Saarbrücken: Galland, 1988.

Crowest, Frederick J. *Verdi: Man and Musician: His Biography with Especial Reference to His English Experiences*. London: Milne, 1897; repr., New York: AMS Press, 1978.

Dahlhaus, Carl. "Drammaturgia dell'opera italiana." In Lorenzo Bianconi and
   Giorgio Pestelli (eds.), *Teorie e tecniche, immagini e fantasmi. Storia dell'opera
   italiana*, vol. VI. Turin: EDT/Musica, 1988, pp. 77–162.
   Foundations of Music History. Cambridge University Press, 1983.
   Nineteenth-Century Music. Trans. J. Bradford Robinson. Berkeley and Los
   Angeles: University of California Press, 1989.
Dallapiccola, Luigi. "Parole e musica nel melodramma." In Fiamma Nicolodi
   (ed.), *Parole e musica*. Milan: Il Saggiatore, 1980. Trans. Alvary E. Grazebrook.
   "Words and Music in Italian Nineteenth-Century Opera." In William Weaver
   and Martin Chusid (eds.), *The Verdi Companion*. New York: Norton, 1979,
   pp. 183–215. Also in Rudy Shackelford (ed. and trans.), *Dallapiccola on Opera*.
   London: Toccata Press, 1987, pp. 133–63.
De Grazia, Paolo. "Una musica di Giuseppe Verdi." *Rivista musicale italiana* 45
   (1941), 230–32.
Della Seta, Fabrizio. "Gli esordi della critica verdiana: a proposito di Alberto
   Mazzucato." In Sieghart Döhring and Wolfgang Osthoff (eds.), in
   collaboration with Arnold Jacobshagen, *Verdi-Studien: Pierluigi Petrobelli zum
   60. Geburtstag*. Munich: Ricordi, 2000, pp. 59–74.
   "The librettist." In Lorenzo Bianconi and Giorgio Pestelli (eds.), *Opera
   Production and Its Resources*. University of Chicago Press, 1998, pp. 229–89.
   "'Parola scenica' in Verdi e nella critica verdiana." In Fiamma Nicolodi and
   Paolo Trovato (eds.), *Le parole della musica I: Studi sulla lingua della letteratura
   musicale in onore di Gianfranco Folena*. Florence: Olschki, 1994, pp. 259–73.
   "Some Difficulties in the Historiography of Italian Opera." *Cambridge Opera
   Journal* 10 (1998), 3–13.
   "Il tempo della festa. Su due scene della *Traviata* e su altri luoghi verdiani."
   Studi verdiani 2 (1983), 108–46.
   "Verdi: la tradizione italiana e l'esperienza europea." *Musica/realtà* 32 (August
   1990), 135–58.
Della Seta, Fabrizio (ed.). *Giuseppe Verdi: "La traviata": Schizzi e abbozzi
   autografi/Autograph Sketches and Drafts*. 2 vols. Parma: Ministero per i Beni e le
   Attività Culturali; Comitato Nazionale per le Celebrazioni Verdiane; Istituto
   Nazionale di Studi Verdiani, 2000.
Della Seta, Fabrizio, Roberta Montemorra Marvin, and Marco Marica (eds.). *Verdi
   2001: Atti del Convegno internazionale/Proceedings of the International
   Conference, Parma, New York, New Haven, 24 gennaio–1 febbraio 2001*. 2 vols.
   Florence: Olschki, 2003.
Döhring, Sieghart, and Wolfgang Osthoff (eds.), in collaboration with Arnold
   Jacobshagen. *Verdi-Studien: Pierluigi Petrobelli zum 60. Geburtstag*. Munich:
   Ricordi, 2000.
Drabkin, William. "Characters, Key Relations, and Tonal Structure in *Il trovatore*."
   Music Analysis 1 (1982), 143–53.
Engelhardt, Markus. *Die Chöre in den frühen Opern Giuseppe Verdis*. Ph.D.
   dissertation, University of Würzburg, 1986. Tutzing: Schneider, 1988.
   Giuseppe Verdi und seine Zeit. Laaber Verlag, 2001.
   "'Something's Been Done to Make Room for Choruses': Choral Conception
   and Choral Construction in *Luisa Miller*." In Martin Chusid (ed.), *Verdi's*

Middle Period, 1849–1859: Source Studies, Analysis, and Performance Practice.
University of Chicago Press, 1997, pp. 197–205.

*Verdi und Andere: "Un giorno di regno," "Ernani," "Attila," "Il corsaro" in
Mehrfachvertonungen.* Parma: Istituto di Studi Verdiani, 1992.

Fabbri, Paolo. "Istituti metrici e formali." In Lorenzo Bianconi and Giorgio
Pestelli (eds.), *Teorie e tecniche, immagini e fantasmi. Storia dell'opera italiana,*
vol. VI. Turin: EDT/Musica, 1988, pp. 163–233.

Fairtile, Linda B. "Two Appendices for Thomas G. Kaufman's *Verdi and His Major
Contemporaries." Verdi Newsletter* 20 (1992), 16–21.

"Verdi's First 'Willow Song': New Sketches and Drafts for *Otello." 19th-Century
Music* 19 (1995–96), 213–30.

"The Violin Director and Verdi's Middle-Period Operas." In Martin Chusid
(ed.), *Verdi's Middle Period, 1849–1859: Source Studies, Analysis, and Performance
Practice.* University of Chicago Press, 1977, pp. 413–26.

"The Violin Director in *Il trovatore* and *Le trouvère*: Some Nineteenth-Century
Evidence." *Verdi Newsletter* 21 (1993), 16–26.

Fish, Stanley. *Professional Correctness: Literary Studies and Political Change.*
Cambridge, Mass.: Harvard University Press, 1995.

Folena, Daniela Goldin. "Lessico melodrammatico verdiano." In Maria Teresa
Muraro (ed.), *Le parole della musica II: Studi sul lessico della letteratura critica
del teatro musicale in onore di Gianfranco Folena.* Florence: Olschki, 1995,
pp. 227–53.

Forgacs, David, and Geoffrey Nowell-Smith (eds.). *Antonio Gramsci: Selections
from the Cultural Writings.* Trans. William Boelhower. Cambridge, Mass.:
Harvard University Press, 1985.

Gable, David. "Mode Mixture and Lyric Form in the Operas of Giuseppe Verdi."
Ph.D. dissertation, University of Chicago, 1997.

Garibaldi, Luigi Agostino (ed.). *Giuseppe Verdi nelle lettere di Emanuele Muzio ad
Antonio Barezzi.* Milan: Fratelli Treves, 1931.

Garlato, Rita. *Repertorio metrico verdiano.* Venice: Marsilio, 1998.

Gartioux, Hervé (ed.). *Giuseppe Verdi, "Les vêpres siciliennes": Dossier de presse
parisienne (1855).* N.p.: Lucie Galland, 1995.

Gatti, Carlo. *Verdi.* 2 vols. Milan: Edizioni "Alpes," 1931; rev. and abr. ed., Milan:
Mondadori, 1951. Ed. and trans. Elisabeth Abbot. *Verdi: The Man and His
Music.* New York: Putnam's Sons, 1955.

Verdi nelle immagini. Milan: Garzanti, 1941.

Gatti, Carlo (ed.). *L'abbozzo del "Rigoletto" di Giuseppe Verdi.* Edizione fuori
commercio a cura del Maestro della Cultura Popolare, 1941.

Gautier, Théophile. *Histoire du romanticisme.* Paris: Éditions d'Aujourd'hui, 1978;
first published 1874.

Gerhard, Anselm. *The Urbanization of Opera: Music Theater in Paris in the
Nineteenth Century.* Trans. Mary Whittall. University of Chicago Press,
1998.

Gerhard, Anselm, and Uwe Schweikert, with Christine Fischer (eds.). *Verdi
Handbuch.* Stuttgart: Metzler; Kassel: Bärenreiter, 2001.

Gerigk, Herbert. *Giuseppe Verdi.* Potsdam: Akademische Verlagsgesellschaft
Athenaion, 1932; repr., Laaber, 1980.

Ghislanzoni, Antonio. "Le trasformazioni di Verdi." *Gazzetta musicale di Milano* 22 (1867), 209–10.

Giger, Andreas. "The Role of Giuseppe Verdi's French Operas in the Transformation of His Melodic Style." Ph.D. dissertation, Indiana University, 1999.

Goldin, Daniela. "Il *Simon Boccanegra* da Piave a Boito e la drammaturgia verdiana." In Goldin, *La vera Fenice: Libretti e librettisti tra Sette e Ottocento.* Turin: Einaudi, 1985, pp. 283–334.

La vera Fenice: Libretti e librettisti tra Sette e Ottocento. Turin: Einaudi, 1985.

Gossett, Philip. "Becoming a Citizen: The Chorus in *Risorgimento* Opera." *Cambridge Opera Journal* 2 (1990), 41–64.

"The 'candeur virginale' of *Tancredi.*" *Musical Times* 112 (1971), 327–29.

"Gioachino Rossini and the Conventions of Composition." *Acta musicologica* 42 (1970), 52–56.

"New Sources for *Stiffelio*: A Preliminary Report." *Cambridge Opera Journal* 5 (1993), 199–22. Also in Martin Chusid (ed.), *Verdi's Middle Period, 1849–1859: Source Studies, Analysis, and Performance Practice.* University of Chicago Press, 1997, pp. 19–43.

"The Overtures of Rossini." *19th-Century Music* 3 (1979–80), 3–31.

"Verdi, Ghislanzoni, and *Aida*: The Uses of Convention." *Critical Inquiry* 1 (1974–75), 291–334.

Gramsci, Antonio. *Quaderni del carcere.* Ed. Valentino, Gerratana. 4 vols. Turin: Einaudi, 1975.

Greenwood, Joanna. "Musical and Dramatic Motion in Verdi's *Il trovatore.*" *Jahrbuch für Opernforschung* 2 (1986), 59–73.

Gronda, Giovanna, and Paolo Fabbri (eds.). *Libretti d'opera italiani dal Seicento a Novecento.* Milan: Mondadori, 1997.

Grover, Michal. "Voicing Death in Verdi's Operas." Ph.D. dissertation, Brandeis University, 1997.

Gualerzi, Giorgio. *Carlo Guasco: Tenore romantico fra mito e realtà.* Alessandria: Cassa di Risparmio di Alessandria, 1976.

Guccini, Gerardo. "La drammaturgia dell'attore nella sintesi di Giuseppe Verdi." *Teatro e storia* 4 (1989), 245–82.

Guichard, Léon. "Victor Hugo e *Le roi s'amuse.*" *Verdi: Bollettino dell'Istituto di studi verdiani* 3/7 (1969), 57–88; English and German trans., 412–65.

Günther, Ursula. "*Don Carlos*: Edizione integrale – Critical Edition." In Marisa Di Gregorio Casati and Marcello Pavarani (eds.), *Nuove prospettive nella ricerca verdiana: Atti del Convegno internazionale in occasione della prima di "Rigoletto" in edizione critica, Vienna, 12–13 marzo 1983.* Parma: Istituto di Studi Verdiani; Milan: Ricordi, 1987, pp. 29–48.

"La genèse de *Don Carlos*, opéra en cinq actes de Giuseppe Verdi, représenté pour la première fois à Paris le 11 mars 1867." *Revue de musicologie* 58 (1972), 16–64; 60 (1974), 87–158.

Hansell, Kathleen Kuzmick. "Compositional Techniques in *Stiffelio*: Reading the Autograph Sources." In Martin Chusid (ed.), *Verdi's Middle Period, 1849–1859: Source Studies, Analysis, and Performance Practice.* University of Chicago Press, 1997, pp. 45–97.

Harwood, Gregory. *Giuseppe Verdi: A Guide to Research*. New York: Garland, 1998.

Hepokoski, James A. "The Compositional History of Verdi's *Falstaff*: A Study of the Autograph Score and the Early Editions." 2 vols. Ph.D. dissertation, Harvard University, 1979.

"Genre and Content in Mid-Century Verdi: 'Addio, del passato' (*La traviata*, Act III)." *Cambridge Opera Journal* 1 (1989), 249–76.

Giuseppe Verdi: "Falstaff". Cambridge University Press, 1983.

Giuseppe Verdi: "Otello". Cambridge University Press, 1987.

"*Ottocento* Opera as Cultural Drama: Generic Mixtures in *Il trovatore*." In Martin Chusid (ed.), *Verdi's Middle Period, 1849–1859: Source Studies, Analysis, and Performance Practice*. University of Chicago Press, 1997, pp. 147–96.

"Overriding the Autograph Score: The Problem of Textual Authority in Verdi's *Falstaff*." *Studi verdiani* 8 (1992), 13–51.

"Verdi, Giuseppina Pasqua, and the Composition of *Falstaff*." *19th-Century Music* 3 (1979–80), 239–50.

"Verdi's Composition of *Otello*: The Act II Quartet." In Carolyn Abbate and Roger Parker (eds.), *Analyzing Opera: Verdi and Wagner*. Berkeley and Los Angeles: University of California Press, 1989, pp. 125–49.

Hepokoski, James A., and Mercedes Viale Ferrero (eds.). *"Otello" di Giuseppe Verdi*. Milan: Ricordi, 1990.

Hopkinson, Cecil. *A Bibliography of the Works of Giuseppe Verdi, 1813–1901*. Vol. I: *Vocal and Instrumental Works*. New York: Broude Brothers, 1973. Vol. II: *Operatic Works*. New York: Broude Brothers, 1978.

Horschansky, Klaus. "Die Herausbildung eines deutsch-sprachigen Verdi-Repertoires im 19. Jahrhundert und die zeitgenössische Kritik." In Friedrich Lippmann (ed.), *Colloquium "Verdi–Wagner" Rom 1969: Bericht. Analecta musicologica* 11. Cologne: Böhlau, 1972, pp. 140–84.

Hudson, Elizabeth. "Gilda Seduced: A Tale Untold." *Cambridge Opera Journal* 4 (1992–93), 229–51.

"Narrative in Verdi: Perspectives on His Musical Dramaturgy." Ph.D. dissertation, Cornell University, 1993.

Huebner, Steven. "Italianate Duets in Meyerbeer's Grand Operas." *Journal of Musicological Research* 8 (1989), 203–58.

"Lyric Form in *Ottocento* Opera." *Journal of the Royal Musical Association* 117 (1992), 123–47.

Hugo, Victor. *Notre-Dame de Paris 1482*. Paris: Garnier-Flammarion, 1967; first published 1831.

Oeuvres complètes. Paris: Robert Laffont, 1985.

Hussey, Dyneley. *Verdi*. London: Dent; New York: Dutton, 1940.

Jensen, Luke. "The Emergence of the Modern Conductor for Nineteenth-Century Italian Opera." *Performance Practice Review* 4 (1991), 34–63 and 223–25.

La Gazzetta musicale di Milano, 1842–1862. 5 vols. *Répertoire international de la presse musicale*. Ann Arbor: University Microfilms International, 2000.

Giuseppe Verdi and Giovanni Ricordi with Notes on Francesco Lucca: From "Oberto" to "La traviata". New York: Garland, 1989.

Jürgensen, Knud Arne. "Come affrontare i balletti verdiani nella mise en scène di oggi?" In Pierluigi Petrobelli and Fabrizio Della Seta (eds.), *La realizzazione scenica dello spettacolo verdiano: Atti del Congresso internazionale di studi, Parma, 28–30 settembre 1994*. Parma: Istituto Nazionale di Studi Verdiani, 1996, pp. 367–71.

The Verdi Ballets. Parma: Istituto Nazionale di Studi Verdiani, 1995.

Kaufman, Thomas G. *Verdi and His Major Contemporaries: A Selected Chronology of Performances with Casts*. New York and London: Garland Publishing, 1990.

Kerman, Joseph. "Lyric Form and Flexibility in *Simon Boccanegra*." *Studi verdiani* 1 (1982), 47–62.

Opera as Drama. New York: Random House, 1956; first published 1952.

"Verdi's Use of Recurring Themes." In Harold S. Powers (ed.), *Studies in Music History: Essays for Oliver Strunk*. Princeton University Press, 1968, pp. 495–510.

"Viewpoint." *19th-Century Music* 2 (1978–79), 186–91.

Kimbell, David R. B. *Verdi in the Age of Italian Romanticism*. Cambridge University Press, 1981.

Klier, Teresa. *Der Verdi-Klang: Die Orchesterkonzeption in den Opern von Giuseppe Verdi*. Ph.D. dissertation, University of Würzburg, 1995. Tutzing: Schneider, 1998.

Kreuzer, Gundula. "Zurück zu Verdi: The 'Verdi Renaissance' and Musical Culture in the Weimar Republic." *Studi verdiani* 13 (1998), 117–154.

Landini, Giancarlo, and Marco Gilardone. *Dal labbro il canto: Il linguaggio vocale delle opere di Verdi*. Turin: Omega Musica, 2001.

Latham, Alison, and Roger Parker (eds.). *Verdi in Performance*. Oxford and New York: Oxford University Press, 2001.

Lavagetto, Mario. *Un caso di censura: "Rigoletto"*. Milan: Il Formichiere, 1979.

Quei più modesti romanzi: Il libretto nel melodramma di Verdi: Tecniche costruttive funzioni poetica di un genere letterario minore. Milan: Garzanti, 1979.

Lawton, David. "The Autograph of *Aida* and the New Verdi Edition." *Verdi Newsletter* 14 (1986), 4–14.

"A New Sketch for Verdi's *I due Foscari*." *Verdi Newsletter* 22 (1995), 4–16.

"On the 'Bacio' Theme in *Otello*." *19th-Century Music* 1 (1977–78), 211–20.

"Tonal Structure and Dramatic Action in *Rigoletto*." *Verdi: Bollettino dell'Istituto di studi verdiani* 3/9 (1982), 1559–81.

"Tonal Systems in *Aida*, Act III." In Carolyn Abbate and Roger Parker (eds.), *Analyzing Opera: Verdi and Wagner*. Berkeley and Los Angeles: University of California Press, 1989, pp. 262–75.

"Tonality and Drama in Verdi's Early Operas." 2 vols. Ph.D. dissertation, University of California, Berkeley, 1973.

"Why Bother with the New Verdi Edition?" *Opera Quarterly* 2 (Winter 1984–85), 43–54.

Lawton, David, and David Rosen. "Verdi's Non-Definitive Revisions: The Early Operas." In Mario Medici and Marcello Pavarani (eds.), *Atti del III Congresso internazionale di studi verdiani, Milano, 12–17 giugno 1972*. Parma: Istituto di Studi Verdiani, 1974, pp. 189–237.

Lessona, Michele. "Parma: Giuseppe Verdi." In Lessona, *Volere è potere*. Florence: G. Barbèra, 1869; repr., with an introduction by Mario Miccinesi, Pordenone: Studio Tesi, 1990, pp. 287–307.

Levarie, Siegmund. "Key Relations in Verdi's *Un ballo in maschera.*" *19th-Century Music* 2 (1978–79), 143–47.

Lippmann, Friedrich. *Versificazione italiana e ritmo musicale.* Naples: Liguori, 1986. *Vincenzo Bellini und die italienische Opera seria seiner Zeit: Studien über Libretto, Arienform und Melodik. Analecta musicologica* 6. Cologne: Böhlau, 1969. Rev. Italian ed., "Vincenzo Bellini e l'opera seria del suo tempo. Studi sul libretto, la forma delle arie e la melodia." In Maria Rosaria Adamo and Friedrich Lippmann, *Vincenzo Bellini.* Rome: ERI, 1981, pp. 313–555.

Lottici, Stefano. *Bio-bibliografia di Giuseppe Verdi.* Parma: Orsatti, 1913.

Luzio, Alessandro (ed.). *Carteggi verdiani.* 4 vols. Rome: Reale Accademia d'Italia – Accademia Nazionale dei Lincei, 1935–47.

Lyttelton, Adrian. "Creating a National Past: History, Myth and Image in the Risorgimento." In Albert Russell Ascoli and Krystyna von Henneberg (eds.), *Making and Remaking Italy.* Oxford: Berg, 2001, pp. 27–74.

Marchesi, Gustavo. "The *Ernani* Years." In Pierluigi Petrobelli (ed.), *"Ernani" Yesterday and Today: Proceedings of the International Congress, Modena, Teatro San Carlo, 9–10 December 1984. Verdi: Bulletin of the Istituto di Studi Verdiani* 4/10. Parma: Istituto di Studi Verdiani, 1989, pp. 19–42.

Marco, Guy. "On Key Relations in Opera." *19th-Century Music* 3 (1979–80), 83–88.

Marcozzi, Rudy T. "The Interaction of Large-Scale Harmonic and Dramatic Structure in the Verdi Operas Adapted from Shakespeare." Ph.D. dissertation, Indiana University, 1992.

Marica, Marco (ed.). *Giuseppe Verdi, "Notturno".* Milan: Museo Teatrale alla Scala; Parma: Istituto Nazionale di Studi Verdiani, 2000.

Martin, George. *Aspects of Verdi.* New York: Dodd Mead, 1988.
  "Verdi and the Risorgimento." In William Weaver and Martin Chusid (eds.), *The Verdi Companion.* New York: Norton, 1979, pp. 13–41.
  Verdi: His Music, Life, and Times. New York: Dodd Mead, 1963.
  "Verdi, *King Lear* and Maria Piccolomini." *Columbia Library Columns* 21 (1971), 12–20.

Marvin, Roberta Montemorra. "Aspects of Tempo in Verdi's Early and Middle-Period Italian Operas." In Martin Chusid (ed.), *Verdi's Middle Period, 1849–1859: Source Studies, Analysis, and Performance Practice.* University of Chicago Press, 1977, pp. 393–411.
  "A Verdi Autograph and the Problem of Authenticity." *Studi verdiani* 9 (1993), 36–61.
  Verdi the Student – Verdi the Teacher. Parma: Istituto Nazionale di Studi Verdiani, forthcoming.
  "Verdi's *I masnadieri*: Its Genesis and Early Reception." 2 vols. Ph.D. dissertation, Brandeis University, 1992.

Mazzini, Giuseppe. *Filosofia della musica.* Ed. Marcello De Angelis. Rimini: Guaraldi, 1977; first published 1836.

Mazzucato, Alberto. "*Il profeta.*" *Gazzetta musicale di Milano* 13 (1855), 187.

Medici, Mario, and Marcello Conati (eds.). *Carteggio Verdi–Boito.* 2 vols. Parma: Istituto di Studi Verdiani, 1978. Trans. William Weaver, with a new introduction by Marcello Conati. *The Verdi–Boito Correspondence*. University of Chicago Press, 1994.

Meloncelli, Raoul. "Giuseppe Verdi e la critica francese." *Studi verdiani* 9 (1993), 97–122.

Meucci, Renato. "Il cimbasso e gli strumenti affini nell'Ottocento italiano." *Studi verdiani* 5 (1989–90), 109–62.

"I timpani e gli strumenti a percussione nell'Ottocento italiano." *Studi verdiani* 13 (1998), 183–254.

Meyer, Leonard B. "A Universe of Universals." *Journal of Musicology* 16 (1998), 3–25.

Mila, Massimo. *L'arte di Verdi*. Turin: Einaudi, 1980.

La giovinezza di Verdi. 2nd ed. Turin: ERI, 1978.

Verdi. Ed. Piero Gelli. Milan: Ricordi, 2000.

Il melodramma di Verdi. Bari: G. Laterza, 1933.

Monaldi, Gino. *Saggio di iconografia verdiana*. Ed. Uberto Visconte di Modrone. Bergamo: Istituto Italiano d'Arti Grafiche, [1913].

Moreen, Robert. "Integration of Text Forms and Musical Forms in Verdi's Early Operas." Ph.D. dissertation, Princeton University, 1975. Ann Arbor, Mich.: University Microfilms, 1976.

Mossa, Carlo Matteo. "'Pure stimerei che vi fosse un preludio': parole e musica nel carteggio Verdi–Cammarano." In Sieghart Döhring and Wolfgang Osthoff (eds.), in collaboration with Arnold Jacobshagen, *Verdi-Studien: Pierluigi Petrobelli zum 60. Geburtstag*. Munich: Ricordi, 2000, pp. 189–212.

Mossa, Carlo Matteo (ed.). *Carteggio Verdi–Cammarano*. Parma: Istituto Nazionale di Studi Verdiani, 2001.

Musini, Nullo. "Giuseppe Verdi a Trieste. Una 'berceuse' inedita del Maestro." *Aurea Parma: Rivista di lettere, arte, e storia* 35 (1951), 199–202.

Napolitano, Almerindo. *Il teatro Verdi di Busseto*. Parma: La Nazionale, 1968.

Nattiez, Jean-Jacques. *Music and Discourse: Toward a Semiology of Music*. Trans. Carolyn Abbate. Princeton University Press, 1990.

Noske, Frits. *The Signifier and the Signified*. The Hague: Nijhoff, 1977.

Oberdorfer, Aldo. *Giuseppe Verdi: Autobiografia dalle lettere*. 2nd ed. Ed. Marcello Conati. Milan: Rizzoli, 1981.

Olsen, Roberta J. M. (ed.). *Ottocento: Romanticism and Revolution in Nineteenth-Century Italian Painting*. New York: American Federation of Arts, 1992.

Ortombina, Fortunato. "'Sgombra, o gentil': un dono di Verdi all'amico Delfico." *Studi verdiani* 8 (1992), 104–17.

Osborne, Charles. *Verdi*. New York: Knopf, 1987.

Osthoff, Wolfgang. "Musica e versificazione: funzioni del verso poetico nell'opera italiana." In Lorenzo Bianconi (ed.), *La drammaturgia musicale*. Bologna: Il Mulino, 1986, pp. 125–41.

"The Musical Characterization of Gilda." *Verdi: Bollettino dell'Istituto di studi verdiani* 3/8 (1973), 1275–314.

"Il sonetto nel *Falstaff* di Verdi." In Giorgio Pestelli (ed.), *Il melodramma italiano dell'ottocento: Studi e ricerche per Massimo Mila*. Turin: Einaudi, 1977, pp. 157–83.

Paduano, Guido. *Il giro di vite: Percorsi dell'opera lirica.* Scandicci: La Nuova Italia, 1992.

    Noi facemmo ambedue un sogno strano: Il disagio amoroso sulla scena dell'opera europea. Palermo: Sellerio, 1982.

Pagannone, Giorgio. "Mobilità strutturale della *lyric form.* Sintassi verbale e sintassi musicale nel melodramma italiano del primo Ottocento." *Analisi* 7/20 (May 1997), 2–17.

Parente, Alfredo. "Il problema della critica verdiana." *Rassegna musicale* 6 (1933), 197–218.

Parker, Roger. *"Arpa d'or dei fatidici vati": The Verdian Patriotic Chorus in the 1840s.* Parma: Istituto Nazionale di Studi Verdiani, 1997.

    "Elizabeth's Last Act." In Mary Ann Smart (ed.), *Siren Songs: Representations of Gender and Sexuality in Opera.* Princeton University Press, 2000, pp. 93–117.

    Infin che un brando vindice' e le cavatine del primo atto di *Ernani.*" In Pierluigi Petrobelli (ed.), *"Ernani" ieri e oggi: Atti del Convegno internazionale di studi, Modena, Teatro San Carlo, 9–10 dicembre 1984. Verdi: Bollettino dell'Istituto di studi verdiani* 4/10. Parma: Istituto di Studi Verdiani, 1987, pp. 142–60.

    "'Infin che un brando vindice': From *Ernani* to *Oberto.*" *Verdi Newsletter* 12 (1984), 5–7.

    "'Insolite forme,' or Basevi's Garden Path." In Martin Chusid (ed.), *Verdi's Middle Period, 1849–1859: Source Studies, Analysis, and Performance Practice.* University of Chicago Press, 1997, pp. 129–46.

    Leonora's Last Act: Essays in Verdian Discourse. Princeton University Press, 1997.

    "Levels of Motivic Definition in *Ernani.*" *19th-Century Music* 6 (1982–83), 141–50.

    "Motives and Recurring Themes in *Aida.*" In Carolyn Abbate and Roger Parker (eds.), *Analyzing Opera: Verdi and Wagner.* Berkeley and Los Angeles: University of California Press, 1989, pp. 222–38.

    "Reading the 'livrets' or the Chimera of 'Authentic' Staging." In Pierluigi Petrobelli and Fabrizio Della Seta (eds.), *La realizzazione scenica dello spettacolo verdiano: Atti del Congresso internazionale di studi, Parma, 28–30 settembre 1994.* Parma: Istituto Nazionale di Studi Verdiani, 1996, pp. 345–66.

    "The Sea and the Stars and the Wastes of the Desert." *University of Toronto Quarterly* 67 (Fall 1998), 750–60.

    Studies in Early Verdi, 1832–1844: New Information and Perspectives in the Milanese Musical Milieu and the Operas from "Oberto" to "Ernani". New York and London: Garland Publishing, 1989.

    "Verdi and the *Gazzetta privilegiata di Milano*: An 'Official' View Seen in Its Cultural Context." *RMA Research Chronicle* 18 (1982), 51–65.

Parker, Roger, and Matthew Brown. "'Ancora un bacio': Three Scenes from Verdi's *Otello.*" *19th-Century Music* 9 (1985–86), 50–62.

    "Motivic and Tonal Interaction in Verdi's *Un ballo in maschera.*" *Journal of the American Musicological Society* 36 (1983), 243–65.

Pascolato, Alessandro (ed.). *"Re Lear" e "Ballo in maschera": Lettere di Giuseppe Verdi ad Antonio Somma.* Città di Castello: Lapi, 1902.

Pasquini, Elisabetta. *Catalogo della discoteca storica dell'Istituto nazionale di studi verdiani*. Vol. I: *Opere complete e selezioni*. Parma: Istituto Nazionale di Studi Verdiani, 2000.

Pauls, Birgit. *Giuseppe Verdi und das Risorgimento: Ein politischer Mythos im Prozess der Nationenbildung*. Ph.D. dissertation, University of Frankfurt am Main, 1996. Berlin: Akademie Verlag, 1996.

Peterseil, Michaela. "Die 'Disposizioni sceniche' des Verlags Ricordi: ihre Publikation und ihr Zielpublikum." *Studi verdiani* 12 (1997), 133–55.

Petrobelli, Pierluigi. "Boito e Verdi." In Giovanni Morelli (ed.), *Arrigo Boito: Atti del Convegno internazionale di studi*. Florence: Olschki, 1994, pp. 261–73.

"L'esperienza teatrale verdiana e la sua proiezione sulla scena." In Pierluigi Petrobelli and Fabrizio Della Seta (eds.), *La realizzazione scenica dello spettacolo verdiano: Atti del Congresso internazionale di studi, Parma, 28–30 settembre 1994*. Parma: Istituto Nazionale di Studi Verdiani, 1996, pp. 17–24.

"More on the Three 'Systems': The First Act of *La forza del destino*." In Petrobelli, *Music in the Theater: Essays on Verdi and Other Composers*. Trans. Roger Parker. Princeton University Press, 1994, pp. 127–40.

"Music in the Theater (Apropos of *Aida*, Act III)." In Petrobelli, *Music in the Theater: Essays on Verdi and Other Composers*. Trans. Roger Parker. Princeton University Press, 1994, pp. 113–26.

Music in the Theater: Essays on Verdi and Other Composers. Trans. Roger Parker. Princeton University Press, 1994.

"The Music of Verdi: An Example of the Transmission and Reception of Musical Culture." Trans. Roger Parker. *Verdi Newsletter* 15 (1987), 3–6.

"On Dante and Italian Music: Three Moments." *Cambridge Opera Journal* 2 (1989), 219–49.

"Pensieri per *Alzira*." In Marisa Di Gregorio Casati and Marcello Pavarani (eds.), *Nuove prospettive nella ricerca verdiana: Atti del Convegno internazionale in occasione della prima del "Rigoletto" in edizione critica, Vienna, 12–13 marzo 1983*. Parma: Istituto di Studi Verdiani; Milan: Ricordi, 1987, pp. 110–24.

"Per un'esegesi della struttura drammatica del *Trovatore*." In Mario Medici and Marcello Pavarani (eds.), *Atti del III Congresso internazionale di studi verdiani, Milano, 12–17 giugno 1972*. Parma: Istituto di Studi Verdiani, 1974, pp. 387–407.

"Toward an Explanation of the Dramatic Structure of *Il trovatore*." In Petrobelli, *Music in the Theater: Essays on Verdi and Other Composers*. Trans. Roger Parker. Princeton University Press, 1994, pp. 100–12.

Petrobelli, Pierluigi (ed.). *"Ernani" ieri e oggi: Atti del Convegno internazionale di studi, Modena, Teatro san Carlo, 9–10 dicembre 1984*. Verdi: *Bollettino dell'Istituto di studi verdiani* 4/10. Parma: Istituto di Studi Verdiani, 1987.

"Ernani" Yesterday and Today: Proceedings of the International Congress, Modena, Teatro San Carlo, 9–10 December 1984. Verdi: *Bulletin of the Istituto di Studi Verdiani* 4/10. Parma: Istituto di Studi Verdiani, 1989.

Petrobelli, Pierluigi, Marisa Di Gregorio Casati, and Olga Jesurum (eds.). *"Sorgete! Ombre serene!" L'aspetto visivo dello spettacolo verdiano*. 2nd ed. Parma: Istituto Nazionale di Studi Verdiani, 1996.

Petrobelli, Pierluigi, and Fabrizio Della Seta (eds.). *La realizzazione scenica dello spettacolo verdiano: Atti del Congresso internazionale di studi, Parma, 28–30 settembre 1994*. Parma: Istituto Nazionale di Studi Verdiani, 1996.

Phillips-Matz, Mary Jane. *Verdi: A Biography*. Oxford University Press, 1993.

Verdi: Il grande gentleman del Piacentino. Piacenza: Banca di Piacenza, 1992.

Pieri, Marzio. *Verdi: L'immaginario dell'ottocento*. Milan: Electa Editrice, 1981.

Piperno, Franco (ed.). "Le orchestre dei teatri d'opera italiani nell'Ottocento: bilancio provvsorio di una ricerca." *Studi verdiani* 11 (1996), 119–221.

Pistone, Danièle. "Verdi et la critique musicale française: aspects et évolution de 1860 à 1993." In Maria Teresa Muraro (ed.), *Le parole della musica II: Studi sul lessico della letteratura critica del teatro musicale in onore di Gianfranco Folena*. Florence: Olschki, 1995, pp. 295–305.

Pizzi, Italo. *Ricordi verdiani inedite, con undici lettere di Giuseppe Verdi ora pubblicate per la prima volta e varie illustrazioni*. Turin: Roux e Viarengo, 1901.

Plantinga, Leon. *Romantic Music*. New York and London: Norton, 1984.

Platoff, John. "Myths and Realities about Tonal Planning in Mozart's Operas." *Cambridge Opera Journal* 8 (1996), 3–15.

Porter, Andrew. "Giuseppe Verdi." In *The New Grove Masters of Italian Opera*. New York: Norton, 1983, pp. 191–308.

"*Les vêpres siciliennes*: New Letters from Verdi to Scribe." *19th-Century Music* 2 (1978), 95–109.

Pougin, Arthur. *Giuseppe Verdi: Vita aneddotica con note ed aggiunte di Folchetto*. Milan: Ricordi, 1881; repr., with preface by Marcello Conati, Florence: Passigli, 1989. Trans. James E. Matthew. *Verdi: An Anecdotic History of His Life and Works*. London: H. Grevel; New York: Scribner and Welford, 1887.

Powers, Harold S. "Boito rimatore per musica." In Giovanni Morelli (ed.), *Arrigo Boito*. Florence: Olschki, 1994, pp. 355–94.

"The 'Laughing Chorus' in Contexts." In *Giuseppe Verdi: "A Masked Ball"/"Un ballo in maschera"*. English National Opera Guide 40. London: Calder; New York: Riverrun, 1989, pp. 23–38.

"Making *Macbeth* Musicabile." In *Giuseppe Verdi: "Macbeth"*. English National Opera Guide 41. London: Calder; New York: Riverrun, 1990, pp. 13–36.

"One Halfstep at a Time: Tonal Transposition and 'Split Association' in Italian Opera." *Cambridge Opera Journal* 7 (1995), 135–64.

"*Simon Boccanegra* I.10–12: A Generic-Genetic Analysis of the Council Chamber Scene." *19th-Century Music* 13 (1989–90), 101–28.

"'La solita forma' and 'The Uses of Convention'." *Acta musicologica* 59 (1987), 65–90.

Redlich, Hans, and Frank Walker. "'Gesù morì,' an Unknown Early Verdi Manuscript." *Music Review* 20 (1959), 232–43.

Reicha, Antoine. *L'art du compositeur dramatique*. Paris: Farrenc, 1833.

Ritorni, Carlo. *Ammaestramenti alla composizione d'ogni poema e d'ogni opera appartenente alla musica*. Milan: Pirola, 1841.

Rizzo, Dino. "'Con eletta musica del Sig. Verdi da Busseto, fu celebrata la messa solenne'." *Studi verdiani* 9 (1993), 62–96.

Robinson, Paul. *Opera and Ideas: From Mozart to Strauss*. New York: Harper and Row, 1985.

Roccatagliati, Alessandro. *Drammaturgia romantica verdiana: "Luisa Miller" e "Rigoletto"*. Bari: Associazione Musicale Il Coretto, 1989.

Felice Romani librettista. Lucca: Libreria Musicale Italiana, 1996.

Rosen, David. "The Genesis of Verdi's Requiem." Ph.D. dissertation, University of California, Berkeley, 1976.

"How Verdi's Operas Begin: An Introduction to the Introduzioni." In Giovanni Morelli (ed.), *Tornando a Stiffelio: Popolarità, rifacimenti, messinscena, effettismo e altre "cure."* Florence: Olschki, 1987, pp. 203–21.

"How Verdi's Serious Operas End." In Angelo Pompilio, Donatella Restani, Lorenzo Bianconi, and F. Alberto Gallo (eds.), *Atti del XIV Congresso della Società internazionale di musicologia*. 3 vols. Turin: EDT, 1990, vol. III, pp. 443–50.

"La *Messa* a Rossini e il *Requiem* per Manzoni." In Michele Girardi and Pierluigi Petrobelli (eds.), *Messa per Rossini: La storia, il testo, la musica*. Parma: Istituto di Studi Verdiani; Milan: Ricordi, 1988, pp. 119–49.

"The Operatic Origins of Verdi's 'Lacrymosa'." *Studi verdiani* 5 (1988–89), 65–84.

"Le quattro stesure del duetto Filippo-Posa." In Marcello Pavarani (ed.), *Atti del II Congresso internazionale de studi verdiani, 30 luglio–5 agosto 1969*. Parma: Istituto di Studi Verdiani, 1971, pp. 368–88.

"The Staging of Verdi's Operas." In Daniel Heartz and Bonnie Wade (eds.), *Report of the Twelfth Congress [of the International Musicological Society], Berkeley, 1977*. Kassel: Bärenreiter, 1980, pp. 239–45.

Verdi: Requiem. Cambridge University Press, 1997.

Rosen, David, and Marinella Pignozzi. *"Un ballo in maschera" di Giuseppe Verdi*. Milan: Ricordi, 2002.

Rosen, David, and Andrew Porter (eds.). *Verdi's "Macbeth": A Sourcebook*. New York: Norton; Cambridge University Press, 1984.

Rosselli, John. *The Opera Industry in Italy from Cimarosa to Verdi: The Role of the Impresario*. Cambridge University Press, 1984.

Rostagno, Antonio (ed.). *Giuseppe Verdi, "Cupo è il sepolcro e mutolo" per canto e pianoforte*. Milan: Museo Teatrale alla Scala; Parma: Istituto Nazionale di Studi Verdiani, 2000.

Runyan, William Edward. "Orchestration in Five French Grand Operas." Ph.D. dissertation, University of Rochester, 1983.

Sala, Emilio. "Verdi and the Parisian Boulevard Theatre, 1847–49." *Cambridge Opera Journal* 7 (1995), 190–91.

Schlitzer, Franco. *Mondo teatrale dell'Ottocento*. Naples: Fausto Fiorentino, 1954.

Schubert, Peter. "Authentic Analysis." *Journal of Musicology* 12 (1994), 3–18.

Seltsam, William H. *Metropolitan Opera Annals: A Chronicle of Artists and Performances*. New York: Wilson, 1947.

Senici, Emanuele. "Verdi's Luisa, a Semiserious Alpine Virgin." *19th-Century Music* 22 (1998–99), 144–68.

Sicchirollo, A. *L'anima di Giuseppe Verdi, ai giovanetti italiani*. Milan: Casa Editrice del Risveglio Educativo, 1901.

Smart, Mary Ann. "Liberty on (and off) the Barricades: Verdi's Risorgimento Fantasies." In Albert Russell Ascoli and Krystyna von Henneberg (eds.), *Making and Remaking Italy: The Cultivation of National Identity around the Risorgimento*. Oxford and New York: Berg, 2001, pp. 103–18.

"'Proud, Indomitable, Irascible': Allegories of Nation in *Attila* and *Les vêpres siciliennes*." In Martin Chusid (ed.), *Verdi's Middle Period, 1849–1859: Source Studies, Analysis, and Performance Practice*. University of Chicago Press, 1997, pp. 227–56.

Smart, Mary Ann (ed.). *Siren Songs: Representations of Gender and Sexuality in Opera*. Princeton University Press, 2000.

Solie, Ruth A. (ed.). *Source Readings in Music History: The Nineteenth Century*. New York and London: Norton, 1998.

Solinas, Rosa. "Arrigo Boito: The Legacy of Scapigliatura." Ph.D. dissertation, University of Oxford, 1999.

Spada, Pietro. *Giuseppe Verdi: Inediti per tenore*. Milan: Suvini Zerboni, 1977.

"Verdi in un salotto romano." In Adrian Belli and Ceccarius (eds.), *Verdi e Roma: Celebrazione verdiana 27 gennaio 1951*. Rome: Teatro dell'Opera di Roma, 1951, pp. 41–48.

Springer, Christian. *Verdi und die Interpreten seiner Zeit*. Vienna: Holzhausen, 2000.

Stefani, Giuseppe. *Verdi e Trieste*. Trieste: Editore il Comune, 1951.

Stivender, David. "The Composer of *Gesù morì*." *AIVS Newsletter* 2 (December 1976), 6–7.

Surian, Elvidio. "Lo stato attuale degli studi verdiani: appunti e bibliografia ragionata (1960–1975)." *Rivista italiana di musicologia* 12 (1977), 305–29.

Toliver, Brooks. "Grieving in the Mirrors of Verdi's Willow Song: Desdemona, Barbara and a 'feeble, strange voice'." *Cambridge Opera Journal* 10 (1998), 289–305.

Tomasi, Gioacchino Lanza. "Verdi al ballo del gattopardo." *Discoteca*, March–April 1963, 18–19.

Tomasini, Daniele. *La cultura umanistica e letteraria di Giuseppe Verdi: Ricerche e contributi*. Cremona: Turris, 1997.

Tomlinson, Gary. "Italian Opera and Italian Romanticism: An Essay in Their Affinities." *19th-Century Music* 10 (1986–87), 43–60.

"Musical Pasts and Postmodern Musicologies: A Response to Lawrence Kramer." *Current Musicology* 53 (1993), 23.

"Opera and *Drame*: Hugo, Donizetti, and Verdi." *Music and Drama*. New York: Broude Brothers, 1988, pp. 171–92.

"Verdi after Budden." *19th-Century Music* 5 (1981–82), 170–82.

Torchi, Luigi. "L'opera di Giuseppe Verdi e i suoi caratteri principali." *Rivista musicale italiana* 8 (1901), 279–325.

Torri, Luigi. "Saggio di bibliografia verdiana." *Rivista musicale italiana* 8 (1901), 379–407.

Toye, Francis. *Giuseppe Verdi: His Life and Works*. New York: Random House, 1930.

Ubersfeld, Anne. *Le roi et le bouffon: Étude sur le théâtre de Hugo de 1830 à 1839*. Paris: Corti, 1974.

Van, Gilles de. "Notes sur Verdi humoriste." In *Omaggio a Gianfranco Folena*. 3 vols. Padua: Editoriale Programma, 1993, vol. II, pp. 1739–48.

Verdi: Un théâtre en musique. Paris: Fayard, 1992. Trans. Gilda Roberts. *Verdi's Theater: Creating Drama through Music*. University of Chicago Press, 1998.

Vanbianchi, Carlo. *Saggio di bibliografia verdiana*. Milan: Ricordi, 1913.

Verdi, Giuseppe. *Gli autografi del Museo Teatrale alla Scala*. Milan: Museo Teatrale alla Scala; Parma: Istituto Nazionale di Studi Verdiani, 2000.

Vitali, Geremia. *La musica ne' suoi principj nuovamente spiegata*. Milan: Ricordi, 1847.

Walker, Frank. "'L'abandonnée': A Forgotten Song." *Verdi: Bollettino dell'Istituto di studi verdiani* 2 (1960), 785–89.

"Goethe's 'Erste Verlust' Set to Music by Verdi: An Unknown Composition." *Music Review* 9 (1948), 13–17.

The Man Verdi. London: Dent; New York: Knopf, 1962; repr., University of Chicago Press, 1982.

Weaver, William. *Verdi: A Documentary Study*. London: Thames and Hudson, 1977.

Weaver, William (ed.). *The Verdi–Boito Correspondence*. University of Chicago Press, 1994. A translation of Mario Medici and Marcello Conati (eds.), *Carteggio Verdi–Boito*. 2 vols. Parma: Istituto di Studi Verdiani, 1978.

Weaver, William, and Martin Chusid (eds.). *The Verdi Companion*. New York: Norton, 1979.

Webster, James. "Mozart's Operas and the Myth of Musical Unity." *Cambridge Opera Journal* 2 (1990), 197–218.

"To Understand Verdi and Wagner We Must Understand Mozart." *19th-Century Music* 11 (1987–88), 175–93.

Weiss, Piero. "'Sacred Bronzes': Paralipomena to an Essay by Dallapiccola." *19th-Century Music* 9 (1985–86), 42–49.

"Verdi and the Fusion of Genres." *Journal of the American Musicological Society* 35 (1982), 138–56.

Werfel, Franz. *Verdi: Roman der Oper*. Vienna: Buchgemeinschaft Donauland, 1923.

Werfel, Franz (ed.). *Giuseppe Verdi Briefe*. Berlin: Zsolnay, 1926. Trans. Edward Downes. *Verdi: The Man in His Letters*. New York: Fisher, 1942; repr., Freeport, N.Y.: Books for Libraries Press, 1970.

Werner, Otto (ed.). *Giuseppe Verdi: Briefe*. Trans. Egon Wiszniewsky. Berlin: Henschelverlag, 1983.

Zoppelli, Luca. "'Stage Music' in Early Nineteenth-Century Italian Opera." *Cambridge Opera Journal* 2 (1990), 29–39.

Index

Abbado, Claudio 216, 229
Académie Royale de Musique (Opéra) 22, 111,
      209, 210, 213
accompaniment
   French, *see* grand opera, accompaniments
   Verdi 123–24
Alagna, Roberto 229
Alfieri, Vittorio, *Virginia* 6
Alighieri, Dante 30, 175, 179, 180
American Institute for Verdi Studies 273–74
analysis
   associational relationships 142; *see also*
         Verdi, Giuseppe, works, operas,
         Rigoletto, key and characterization
   double cycles of keys 145–46
   general considerations 139–43
   historical authenticity and inauthenticity
         141–42
   intertextual 151–52
   key sequences influenced by prominent
         pitches 143–45
   long-range tonics 146–49; *see also* Verdi,
         Giuseppe, works, operas, *Rigoletto*,
         long-range tonics
   motivic coherence, *see* Verdi, Giuseppe,
         works, operas, *Ernani*, motivic
         coherence; Verdi, Giuseppe, works,
         operas, *Otello*, motivic coherence;
         Verdi, Giuseppe, works, operas,
         Rigoletto, motivic coherence
   pluralism of approaches 140, 151,
         152–53
   presentist 139–40
   purposefulness and randomness 141
   structural coherence of standard
         forms 142
   subjectivity 140
   tonal design 143–52; *see also* Verdi,
         Giuseppe, works, operas, *Otello*,
         tonal design
   vicarious recomposition 141
"angel in the house" archetype 40
Angiolini, Carlo 171
Anicet-Bourgeois, Auguste, and
         Francis Cornu, *Nabuchodonosor*
         111
antimasque 163
aria form, *see* set piece design, aria
Ariosto, Ludovico 30, 72, 76
Assembly of the Parma Provinces 12
Auber, Daniel-François-Esprit 25, 180

Austro-German instrumental tradition 26, 140,
      141, 154, 175, 177

Bach, Johann Sebastian 140
Balbo, Cesare 39
Balestra, Luigi 171
ballet
   French, *see* grand opera, ballet
   Italian *danse aérienne* 163
   Verdi 121–23, 162–64; *see also* Verdi,
         Giuseppe, works, operas, *Les vêpres
         siciliennes*, Act II finale, ballets
Barbieri-Nini, Marianna 10
Barezzi, Antonio 3, 5
Barrot, Odilon 201
Basevi, Abramo 49, 56, 269
Bassi, Calisto, *Il solitario di Eloisa* 170
battle scenes 161
Baudelaire, Charles 83
Belgioioso, Count Lodovico 172
Bellaigue, Camille 270
Bellini, Vincenzo 25, 49, 157
   Il pirata 31
   La sonnambula 74, 107
Berlioz, Hector 31
Bermani, B. 269
Berna Agreement 24
Bianchi, Tomaso 171
Bing, Rudolf 209
Bizet, Georges, *Les pêcheurs de perles* 211
Boito, Arrigo 9, 26, 28, 72, 83–87, 175, 180,
         237–44, 259, 262
   Mefistofele 26
Bondy, Luc 229
Borromeo, Count Renato 169, 180
Brambilla, Teresa 10
Budden, Julian 230
Byron, Lord George 31
   The two Foscari 158

Cammarano, Salvatore 8, 39, 72, 73–76, 112,
         258, 262–63
Canti, Giovanni 170, 171
Caponi, Giacomo (Folchetto) 270
Capponi, Giuseppe 178
Carara-Verdi family 263
Carcano, Giulio 21
Casa di Riposo per Musicisti 13, 14
Casa Ricordi, *see* Ricordi publishing house
Castil-Blaze 128
cavatina 51

Cambridge Companions to Music

Instruments

The Cambridge Companion to Brass Instruments
Edited by Trevor Herbert and John Wallace

The Cambridge Companion to the Cello
Edited by Robin Stowell

The Cambridge Companion to the Clarinet
Edited by Colin Lawson

The Cambridge Companion to the Guitar
Edited by Victor Anand Coelho

The Cambridge Companion to the Organ
Edited by Nicholas Thistlethwaite and Geoffrey Webber

The Cambridge Companion to the Piano
Edited by David Rowland

The Cambridge Companion to the Recorder
Edited by John Mansfield Thomson

The Cambridge Companion to the Saxophone
Edited by Richard Ingham

The Cambridge Companion to Singing
Edited by John Potter

The Cambridge Companion to the Violin
Edited by Robin Stowell

Composers

The Cambridge Companion to Bach
Edited by John Butt

The Cambridge Companion to Bartók
Edited by Amanda Bayley

The Cambridge Companion to Beethoven
Edited by Glenn Stanley

The Cambridge Companion to Berg
Edited by Anthony Pople

The Cambridge Companion to Berlioz
Edited by Peter Bloom

The Cambridge Companion to Brahms
Edited by Michael Musgrave

The Cambridge Companion to Benjamin Britten
Edited by Mervyn Cooke

The Cambridge Companion to John Cage
Edited by David Nicholls

The Cambridge Companion to Chopin
Edited by Jim Samson